Hanging in th

A History of
Abolition of Capital Punis.

Brian P Block has a doctorate in pharmacology and has spent over 20 years testing the safety of new medicines. He holds degrees in pharmacy (London), criminal justice (Brunel) and Chinese (Westminster), and is a former Fulbright scholar and a post-doctoral research fellow at Yale University. He is a magistrate and a regular contributor to the weekly journal *Justice of the Peace*.

John Hostettler practised as a solicitor in London, as well as undertaking political and civil liberties cases in Nigeria, Germany and Aden. During this time he played a leading role in the abolition of flogging in British colonial prisons. His subjects as a legal biographer and historian have included Sir James Fitzjames Stephen and Sir Edward Carson. A magistrate and a part-time chairman of Social Security Appeal Tribunals, he is the author of *The Politics of Punishment* (1964) and *The Politics of Criminal Law* (1992).

Former prime minister **Lord Callaghan** was Home Secretary at the time of the abolition of capital punishment for murder and voted consistently in favour of abolition from the time he entered Parliament in 1945.

Hanging in the Balance

A History of the
Abolition of Capital Punishment in Britain

Brian P Block
John Hostettler

With a Foreword by
Lord Callaghan of Cardiff KG

WATERSIDE PRESS

Hanging in the Balance

Brian P Block and John Hostettler

Published 1997 by
WATERSIDE PRESS
Sherfield Gables, Sherfield-on-Loddon, Hook
Hampshire, RG27 0JG, United Kingdom
Telephone 0845 2300 733 **Fax** 01256 883 987
Web WatersidePress.co.uk **Email** enquiries@watersidepress.co.uk

ISBN 978-1-872870-47-2 (paperback)

Cataloguing-in-Publication Data A catalogue record for this book can be obtained from the British Library

Cover John Good Holbrook Ltd, Coventry

Printed and bound in Great Britain by
CPI Antony Rowe, Chippenham and Eastbourne

Hanging in the Balance

CONTENTS

Foreword

Murder is a most dreadful crime from which heart and mind recoil, and down the centuries, the penalty of death by hanging was exacted from the guilty murderer, both as retribution and as a fearful example to others. Execution was the ultimate sentence; one which, by its finality, could never be revoked, and it was this very characteristic which, 30 years ago, led Parliament to abolish the death penalty.

This book tells the story of how Parliament, from the eighteenth century onwards, often somewhat ahead of public opinion, moved through the years to the final termination of capital punishment. Three hundred years ago, there were those who asserted that even the execution of an innocent person could be justified by the need to ensure the security of civil life. Women and even children were hanged for trivial crimes and a man could be, and was, executed for stealing sixpence in the street.

As the years passed, such excessive cruelty was checked. During the eighteenth century juries showed increasing reluctance to convict prisoners charged with capital offences. And it was in this same century that the argument took hold, which has lasted interminably, about such various matters as the effectiveness of hanging as a deterrent, about hanging as an appropriate punishment, and about its consequences as a final act. During the nineteenth century the argument for prohibition was given added force by the recognition that Britain's penal law was more severe than that of any other European country.

It is with tracing the Parliamentary history of the struggle for abolition with which Block and Hostettler are mainly concerned. They concentrate particularly on the successful efforts of the reformers in the period immediately after World War II, which led to the final victory.

The undoubted hero of the campaign was Sydney Silverman—small in stature, uptilted head, erect carriage, a quick pattering footstep and a prominent pointed beard which was almost a weapon in itself. In the Commons he always perched himself (perched is the word) on the corner seat just below the gangway adjoining the Government Front Bench, his feet hardly touching the ground. From that advantageous position he was always ready to jump to his feet at any moment. He was fearless in the face of hostility, of which there was plenty, and coupled this with great skill as a Parliamentarian and with considerable legal knowledge and practical experience, brought from his profession as a solicitor.

He carried a formidable armoury that convinced many of us just back from the war in the late 1940s that hanging should go. I cannot say that until then, hanging had impinged on my thinking, and it was only when I reached Parliament in 1945 and was confronted by the need to take a position, that I concluded that hanging should be abolished. In the debates of 1948, I voted for abolition for the first time and after that decision, did so steadily thereafter, whenever the issue came before the House.

As the authors show, it was not only the sustained campaigning and arguments which eventually carried the day. There was also a growing uneasiness among the public and in Parliament that miscarriages of justice might have taken place, and innocent people (such as Timothy Evans) had been hanged. The controversy over Bentley and Craig also had an affect on Parliamentary and public opinion, as did the execution of a woman, Ruth Ellis, in 1955. Some former home secretaries, both Conservative and Labour, who had been responsible for taking the final decisions which had resulted in certain hangings, announced that they had changed their minds; and later the judges concluded that attempts to define the scope of hanging were leading to such uncertainty and anomalies, that they, the judges, would prefer abolition to the continuance of the existing law.

The result was that by the time of the election of the Labour government of 1964, there was a growing agreement that the existing law could not be allowed to continue. Sydney Silverman brought forward yet another Bill for abolition. The cabinet, in which I was serving as chancellor of the exchequer, contained a number of abolitionists, including the prime minister Harold Wilson, and a most powerful advocate in the person of Gerald Gardiner, the Lord Chancellor. As a government, we had no hesitation in offering support for Silverman's Bill. Together with a free vote for government supporters, the Conservative opposition also announced that their followers would enjoy the same freedom.

The authors of this book describe in detail the long and tortuous Parliamentary proceedings which followed, and the struggle and the confrontations before both Lords and Commons agreed in 1965 to end the death penalty but only for a limited period of five years. This uneasy compromise of a five year period almost immediately became a source of controversy which was intensified for me personally when I became home secretary in the autumn of 1967.

I thought about the matter carefully and knew that I would find it extremely difficult, if not impossible, to fulfil my responsibilities if a case of hanging was likely to come before me when the five year period ended, with the certainty that we would revert to the former unsatisfactory law and practice. I talked with Harold Wilson, who encouraged me to sound out opinion to see what support there would be to put an immediate end to hanging without waiting for the five year period to run its course. I found enough room to go ahead. In retrospect, I think what finally decided me was when I learned that the leaders of the Conservative party and of the Liberal party would both be likely to support immediate abolition.

This helped to remove a serious objection, namely that the five year period was likely to come to an end at about the same time as the next general election. The known attitude of Ted Heath and Jeremy Thorpe meant that the danger of hanging becoming a dominant issue when the election arrived was largely negated, and so it turned out. My proposal to abolish the compromise period of five years was given full support by the cabinet and I brought it before the Commons. In the chamber the issues were lengthily debated and decided by free votes in all the parties. The opposition to abolition was stubborn in the Commons and even more so in the Lords, but eventually the proposal in favour of permanent abolition was carried though both Houses of Parliament on 18 December 1969. The Bill became law and a permanent memorial to the unflagging campaign waged by Sydney Silverman and his group of Parliamentary supporters.

It seems likely that public opinion in the country has not even yet been won over to Parliament's view. On the other hand, it should not be forgotten that there are men who would have been hanged although they are innocent, but who are alive today because the law was changed. Members of Parliament show themselves to be only too aware of this and it is not surprising that whenever a proposal to reinstate hanging comes before Parliament, it has been rejected on every occasion by a large majority.

Block and Hostettler tell the story of how it happened and our thanks are due to them for reminding a new generation of how a splendid campaign was finally fought and won.

Rt. Hon. Lord Callaghan of Cardiff KG
October 1997

Preface

On 13 August 1964, at the first stroke of eight in the morning, two men, one in Manchester and the other in Liverpool, fell feet first through the floor into empty space, and stopped even before the second stroke struck, dead.

Crime, verdict and sentence

Peter Anthony Allen, who was 21, lived with his wife Mary and their two children in Clarenden Road, Preston, and Gwynne Owen Evans, who was 24, lived with them as a lodger. Some time earlier, on 7 April they all drove up to Seaton, a small town near Workington in what was then Cumberland. While Mrs Allen waited in the car, her husband and Evans visited John Alan West, as she believed to borrow some money. Whatever went on in West's house in King's Avenue, West was killed: battered and stabbed, and Allen and Evans took away with them two bank books and a watch. More important than what they took away, however, was what they left behind: Evans' raincoat with a medallion in the pocket bearing his name. Both were quickly arrested and three months later brought to trial in Manchester.

The case lasted for six days but drew little national attention. *The Daily Herald*[1] and the *Daily Mirror*[2] each carried a bare report of the verdict. But Preston's main local paper, the *Lancashire Evening Post,* reported the result fully. The front page carried a banner headline, 'Preston Men Sentenced to Die' with the sub-heading, 'Wife led weeping from court as husband goes below.'[3] There were pictures of the men, both dairymen, who had pleaded 'not guilty' to capital murder. Under the Homicide Act 1957 not all murders were capital offences but murder committed in the furtherance of theft, among others, was, and Allen and Evans had stolen from their victim. The jury had heard evidence from 40 witnesses and the judge told them that three verdicts were possible: not guilty; guilty of capital murder; guilty of murder, and pointed out that at the heart of the case was the problem of who committed the murder—was it Allen or Evans, or was it both? He explained that if two men agreed to kill or do grievous bodily harm to someone, both are guilty even if only one deals the fatal blow. Allen said that he never intended to do grievous bodily harm; all he admitted to was hitting West with his fist and one or two blows with a cosh, and then he stopped. Evans said he had not touched West at all and had had no intention that he should be killed or harmed.

The judge warned the jury to examine the evidence of Mrs Allen with great care as she was interested in getting her husband off. Since she had heard it made public knowledge by Evans in court that she and he were more than landlady and lodger and had slept together, she had a deep, bitter hatred for Evans. Both men had lied and if the jury found they had taken an active part in an attack on West, the judge explained, they would then find them each guilty of the offence with which they were charged, capital murder. This they did. The jury, consisting of nine men and three women, retired for three hours before bringing in that verdict.

11

The judge, passing sentence, said, 'As both of you know, for the crime of which you have in my judgement been quite rightly convicted, the law provides only one sentence—that you suffer death in the manner authorised by law'. Both men paled as sentence was passed but said nothing. Mrs Allen, who had sat at the back of the court straining to get a glimpse of her husband, was led away weeping by a policewoman as both men went quietly down to the cells.[4]

Later, the two men were taken to their respective prisons, Allen to Walton and Evans to Strangeways, where they would stay in their condemned cells for the last few weeks of their lives, never alone, always in the company of two prison officers who would talk and play cards or draughts with them when they were awake, and watch them whilst they slept.

Dismissing their appeals, the Lord Chief Justice, Lord Parker, remarked that it would be difficult to imagine a more brutal murder.

No reprieve

Two days before their execution, it was announced by the home secretary, Henry Brooke, that he would not interfere with the course of justice and that there would be no reprieve. This statement provoked little interest nationally; and there were two-line announcements of the fact in the *Manchester Evening News*,[5] *The Guardian*[6] and *The Times*[7] which stated bleakly that there would be no reprieve for the two men and that they would be executed at Liverpool and Manchester respectively on August 13.

But in Preston it was front page news. Under the headline 'Brooke Denies Reprieves. He rules: Preston men to hang for "brutal" murder' the *Lancashire Evening Post*[8] carried pictures of both men and of people in a Preston street collecting signatures for petitions for clemency. In more emotional language than the nationals, the Lancashire paper stated that 'hopes for mercy were dashed when the home secretary announced that there would be no reprieve for Allen and Evans who will be hanged on Thursday morning, August thirteenth.' The story went on to say that the case had aroused much controversy in and around Preston since their appeals were dismissed. Petitions for mercy had been circulated for signatures and groups pressing for both the abolition of capital punishment and for it's extension had been active; but neither side was surprised that there would be no reprieve.

A local minister, the reverend Geoffrey Grimes, said that one outcome would be the setting up of a Preston branch of the Campaign for the Abolition of Capital Punishment. He still believed in mercy, forgiveness and love far above revenge, he said. On hearing of the home secretary's decision, Councillor Joseph Holden, leader of the group demanding the death sentence, reacted with one word, 'Good'. He added, 'I don't like to see anybody hang but I do feel that hanging should be the penalty for murder'.

Meanwhile, the house where Mr and Mrs Allen had lived, and where Evans had lodged, was empty and up for sale.

The scaffold

The next day, the day prior to the executions, the executioners arrived at the two prisons, and met their respective assistants. Over cups of tea in the rooms set aside for them they discussed the routine they would follow. At each prison, the engineer, who looked after the scaffold and its equipment, handed the executioner details of the condemned man's height and weight. Tables were provided by the Home Office which calculated the drop needed based on the condemned man's size, but the final decision was the executioner's.

When the drop was correct the neck was broken cleanly and death, or at least unconsciousness, was instantaneous. If the drop was too short the neck would not break and the man would be strangled; too long and the head would be torn off. Most drops were about six feet. Before the precise length of the drop was decided the executioner would need to view the prisoner. But before that they all went off to the execution chamber to examine the kit.

Whilst the equipment was being examined the local paper, the *Lancashire Evening Post*, came onto the streets of Preston, containing a number of letters on the subject.[9] Because of the policy of newspapers to balance the letters printed where the subject is controversial unless they are overwhelmingly supporting one side, it is not possible to gauge the balance of local views. Frank Curry Jr wrote that the death penalty was neither a necessary nor a unique deterrent and was completely irremediable. He implored the British public to do something 'for surely to kill a man by judicial strangulation is a punishment incomparably worse than the crime itself'.

The executioners, one in Liverpool and the other in Manchester, went through the same routine. They first examined the ropes—more than one to choose from—making sure there was no fraying. The noose itself was covered with thin leather and made by running the end of the rope through a metal eye set into the rope itself. The 'hangman's noose' with the rope running through the coils, had not been used in Britain for many years. The other end of the rope, which was six feet in length, was attached by another metal eye to a chain fixed to the ceiling; adjustments to the length of the drop were made by fixing the rope higher or lower on the chain. When a rope had been selected the trapdoor was examined.

Mrs A. Livesay's letter was brief. 'What a lot of fuss over two Preston boys who have to hang! There should be no reprieve for murderers.' Her view was echoed by David Whittle who instructed readers to read Deuteronomy xix:11-13[10] in order to show why the men must be taken from Preston (they were no longer in Preston) and 'given to the avenger of blood'. Further support for the death penalty came from an A. Sutcliffe who pointed out that hanging would not bring back the victim but would make sure the killers did not murder again. He added, rather incongruously, 'Such men are never fit to be released'.

The next job was to inspect and test the mechanism, to ensure that the trapdoor opened smoothly when the lever was activated. The hole in the floor was covered with two hinged flaps, each about eight and a half feet by two and a half. These doors were held up, meeting in the middle, by metal plates on either side which were held in position by metal bolts. When the lever was pushed

13

over, the bolts opened and the trapdoors fell, to be caught vertically by rubber-backed spring clips on either side. The lever had a safety catch in the form of a cotter pin which had to be removed before the lever could be shifted.

The two executioners checked the safety catches, removed them, pushed the lever and ensured that the flaps were caught by the clips on the sides of the pit. The traps were closed again. An approximate length of rope was measured off and attached to the chain, a sandbag slightly heavier than the prisoner was attached to the lower end of the rope, fastened to the noose. The executioners pushed the levers again, the traps opened and the bags dropped, to be left in position overnight, stretching the two ropes.

A final correspondent, D.T. Smith, whose views on crime and punishment were also questionable, 'was alarmed, if not disgusted, at the attitude of apparently uncivilised Prestonians who refused to sign the [petitions for clemency]. They need putting in the stocks.'

The next job was to take a look at the prisoner so that the executioner could calculate the drop accurately—to the nearest half-inch—by taking into account not only his height and weight but also his build, and in particular the musculature of the neck. Thickset men with swarthy necks needed a longer drop than more slimly built ones of the same weight. This viewing of the prisoners took place without the prisoners' knowledge, either through a peep-hole in the cell door or while the prisoner was in the exercise yard. The demeanour of the prisoner also gave a clue as to his possible behaviour the following morning. That done, a final calculation as to the length of the drop was made and the routine for the next morning discussed with the assistant; everything had to be done quickly and smoothly.

The executioners went to bed early for they were to make an early start. The weather was cool for mid-August, but not cold. The overnight temperature was just below 60 degrees Fahrenheit and there was a breeze from the North-west. But no crowds gathered overnight, just two men who kept vigil outside Walton jail. They were Robert W. Bart, aged 44, and Roger Moody, aged 21, both officials of the Campaign for the Abolition of Capital Punishment who had travelled from Bristol.

Final checks
Very early the next morning executioners and assistants went to the execution chambers; those about to die were given their last breakfasts, their civilian clothes to die in and the comfort of a priest for their last hour on earth.

Hangmen and assistants worked quietly, for the execution chamber was adjacent to the condemned cell, joined by a door hidden by a wardrobe on the side of the cell. Each assistant detached the sandbag from the rope and placed it near the stretcher already in place to remove the body. He then stood on a stool, detached the sides of the trapdoors from their spring catches and held them up horizontally; above, the executioner slid in the bolt and replaced the cotter pin, only just in position so that it could be removed quickly. The rope length was then readjusted allowing for the final calculation after having seen the condemned man and also for the stretching of the rope. A note was made for the

14

official record of the length of the drop. The rope was coiled until the noose was at shoulder level and the coil tied to the rope with a length of thin twine that would break immediately as the body fell. Finally, chalk marks were made under the noose so that the prisoner's toes could be placed in the exact position where the arches of his feet would be directly over the crack between the flaps, and the two planks across the traps where the prison officers would stand, one on either side of the prisoner, were checked. Executioners and assistants then went for breakfast.

The executions
At five minutes to eight, in each of the two prisons, executioners and assistants were alerted and, accompanied by a prison officer, walked up the corridor that led to the condemned cell. At half a minute to eight the prison governor, the doctor and some senior prison officers came along the corridor and joined them. After a further quarter of a minute, at a nod from the governor, the small party entered the condemned cell and the executioner confronted his victim for the first time. From that moment events moved at a rapid pace and the actions in Manchester and Liverpool were virtually simultaneous.

On entering the cell the executioner strode over to the prisoner and pinioned his wrists behind his back with a leather strap and said 'Follow me'. They walked a few steps through the door that had been exposed and opened by an officer as the party entered the cell, and the officers escorting the prisoner stopped him as his feet drew level with the chalk marks on the trap, and stood one on either side on the cross planks. As the prisoner stopped, the assistant strapped his ankles and the executioner, who had crossed the trapdoor, turned and faced the prisoner, took a folded white hood from his pocket and slipped it over the man's head. The noose was pulled over the hood, tightened and held in place with a rubber washer, making sure that the eyelet was under the left angle of the jaw. This was because during the fall the rope moves clockwise around the neck finishing level with the chin, with the effect that the neck is jerked backwards; if the rope were to end up at the back, the neck would jerk forward and the prisoner would strangle.

As the clock began to strike the hour, with a single smooth movement the executioner crouched and pulled out the cotter pin with one hand and pushed the lever with the other. The trapdoors fell open with a bang and were held by the spring clips. From a stationary start it takes six tenths of a second for a man to fall six feet by which time he is travelling at about 13 miles per hour. At the end of the drop the body continues to fall for a fraction of a second but the head is stopped suddenly by the rope which, now under the chin, jerks the head sharply backwards, breaking one or more cervical vertebrae and severing or crushing the spinal cord. Before the clock had finished striking eight, and not more than 12 seconds after the execution parties entered the condemned cells, the prisoners were dead. Shortly afterwards doctors pronounced the prisoners' lives were extinct, and formal inquests reported that they had died as the result of judicial hanging. A few hours later they were each buried in the precincts of the prison in which they had been hanged, the prison chaplains conducting brief services.[11]

15

The reaction

By 1964 hanging had become a rare event in Britain; there had been only two hangings in 1963 and two in 1962. The national press might have been expected to carry the story more fully than they did, but then two days earlier, Charles Wilson, one of the Great Train Robbers, had been dramatically snatched from Winson Green prison, Birmingham, and it was this story that made the headlines for days. On the evening of the executions, however, the *Manchester Evening News*[12] carried a short report under the heading 'Three-City Vigil as Killers Hang' (which actually mentioned four cities). 'Only a handful' of people were outside the main gate of Strangeways in Southall Street, Manchester, as Evans was executed and there was no demonstration. Two anti-capital punishment supporters kept an all-night vigil and in Bristol opponents of hanging stood silent and bareheaded outside the cathedral.

In the *Daily Herald*[13] the report of the executions was not only committed to an inside page but was beneath a more prominent report that May had had the worst record ever of road accidents with 619 deaths and 34,000 injuries. Compared with two people being hanged, the road toll was considered to be more important.

As Allen was hanged at Walton gaol in Liverpool it is less surprising that the *Liverpool Daily Post*[14] gave the story front page coverage. This paper alone reported that the men's mothers had sent a letter to the Queen pleading for clemency, and that the Reverend Grimes led 23 people in silent meditation in Preston Market Square. About 42 people were outside the prison when Allen was hanged, having joined the two anti-hanging supporters who had been there all night. At 7.30 a.m. two girls arrived with banners proclaiming 'No more hanging' and 'Why take another life?'. The *Guardian*,[15] then a Manchester-based paper, carried a similar story, adding, oddly in the circumstances, that the victim was a laundry van driver and that 20 or so people outside Strangeways claimed they were there because they were interested in seeing if there were any demonstrations.

On the letters page of the local Preston paper the arguments continued.[16] C. D.Wilding was appalled that the Reverend Grimes contemplated holding a vigil at the Preston Cenotaph which was erected to the memory of those who died for King and country, not to that of brutal, cold-blooded killers. But the editor pointed out that as soon as the reverend realised this might give offence he changed the venue of the vigil.

Mrs R. M. Parker had no doubt that Grimes would pray for the two men's souls and for the people who still believe in the senseless and barbaric practice of hanging. An M. Day relied on Exodus xxi:12 for his opinion: 'He that smiteth a man so that he die shall surely be put to death' and Ron Yates pointed out that Britain, France and Spain were the only countries in Europe to retain the death penalty. Hanging was cold-blooded and sadistic and the Homicide Act 1957 was neither rational not ethical.

However, the silent vigil organized by the Reverend Grimes in Preston's Flag Market was disturbed. Mrs Emily Hammond, aunt of a girl shot dead in Preston three years earlier, approached the meditators and told Grimes: 'I am disgusted with you. See if you'd like it if one of your children was shot at your door. All murderers should hang'.

Although the executions were taking place elsewhere, four uniformed policemen stood outside the door of Preston prison 'as a precautionary measure'. As a distant clock struck eight, eight men and four women outside HMP Strangeways kept vigil with their heads bowed, whilst outside Walton jail in Liverpool, among the 30 bystanders and 12 members of the press, one man removed his cap as they all stood, silent.[17]

But what nobody knew, neither those who waited outside nor those who participated within, was that each, in his own way, had witnessed the very last judicial executions to take place in the United Kingdom.

ENDNOTES

1 *Daily Herald,* p. 4, 8 July 1964

2 *Daily Mirror,* p. 9, 8 July 1964

3 *Lancashire Evening Post,* p. 1, 7 July 1964

4 ibid, p. 1

5 *Manchester Evening News,* p. 1, 11 August 1964

6 *The Guardian,* p. 1, 12 August 1964

7 *The Times,* p. 6, 12 August 1964

8 *Lancashire Evening Post,* p. 1, 11 August 1964

9 *Lancashire Evening Post,* p. 1, 12 August 1964

10 Deuteronomy xix:11-13: 'But if any man hates his neighbour, and lies in wait for him, and attacks him, and wounds him mortally so that he dies, and the man flees into one of these cities, then the elders of his city shall send and fetch him from there, and hand him over to the avenger of blood, so that he may die. Your eye shall not pity him, but you shall purge the guilt of innocent blood from Israel, so that it may be well with you.'

11 Descriptions of the execution procedure are culled in part from *Executioner: Pierrepoint,* Albert Pierrepoint, London: Harrap, 1974

12 *Manchester Evening News,* p. 11, 13 August 1964

13 *Daily Herald,* p. 7, 14 August 1964

14 *Liverpool Daily Post,* p. 1, 14 August 1964

15 *The Guardian,* p. 18, 14 August 1964

16 *Lancashire Evening Post,* p. 7, 13 August 1964

17 The events described in this paragraph were collated from several newspapers.

CHAPTER 1

Capital Crimes

For the public at large the gallows and 'hanging by the neck until dead' involve a unique mystique of horror. As a form of lawful execution they have enjoyed a long history in England.

Poisonous ingredients

In the early Middle Ages hanging held a prominent place in the primitive laws of blood and revenge, ahead of other gruesome punishments. In Anglo-Saxon communities hundred and shire courts were often by-passed. A thief captured in the course of a 'hue and cry' could be hanged summarily. Incredibly, so too could a free peasant farmer who left his home without explanation. Whereas the runaway thief would have been seen committing the offence, and often had the stolen property with him, it would simply be assumed that the farmer had committed a crime. Explanations were not regarded as useful.

Creating a rare interlude, after his victory at the Battle of Hastings in 1066 William the Conqueror abolished the death penalty altogether but not in a spirit of mercy. He favoured mutilations of the body, believing that as they were more visible and lasting they were also more effective as a deterrent. William Rufus made no change but by 1108 hanging was re-instated by Henry I, particularly for homicide. It was accompanied by beheading, burning at the stake and drowning, not to mention other unpleasant punishments that fell short of death.

Notwithstanding the horrific nature of these other penalties, hanging was considered the most degrading form of death, probably because it was more messy and squalid, as we shall see. Decapitation was regarded as a right reserved for the wealthy, and burning at the stake was considered to be suitable for women. As Sir William Blackstone expressed it, 'For as the decency due to the sex forbids the exposing and publicly mangling of their bodies, their sentence is, to be drawn to the gallows and there to be burnt alive'.[1]

Down the ages the barbarous and irrational criminal law of England was woven around capital punishment as a means of social control by a mixture of terror and legality. Death was the only punishment for treason, for all felonies except petty larceny and mayhem, and for many lesser transgressions. This meant that a murderer on the one hand, and a person who stole an article worth 12 pence or more on the other, were both to be executed. Clearly, means had to be employed to mitigate the harshness of such law if its legitimacy was to survive. One of these was 'benefit of clergy'. Yet paradoxically, its very effect in reducing the incidence of capital punishment was to ensure the durability of the death penalty and dampen demands for its reform for centuries. Another means of escape was the royal pardon.

Benefit of clergy was conceded for clerics by Henry II after the murder of Thomas á Becket. It was not only quickly adopted by the judges but its scope

18

was expanded by them and by the statute *pro clero* of 1350[2] the privilege was extended to secular as well as religious clerks. These included door-keepers, readers and exorcists who were assistants to the clergy.

Not all offences were included (treason and misdemeanours were excluded) but for those that were the statute ensured that any convicted criminal who could read the first verse of the 51st psalm—the 'neck verse' as it became known—would be released. It was even known for judges to send an illiterate prisoner who had been found guilty back to the cells to learn the verse by heart before returning to the court to be set free, although this would have been rare.[3] The verse reads:

Have mercy on me, O God according to thy loving kindness; according to the multitude of thy tender mercies, blot out my transgressions.

This bizarre 'benefit' was to bedevil the penal law for centuries despite Blackstone, seeing it as a merciful mitigation of harsh penalties, persuading himself and others that the law 'in the course of a long and laborious process, extracted by noble alchemy rich medicines out of poisonous ingredients'.[4] More perceptively, the eminent jurist, Sir James Fitzjames Stephen, stated baldly that the benefit 'reduced the administration of justice to a farce'.[5]

Not surprisingly, after a period of time some kings and governments eventually despaired of the richness of a medicine which set so many dangerous criminals free. A statute in the reign of Henry VII (1485-1509)[6] attempted to draw a distinction between those who were in orders and those who were not. It provided for the latter that the benefit could be pleaded once only, with the thumb branded with a red-hot iron with 'M' for murder and 'T' for theft to ensure recognition on a second occasion. The branding was carried out in court and when completed the warder would look up to the judge and cry, 'A fair mark, my Lord?' If the judge nodded the prisoner was released.

Henry VIII (1509-1547) was even more radical and removed 'clergy' in certain cases from all people whether in orders or not. Thereafter, at various times, the benefit was revoked for all cases of adultery, murder and witchcraft. Nevertheless, it was not fully abolished until 1827.

Royal pardons, for their part, were quite often granted when the felon was wealthy enough to pay for the privilege or to pay witnesses—practices clearly open to abuse. On other occasions they could restore a convicted person to liberty where there remained a doubt about guilt. In such cases they were used to show the people how merciful their monarchs were. It was not until 1761 that the power of recommending a reprieve to the Crown passed to the home secretary. Gradually, as the centuries passed, various disgraceful and obscene methods of judicial killing were abandoned until by the mid-nineteenth century only hanging remained, except for treason where the offender was still hanged, drawn and quartered.

The guillotine, which was operated mainly in Halifax and Scotland, ended its life in 1710 and burning of women at the stake was abolished in 1790. Disembowelling alive was ended in 1814 and the axe was last used on the Cato

19

Street conspirators in 1820. Gibbeting was brought to an end in 1834. However, the frightful method of hanging, beheading and quartering of those found guilty of treason was not finally dispensed with until 1870. What prompted these apparently humane changes will be considered shortly.

During the lengthy reign, or misrule, of King Henry III (1216-1272), the celebrated jurist and judge, Henry de Bracton, enumerated eleven common law offences and about thirty statutory crimes, almost all of which were capital—still a small body of criminal law by later standards. By the time of Sir Edward Coke (sometime Lord Chief Justice), when Queen Elizabeth was on the throne (1558-1603), there remained some 30 statutory offences which attracted the death penalty. This number of capital felonies was sufficient to enable the Tudor and early Stuart monarchs lawfully to indulge in bloody terror and torture. Coke lamented the hanging of

> so many Christian men and women strangled on that cursed tree of the gallows, insomuch as if in a large field a man might see together all the Christians, that but in one year, throughout England, come to that untimely and ignominious death, if there were any spark of grace or charity in him, it would make his heart bleed for pity and compassion . . .

> True it is that we have found by woeful experience, that it is not frequent and often punishment that does prevent like offences. Those offences are often committed that are often punished; for the frequency of the punishment makes it so familiar as it is not feared.[7]

In so speaking Coke was an early, if isolated pioneer in deploring not only the frequency with which capital punishment was inflicted but the fact that this very often prevented it acting as a deterrent. Nevertheless, he believed death was the right punishment for crimes of great abomination. As with Sir Matthew Hale, later Lord Chief Justice, he was no doubt influenced in this respect by the Bible. Homicide was to be punished with death as Genesis ix: 6 provides that 'Whosoever sheddeth man's blood, by man shall his blood be shed'.[8] During the reign of Henry VIII alone, over 72,000 people were hanged in the name of the law.[9] In 1531 when Richard Rouse, a cook in the household of Bishop Fisher, was accused of attempting to poison his master, Henry had a statute enacted[10] to have him punished by boiling to death in hot water. According to Coke a young woman named Margaret Davy was also boiled to death in Smithfield for the 'poisonyng of her mistris' and some others suffered the same fate.

Eighteenth century ferocity
In spite of some moderation in the use of the death penalty during the Commonwealth and the Protectorate (1649-1659) and the reigns of the later Stuarts (1660-1688), by the eighteenth century there was a reversal which resulted in England's 'Bloody Code'. The infamous Waltham Black Act of 1723 is the most extreme example; it added 50 new capital offences to the statute book. Its principal purpose was to protect the hunting forests and parks of prime minister Sir Robert Walpole and his nouveau-riche friends from poachers.[11]

20

Even stealing fruit from trees and damaging ponds to allow fish to escape became capital crimes. And 60 more new crimes were made capital during the reign of George III alone (1760-1820).

Under these numerous new statutes well over 200 offences became punishable with death. In an age of commerce and increasing prosperity, the protection not only of the political order but also of property was seen to be paramount by those who had become newly enriched. As *The Times* was eventually to admit on 25 July 1872, under the Bloody Code 'It was not justice that was administered; it was a war that was waged between two classes of the community'.

Liberal-minded Whig and Radical politicians found they could not stomach this new tyranny. In a famous and impassioned speech in the House of Commons on 23 May 1821, Sir Thomas Fowell Buxton, a leading Evangelical politician, told members that the previous century had witnessed a four-fold increase in the criminal law, and in the previous year alone 600 people had been condemned to death by the courts. Of 20 volumes of penal statutes to which he referred, only three contained Acts which existed prior to 1700.

Buxton mocked that as severity was deemed by the country's rulers to be wisdom and capital enactment the best method of repressing crime, it followed that the country should be distinguished by the rarity of crime. Moreover, he was quick to point out that as the greater part of the existing criminal code was rank innovation it could not be part of the 'good old beloved common law' as the men of severity tried to pretend. 'Men there are living', he declared, 'at whose birth our code contained less than seventy capital offences; and who have seen that number more than trebled'.

In the same speech, Buxton explained that the law of England also displayed 'no unnecessary nicety' in apportioning the punishment of death.

'Kill your father', he said, 'or catch a rabbit in a warren—the penalty is the same! Destroy three kingdoms, or destroy a hop-bine—the penalty is the same! Meet a gypsy on the high road, keep company with the said gypsy, or kill him, no matter which—the penalty by law is the same!'[12]

These capital statutes were, in part, wild responses to a rapid impoverishment of the poor and an apparently equally rapid growth in the crime rate, which at the time many saw as cause and effect. Henry Fielding for instance, well-known as a novelist and as a humane Bow Street magistrate, describing families in want of every necessity of life and oppressed with hunger, cold, nakedness, filth and disease, concluded: 'They starve and freeze and rot among themselves; but they beg and steal and rob among their Betters'.[13]

Sir James Mackintosh was later to write of the period that if he was capable of doing nothing else every member of Parliament could create a capital felony.[14] Indeed, Sir Samuel Romilly complained that when a colliery owner introduced a Bill to make the destruction of mining machinery a capital crime it passed through all its stages without a single statement, inquiry or remark being made by anyone, even though the offence was already punishable by transportation.[15]

Not without reason, law reformer H. B. Andrews complained angrily in 1833 that in England the law

grinds the poor, rich men make law. Here is the secret of our bloody code of the perverse ingenuity by which its abominations have so long been defended: 'Who so stealeth a sheep, let him die the death', says the statute: could so monstrous a law have been enacted had our legislators been chosen by the people of England? But our lawmakers hitherto have been our landlords. By the sale of his sheep, the farmer pays his rent; by the rent of the farmer, the luxury of the member is upheld; touch one link touch all.[16]

As barrister Charles Phillips was to sum up in 1856, 'We hanged for everything—for a shilling—for five shillings—for five pounds—for cattle—for coining—for forgery, even for witchcraft—for things that were and things that could not be'.[17]

Children
Among offenders were to be found a large number of juveniles. Fowell Buxton claimed in the House of Commons that in London alone there were from eight to ten thousand children earning their daily bread by their daily misdeeds, living by petty pilfering and growing into serious criminals.[18] But even for offences of a trivial nature they were shown no more mercy than adult men and women.

Children under seven years of age could not be punished since they were presumed incapable of distinguishing between right and wrong. When over the age of 14 they were treated as adults, and between those two ages they could be sentenced to death and taken to slaughter on the gallows if malice was proved.

At the Bury Assizes in 1748, William York, a boy of ten, was convicted, and sentenced to death by Lord Chief Justice Willes, for the murder of a girl of about five. The girl's body was found cut and mangled 'in a most barbarous and horrid manner' under a heap of dung near the house in which they both lived. William at first denied guilt. Later however, under close interrogation he admitted murder to the coroner.

The justice of the peace before whom the child was taken the next day clearly felt some doubt about the confession, which was the sole evidence, perhaps because the motive given by William—that he killed the girl because she had fouled herself in bed—proved to be untrue. Willes also may have had some misgivings since he postponed execution to take the opinion of all his brother judges.

Meeting at Serjeant's Inn in the following Michaelmas term the judges unanimously found the verdict justified and William deserving of capital punishment. Taking the life of a ten-year-old, they said, might savour of cruelty but the example might be a deterrent. Not everyone agreed, however, including King George II who granted William a royal pardon on condition that he entered the navy.[19]

On 18 January 1801 *The Times* reported that an urchin of 13 named Andrew Brunning was sentenced to death for stealing a spoon from a house. The celebrated diarist Charles Greville recorded seeing several boys sentenced to be hanged and remarked, 'never did I see boys cry so'. And the poet Samuel Rogers saw a 'cartload of young girls, in dresses of various colours, on their way to be hanged at Tyburn Tree'.[20]

It is salutary to recall that in 1785 the solicitor-general, Sir Archibald Macdonald, told the House of Commons that out of every 20 offenders executed in London, 18 were under the age of 21.[21]

Flexibilty

Other factors that encouraged support for severity in penalties were the lack of suitable more modest punishments, a general sense of insecurity flowing from the absence of extensive policing, and the use of discretion in both the prosecuting process and punishment itself. This last helped to give the criminal law an extraordinary flexibility, which we would now call inconsistency, and constituted a vital aspect in legitimizing the rule of the aristocracy who at will could punish severely or exercise leniency as magistrates and judges and in their role as a squire.

In effect, the English criminal law of the eighteenth century was a striking combination of terror and discretion, imagery and force, ideals and hard practice. Interestingly, the impact of these conflicting features produced among the people an impression of justice, when contrasted with the pervading torture, secret trials and imprisonment without trial found in the arbitrary and big-brother police autocracies of the continent. Despite the horror of the death penalty, the rule of law, trial by jury and *habeas corpus* were perceived to be just and conducive to freedom, as indeed they are.

Douglas Hay argues that the gentry who enacted so many of the capital statutes of the eighteenth century never intended that they should be strictly enforced since too many executions would have produced revulsion and led to revolt. With no central police force, the governing class essentially wanted to be able to display and threaten terror but then restrain its use in order to secure obedience to their authority. This, he claims, is why Paley's arguments (of which more later) were so successful for so long in resisting reform in a criminal law system which the gentry used as ideology in place of religion.[22]

The Italian marquis

During the eighteenth century ideological banners were unfurled in England in support of this use by the ruling class of flexibility in applying the law. It was an unfortunate response to the change towards a more humane and rewarding policy which the spirit of the Enlightenment was beginning to engender on the continent. There, Count Cesare Beccaria, a 26-year-old Italian nobleman with no legal experience, caused a sensation in 1764 with his book *Dei Delitti e delle Pene* ('Of Crimes and Punishments'). Published anonymously at first for fear of reprisals, the work was a brilliant indictment of inhumane punishments and it gave birth to the crusade against capital punishment. It was destined to set Europe ablaze, despite the Inquisition forbidding its distribution under pain of death. The Catholic Church branded the unknown author a madman and a stupid imposter. It stigmatised the writing as having 'sprung from the deepest abyss of darkness . . . [it was] horrible, monstrous, full of poison'.

Notwithstanding, the book became an instant success and within a year its now acknowledged author was famous throughout the world. Unfortunately, at the same time it also met strong opposition in England where it clashed with the prevailing Lockeian philosophy that the protection of property was the primary role of the state and of the courts.

Beccaria argued that the death penalty was not a deterrent to criminals, only a barbarous act of violence and injustice. 'Countries and times', he wrote, 'most notorious for the severity of punishments were always those in which the most bloody and inhuman actions and the most atrocious crimes were committed; for the hand of the legislator and that of the assassin were directed by the same spirit of ferocity'.[23] He saw society as held together by the social compact which was made between ruler and ruled in order to rise above the barbarism which existed where there were no laws. He was sure, however, that no-one ever gave to others the right to take away his life. To avoid the excess of ferocity, he held that every punishment ' . . . should be public, immediate and necessary; the least possible in the case; proportioned to the crime and determined by the laws'.[24] Its primary purpose was to benefit society, not to torment offenders.

He applauded the rule of law and absence of torture in England. But he opposed the arbitrary discretionary system in operation here and proposed instead the concept of certainty of punishment. He argued that a small inevitable punishment would make a stronger impression than the fear of one more severe if attended with the hope of escaping. To replace certainty with the point of view, or prejudice, of the judge was dangerous.

Beccaria's inspiration spread swiftly across the continent and in many countries new penal codes were enacted by admirers, such as Catherine the Great in Russia and Frederick the Great in Prussia, which for the time being forbade torture and death as punishments for crimes.

Severity
By way of contrast, in England the concept of severity accompanied by discretion in punishment received a good deal of ideological backing from a number of sources. Even breaking on the wheel, hanging in chains alive and starving were advocated by one writer.[25]

George Ollyffe MA also advocated a more prolonged and painful form of hanging as well as longer and more excruciating executions as a means of strengthening deterrence. Not only breaking offenders on the wheel was advanced but their removal from the wheel whilst still alive to be suspended in gibbets. All to produce, he savagely wrote—'ten thousand of the most exquisite Agonies, as there are Moments in the several hours and days during the unconceivable Torture of their bruised, broken and disjointed Limbs to the last Period'.[26]

Yet even though the existing methods of execution were sufficiently brutal, a century was to pass before the abolitionist and former member of Parliament, Thomas Wrightson, was to respond to Ollyffe. It was not enough, he wrote, to know which punishment inspired the greatest degree of terror. If that punishment which excited the greatest fear were necessarily the best then it would be necessary to use breaking upon the wheel, burning alive, boiling alive and disembowelling alive.

These tortures, he continued, were no longer employed however, because the brutalizing effects of such horrible spectacles upon public morals produced an evil so great as to outweigh any possible advantages. Equally to the point, he added that like the death penalty itself they also suffered from being transient as examples and irremissible.[27]

Another enthusiast for the death penalty was the reverend Martin Madan, himself a barrister, cousin of the poet William Cowper and, perhaps surprisingly, a Quaker. He believed that all capital laws should rigidly and invariably be enforced.[28] The rigour of the criminal laws, he wrote in a widely-read book, was extremely beneficial. Severity produced fear and made an example of the guilty. Hence the punishment of the law should be executed relentlessly in every case without any relaxation. He abhorred the frequency of pardons which he claimed left the capital statutes 'little more than scarecrows set in a field to frighten the birds from the corn'.[29] His book also caused a sensation, but of a different kind from Beccaria's. As a result of its influence on the judges it produced a temporary bloodbath until countered by Samuel Romilly. According to Romilly

Lord Ellenborough . . . has lately, in the House of Lords, in his usual way of unqualified and vehement assertion, declared that it was false that this book had any effect, whatever, upon either judges or ministers. To this assertion I have only to oppose these plain facts: in the year 1783 . . . before the work was published, there were executed in London only fifty-three malefactors; in 1785 . . . after it was published, there were executed ninety-seven: and it was recently after the publication of this book that was exhibited a spectacle unseen in London for a long course of years before, the execution of nearly twenty criminals at a time.[30]

Uncertainty

The most potent propagandist for the death penalty, however, was another churchman, Archdeacon William Paley, who expounded his views in his *Principles of Moral and Political Philosophy*.[31] The book was dedicated to the Bishop of Carlisle, the father of Lord Chief Justice Ellenborough whose speeches along with those of Lord Chancellor Eldon in the House of Lords in favour of capital punishment were based upon Paley's philosophy. This remarkable work ran through fifteen editions in Paley's own lifetime and was adopted as a textbook by Cambridge University. Its influence remained prevalent for nearly a century.

Only two possible methods of applying the penal laws were perceived by Paley. First, to sentence to death for few actual offences and invariably inflict it in those cases; alternatively, to provide such punishment for every crime which, under any circumstances, might merit death but inflict it upon only a few examples of each kind. Paley saw the second approach as the more suitable for England and gave his blessing to its growing acceptance. He believed that by means of the danger of death hanging over the criminal acts of many people it followed that 'the tenderness of the law cannot be taken advantage of'. If an innocent person were hanged as a result, said Paley, he should be considered as falling for his country, since the general effect was to uphold the welfare of the community![32] 'Acting the patriot for others', grimly observed Romilly, on whom Beccaria's philosophy was to serve as an intellectual stimulus.[33]

Paley actually went so far as to claim that his design showed 'wisdom and humanity', although he rather spoilt the effect by going on to advocate that murderers should meet death by being thrown into a den of wild beasts where they would perish in a manner dreadful to the imagination but concealed from view! This harsh doctrine was eagerly adopted by the aristocratic rulers of this country (and the clergy) to justify their system. It was put into effect by the judiciary, including Lord Ellenborough, Lord Eldon and others who, in the House of Lords, opposed any reform of the criminal law whatsoever. Whilst this battle of ideas between enlightenment and severity was fermenting, what did capital punishment, as the focal point around which the criminal justice system was finely spun, mean for the people of England?

ENDNOTES

1   *Commentaries*, iv: 78, 1770

2   25 Edward III, st. 3: c. 4

3   Dyer, *Reports*, 205, pl. 6, 1561

4   *Commentaries, op. cit.*, 364

5   *History of the Criminal Law of England*, i: 463, 1883

6   4 Henry VII: c. 14

7   3 Institute, *Epilogue*, 1797 edn.

8   cf. also Exodus xxi: 12, 14/17 and Deuteronomy xix: 11/12

9   *Survey of London*, John Stowe, 1603.

10 22 Henry VIII, c. 9

11 Many of the poachers were poor labourers who had lost their ancient rights to the fruits of the earth by the enclosures of common land.

12 *Hansard*, [5] 900-52 (23 May 1821)

13 *A Proposal for Making an Effectual Provision for the Poor etc.*, p. 10, 1753

14 *Miscellaneous Works*, iii: 371, 1846.

15 *Memoirs*, iii: 260, 1840

16 *Criminal Law: Being a Commentary on Bentham on Death Punishment*, 1833

17 *Vacation Thoughts on Capital Punishment*, iv, 1856

18 *Hansard, op. cit.*, 903

19 *Crown Law*, Sir Michael Foster, 70, 1762

20 Quoted in *History of Torture*, L. A. Parry, 15, 1933

21 *Parliamentary History*, [25] 889, 1785-6

22 'Property, Authority and the Criminal Law', in *Albion's Fatal Tree*, 56, 1975

23 *Dei Delitti e delle Pene*, 99, 1769 edn.

24 ibid, 179

25 *Hanging Not Punishment Enough*, Anon, p. 6, 1701 (reprinted 1812)

26 'An Essay Humbly Offer'd, for an Act of Parliament to prevent Capital Crimes etc.', pp. 6-11, 1731

27 *On the Punishment of Death*, xiii, 1833

28 *Thoughts on Executive Justice*, 1785

29 ibid, 137

30 *Memoirs*, i: 89, 1840

31 bk. vi, ch. 9, p. 526, 1786 (2nd edn.)

32 A century later a correspondent to *The Times* claimed that if a murderer were to be hanged to deter others, his benefit to the community should be recognised and his execution administered with honour and dignity

33 'Observations on the Criminal Law of England, as it relates to Capital Punishment; and on the Mode in which it is administered', Note D, 75, 1810.

CHAPTER 2

Gruesome Scenes

The stark reality in England was ghoulish in the extreme. Public strangulation in cold blood on the gallows was obscene and cruel, apart from which it also sometimes dispatched the innocent. But the authorities regarded not only the destruction of offenders but the publicity surrounding it as crucial for deterrence.

The noose tightens

Convicted pirates, for example, were openly hanged on the gallows at Execution Dock, low on the Thames near Wapping, until the rising tide washed over and drowned them in full view of seamen on the river. For offenders generally, their corpses were frequently hung at crossroads and entrances to towns to secure maximum exposure to townspeople and travellers. They were a sight that engaged the curiosity of many foreign visitors.

In London, large numbers of often terror-ridden men and women were hanged in the presence of huge, excited crowds, sometimes numbering up to 100,000 people. For centuries the executions were centred on the Tyburn Tree [1] at the North-east corner of Hyde Park near Marble Arch, where the three triangular-shaped beams forming the gallows could hang as many as 24 felons at one time. Generally speaking, executions took place every six weeks. Then, after 1783, the execution site was moved to outside Newgate Gaol. Similar scenes took place in other major cities and towns throughout the country, normally in front of town halls or in market squares.

Tyburn had commenced its gruesome role as early as the year 1108 when the Normans considered the scaffold to be the tree of justice. Aside from 'justice' however, it provided evidence—as in the Colosseum at Rome—that there are always people in all classes of society who enjoy witnessing spectacles of cruelty. Henry Fielding, who supported capital punishment as a deterrent, claimed that the purpose of carrying out the execution in public was 'to add the punishment of shame to that of death'; but, significantly, he realised that the opposite was often the result.

The day appointed by law for the thief's shame is the day of glory in his own opinion', he wrote. 'His procession to Tyburn, and his last moments there are all triumphant; attended with the compassion of the meek and tender-hearted, and with the applause, admiration, and envy of all bold and hardened . . . And if he hath sense enough to temper his boldness with any degree of decency, his death is spoken of by many with honour, by most with pity, and by all with approbation.[2]

Undoubtedly, the elevating of murderers to the status of popular heroes must have had a detrimental effect on public morality. But with thieves it was a different matter since, as the public well knew, many were condemned to death for trifling and poverty-induced offences. As Fielding understood, the object of

28

the state ritual was not always accepted by the condemned and the crowds, and this contradiction was to bedevil the issue for generations. The world and his wife would gather in festive mood but public feeling against hanging was vividly expressed in many widely-sung ballads and the ever-popular Punch and Judy shows where, after much crude mayhem, including child and wife murder, Punch finally outwits and hangs the archetypal hangman, Jack Ketch himself.

At that time these shows were not children's entertainment but were watched principally by adults who had seen public hangings.[3] Their pleasure at seeing Punch escape the gallows and knock down the Lord Chief Justice, representing the majesty of the law, gives us a fascinating insight into public attitudes.

The gallows

As we have seen, in one form or another the scaffold as employed at Tyburn had been in use since the reign of Henry I in the twelfth century. Over the years it had ended the lives of more than 50,000 men, women and children. Some of the more prominent of them included Perkin Warbeck, John Felton, who assassinated the Duke of Buckingham, and Earl Ferrers. It also claimed Jack Sheppard, the highwayman who was a Houdini of incredible prison escapes that captured the public imagination. These made him a folk hero, although eventually even he could not cheat 'The Deadly Never-green'. After his execution he dangled on the gallows for 15 minutes before a soldier cut him down and the crowd tried in vain to resuscitate him.

For executions at Tyburn an open horse-drawn cart would be placed beneath the tree and, after ropes secured to the beams had been strung around the necks of the prisoners and caps drawn over their faces, the hangman lashed the horse which galloped away with the cart, leaving the delinquents dangling in the air. Yet, as Fielding explained, the horror of their impending fate did nothing to deflate some of those facing execution who flaunted their defiance and dressed as if on the way to a wedding. To do so was regarded as the acceptable face of hanging. But not all the victims were so brave on the journey to such a brutal death where careful calculations of body weight and the length of the drop had not yet been thought of and were not made at that time. In these primitive hangings one end of the rope was formed into a slip knot and put around the neck of the felon who was to be left dangling when the cart was removed and left to die of slow strangulation. Although the length of the rope was roughly nine feet, the 'drop' was often only a few inches and death was regularly messy and prolonged with the still-alive body suffering violent convulsions. Many a wretch was to have what was described in the ribald imagery of the time as, 'a wry mouth and a pissen pair of breeches' and to 'loll out one's tongue at the company'. Despite a more sober approach the words from A. S. Taylor's prestigious study, *The Principles and Practice of Medical Jurisprudence* produce a similar impact. Dr Taylor describes the effects of hanging as being

lividity and swelling of the face, especially of the ears and lips, which appear distorted: the eyelids swollen, and of a blueish colour; the eyes red, projecting forwards, and sometimes partially forced out of their cavities, the pupils dilated, the tongue enlarged, livid and either compressed between the teeth, or sometimes protruded; the lower jaw retracted, and a bloody froth or frothy mucus sometimes escaping from the lips and nostrils . . . the fingers are generally much contracted or firmly clenched . . . the urine and faeces are sometimes involuntarily expelled at the moment of death.[4]

As a 1752 Act for the better preventing of murder[5] made clear, the state's purpose with these gruesome spectacles was to cause terror in the minds of the public although, in fact, they often provoked a self-protective reaction of irreverence and defiance in the watching crowds.

Dread of dissection

Why then did so many flock to these outings with their revelry, ribaldry and often rioting? Although a morbid desire to witness a revolting spectacle was frequently the motive, another reason was to prevent the surgeons acquiring the bodies for dissection at the Surgeon's Hall adjoining Newgate Gaol. Surgeons required cadavers for their courses of instruction in anatomy to medical students and corpses were always in short supply. At least 2,000 were required each year and less than half that number were to be found. Only three types of source were available. Two were illegal and involved grave-snatching by so-called 'resurrection men' or murdering victims in order sell their bodies, as with the notorious Burke and Hare in Edinburgh and Bishop and Williams in London.

The other means was both cruel and class-ridden—but legal. The Murder Act 1752 quite openly declared: 'It is become necessary that some further Terror and peculiar Mark of Infamy be added to the Punishment' of hanging. It encouraged judges to order the use of the gibbet, until then not recognized by statute, in which many tar-soaked bodies were publicly exhibited in iron cages, often for months, as a grisly warning to the lower orders. Sometimes the cages would be hung on posts 30 feet high and spiked with thousands of nails to prevent the recovery of the bodies by relatives under cover of darkness. Following the 1752 Act, at Newgate after an execution the body would be taken to 'The Kitchen' where it was put into a cauldron of boiling pitch prior to being placed in chains described as its 'last suit'. It was then gibbeted.

It seems remarkable that Blackstone could describe hanging in chains as not only a terrifying example to criminals but as being encouraged by the authorities as 'a comfortable sight to the relations and friends of the deceased'.[6] This appears to be unlikely in the extreme, even if the family and friends were distressed that the felon had committed the crime for which he or she was executed. After the enactment of the statute doubts arose as to whether the sentences of gibbeting and dissection might be given alternatively. In *Swan v Jefferys*[7], however, it was held that according to the Act only dissecting should be made part of the judgment and that gibbeting should be left to the discretion of the judge. No doubt it was difficult to dissect a body which had been soaked in tar and left to the elements. In fact, the method of mutilating the body in public following death considered by Parliament to be the most desirable form of aggravated capital punishment was dissection. It was intended to intimidate

30

the 'scum of the people' and act as a general deterrent. This was the 'further Terror' the preamble to the Act prescribed. Consequently, section 4 provided that in all cases the bodies of executed murderers were to be used for dissection and not receive a burial. Thereupon the surgeons cheerfully sent their agents to the scaffold to collect the bodies and return them to Surgeons Hall to be cut up in full view of the public gallery.

Not surprisingly, this produced a reaction among those condemned to death since the dread of mutilation, with mystic overtones, was frequently greater than the fear of death itself. It might prevent resurrection which was believed in by many. Or it might lead to impairment in the after-life. As a result, those about to die on the scaffold often pleaded with relatives or friends to ensure they received a burial in one piece. Close relatives and family would then travel vast distances if necessary to engage in spectacular and ingenious activities to prevent corpses falling into the hands of the surgeons. For example, when Matthew Lee, a shoemaker, was hanged in 1752 for stealing a watch his brother and sister travelled from Lincoln to protect his body and give it a Christian burial.

Stories abound of relatives and surgeons' agents chasing each other's carts through London to recover or steal corpses. The contests, said Fielding, were fierce and bloody and frightful to look at. Sometimes surgeons' agents even masqueraded as parents or other relatives of the dead to secure the bodies without the use of force, which at other times they would engage in without hesitation.

Bungled hangings
Another reason for fearing the surgeons was that a hanging was not carried out in a scientific manner and revival after an incomplete hanging was by no means unknown. Indeed, it appears to have occurred quite often, since death was by asphyxiation and not from a broken neck. Moreover, it could sometimes be planned with the connivance of the hangman, provided he was paid sufficiently.

In one case in 1709 John Smith, a one-time packer, sailor and soldier, was left swaying on Tyburn Tree for two hours following his 'execution' for burglary. After he was cut down he was taken to a nearby house and bled, as was the custom. He soon recovered and related that on the gallows he saw a great blaze, or glaring light which seemed to go out of his eyes with a flash. For the remaining ten years of his life he was known as 'Half-hanged Smith'.[8]

Thomas Reynolds, a collier, was hanged in 1736 for violating the Waltham Black Act by wearing 'a woman's gown and a woman's straw hat' in a turnpike riot. After his 'death' he was cut down by the executioner but as his coffin was being fastened he thrust back the lid. The executioner tried to remedy his mistake but the angry crowds prevented him from doing so and carried Reynolds to a nearby house. There he vomited three pints of blood before being given brandy, but nonetheless he shortly expired.[9]

In November 1740, a 17-year-old, William Duell, floundered on Tyburn Tree for half an hour before the surgeons took him for dissection. After he had been laid on a table to be cut up the surprised surgeons heard him groan. Upon being bled of several ounces of blood he recovered sufficiently to be transported for life instead of being hanged again.[10] Clearly, therefore, hanging might not mean the end, and this is confirmed by Taylor.[11]

Another reason why people attended executions was to touch the body of the hanged. The gallows would often be stormed, particularly by superstitious mothers who wanted to have the still quivering hand of a body touch them or their children. *The Gentleman's Magazine* reported that following a man being hanged at Tyburn on 4 May 1767 'a young woman, with a wen upon her neck, was lifted up while he was hanging, and had the wen rubbed with the dead man's hand, from a superstitious notion that it would effect a cure'.[12] The 'death sweat', as it was called, was widely believed to bring good luck and health to the one touched. Even pieces of the scaffold were taken away as a remedy for toothache!

Fear of death

Despite these incentives to attend executions, it is often suggested that the large crowds in carnival atmosphere at hangings revealed a callous population accustomed to death. Author A. Griffiths, for example, saw a morbid curiosity among the upper classes and a fierce hungry passion in the lower. He wrote that the latter formed, 'a ribald, reckless, brutal mob, violently combative, fighting and struggling for foremost places, fiercely aggressive, distinctly abusive. Spectators often had their limbs broken, their teeth knocked out and sometimes they were crushed to death'.[13]

Certainly large crowds were to some extent induced to attend by the widespread sale of the 'last dying speeches and confessions' of notorious felons. These were usually taken down and written up by the prison chaplain, known officially as the 'Ordinary' but sometimes as 'the great Bishop of the cells'. They were then sold on the streets by the ubiquitous 'Last Dying Speech Man' for a halfpenny or a penny. So enormous was their success that the moralising *Newgate Calendar* and numerous cheap broadsheets each sold ten times as many copies as *The Spectator* or *The Rambler*.

But there was not always a raging desire to enjoy the spectacle of death. Often, as with the execution of the Cato Street conspirators whom many believed were framed,[14] the crowds would vent their fury at the authorities with cries of 'murder' and attempts to attack the hangman. In the Cato Street case two troops of Life Guards had to be deployed to control the angry crowds. And when the Reverend William Dodd was about to be executed for forgery on 27 June 1777, 2,000 troops were stationed near Tyburn to forestall any rescue attempt. Such doubts as to guilt, or feelings that the penalty was excessive, were by no means uncommon.

The intention of the authorities was clearly to inspire terror as a deterrent and their frequent failure to do so was recorded by a contemporary pamphleteer. The writer Edward Gibbon Wakefield, who was a cousin of the prison reformer Elizabeth Fry, wrote in a fictitious letter to a judge:

What with funerals all in black, loud grief for the dead and marks of disgust at the sight of a corpse, people are brought up to dread death . . . Fearing death so much,

we could not live if we expected to die: we should die of the unceasing terror . . .
When you make a law to punish with death, you fly in the face of nature; and she
beats you hollow. You mean to frighten the people, and you frighten them
overmuch. You want them to think of the punishment, but it is so dreadful they will
not think of it . . . Fail not to watch the people. The men, women and children, good,
bad and indifferent, who have gathered to behold the sacred majesty of the law. You
will see such flashing of eyes and grinding of teeth; you will hear sighs and groans,
and words of rage and hatred, with fierce curses . . . [15]

A year earlier Wakefield had published a tract called *Facts Relating to the
Punishment of Death in the Metropolis* which had a powerful impact on the
public. Much of his knowledge of the ineffectiveness of capital punishment as a
deterrent arose from his mixing with prisoners in gaol as one of them. The tract,
which is described by the *Dictionary of National Biography* as remarkable both
for its insight and for its extraordinary power of portrayal, demonstrated that
punishment is a deterrent by its certainty, not its severity.

However, the reason for Wakefield's spell in gaol is not an edifying one. In
1826 he was sentenced to three years' imprisonment for foolishly beguiling
from school Ellen Turner, the daughter of a wealthy Cheshire manufacturer, and
inducing her to marry him at Gretna Green before going with him to the
colonies. He achieved her consent by saying that her father's future depended on
her doing so. The couple got only as far as Calais and the marriage, which had
not been consummated, was subsequently annulled by a special Act of
Parliament. Later, Wakefield became an outstanding colonial statesman.

Journey to Tyburn Tree
The public interest in hangings at Tyburn often commenced in Newgate prison
the day before. Dissipation and debauchery in the sqalid and unhealthy gaol
were a constant feature[16] and on the eve of execution a condemned prisoner
could indulge himself. A not untypical account is that of what was called 'The
Monster's Ball'.

Rhenwick Williams, known as the 'Monster of London' for stabbing several
women, sent invitations to join him in the gaol to some 20 couples among whom
were friends (who had unavailingly given him alibis), relatives and other
prisoners. They all took tea, after which there was dancing followed at night by
supper with wine.[17] Bernard Mandeville refers to 'substantial Breakfasts' and
'Seas of Beer' available on many such occasions.[18] At one time a John Rann
had seven girls dine with him in the gaol.

Paul Lewis, a Sussex parson's son who became an officer of the Royal
Navy and later turned highwayman, spent his last hours in Newgate sitting at the
head of a table drinking and gambling, singing obscene songs, and cursing the
Ordinary whom he threatened to take to hell with him. However, it was not all
fun and games; Lewis lost his nerve as time passed and was reduced to a
nervous wreck before being executed.

Prisoners were also put on exhibition in an open pew draped in a black cloth
in the prison chapel, with a coffin nearby. The public were admitted to this
'theatre' on paying a fee to the gaolers. Often they included peers, MPs,

fashionable ladies and foreign dignitaries. On other occasions, large throngs of people would crowd into the cell of a criminal under sentence of death or he or she might be placed in a separate room for public viewing, rather as mad men and women were on exhibition in asylums. At the execution of Francois Courvoisier (of whom more later), William Makepeace Thackeray mentioned 'six hundred noblemen and gentlemen' being admitted within the walls of the prison.[19]

According to Edward Gibbon Wakefield, the judge provided the animals for the slaughter, the Ordinary broke their hearts in order that they might stand quiet on their execution, whilst Jack Ketch, the hangman, butchered them.[20]

At midnight prior to the execution, the bellman of St Sepulchre's would sing outside the cells of the condemned the following macabre verses:

> All you that in the condemn'd hold do lie,
> Prepare you, for tomorrow you shall die.
> Watch all, and pray, the hour is drawing near,
> That you before the Almighty must appear.
> Examine well yourselves, in time repent,
> That you may not t'eternal flames be sent.
> And when St Sepulchre's bell tomorrow tolls,
> The Lord have mercy on your souls!
> Past twelve o'clock! [21]

On the day of execution came the three-mile procession to meet the public hangman at 'Tyburn Fair'. As the condemned prisoners set off from Newgate the bells of St Sepulchre's would ominously toll 12 times with double strokes in a forlorn attempt to quell the obscene behaviour of the crowds. Holborn Road, along which the procession wound, was known as 'the heavy hill' and 'riding a cart up the heavy hill' was said of those going to be hanged. Drunken, rowdy crowds would follow the condemned, often singing.

Prisoners could, in fact, dress as they liked (as they could right up to the abolition of the death penalty) and, as we have seen, some took the opportunity to appear at their best, often in finery. A wealthy criminal might make the journey in his or her own carriage, although it would be preceded by a coffin in a hearse. For example, the unstable Earl Ferrers, who had murdered his steward, travelled to his death wearing his white wedding suit richly embroidered with silver in a landau drawn by six horses. Unfortunately, at the scaffold faulty mechanism resulted in his suffering particularly slow strangulation before being cut down and taken to Surgeons' Hall for dissection.

Poorer convicts usually sat on the coffin in the hearse with a rope hanging from their necks. Some prisoners managed to retain their dignity; others were a more pitiful sight. As the procession stopped at the Hospital of St Giles in the Fields, all the condemned were offered a 'great bowl of ale to drink at their pleasure, as their last refreshment in life'. When the Hospital was closed down, the ale was provided at the aptly named 'The Bowl'—a nearby public house. Bernard Mandeville provides an eye-witness account of the procession:

34

All the way from Newgate to Tyburn is one continuous Fair for whores and rogues of the meaner sort. Here the most abandoned rakehells may light on women as shameless . . . No modern rabble can long subsist without the darling cordial 'geneva'. The intelligible sounds that are heard among them are oaths and vile expressions. As these undisciplined armies have no particular enemies to encounter but cleanliness and good manners, so nothing is more entertaining to them than the dead carcasses of dogs and cats, or for want of them, rags flung as high and as far as a strong arm can carry them, and commonly directed where the throng is thickest. [22]

At the place of execution, wrote Fielding, 'the psalm was sung amidst the curses and quarrelling of hundreds of the most abandoned and profligate of mankind, upon whom, so dead are they to every sense of decency, all the preparation of the unhappy wretches seems to serve only for subject of a barbarous kind of mirth, altogether inconsistent with humanity',[23]

Once the prisoners were on the scaffold the parson would endeavour to convince them that they were going to their death not only as a deterrent to others but for their own good in the next life—provided they repented first. One prisoner is said to have retorted to the parson that he liked the life here well enough if they would only let him stay. Another, upon being asked if there was some comfort he wanted, answered that all he wanted was for some other man to hang in his place. Despite such occasional spirited replies both the processions and the hangings on Tyburn Tree were macabre spectacles with little or no deterrent effect, and the poet William Blake was appalled by some processions he witnessed when as a child he lived in Stratford Place near Tyburn. [24] Jonathan Swift, on the other hand, gives a satirical picture of the journey in his 'Clever Tom Clinch, Going to be Hanged', 1727:

As clever Tom Clinch, while the rabble was bawling,
Rode stately through Holborn to die in his calling,
He stopt at the George for a bottle of sack,
And promised to pay for it when he came back.
His waistcoat, and stockings, and breeches were white;
His cap had a new cherry ribbon to tie't . . .
He swore from his cart 'It was all a damn'd lie!'
The hangman for pardon fell down on his knee;
Tom gave him a kick in the guts for his fee . . .
My conscience is clear, and my spirits are calm,
And thus I go off without prayer-book or psalm;
Then follow the practice of clever Tom Clinch,
Who hung like a hero, and never would flinch. [25]

The hangman at that time was often a criminal who had been reprieved on condition that he undertook the office. One such was John Price who was eventually hanged himself in 1718. This method of recruitment meant professional skill was usually lacking and the celebrated pirate Captain Kidd, for instance, experienced the breaking of the rope before he could finally be disposed of in 1701. Another pirate, John Gow, suffered the same fate when friends pulled his legs too forcibly, anxious to put him out of his misery.

The long drop

By 1783 the prosperous householders in the fashionable districts around Tyburn and on the route of the processions found the crowds on execution days a considerable nuisance, as did Edmund Burke, the City of London and the sheriffs of London and Middlesex, Sir Bernard Turner and Thomas Skinner. By this time they considered the hangings had lost their terror and, with the processions, merely encouraged vice. As a consequence, in that year the Fox-North Coalition government had the scaffold removed to a large open space in front of the Debtor's Door of Newgate prison, adjoining the site now occupied by the Central Criminal Court in the Old Bailey.

Apart from the sensibilities of affluent householders, the authorities believed that executions at the new spot adjacent to the place of confinement of the inmates of the prison would help the convicts to see the error of their ways and repent. Repentance was considered to be another crucial contribution to general deterrence in a society more religious than that of today. Ordinaries sometimes went to cruel lengths to secure a semblance of it, often in the presence of spectators during the hours before execution.

The crowds outside Newgate continued to be at least as large as those around Tyburn and it was still believed by the government that the perceived chilling cautionary effect of hanging in public would remain. Enterprising citizens owning adjoining properties made seats available for those who could pay. In one case fourteen shillings a place was charged at the 'King of Denmark' and one pound at Luttman's eating house which was nearer to the scaffold. But the affluent voyeurs were not those whom it was desired to deter.

In the event, all that was lost in the move were the mischievous processions which the sheriffs so disliked. Dr Johnson, however, thought the change was rank innovation since if executions did not draw spectators they were not answering their purpose. For him, the old method was more satisfactory to all parties. 'The public', he said, 'was gratified by a procession, the criminal is supported by it. Why is all this to be swept away?'[26] He need not have been too concerned since the crowds outside the more central Newgate were often denser than they had been at Tyburn.

At the same time as the removal of public executions to Newgate a refinement in the method of execution was introduced. This was the adoption of the 'long drop' technique, first used to hang ten men outside that gaol. The inventor is not known but it was said to have been introduced from Ireland where it had first been suggested by surgeons. The device draped with black cloth consisted of small collapsible platforms about a foot in height which were placed on top of the actual scaffold. The mechanism by which the platforms operated is described by John Laurence in these words:

> The small square of planking on which the malefactor stood was supported by one or more beams of wood, to which ropes were tied. When all was ready the executioner retired beneath the scaffold, and, on the word being given, pulled the ropes which dragged away the props and the drop fell.[27]

36

Although undoubtedly crude, the drop (or trap-door) continued to be used to execute prisoners in front of the gaol and was intended to be a good deal more efficient than the earlier method of hanging. It was also meant to be humane in that death was supposed to be instantaneous and more certain, being now by a broken neck and not by asphyxiation; when it worked properly.

In any event, improvements continued to be made and in 1824 the drop constructed for the execution of John Thurtell, who murdered William Weare, was

ingeniously erected to the purpose for which it was intended and was calculated to terminate the existence of the unhappy culprit in the shortest possible period. There was now a temporary platform with a falling leaf, supported by bolts, and upon this the prisoner was to be placed. The bolts were fixed in such a manner as to be removed in an instant, and as instantaneously the victim of his own crime would be launched into eternity. Above this platform was a cross beam, to which the fatal cord was affixed.[28]

To see it, said William Makepeace Thackeray later, gave 'a kind of dumb electric shock, which causes one to start a little, and give a sort of gasp for breath'.[29] What is worse, the condition of the rope and the length of the drop, related to the weight of the prisoner, were left to the discretion of the hangman. Although there was an official 'Table of Drops' governing the length it was often ignored by executioners.

At the execution of Robert Goodall in Norwich Castle on 30 November 1885, hangman James Berry used a drop of five feet eight inches. As a consequence Goodall's head was wrenched from his body. Berry had made a rough guess at the length of drop required, wrote the *Pall Mall Gazette* the following day, and this led to the 'hideous and revolting result'. The *St James Gazette* added its voice of disquiet.

A year earlier *The Standard* newspaper carried the story of the 'long struggle' of a man executed in Kirkdale gaol near Liverpool.[30] The horrifying examples of bungled executions, when the earlier drop was only a few inches, were clearly being re-enacted later with the long drop. However, although the sometimes lengthy suffering of victims on the scaffold became less frequent, bungling was not a thing of the past, since some hangmen continued to be inefficient. In any event, it remained a degrading spectacle.

The change of location to Newgate sometimes proved problematic. In 1807 when two murderers, Holloway and Haggerty, were to be executed for killing a lavender merchant some 40,000 people collected in the vicinity. When a pieman stooped down to pick up pies which had scattered from his basket, several men and a woman with a baby at her breast fell over him. In an endeavour to escape from the intense pressure that built up, some spectators tried to push their way out and the crowd panicked. Nearly one hundred people, including women, were killed by suffocation or being trampled to death. The horror and disgrace of public executions continued.

An estimated 100,000 spectators assembled to view the execution of the banker Henry Fauntleroy in 1824 and blocked all the approaches to the prison.

At Courvoisier's hanging in 1840 sums of two pounds and more were paid for a window overlooking the 'display'.[31] As an eye-witness, Thackeray described the wealthy spectators as, 'young dandies with moustaches and cigars; some quiet, fat, family-parties, of simple, honest tradesmen and their wives . . . sipping their tea'.[32]

When Maria and Frederick Manning were executed at the scaffold on the roof of Horsemongers Lane gaol in London in 1849 for murdering a friend named O'Connor, a young woman was crushed to death against barriers erected by the police to prevent trouble.[33] On this occasion some 30,000 people were present to witness the hangings and more than 2.5 million broadsheets, containing rhymed verses and describing the last moments, the execution and the 'confessions' were sold.[34] In his 'confession' Manning was depicted as saying that the victim, who had been shot by Mrs Manning, 'moaned . . . I never liked him well, and I battered his head with a ripping chisel'. Before their executions the Mannings were made to walk over their graves as they had made their victim do over his.

According to *The Times* the crowds at the hangings made the atmosphere like that of a fairground and included 'the dregs and offcoursings of the population of London . . . Irish labourers smoking clay pipes and muzzy with beer, pickpockets plying their light-fingered art, little ragged boys climbing up posts . . .' As to the hangings, the newspaper continued; 'In an instant Calcraft withdrew the bolt, the drop fell . . . They died almost without a struggle . . . The mob during the terrible scene exhibited no feeling except one of heartless indifference and levity'.[35] In fact, hangman William Calcraft was not always so effective.[36] William Bousfield was executed by him on 31 March 1856 having been carried to the scaffold with his face swathed in cloth after burning himself in the fire in his prison cell. Once he was placed above the drop Calcraft acted swiftly having received a letter containing a threat to shoot him on the scaffold. After putting the rope around Bousfield's neck he drew the bolt and ran off. Bousfield hung motionless for a short time and then drew himself up and rested his foot on the drop. One of the attendant turnkeys rushed forward and pushed him off but again he secured a foothold. The chaplain made the scared Calcraft return but four times Bousfield managed to raise himself. When he was forced off for the last time Calcraft threw himself around his legs and by the force of his weight finally succeeded in strangling him.

Incidentally, Calcraft served as hangman for longer than anyone else—for 45 years from 1829 to 1874. The City of London paid him a retainer of a guinea a week for his services and a further guinea for each execution. He was also in great demand in other parts of the country and he sold the dreaded rope by the inch. The hanged men's effects were purchased by Madame Tussauds and other exhibitions. Presumably Calcraft was quite wealthy and was said to be very fond of his child and grandchildren as well as his many pets.

He was succeeded by William Marwood in 1879. Marwood was more sympathetic to his victims but nevertheless said that he was only doing God's work and claimed that he slept as soundly as a child and was 'never disturbed by phantoms'. His retainer from the City of London was twenty pounds a year and

38

ten pounds for each execution. This was remarkably high and some 80 years later the hangman was getting no more. Yet Marwood had asked to be paid a retainer of £100 per annum and Berry £400 per annum. Both requests were turned down. Traditionally, executioners were selected informally with the decision resting with the High Sheriff of the county concerned. But with the shocking example of James Berry, the chief executioner of the 1880s, mentioned earlier, the Home Office decided that its intervention was required. Berry was believed to be a drunkard and to be selling pieces of rope as souvenirs. He was also responsible for a number of serious incidents during executions, including decapitations.[37] Of course, he was by no means alone in this but perhaps Calcraft and others did not come to the attention of the Home Office. In any event, by January 1890 the Home Office had introduced a formal system of selection and training for hangmen.[38]

ENDNOTES

1 Named after the nearby river Tyburn

2 *An Inquiry into the Causes of the Frequent Executions at Tyburn*, p. 265, 1725.

3 *The Hanging Tree: Execution and the English People 1770-1868*, V. A. C. Gatrell, p. 120, 1994.

4 ii: 39, 1883.

5 25 Geo. II, c. 37

6 *op. cit.*

7 *Crown Law*, Foster, p. 107, 1762

8 *Tyburn Tree; Its History and Annals*, Alfred Marks, p. 221/2, 1908

9 'The Ordinary of Newgate, His Account of the Behaviour, Confession, and Dying Words, of the Malefactors who were executed at Tyburn', 26 July 1736; also the *Gentleman's Magazine*, vi: 422 (1736)

10 *Reade's Weekly Journal* (30 December 1740)

11 *op. cit*

12 276, 1767

13 *The Chronicles of Newgate*, 2 vols., 1884

14 For details see *Thomas Wakley - An Improbable Radical*, John Hostettler, c. 2, 1993

15 'The Hangman and the Judge: Or a Letter from Jack Ketch to Mr Justice Alderson', pp. 3/5, 1833

16 cf. 'Finding Solace in Eighteenth-Century Newgate', W. J. Sheehan, in *Crime in England, 1550-1800*, J. S. Cockburn (ed.), 16229/245, 1977

17 Reported in *The Oracle* (20 August 1790)

18 *An Enquiry into the Causes of the Frequent Executions at Tyburn etc.*, pp. 18-19, 1725

19 'Going to see a Man Hanged', *Fraser's Magazine*, xx: 1 (August 1840)

20 *op. cit*, 2

21 BM. Add. MSS. Francis Place Papers. 27, 826. fol. 14

22 *op. cit.*

23 *op. cit.*

24 'Milton', *Blake's Poems and Prophesies,* p. 113, 1927

25 *Poetical Works,* p. 202, 1833 edn.

26 Boswell's *Life of Johnson,* p. 1211, 1961 edn.

27 *A History of Capital Punishment,* p. 45, 1932

28 *The Newgate Calendar,* vi: 316, 1824

29 *Going to see a Man Hanged,* op.cit

30 8 December 1884.

31 Radzinowicz, i: 204, 1948

32 *op. cit*

33 *The Times,* 16 November 1849

34 Radzinowicz, iv: 349, 1968

35 *The Times, op. cit.*

36 *The Law on Trial, or Personal Recollections of the Death Penalty, and its Opponents,* Alfred H. Dymond, p. 160, 1865

37 HO 144/18/46327

38 HO 144/212/A48697D.

CHAPTER 3

Moves To Minimise Capital Punishment

As noted in *Chapter 1* Romilly, who was a barrister by profession, readily embraced the penal philosophy of Beccaria.

Sir Samuel Romilly

Born in Frith Street, Soho, in 1757, he was the son of a Huguenot immigrant from France. It may be significant that his early education was in the hands of a gloomy nurse who attempted to improve his mind by reading to him long pieces from the *Newgate Calendar*. Romilly was also considerably influenced by his close friend, the law reformer Jeremy Bentham, whom he often met in the Bowood Whig circle of Lord Shelburne. Bentham believed severe laws encouraged criminals rather than deterred them. Hanging also had the undesirable effect of producing sentiments of pity for the sufferer, with the spectators sharing his or her ordeal. He gave a scientific basis to the whole subject of penal law for which some form of realistic and humanitarian approach had long been required. In the process he made criminal jurisprudence a good deal more exact.

Although totally opposed to the death penalty,[1] he believed that when it existed it should at least be made clear to precisely what crimes it applied. He wrote with deep irony and in his sometimes obscure style that

> hanging men for they knew *what*, would be *theory*: hanging men for nobody knows what, is *practice*; and how bad a thing theory is, and how good a thing practice, no one who has had the advantage of sitting at the feet of Lord or Lady Eldon can be at a loss to know.[2]

He also explained that the desirable qualities lacking in capital punishment were, *inter alia*:

1. It could not provide for compensation as its source was destroyed.
2. Executed men could not be reformed and rendered of some use to society.
3. The death penalty was unequal since men were unequal and it was not variable or remissible.
4. Judges were not infallible and many innocent victims had perished.[3]

However, despite Bentham's friendship and support Romilly still had to battle against the ideas of Madan and Paley whose influence on the judiciary was alarming. He had already attacked Madan's proposals in an essay which he sent to each of the judges who soon recoiled from the increased severity they had adopted earlier. He maintained that imprisonment—then little used for criminals unless on remand or for debt—was an appropriate and adequate substitute for the death penalty in most cases. Romilly's booklet had the distinction of being translated into French but, significantly, was banned by the Paris police.

Unusually for the time, Romilly saw the principal aim of punishment as the reformation of the criminal—and he believed that the excessive severity of the criminal law, far from acting as a deterrent as Madan claimed, was the main cause of the increase in crime. Madan's view, he wrote, 'breathes a spirit contrary to the genius of the present times'. His doctrine 'is not supported by dispassionate argument; instead he uses far-fetched hyperboles, ferocious language, all the most specious colourings of rhetoric'.[4]

Although still only a young man Romilly also tackled Dr Paley head on. When Paley declared that the execution of an innocent person was justified by the security of civil life, Romilly angrily responded that the escape of ten guilty criminals was no trivial ill but it was less destructive of the security and happiness of the community than that one innocent man should be put to death. 'When guilty men escape', he wrote, 'the law has merely failed but when an innocent man is condemned, it does great harm and creates a sense of insecurity in the population at large'.[5] He also described the devastating consequences not only for the executed man, but for his equally innocent wife and children whose lives would be lived out in misery and ignominy.

In 1806, although not a member of Parliament, Romilly was appointed solicitor-general in Greville's 'Ministry of All the Talents' and knighted. At the instigation of the Whig leader Charles James Fox he was subsequently returned to the House of Commons as member for Queensborough. He explained that he was determined to devote his life in Parliament to attempting to ameliorate what he described as 'Our sanguinary and barbarous penal code, written in blood'. He did, in fact, accept that capital punishment was necessary for some particularly heinous crimes but stigmatised its contemporary use as a 'lottery of justice'. His first attempts at reform between 1808 and 1812, were successful in having the death penalty repealed for the offences of picking pockets, theft from the premises of calico printers and vagrancy by a soldier or sailor. He also secured an end to the punishment of disembowelling alive. Thereafter he had to fight against the entrenched opposition to his humanitarian crusade of the House of Lords and, in particular, Lords Ellenborough and Eldon.

By this time Romilly's early attacks on Madan and Paley had developed into a more mature penal theory. This he fully expressed in his famous speech in the House of Commons on 9 February 1810 when moving for leave to bring in three Bills to abolish the death penalty for stealing five shillings or less in shops, for stealing to the value of forty shillings in a dwellinghouse and for stealing from a vessel on a river or canal.[6] His lengthy and powerful refutation of Paley caused W. Windham to exclaim that Paley's works had 'done more for the moral improvement of mankind than perhaps the writings of any other man that had ever existed'.

In his speech Romilly's main thrust was an attack on the frequency of capital punishment. 'There was no country on the face of the earth', he said, 'in which there were so many different offences according to law to be punished with death as in England'. Some statutes could not be read without horror and a failure to understand how they had come to be enacted.

'Such, for instance', he continued, 'as the Act which makes it a capital offence in any person, male or female, to be seen in the company of gypsies for the space of a month. That Act has, however, been enforced for nearly a century; and it is lamentable to think that no less than thirteen persons had been executed under its cruel provisions at one Assizes'. Confirming the figures of John Stowe he said that about 72,000 people were executed in the reign of Henry VIII, which was at a rate of about 2,000 people a year. He then gave the following figures for more recent times.

'In London and Middlesex, from 1749 to 1772', he said, 'the number of persons convicted of capital crimes was 428 of whom 306 were executed'. On the other hand, in London from 1801 to 1809 only about one-eighth of those convicted were executed. In 1808, 87 had been convicted with only three executed. The figures showed, he said, 'how little the penal laws had operated in preventing crimes'. For stealing in a shop or dwellinghouse the law might be made more effective if capital punishment were removed, for people offended now certain that they would not incur the punishment.

For stealing in a dwellinghouse, he continued, in London and Middlesex, in seven years, only eight had been executed out of 1,802 convicted. In other parts of the Kingdom it was one out of 3,000. It might be said the law had been 'unexecuted'. Judges, jurors, prosecutors and the Crown all felt that it was impossible in such cases for the statutes to be carried into effect. Then there was the question of the uncertainty of penalty. As an example Romilly instanced the case where different judgments had been pronounced upon the same offence by different judges. On the Norfolk Circuit two men were indicted for stealing poultry. One of them escaped, the other was tried by Lord Loughborough and convicted. Having until then been a man of good character, and this was his first offence, he was sentenced to only six months imprisonment. The other man, hearing this and desiring to see his family, surrendered. He was tried before Mr Justice Gould who thought that as this was a first offence it would be for the public good to punish him severely as an example and he was transported for seven years. This, said Romilly, was in line with Paley's doctrine, whereas every man should by positive law know what to expect.

In the debate the Chancellor of the Exchequer, Spencer Perceval, predictably defended judicial discretion and the solicitor-general, Sir T. Plomer, accused Romilly of endeavouring to cast 'discredit and odium' on the whole of the criminal law.

Demand for certainty
Romilly continued to deny that the exercise of discretion in the carrying out of the laws could produce a regular, matured and well digested system. On the contrary, he stressed the importance of certainty and asked how it could be said that the species of punishment was clearly determined for every offence, when, in practice, it was for the judge to say whether a criminal was to suffer death, or possibly transportation or imprisonment. Liberal opinion was also disturbed at

43

the problems raised by the uncertainty surrounding whether the sentence of death would actually be carried out. Furthermore, Romilly realised that although by law a man should only be punished if convicted of a crime clearly alleged against him, criminals were frequently executed for aggravations not set out in the indictment. Equally, there was rarely any real alternative to the pronouncement of the death penalty for felony at this time regardless of extenuating circumstances or the particular facts of a case.

Many trivial crimes were punished with death, with no discrimination on the grounds of sex or age. For instance, in 1749 a John Cross was hanged for robbing a man of sixpence on the highway. In 1783 a John Kelly was similarly hanged at Tyburn for stealing sixpence and a farthing in a public street.[7] Over the years numerous women and children were hanged for similar petty thefts. As an alternative to such atrocities, Romilly urged that if a punishment were really certain then it could be very light indeed. Furthermore, juries would be more willing to convict and not, by 'pious perjury', reduce the value of property stolen to below the then capital limit of 12 pence. In 1833 Lord Suffield actually submitted to Parliament a list of 555 perjured verdicts returned at the Old Bailey over a period of 15 years. For instance, the verdicts of juries for offences of stealing 40 shillings or more from dwelling houses often reduced the amount to 39 shillings only.[8] And, it was not unknown for a jury to treat a stolen sheep as merely its skin to prevent the thief being hanged.

Romilly further asserted that capital laws formed a kind of standard of cruelty to justify a harsh and excessive exercise of authority. Thus they became obstacles to social progress and also tended to increase the scale of all other punishments. His Bills over the years, although well supported in the Commons by such leaders as William Wilberforce and George Canning, were lost largely because the bishops combined with Lord Chancellor Eldon and Lord Chief Justice Ellenborough to defeat them in the House of Lords. For instance, a Bill to abolish the death penalty for shoplifting to the value of five shillings and under was passed by the Commons and defeated in the Lords on no less than six separate occasions. Writing of the bishops, Romilly said:

> I rank these prelates amongst the members who were solicited to vote against the Bill, because I would rather be convinced of their servility towards government, than that, recollecting the mild doctrines of their religion, they could have come down to the House spontaneously, to vote that transportation for life is not a sufficiently severe punishment for the offence of pilfering what is of five shillings' value, and that nothing but the blood of the offender can afford an adequate atonement for such a transgression.[9]

The Bill was finally passed in 1832, long after Romilly's death. Lord Ellenborough, in particular, was bitterly hostile to any change in the criminal law on the ground that such law was sanctified by its antiquity. In attacking a Bill to abolish the pillory in 1815 he held up its ancient origin as a merit and took the opportunity to declaim against any innovation in the penal system.

Romilly asked his Lordship whether he was still in favour of such 'bulwarks of the Constitution' as disembowelling alive, or the burning of women at the stake for felony, and whether the removal of those 'bulwarks' had endangered the Constitution. Ellenborough also managed to see the horrors and sufferings in transportation as 'only a summer airing by an easy migration to a milder climate'.[10] In fact, of course, throughout history—on each occasion a crime was removed from the capital list—woeful forecasts were made of a descent into the pit of lawlessness only to be proved groundless. Nothing can condone murder, but cold-blooded violence by society can only help breed such a crime, not prevent it. It becomes a form of primitive retribution as if the state chose to steal from a thief or decided to burn down the home of an arsonist. As Thackeray put it, after watching the execution of Francois Courvoisier for murder, 'I fully confess that I came away down Snow Hill that morning with a disgust for murder, but it was for the murder I saw done'.[11]

Romilly's speech of 9 February 1810 made a deep and lasting impression in the country at large, as well as in the Commons. It also received considerable support from the influential journals of the day, the *Monthly Review* and the *European Magazine*, both of which were favourable to reform of the criminal law. The *Monthly Magazine* was wildly favourable, the Whig *Edinburgh Review*, the *Quarterly Review* and the *Westminster Review* were all enthusiastic in their praise—to which must be added the support of the London liberal newspapers the *Morning Herald* and the *Morning Chronicle*.

Published as a booklet entitled *Observations on Criminal Laws,* the speech was described by Henry Brougham (later Lord Chancellor) as a 'beautiful and interesting tract'.[12] It marked the beginning of the growth of a deep-rooted tide of public opinion anxious for reform. In the event, in the face of furious opposition Romilly did achieve some further successes, notably six statutes to improve the criminal law. This was less than he deserved but his arguments were to recur again and again in the speeches and proposals of the great criminal law reformers who followed him, including Sir Robert Peel and Lord John Russell, as well as his contemporary and friend, Jeremy Bentham who died on the day the Reform Act became law in 1832.

It was a tragedy when Romilly himself died, by his own hand, on 2 November 1818, just four days after the death of his beloved wife. *Felo de se* was, of course, a capital crime itself at the time but only if the person was of sound mind. Romilly's grief was unbearable and he may well not have been so at the moment of his death.

Arbitrary selection

By the 1820s the main issues concerning reformers were the inhumanity of the sheer number of capital statutes, the question whether the death penalty was effective as a deterrent and necessary at all, and the effect of the uncertainty of punishment caused by the arbitrary selection to be executed of only a proportion of those convicted. On the last point, Dr Stephen Lushington, member of Parliament and a tireless abolitionist, was to tell of having seen 35 men in Newgate awaiting execution when the governor had pointed out four or five of them who were likely to be hanged. He was right about the first number but in the event it was a different four who were actually hanged. That sort of thing, Lushington said, made juries unwilling to convict.[13]

After Romilly died, Sir James Mackintosh donned his mantle and was soon instrumental in securing the appointment of the 1819 Select Committee of the House of Commons on the Criminal Law relating to Capital Punishment, of which he became chairman.[14] The remit of the committee was achieved against the strong opposition of Lord Castlereagh who wanted a more diffused committee with far wider terms of reference on the administration of the criminal law generally.

Mackintosh told the committee of his experience in India when Recorder of Bombay for seven years. During that period the carrying out of capital punishments was discontinued and in consequence the committing of capital offences greatly diminished. This was particularly true of murder, notwithstanding a doubling of the population and the introduction of 4,000 European troops into Bombay. Capital convictions for the whole seven years were only 109 (murder accounting for six) with no executions taking place. The preceding seven years had seen sixteen convictions for murder with 12 executions. When it was published, the committee's report called for the abolition of the death penalty for a number of crimes including some thefts and forgeries as well as numerous property offences, and being found disguised in the Mint. However, it met with a good deal of Parliamentary opposition and at the time achieved very little in changing the law. Nevertheless, it had a powerful effect on public opinion and in 1820 resulted in the enactment of the three Bills relating to shoplifting and theft so often advocated by Romilly.

Sleep of a century

Subsequently, Sir Robert Peel was appointed home secretary in January 1822, and with a firm determination declared that he would improve the penal law and break 'the sleep of a century'. He told the House of Commons that he wished to remove the punishment of death in all cases where it was practicable and later admitted that, 'it is impossible to conceal from ourselves that capital punishments are more frequent and the criminal law more severe, on the whole, in this country than in any country in the world'.[15]

Nevertheless, he had a sensitive awareness of how far Parliament would follow him and this displeased Bentham. Understandably, although he probably underestimated the support available to him, Peel was anxious to avoid the problems that had beset Romilly. Moreover, he admitted that he despaired of finding any secondary punishment that would be a suitable alternative to death, although he did accept that transportation was appropriate for some crimes.[16] This was before the widespread building of penitentiaries, later to provide a substitute in the form of imprisonment, greatly expanded.

As it happens, Peel secured the consolidation and repeal of a considerable number of statutes which had the significant effect of reducing the incidence of capital punishment. The Waltham Black Act was one so repealed and the farce of benefit of clergy abolished. His achievements were remarkable and his very success increased the clamour for further reform. As part of this, the movement for abolition was now reaching new heights. The Committee for the Diffusion of Information on the Subject of Capital Punishments was formed and William Ewart, a barrister and the Liberal MP for Dumfries, commenced his campaign—against the opposition of Peel who feared a backlash—to secure a further reduction in the number of capital offences. He was supported by a long line of prominent figures, including Fowell Buxton, Mackintosh, Brougham and Lord John Russell. The committee's members included Dr Stephen Lushington and as a typical example of its activities it held a public meeting at Exeter Hall, London on 30 May 1831 with Dr Lushington as a speaker. A resolution was passed with acclaim calling upon Parliament to give attention to the punishment of death which was 'at variance with justice, religion and the feelings of the nation'. Another member of the Committee was Basil Montague who was instrumental in saving many convicted prisoners from the gallows. At the age of sixty he generalised his experiences in an influential book of wider implications than its title *Thoughts on the Punishment of Death for Forgery* suggests.[17]

The irrepressible Ewart brought in a Bill, on 27 March 1832, to repeal capital punishment for stealing in a dwellinghouse to the value of five pounds and for horse, sheep and cattle stealing. This represented an important step since out of the 9,316 death sentences passed in the period 1825-1831, as many as 3,178 related to these offences. On the 'principle' of flexibility, 70 of these sentences were carried out from a total of 410 for all offences. Nevertheless, Peel intervened no less than three times in the debates to oppose the Bill,[18] mistakenly convinced that he had gone as far as public opinion would allow. He asserted that the proposal was 'a most dangerous experiment', and that 'as civilisation increased, the facility for the commission of crime increased more rapidly than the facility for the protection of it'. Despite this, in the light of his overall success it is difficult to understand why some writers consider that Peel was largely ineffective or even desired to outflank the reform movement and make the law more of a terror.[19] He wanted a more efficient criminal law system but so did Romilly, Bentham and other reformers. Literature also played its part. Horace Walpole deplored 'the monthly shambles at Tyburn' as scenes that shocked humanity.[20] Dr Johnson declaimed that 'to equal robbery with murder is to reduce murder to robbery; to confound in common minds the gradations of iniquity and incite the commission of a greater crime to prevent the detection of a less'.[21] Oliver Goldsmith questioned the right of the state to punish offences against property with death at all.[22]

On 2 August 1833 Lord Suffield was to introduce into the House of Lords a Bill to abolish the death penalty for housebreaking.[23] In the course of his speech he referred to a case in the previous May where a nine-year-old boy named Nicholas White had, whilst playing with some other children, pulled some printers' colours out of a broken window. Despite their value being only two pence the boy was tried at the Old Bailey, convicted and sentenced to be hanged under the statute Lord Suffield was attempting to repeal. Nicholas White was later reprieved.

Both the Duke of Wellington and Lord Wynford opposed Suffield's Bill. It is significant, however, that neither of them cared to grapple with the facts and arguments put forward by Suffield nor did they venture to press the House to a division. In the event, the Bill received the royal assent 12 days after it was introduced—a remarkably speedy enactment.

Petitions

Further progress was called for by journals and newspapers and so many petitions for abolition were flowing into the House of Commons that Henry Brougham exclaimed that 'the Table groaned with them'.[24] Indeed, as many as 24,492 had been presented in the five years ending in 1831 although not all related to capital punishment.[25] Perhaps the most significant of those that did so was that from 214 cities and towns calling for the abolition of death for forgery.[26] It included the signatures of some 1,000 bankers who claimed they suffered most from the crime but found from experience that the possibility of inflicting the death penalty for it often prevented the prosecution, conviction and punishment of the criminals and thus endangered the very property it was intended to protect. Of interest is what George Cruikshank wrote:

> About the year 1818 I was returning home between 8 a.m. and 9 a.m. down Ludgate Hill, and saw several human beings hanging opposite Newgate, and to my horror two of them were women. On inquiring, I was informed that it was for passing forged one pound notes! It had a great effect on me, and I determined, if possible, to put a stop to this shocking destruction of life for merely obtaining a few shillings by fraud. I felt sure that in many cases the rascals who had forged the notes induced these poor, ignorant women to go into the gin shops and get 'something to drink' and then pass the notes and hand them the change.[27]

The illustrator made a sketch of a 'Bank-note not to be Imitated', the publication of which created a sensation and caused the Bank of England to discontinue the issue of one pound notes. By 1832 death for most types of forgery was abolished. The bankers' claim about the difficulty in securing convictions was confirmed by an earlier petition from jurors which said:

> . . . laws a disgrace to our civilisation, by retaining the opprobrious distinction of being the most sanguinary in Europe. That Christianity, common reason, and sound policy demand that the laws which affect the liberties and lives of men should proportion the punishment to the offence, and not teach cruelty to the people by examples of vindictive legislation . . . That in the present state of the law, juries feel extremely reluctant to convict where the penal consequences of the offence excite a conscientious horror on their minds, lest the rigorous performance of their duty as jurors should make them accessory to judicial murder.[28]

Despite such strong and informed feelings Peel himself led the opposition to the outcry. He knew much remained to be done but was afraid that if Parliament proceeded too rapidly a strong prejudice would arise in the country against the new measures and, as he had said earlier, the 'great object of justice and humanity might be defeated'.[29]

Many middle class groupings were concerned that their property was unsafe because more and more juries were failing to convict for theft as well as forgery. This abolitionist trend in the middle class arose not out of squeamishness or sentimentality but from the practical reasoning, borne out by the facts, that extreme severity made prosecutions less likely and juries reluctant to convict. The many petitions arguing, as we have seen, that the severity of the laws made them unenforceable, added to the swell of complaints entering Parliament and a number of capital statutes were repealed in the face of continuing strong opposition from the House of Lords. Members of the Lords, in the main, were landowners and bishops who were not threatened in the same manner, but occasionally they succumbed to pressure from outside. Nevertheless, despite the repeals, crimes which still attracted the death penalty by 1832 included rape, buggery, murder, robbery, some types of forgery, attempted murder resulting in injury and housebreaking with larceny to any value.

ENDNOTES

1 *Rationale of Punishment*, p. 196, 1830

2 BM. Add. MSS. 40393 f.65

3 *op. cit.*

4 *Observations on a Late Publication Intitled Thoughts on Executive Justice*, 1786

5 *ibid.*

6 *Hansard*, [15] 366/74

7 *Gentleman's Magazine* (7 March 1783)

8 *Hansard* [20] 278-82

9 *Memoirs*, ii: 331. 1840.

10 *ibid*, 333-4

11 *op. cit.*

12 *Edinburgh Review*, 19: 389-415 (1811/12)

13 *Evidence to the Criminal Law Commissioners*, Parliamentary Papers, XXXVI: 183, (1836)

14 P.P. VIII, i, 1819

15 *Hansard* [23] 1176 (1 April 1830)

16 Transportation was more widely imposed after 1839 when it was made a punishment for 38 classes of felony and 96 classes of misdemeanour

17 *Thoughts on the Punishment of Death for Forgery*, 1831

18 *Hansard*, [11] 952-3; and *Hansard* [13] 195-7 and 198-200

19 e.g. *The Crusade Against Capital Punishment*, Elizabeth Tuttle, vii, 1961; and *The Hanging Tree*, V. A. C. Gatrell, p. 568, 1994

20 *Memoirs of the Last Ten Years of George II's Reign*, i. 224

21 *The Rambler*, No. 114, 20 April 1751

22 *The Vicar of Wakefield*, c. xxvii, 1852 edn.

23 *Hansard*, [20] 278-82

24 *Hansard*, [24] 1058 (1830)

25 Radzinowicz, i: 528.

26 *Journals of the House of Commons*, [85] 463 (24 May 1830)

27 Quoted by John Laurence, *op. cit.*, 13

28 *Hansard*, N.S. [6] 1174-76, 6 September 1831. Introduced by Brougham

29 ibid, [16] 635/6 (1826/7).

CHAPTER 4

Rush To Reform

The extension of the franchise and the redistribution of seats resulting from the great Reform Act of 1832 produced a Whig administration set upon liberal social reform. This included sweeping away the barbaric feudal relics that constituted so much of the law of crime and punishment.

Criminal Law Commission

As a consequence of the reform mania that gripped the country, in 1833 Lord Chancellor Brougham was able to secure from William IV the appointment of a Royal Commission on Criminal Law and he remained its champion throughout his and the Commission's long lives. There were five commissioners selected by Brougham. Andrew Amos was a barrister and the first Professor of English Law at the University of London on its foundation in 1828. Henry Bellenden Ker, also a barrister, enjoyed a large practice and reputation. Thomas Starkie was a county court judge and Downing Professor of Laws at Cambridge. William Wightman was a successful advocate and eventually a judge of the Queen's Bench. John Austin was the celebrated Benthamite jurist. All were brilliant lawyers in their own fields and, as Brougham well knew, all believed in the need for serious reform of the criminal law. In fact, they formed a coherent radical group pursuing a philosophical position, who powerfully enhanced the humanitarian movement of the early nineteenth century by spearheading the mitigation of the cruel criminal law and the legislative extension of individual liberty.

By this time Peel's 'sleep of centuries' *(Chapter 3)* had been only partially broken but his successors were continuing to build on his achievements. Coining (the making of forged money) had ceased to be capital in 1832 and housebreaking, returning from transportation, sacrilege and letter-stealing followed in the years 1833 to 1834. Nonetheless, a huge number of capital enactments remained on the statute book and Paley's ideology was still potent in some circles.

Refuting Paley

Public opinion generally was finally becoming ready to reject the Paleian doctrine. The scene was now set for the onslaught on the death penalty by the new home secretary, Lord John Russell, with help from the commissioners who quickly produced a report[1] based on the principles of Beccaria and Bentham. They demolished the Paleian faith and carefully considered the secondary punishments which might replace death. It was a skilful analysis of the case for abolition for most crimes without endangering public security or morality. They took, and published, a considerable body of evidence from interested parties and carefully chosen reformers. They declared that it was contrary to the plainest

51

principles of criminal jurisprudence indiscriminately to punish offenders whose crimes differed widely not only in respect of moral guilt but also in their harmful consequences to society, and to inflict death for offences which might adequately be repressed by milder means.

They questioned whether capital punishment could be of any use where it applied to many offences but was not normally inflicted. After canvassing the views of many witnesses on the point, they concluded that selection of a few culprits who alone suffered death did not diminish but, on the contrary, actually tended to increase the number of offenders. The fear of death, they said, was not strong when remote and uncertain, as was evidenced by men who engaged in the most hazardous occupations without regard to danger to life. Or as Lord John Russell put it, 'Death itself, for many, has no terrors; the passions of revenge, honour, love, despair, triumph over and despite it'.[2] On this point John Miller, a barrister of Lincoln's Inn, had earlier written in *An Inquiry into the Present State of the Statute and Criminal Law of England* that

> Under the capital statutes for theft, in the years 1810 to1818 inclusive, only 18 of 1196 capitally convicted were executed—1 in 66. These Acts, instead of being a terror to the 65 criminals over whose heads their threatenings for a time suspended, must with greater justice have been regarded as a surprise upon the sixty-sixth object who became obnoxious to their vengeance.[3]

The commissioners could not find that the earlier repeal of a number of capital statutes had resulted in any subsequent increase in the number of offenders. On the contrary, they produced figures which went far to demonstrate that, as the proportion of those executed to those convicted had reduced, the number of offenders had diminished.

Certainty essential

As a consequence, they came to the conclusion that the punishment of death should be limited to crimes of special atrocity such as treason, although they were also of the opinion that it could not immediately be dispensed with if, indeed, its total abolition could ever be expedient. They believed that the death penalty might have a salutary effect in restraining offenders from acts of particular outrage and cruelty if it were known that on conviction they would almost certainly be executed. In the spirit of Beccaria and Romilly, certainty was the deterrent.

They might have added that uncertainty is contrary to justice. As Sir Francis Bacon had said, 'Certainty is so essential to a law that a law without it cannot be just. A law ought to give warning before it strikes, and it is a true maxim that the best laws leave least to the breast of the judge'.[4] A sentiment to be echoed by Beccaria two centuries later. The commissioners further argued strongly against the practice of the courts, which had incensed Romilly, in allowing aggravating circumstances which were not included in the indictment to determine whether death should follow. This, they said, undermined any possibility of certainty.

They also sounded a note of warning that is as relevant today as it was in 1836. Public opinion on subjects of criminal jurisprudence, they said, was not always informed by the most enlightened views and would of itself be an insufficient ground for determining the measure of punishment.

Lord John Russell's legislation

On 19 September 1836 the home secretary, Lord John Russell, wrote[5] to inform the Commissioners that the government wished to introduce a Bill on capital punishment and that he wanted them to consider what the principal heads of such a Bill should be.

This official letter was followed a day later by a personal letter[6] in which Russell set out his own views on the proposals in the commissioners' report. Although he said he largely agreed with their suggested limitations of capital punishment, he asked for more detail on the aggravations to be specified by statute that would leave offences such as robbery, arson and rape still capital. At the same time he made it clear that he would not preclude the commissioners from considering the question of abolishing capital punishment to a greater extent than they had proposed. Nevertheless, he doubted whether public opinion was ready for abolition in cases of burglary or robbery where great violence was used. And he believed that the shedding of a man's blood with premeditated violence could not cease to be capital without resulting in an increase in such crimes.

If the incidence of the death penalty was to be substantially reduced, suitable secondary punishments had to be considered. Russell thought that transportation should often be used as an alternative to death although he saw the existing system of transporting 'a numerous army of thieves and poachers into New South Wales and Van Diemen's Land as fraught with bad, and even dangerous consequences'. Accordingly it should be retained only for grave offences. He was not much happier with long prison sentences. In his view the threat of detention in gaol for ten years rarely acted as a deterrent and was vindictive rather than exemplary. Imprisonment for such a term inflicted too much suffering, since a man's mind and strength were wasted by such confinement and he was hardened for the remainder of his life. He did not mention the notorious Hulks moored in the Thames but said he believed that the punishment of the galleys, resorted to in 'some foreign states' was even more objectionable than straightforward imprisonment. It had the effect of corrupting and degrading the criminal as well as shocking and brutalizing the spectators of such a horrible sight.

It is clear from Lord John Russell's letter that he needed the commissioner's prestige against anticipated difficulties in the House of Lords that had so bedevilled Romilly. He had already informed the Commons that punishment by death was indiscriminate. In 1836, for example, 494 people were condemned to death but only seventeen executed.[7] As the *Westminster Review* had put it after comparing figures from the United States of America, whilst in that country the chance of the punishment being inflicted was 'three to one against the criminal, in England it was nine and a half to one in his favour'. This exhibition of 'mockery' in our courts of justice, it wrote, was not in harmony with the intelligence and feelings of the age.[8]

The commissioners replied to the home secretary's letter on 19 January 1837.[9] They said they were prepared to put the principles of their report into a legislative form that might be carried at once. To this end they submitted the heads of Bills to decrease the number of capital offences, classify crimes into grades and introduce precise definitions of offences.

Their first draft B ill proposed to abolish capital punishment for eight specified crimes substituting discretionary punishments varying between transportation for life and imprisonment for five years. Their second Bill proposed abolition for certain forgeries which still remained capital and the third restricted the extent of capital punishment for malicious injuries, burglary, robbery, stealing from the person, arson and piracy. The combined effect of both Bills would be to remove the punishment of death from more than three-quarters of the existing capital crimes.

Substantial progress
Armed with these drafts, and the influential public support of the commissioners, Lord John Russell sponsored far-reaching Bills in the House of Commons during the course of 1837 to provide for the removal of the death penalty from 21 of the 37 offences still capital and for restrictions in the use of such punishment in the 16 remaining.[10]

On March 23 he told the House[11] that the introduction of his Bills followed directly from the appointment of the commissioners. The result of their 'laborious investigations' of the criminal law was their conclusion that capital punishment should be limited to a small number of offences. He described Paley's policy as one of injustice as fully demonstrated by Sir Samuel Romilly—'to his immortal credit and the great advantage of the country'.

Inflicting capital punishment indiscriminately, he continued, meant that neither offenders, nor the country in general, could know what crimes or aggravations of them would result in death and thus deterrence became ineffective. Furthermore, there was a great disproportion between the number of people sentenced to death and the number executed. By way of illustration he drew on some comparative figures:

In 1835, the whole number condemned was 523; but the number executed was only 34. In 1836, the number of persons condemned to death was 494; while the number executed was only 17. With respect to certain offences, the punishments which had taken place were in great disproportion to the convictions. With respect to murder, for instance, twenty-five persons were convicted in 1835 . . . 21 out of the 25 were executed. But with respect to burglaries, 193 were convicted and sentenced to death, but only one was executed . . . As to cases of robbery, 202 were convicted and no person executed.[12]

All this, he said, placed in a very painful situation the judges and the Secretary of State who were obliged to administer a law which generally was not carried into effect, except in some few cases where it became expedient to enforce it with the extreme penalty of death. What was needed, he added, was to define the law so that it could be said, generally, that people who committed specified offences made themselves liable to capital punishment. Then it would be a question for the discretion of the judge, and afterwards the Secretary of State for the Home Department, to consider whether or not there were circumstances that entitled the culprit to mercy.

Russell then turned to the question of whether earlier Acts abolishing the death penalty in certain cases had led to an increase or decrease in the incidence of the crimes involved. He chose forgery as a prime example.

The Act abolishing capital punishment for most forms of this crime was passed in 1832. 'Now', he said, 'when we consider the awful infliction of capital punishment that used to take place for forgery, it is consolatory to think that it can be done away with, without increasing the number of offences, and, at the same time, increasing the security of the bankers and persons engaged in trade and commerce'.[13]

Stating that strong public feeling among all classes favoured a reduction in the number of capital punishments, Russell outlined the proposals of the commissioners as the basis for action. Nevertheless, he believed the law should occasionally be strengthened.

He instanced the case of a man who deliberately set out to destroy his wife. To do so he had assaulted her with a red hot poker, had beaten her furiously until she was insensible and had set her clothes on fire. He was prevented from finally killing her only by the intervention of neighbours. However, because no incised wound was inflicted the case was outside capital statutes and the culprit could only be punished for an aggravated assault. This defect in the law, he said, should be remedied by an amending statute.[14]

One point on which Russell disagreed with the Commissioners was on the length of imprisonment. They had, he said, proposed a maximum of ten years.[15] But, repeating what he had written in his letter to them, he thought five years was a better option since ten years hardened a criminal and destroyed his powers and the capacities of the mind. This was one example of Russell's remarkably modern thinking some 70 years before the introduction of modern psychology.

In the event, the House of Lords was to reduce the term to three years, aware that in many cases longer terms of transportation were likely to be imposed in serious cases. The Lords also limited solitary confinement to a month at any one time and not more than three months in any one year.[16] An impressive change seems to have come over the Upper House since the days of dispute between Romilly and Lord Ellenborough.

This speech of Russell's was fully reported in *The Times* the following day but, although throughout the nineteenth century the newspaper opposed any reduction in capital punishment, it passed no comment on this occasion. Its Leaders that day were more concerned with the Irish Tithe Bill and the Belfast Waterworks Bill; the Poor Law Amendment Bill was also much in evidence. It is also noteworthy that no letters concerning the speech were published.

Ewart's amendment

To Russell's dismay, since he saw his Bills threatened, on May 19 William Ewart proposed a motion[17] to remove capital punishment from all offences short of murder. In a very low and level tone, he indicated that for a number of years he had been deeply concerned with the national character and national habits. He believed that in the present state of society the punishment of death might be abolished altogether. He pointed out to the House that, although for many offences capital punishment had already been abolished, since 1829 crime had decreased.[18] However, a reason why murder only should be punished with death was that the continuance of capital punishment in other cases gave the criminal an inducement to destroy evidence against him by killing his victim. In any event imprisonment for life was a much greater punishment than death itself, as criminals acknowledged.

The home secretary opposed the motion on the ground that his own proposals had the support of public opinion and if the motion were carried there would be a growing opinion in favour of the death penalty. True to the caution expressed in his letter to the commissioners, and like Peel before him, he implored the House to move slowly to prevent such a revulsion of public feeling against any abolition. Russell was clearly agitated when in reply radical members urged that public opinion had supported Parliament in all earlier changes towards greater leniency in the criminal law. When he finally sat down Fowell Buxton rose to support Ewart. But then Dr John Bowring, friend and literary executor of Bentham, said he favoured the abolition of capital punishment in all cases, including murder since the spectacle of an execution depraved the mind more than it deterred. He explained that he looked upon the desire for severe punishments as nothing less than a desire for vengeance, and the most humane laws were those which were the most efficient in the prevention of crime.

Radical MP J. A. Roebuck, supported by Daniel O'Connell and Dr Lushington, also stood for total abolition saying that the prevention of the offence, not the torture of the offender, was the object of punishment. In the debate on the motion only the attorney-general, Sir John Campbell (afterwards Lord Chancellor), and the solicitor-general, Sir Robert Monsey Rolfe (afterwards Lord Cranworth) supported Russell against Ewart, although all members who spoke said they also backed the home secretary's Bills whilst wanting to go even further. In fact, so strong was the feeling for total abolition that Ewart felt obliged to explain at the end of the debate that he gave credit to the government for its proposed Bills and reminded the House that he had not expressed himself in favour of abolishing the death penalty for murder.

In spite of Russell's opposition the amendment for total abolition secured an astonishing 72 votes against 73. Yet, once again there was no editorial thunder from *The Times* or correspondence in its columns on this significant debate.

Achievement of the century

Since in February 1837 Russell had told the House of Commons that the retention of the existing 'awful punishment of death should not be left long in debate or dispute'[19] once Ewart's motion was out of the way his seven Bills became law with great speed, being passed on July 17. Shortly afterwards the death penalty was inflicted only in cases of murder and treason. During the 1840's the number of capital sentences each year was around 60 against an average total of over 20,000 sentences a year. The number actually hanged each year varied from nine to 16 and these were all murderers.[20] This was fewer than in the early twentieth century.

In the event, the labours of the commissioners had proved to be of considerable help to the government in securing substantial inroads into the use of capital punishment. It was a fitting conclusion to the work of reform started by Romilly who, as we have seen, had never advocated total abolition. Clearly, the Whig government had thought it advisable to enlist the support of the commissioners against retentionists inside and outside Parliament. Their detailed examination of the problem and cogent arguments for their proposals undoubtedly had an important effect in securing the support of the public and MP's for Russell's Bills. Lord John succeeded in changing the climate and the law relating to the death penalty and in this respect his legislation was the outstanding achievement of the century.

As a measure of its success, and of earlier Bills such as those of Ewart and Lord Suffield, whereas in 1831 over 1,600 people were sentenced to death (although many were not executed), by 1838 the number sentenced had reduced to 116. Yet, like Peel before him, Russell had gone as far as he felt the majority in the country wanted, and he continued to oppose Bills introduced later by Fitzroy Kelly and others for abolition in regard to serious offences against the person, although he conceded it for rape at the suggestion of the judges.[21]

But, despite Russell's success causing the fire to be taken out of the movement for reform for a long time to come, it would not be the end. The strong support in the Commons for Ewart's amendment revealed the desire of the newly enfranchised middle-class for an even more substantial reduction in the use of capital punishment as part of its general endeavour to reduce crime and extend the work ethic in a fast-expanding industrial economy. The issue was not to be finally resolved, however, until well into the twentieth century.

ENDNOTES

1   P.P., xxxvi, 183 (1836)

2   *Hansard*, [37] 713 (23 March 1837)

3   p. 123, 1822

4   *Letters and Life of Bacon*, Spedding, 1869

5   P.P., xxxi, i (1837)

6   ibid

7   *Hansard*, [37] 711 (23 March 1837)

8   Vol. xvii, 380 (October 1832)

9   P.P., xxx (1837)

10 *Hansard,* [37] 709 (1837)

11 ibid

12 ibid , 711

13 ibid , 716

14 ibid , 723

15 In fact, they had generally preferred a maximum of five years

16 *Hansard,* [38] 1915 (15 July 1837)

17 ibid, [38] 907

18 ibid , [38] 908, 911

19 *Hansard,* [36] 89 (2 February 1837)

20 Radzinowicz, *op. cit.,* iv: 330

21 *Hansard,* [55] 1079 (1840) and [57] 47-57 (1841).

CHAPTER 5

Executions in Private

Perhaps inevitably, despite the continued efforts of William Ewart, attention shifted to the public spectacle of hanging and its brutalizing effects on spectators.

Terror by example

In the first half of the nineteenth century most people believed in the deterrent effect of hangings in public.When the first motion to abolish public executions and avoid releasing 'fierce hungry passions' was introduced in Parliament by Henry Rich on 16 February 1841 it was greeted with laughter and rejected outright.[1] Even Ewart opposed the Bill, but in his case only from a reasonable and persistent fear that taking away the public exhibition might weaken the pressure for total abolition of capital punishment, as indeed subsequently occurred.

The position of the government of the day was made clear in 1844 when, after the execution in Nottingham of William Saville for the murder of his wife and children, a large number of people were trampled to death and injured in a stampede by the watching crowd. It was urged by the mayor of the town that the area for executions in front of the county gaol was too restrictive for the purpose. A new location was suggested to the home secretary, Sir James Graham, whose permission was required for the change of venue. The new site was certainly large enough but the Nottingham magistrates were concerned that it could be viewed only from a distance. In reply Graham sent the magistrates some guidelines for executions. 'The principal object of capital punishment', he said in his memorandum, 'is the terror of the example'.[2] He continued that it was necessary for that purpose that a large multitude of spectators should assemble sufficiently near the scaffold to recognise the criminal. Some of them should also be able to hear any words of warning about the consequences of crime that the criminal might wish to address to them. Clearly, little had changed in government thinking in over a century.

Charles Dickens intervenes

Public sentiment was beginning to alter, however, as the country began to benefit materially from the Industrial Revolution and its position as the 'workshop of the world'. Prosperity for many was growing, as was the gap between rich and poor which some found distressing. A new sensibility about what was humane was arising. As we have seen (*Chapter 2*), in 1840 William Makepeace Thackeray attended with Richard Monckton Milne the hanging at Newgate of Francois Courvoisier, a Swiss butler who cut the throat of his employer Lord William Russell in his bed. According to the diarist Charles

Greville, the murder excited a prodigious interest and frightened all London out of its wits. He wrote on May 15, 'Visionary servants and air-drawn razors or carving-knives dance before everybody's imagination, and half the world go to sleep expecting to have their throats cut before morning'.[3] Courvoisier confessed to the murder which, he said, he had been inspired to commit by reading a bloodthirsty novel. Thackeray, writing in bitter terms about his experience as a spectator at the hanging, said:

> The whole of the sickening, ghastly, wicked scene passes before the eyes again; and, indeed, it is an awful one to see, and very hard and painful to describe . . . It seems to me that I have been abetting an act of frightful wickedness and violence, performed by a set of men against one of their fellows; and I pray God that it may soon be out of the power of any man in England to witness such a hideous and degrading sight . . . I feel myself ashamed and degraded at the brutal curiosity which took me to that brutal sight; and I pray to Almighty God to cause this disgraceful sin to pass from among us, and to cleanse our land of blood.[4]

Charles Dickens also spoke for many of the middle-class when he proposed ending public executions with their 'odious levity'. Like Thackeray he, too, attended the hanging of Courvoisier. At the scaffold, as the condemned prisoner stepped out from the gaol to the platform, the bell of St Sepulchre's was sounded and the crowd roared its approval. Courvoisier lifted up his manacled hands and appeared to pray before turning around with a wild, imploring look. He then had a nightcap placed over his head and face and was hanged, cut down and carried back into the prison on a wooden bier. Dickens was disgusted with what he saw of the surging throng from his window above the multitude. 'I did not see', he wrote six years later, 'one token in all the immense crowd of any emotion suitable to the occasion. No sorrow, no salutary terror, no abhorrence, no seriousness, nothing but ribaldry, debauchery, levity, drunkenness and flaunting vice in 50 other shapes. I should have deemed it impossible that I could have ever felt any large assemblage of my fellow-creatures to be so odious'.[5]

It was later, in the year 1849, after attending the executions of Maria and Frederick Manning, that Dickens,[6] who seems to have been drawn to watching such spectacles,[7] became publicly ready to support executions being carried out in private. In an indignant letter to *The Times* he described in detail the crude behaviour in what he said he believed was 'a sight so inconceivably awful as the wickedness and levity of the immense crowd collected at that execution this morning could be imagined by no man, and could be presented by no heathen land under the sun'. He went on to say:

> I simply wish to turn this dreadful experience to some account for the general good, by taking the readiest and most public means of adverting to an intimation given by Sir G. Grey in the last session of Parliament, that the government might be induced to give its support to a measure making the infliction of capital punishment a private solemnity within the prison walls (with such guarantees for the last sentence of the law being inexorably and surely administered as should be satisfactory to the public

at large) . . . and beseech him as a solemn duty which he owes to society, and a responsibility which he cannot for ever put away, to originate such a legislative change himself.'[8]

The Times could not agree. In its reply it accepted that Dickens was a great novelist and that the execution he had witnessed was horrid—'an act of judicial slaughter'—but, it said, public executions could ensure 'useful terror and a convenient humility'. It continued:

> It appears to us as a matter of necessity that so tremendous an act as a national homicide should be publicly as well as solemnly done. Popular jealousy demands it. Were it otherwise, the mass of people would never be sure that great offenders were really executed, or that the humbler class of criminals were not executed in greater numbers than the State chose to confess.[9]

'National homicide' was a useful euphemism for judicial murder.

Dickens felt obliged to send to *The Times* a second letter urging private executions and this was published on November 19. An execution within the walls of a prison, he wrote, should be conducted with every terrible solemnity that careful consideration could devise. And a murderer should not have his sayings and doings served up in print on Sunday mornings for the perusal of families. Furthermore, 'Mr Calcraft, the hangman, (of whom I have some information in reference to this last occasion i.e. the Mannings' execution) should be restrained in his unseemly briskness, his jokes, his oaths and his brandy'.

Although in 1845 Dickens had written of his aversion to capital punishment as such,[10] by 1849 he now confirmed Ewart's worst fears by breaking with abolition as a consequence of his conversion to private executions.[11] Ewart returned to the fray by urging that total abolition would itself entirely resolve the dispute as to where executions should take place. However, he made no attack on the novelist—an omission rectified by Richard Cobden and John Bright who unjustly linked his name with that of Calcraft.

Select Committee
Dickens claimed to have whipped up a roaring sea of controversy but it was not until 1856, which saw the end of the Crimean War, that the House of Lords was persuaded to appoint a Select Committee to enquire into 'the mode of carrying into effect capital punishment'. The proposal was made by Samuel Wilberforce, the Bishop of Oxford and son of the anti-slavery crusader William Wilberforce. The bishop feared that public executions were threatening to undermine capital punishment altogether. 'A few more such scenes' he had earlier told the House of Lords, 'would have the effect of making men's minds recoil from that which I believe to be essential to the highest principles of justice as well as to the necessities of human expediency'.[12] On July 7 of that year, the committee recommended the introduction of private executions, provided that the jurors and witnesses in the case attended, bells were tolled to let the people know an execution was taking place and the bodies of those executed were exposed to

public view. However, under pressure against the proposal from both the press and abolitionists—although from opposing positions—the House took no action and the government concluded that such safeguards would not prevent large crowds continuing to be lured to the place of execution. Thomas Carlyle joined the fray, recalling rather disingenuously that the ancient Germans had no scruple about public executions.[13]

Hanging of a poisoner

Nevertheless, the horrors of such executions had not diminished. In 1856 the London weekly, the *Leader*, published from its reporter on the spot the following sensationalist but accurate details of the hanging of the infamous mass-poisoner William Palmer in Stafford:

And now the hangman grasps the rope—Palmer bends his head—the noose is slipped over—his face grows yet more ghastly—his throat throbs spasmodically—he moves his neck round, as a man with a tight collar—the hangman is hurrying off the drop—he suddenly bethinks himself of the cap—turns back—clutches at the criminal's right hand, as if asking for pardon—'God bless you, goodbye' says the prisoner, in a low, distinct voice—the cap or white bag, is pulled over his head—the peak blows out from his chin by the violent and rapid respiration—another second, the bolt is drawn, down falls the drop with a slight crash—the arms are thrown up from the elbow, with the hands clenched—the body whirls round—the hangman from below seizes the legs—one escapes from his grasp, and by a mighty spasm is once drawn up—the chest thrice heaves convulsively—the hangman looses his hold—the body again whirls round, then becomes steady, and hangs a dull, grey, shapeless mass, facing the newly-risen sun.[14]

Yet by the time Palmer was hanged the memories of Thackeray and Dickens had dimmed and they both changed their minds, declaring that they had been wrong to advocate total abolition. Dickens had come to believe that abolition would never be accepted in England but the brutalizing sight of a public execution was what could be prevented.[15] Still *The Times* did not agree and in 1860 penned the following sentiments:

No crime in many years has been more unmitigated in its atrocity than that for which William Godfrey Youngman suffered death yesterday in the presence of a vast and unsympathetic multitude. Now, we put it to the most sensitive conscience whether any genuine sentiment is violated by consigning such a human being to instant death, instead of maintaining him in hopeless servitude at the expense of the country? Are we to make a providence of ourselves by weighing a slender chance for his future repentance against the beneficial effect of his execution? We know well the conventional argument that may be used against us, and which will seem to derive new force with the incidents of yesterday.

Can we believe, it is urged, that this mob whose brutal merriment surged round Horsemongers Lane Gaol on the eve of the execution were edified rather than demoralised by this spectacle? If, so far as it goes, there is an argument not against the use but against the publicity of executions, we are deeply convinced that however it may affect spectators, the shameful death of murderers must materially contribute to keep out that execration of wilful homicide which alone secures us against its frequent occurrence.

The motives for murder are stronger than for many lesser offences. Hatred is no uncommon passion and the characteristic of hatred, as moralists tell us, is an impatience of the very existence of its object. Let the inquisition 'of blood' be robbed of its terrors and we shall soon find what it is that now overawes the homicidal instinct. [16]

In a thunderous outpouring Thomas Carlyle also expressed the view of retentionists when he wrote of the murderer:

We . . . dare not allow thee to continue longer among us. As a palpable deserter . . . fighting thus against the whole Universe and its Laws, we send thee back into the whole Universe, solemnly expel thee from our community; and will in the name of God, not with joy and exaltation, but with sorrows stern as thy own, hang thee on Wednesday next, and so end . . . 'Revenge', my friends! revenge, and the natural hatred of scoundrels and the ineradicable tendency to . . . pay them what they had merited: this is forevermore intrinsically a correct, and even a divine, feeling in the mind of every man. [17]

But, after all, Carlyle had also written an outrageous panegyric about the 'wonderland atmosphere' of a prison he actually visited in 1849 as part of his campaign against the introduction of penitentiaries.

Royal Commission
Early in 1864, when almost another decade had passed since the House of Lords Select Committee had met and the Society for the Abolition of Capital Punishment[18] had been founded by Ewart and others, a sea change in popular perceptions about public executions occurred when three controversial hangings caused scenes of considerable disgrace. The press and MPs veered with the wind; but not the government which, attempting to stem the storm, pointed out that the judges favoured retention of both the death penalty and public executions. John Bright immediately responded that every amelioration in the criminal law had been carried against the advice of the judges. [19]

The pressure on the government remained intense, however, and in May, following a motion by William Ewart for a Select Committee to consider abolition, it announced the appointment of a Royal Commission[20] to enquire into public executions and capital punishment, although in regard to the latter the commission's terms of reference did not include the question of total abolition but whether the number of crimes classified as murder could be reduced.

Whilst the Commission was sitting came the hanging of young Franz Muller at Newgate on 14 November 1864 for robbery and murder on a London railway train (he was the first person to have committed a murder on a train, and the first to be arrested by use of the Atlantic cable after he had fled to the United States of America). It revealed how little had changed. Whilst Muller was in prison, his church minister complained to the authorities about 'A cruel and crying evil in Newgate. Again and again', he said, 'on Monday morning in those last solemn moments our prayers were interrupted by the savage yells of the multitude assembled to witness the execution'.

At the execution, according to *The Times*, 'Before the slight slow vibrations of [Muller's] body had well ended, robbery and violence, loud laughing, oaths, fighting, obscene conduct and still more filthy language reigned round the gallows far and near. Such too the scene remained with little change till the old hangman (Calcraft) slunk again along the drop amid hissing and sneering inquiries of what he had had to drink that morning. After failing once to cut the rope he made a second attempt more successfully, and the body of Muller disappeared from view'.[21]

Also present was the respected George Jacob Holyoake who expressed sentiments of disgust similar to those voiced by Charles Dickens in 1840. In his *Public Lessons of the Hangman*, published as a penny pamphlet in 1864 and in part included in his memoirs, Holyoake wrote that the crowds saw, 'the frame quiver and the blood rush to the neck. A thrill passes through the congregated scoundrels whom the government has thus undertaken to entertain'.[22] Those scoundrels, he wrote, were the knave and the burglar, the pickpocket, the prisoner on leave, the drunkard and the wife-beater all of whom had 'found means to profit [in education] by this great State opportunity . . . An influence stronger than lust, more alluring than vice, more tempting than plunder, is exercised by this seductive instructor'. 'Why', he asked, 'did the Archbishop of York condemn sensational novels and utter not one word against this vile, this real, this overriding villainous sensation provided by the government in every county of the Kingdom?'[23]

Meanwhile, among the distinguished members of the Royal Commission were its chairman, the Duke of Richmond, John Bright, Charles Neate, MP for Oxford, Dr Stephen Lushington and William Ewart himself. But only four were abolitionists, the remainder merely supporting the ending of public executions. Over a period of two years extensive testimony was taken from judges, prison governors, police officers, clergymen and a former home secretary as well as the current holder of the office, Sir George Grey.

The judges who gave evidence before the Commission were strongly in favour of retaining capital punishment but on public executions they differed.[24] Baron Bramwell, for example, declared, 'Nothing deters so much as that which ends everything for which most men presently care—life. Common experience and common knowledge tell us so'.[25] Whilst agreeing, Lord Cranworth thought the time had come for private executions but only because disgust at public executions might dispose people to want the death penalty abolished altogether.[26]

James Fitzjames Stephen, then Recorder of Newark, pressed for continuing the public spectacle as a deterrent since he considered a shameful death was 'much harder to go through than one in private'.[27] On the other hand, he would have reduced the scope of the crime of murder, confining it to felonious homicides of great enormity. As to capital punishment itself, he was strongly in favour of its retention and its extension to more felonies since it too was a deterrent as people associated it with an ignominious death. It also satisfied society's demand for revenge. With undue optimism he was to write later that 'If society could make up its mind to the destruction of really bad offenders' (not only murderers), 'they might, in a very few years, be made as rare as wolves'.[28] Stephen was supported before the Commission by the reverend J. Davis MA an Ordinary of Newgate, who said he had attended 24 executions at the prison and was convinced that 'incorrigibles' could not be restrained if capital punishment was abolished.

Baron Martin, of the Court of Exchequer, claimed that murder was a crime of the lower classes who should know that committing it brought punishment of death on the public scaffold. He naively confessed he had never conversed with the lower classes to ascertain their feelings but was nevertheless convinced that death was a great deterrent to them. When Ewart asked him if women and children should be permitted to attend executions the judge faltered. He said he knew that they were excluded from certain cases in court and thought that might be extended to executions. Seizing his opportunity, Charles Neate MP was quick to ask him, 'If women are to be hanged ought they not see what it is?' 'Perhaps so', replied the bemused Baron.

During Lord Wensleydale's evidence he was asked by the Duke of Richmond whether he thought there were better substitutes for capital punishment? His startling reply was that he believed, 'there are tortures which are capable of producing a much greater effect, but they are punishments which the public would not tolerate'. He instanced 'cutting off a man's members, depriving him of his eyesight, cutting off his limbs'.

Sir George Grey's evidence was likely to be of considerable influence as coming from the home secretary. He did not think the death penalty could safely be dispensed with in cases of murder but he detected, he said, a growing public feeling in favour of private executions. The moral attitudes and conduct of the lower classes had improved and, as a result, crime was decreasing. Moreover, he had received reports that in some parts of the United States[29] and Australia private executions were proving successful, particularly as they had removed the degrading spectacles surrounding the gallows. In fact, a great many reports from abroad had been sought by the commissioners and they were full of praise for the benefits accruing from hangings being transferred from public places to prisons.

Innocents executed

Despite the absurd statement of Lord Palmerston, when he had been home secretary in 1853, (to be repeated a hundred years later by another home secretary, Sir David Maxwell Fyfe) that there were no instances of a wrongful conviction,[30] concern that innocent men were sometimes executed caused eleven witnesses to address the question before the Royal Commission. However, only one of them favoured the establishment of a Court of Criminal Appeal. That witness was Sir Fitzroy Kelly QC, a distinguished former attorney-general who afterwards became a judge. He said that between 1802 and 1840 no

65

fewer than 42 people had been sentenced to death who were afterwards proved to have been innocent. He suggested that if there were a Court of Appeal 'the cases in which innocent men are convicted and punished would be greatly diminished'.[31] Lord Bramwell and other judges disagreed. They were concerned that such a court would increase uncertainty and dismay prosecutors.[32]

Kelly gave examples including a man named Chalker who was executed in 1835 at Ipswich for the murder of a gamekeeper. Another man afterwards confessed to the crime on his death-bed and it was established that Chalker had not been involved in any way. William Tallack, the Secretary of the Society for the Abolition of Capital Punishment also gave instances of innocent people being found guilty. One case was of a Charles Mallet who was sentenced to be executed after being found guilty at the Central Criminal Court in 1854. He was not charged with murder but with 'atrocious assault and robbery'. The victim, a Mrs Harrison, identified him despite having been insensible when she was found and in spite of the accused having an alibi. In the event, he was not executed but transported, which was fortunate for his life since three months later Mrs Harrison made a similar charge against another man and investigations showed her accusations to be unfounded. It was then proved that the story against Mallet had been a fabrication from beginning to end and he was pardoned. Her motive and who had assaulted her were not revealed.

Subsequently, in the year of the Royal Commission's Report itself (1866) a Mrs Biggadyke was hanged for poisoning her husband, a crime to which a convict later confessed. At the same time *The Times* reported that the reprieve of a John Banks was received with some surprise, since the judge in passing sentence said that there never was a clearer case of murder proved. Faced with this explicit declaration, it wrote, it was not generally expected that the memorial praying for a reprieve would be favourably entertained.[33] Was he found to be innocent?

Eventually, a Court of Criminal Appeal was established in 1907 after the proven misconviction of the innocent Adolf Beck and Birmingham solicitor, George Edalji, as well as the unsavoury and unsafe conviction of Mrs Florence Maybrick in 1889 when the judge was mentally unwell.[34]

Dilemma
Abolitionists also gave evidence to the Royal Commission and, despite its narrow terms of reference, attacked capital punishment itself. Tallack, for example, claimed that experience over the previous 30 years revealed that abolition for many crimes had offered a greater certainty of the conviction of the worst offenders. It would be the same if capital punishment were abolished for murder, as experience in other countries showed. Nevertheless, some abolitionists did accept that public executions had a desirable, morbid and compulsive effect on spectators. It was pointed out that in one town, out of 167 felons under sentence of death no fewer than 164 of them had witnessed a public execution. And questioning the reverend Davis, John Bright cited the case of a young man named Wicks who went to see an execution, afterwards saying 'It is nothing, it is only a kick'. He then went home and shot his master dead.

But most abolitionists did not approve of public executions although they found themselves in the continuing dilemma which arose from their conviction that private executions would detract attention from their main aim. To strengthen the opposition to hangings in prison they also claimed that the working class would believe that the rich were not executed if they did not see it happen with their own eyes. Indeed, it was true that many of the poor were still convinced that only publicity would prevent wealthy criminals escaping the noose and stories were rife of such felons being seen in public places long after their 'execution'. There is no evidence, however, to confirm this.

Eventually, although saying that they forbore to enter into the abstract questions of the expediency of abolishing or retaining capital punishment on which there were differences of opinion among them, the majority of the commissioners found it 'impossible to resist such a weight of authority' received on the desirability of private executions. Accordingly, they decided to recommend that public executions be brought to an end. William Ewart, Dr Lushington, John Bright, Charles Neate and James Moncrieff opposed the majority report, recommending instead that 'capital punishment might safely and with advantage to the community be at once abolished'. Thereafter they continued their opposition to ending public executions which they felt obliged to claim served as a great moral lesson. For other reasons *The Times* also rejected the majority recommendation. Men not frightened of death, it wrote, would be frightened by the prospect of dying in public on the gallows.[35]

Degrees of murder

The Royal Commission also proposed that the punishment for murder be divided into two degrees with death only for the first degree, as in the United States. Murder in the first degree would encompass deliberate killing with malice aforethought, if found as a fact by the jury, and homicide in the course of perpetrating arson, rape, burglary, robbery or piracy. James Fitzjames Stephen examined this proposal in a lengthy article in *Fraser's Magazine* of February 1866.[36] He found it unsatisfactory, saying it would make the definition of murder more complicated and cause numerous injustices. Indeed, if the motive of the murderer were not brought to light, the worst killings would fall within the second degree. This view was destined to prevail until the enactment of the Homicide Act of 1957.

ENDNOTES

1   *Hansard*, [56] 647-66 (1841)
2   PRO. HO. 45/681
3   *Greville's England*, The Folio Society, C. Hibbert (ed.), p.180 (1981)
4   'Going to see a Man Hanged', *Fraser's Magazine, op. cit.*
5   Letter to the *Daily News*, 28 February 1846

6 Dickens used Maria Manning, who was Belgian, as the model for Hortense, the murderous Frenchwoman in *Bleak House*

7 He also attended a public execution by guillotine in Rome. 'Nobody cared or was at all affected', he wrote, 'There was no manifestation of disgust, or pity, or indignation, or sorrow', *Pictures from Italy*, 1846

8 14 November 1849

9 ibid

10 Letter to Macvey Napier, 28 July 1845. In 'Mamie Dickens and Georgina Hogarth', *The Letters of Charles Dickens*, iii: 78-9, 1882

11 *The Times*, 19 November 1849

12 *Lords* [133] 311, 15 May 1854

13 'Model Prisons', in *Latter- Day Pamphlets*, 1872 edn.

14 Quoted by Thomas Boyle. *Black Swine in the Sewers of Hampstead: Beneath* the *Surface of Victorian Sensationalism*, 89, 1990

15 *The Letters of Charles Dickens*, Walter Dexter, 1845-47, ii: 185, 1938 edn.

16 5 September 1860.

17 *Latter-Day Pamphlets*, pp. 66/7, 1872 edn.

18 Later the Howard Association and now the Howard League for Penal Reform

19 *Hansard*, [174] 2092 (1864)

20 P.P., xxi (1866)

21 *The Times*, 16 November 1864

22 *Sixty Years of an Agitator's Life*, ii, p. 117, 5th Impression, 1902

23 *Public Lessons of the Hangman*, pp. 6/7, 1864

24 P.P, xxi, 14 (1866)

25 ibid, 672

26 ibid,14

27 *A History of the Criminal Law of England*, ii, p. 89, 1883

28 ibid

29 The last public hangings in the USA as a whole did not take place until 14 August 1936 in Kentucky with 20,000 spectators, and on 21 May 1937 in Montana where there were 500 spectators

30 The myopia was not confined to Lord Palmerston. Lord Wensleydale told the commissioners that he was not aware of a single capital case in which he thought the verdict ill-founded

31 P.P., *op. cit.*, 1101

32 ibid, 229

33 8 August 1866.

34 See *Politics and Law in the Life of Sir James Fitjames Stephen*, John Hostettler, 1995

35 26 January 1866

36 *Report of the Capital Punishment Commission*, lxxiii, 232.

CHAPTER 6

Abolition of Public Hangings

The report of the commissioners was published on 8 January 1866.[1] During the sittings of the Royal Commission John Hibbert, Bonham Carter and Viscount Hinchfield had introduced a Bill in the Commons to provide for executions to be carried out inside prison walls. Other provisions were that the sheriff, gaoler, chaplain and surgeon would be required to be present, the death certificate would have to be signed immediately after the sentence had been carried out and the coroner was required to produce a report within 12 hours. Printed copies of the death certificate and the coroner's declaration would then be exhibited near the principal entrance to the prison.[2] In an attempt to gain support, Hibbert urged in the House of Commons that the solemnity and formality of private executions would be more of a deterrent than public ones.

Privacy more decorous
The home secretary, Sir George Grey, asked Hibbert to withdraw the Bill since the government would shortly bring forward their own based on the report of the commission and Hibbert's proposals. He complied. The government then on 23 March 1866 introduced the Law of Capital Punishment Amendment Bill in the House of Lords.[3] True to Grey's promise this incorporated the recommendations of the Royal Commission including the changes in the definition of murder, executions within prisons and other reforms.

In a lengthy and argumentative debate Lord Cranworth, by now Lord Chancellor, revealed a new, hearty support for private executions. But Lord Malmesbury urged that they be rejected, with the curious reasoning that 'We must not give way to the natural sentiments which civilisation prompts'.[4] In contrast to the abolitionists he also feared they would lead to the end of the death penalty itself.

Lord Dunsany explained the horror of men hanging on the gallows for 15 to 20 minutes. Criminals thus died, he said, from suffocation, from dislocation of the neck or apoplexy caused by an excessive flow of blood to the brain. He believed this arose from a lack of skilled executioners, but it is not clear why he thought private executions would be more 'solemn and decorous',[5] or even more humane.

On the Bill being sent to the House of Commons in July, William Ewart asked the home secretary, Spencer Walpole, what the intentions of the government were towards it. Walpole replied, with another example of curious reasoning, that it would not be proceeded with as it was out of tune with the recommendations of the Royal Commission. His suggestion that it was also too encumbered with amendments was more to the point.[6] In any event, it was withdrawn on July 30. Nine days later *The Times* printed the following story under the heading 'Shocking Scene at Execution':

69

At Stafford yesterday about 2,000 people assembled in front of the gaol to witness the execution of William Collier who had taken the life of Thomas Smith a young man of only 25 years of age. It appears that the rope with which Collier was to be hanged had not been delivered to the prison until 8.30 p.m. the previous evening. The assistant warders in consequence spliced the rope left after the last execution to a piece of old rope. The noose was formed of the former, and the latter was attached to the beam, round which it was twisted twice. Then the ends were fastened with string and past the unwound rope, but, it would appear, very insecurely.

The procession reached the scaffold at eight o'clock the next morning and the hangman, Smith, a cattle dealer from Dudley, pulled the drop in the usual way. The floor fell, but instead of the culprit's head being seen above the scaffold, it altogether disappeared. There was a cry, "The man's down!" and "The rope's broken!" The powerful tug which resulted from the falling of the culprit through the scaffold floor had in fact been too much for the fastening by which the rope held to the beam.

The intertwined threads became liberated, the knot slipped and Collier fell to the ground. The executioner, after a moment of bewilderment, ran down the steps beneath the platform where he found Collier upon his feet but leaning against the side of the hoarding, the cap over his face, the rope round his neck. He seemed to be unconscious.

The assistant warders ran into the prison to retrieve the new halter that had been delivered the previous night. The hangman quickly took the rope from the culprit's neck around which the tight rope had left a deep-red mark, whilst the assistant warder fastened the rope to the beam, this time securely. The drop fell again and after a further two-and-a-half minutes the culprit was evidently dead. About four-and-a-half minutes intervened between the two falls.[7]

No explanation was given as to why the new rope was not used on the first occasion but clearly bungled hangings were still occurring, and continued to do so. A Prison Department circular dated January 1879 refers to an accident at a hanging 'by reason of an old and faulty rope having been used, which broke and caused a painful scene'. On this occasion it was proposed that suitable ropes be made available from Newgate.

Belated government action
As is often the case with such reports the government proved reluctant to act upon the Royal Commission's recommendations. It was not until the following year, 1867, that the government introduced two new and separate Bills. One was the Murder Law Amendment Bill, which was soon abandoned because of the complications surrounding degrees of murder. The other was the Capital Punishment Within Prisons Bill which set out the measures considered necessary to ensure that executions in private would be carried out with sufficient precautions to satisfy the public that they were genuine. This, too, was withdrawn.

Then things changed in May 1867, when Garthorne Hardy was appointed home secretary. He had been a member of the Royal Commission and later became Earl Cranbrook. Although he favoured retention of the death penalty he reintroduced the Capital Punishment Within Prisons Bill on 26 November 1867. Private executions, he argued[8] would act as a more effective deterrent than public hangings because the consequent 'mystery and indefiniteness attending the punishment serves only to increase its terrors in the eyes [of the people]'.[9] Moreover, he added, public executions attracted the very worst classes, many of whom were themselves on the road to the gallows. They attended only to make a jest of what to every worthy person was a matter of gravest regret. Far from absorbing a moral message they kept one another's courage up by singing low songs and laughing at low jests.

Serjeant Gaselee disagreed that private hanging would hold more terror. Furthermore, with private executions, he said, repeating the well-worn argument,

> the opinion was prevalent in some quarters that if a rich man were condemned to death, he would be able to procure a substitute, as in China. He viewed this as a poor man's question, for the poor man had a right to be hung in public. If innocent he had a right to appear before the people and declare his innocence, or if guilty to acknowledge his crime and warn others by example.[10]

However, his amendment to postpone the Bill was defeated by 181 votes to 25, with both Benjamin Disraeli and W. E. Gladstone voting against him. Abolitionists continued to press that the measure be dropped in favour of a complete end to the death penalty and moved an amendment to that effect. This was opposed by Disraeli and Gladstone, who both approved of the Bill, as well as by John Stuart Mill—a former supporter of abolition.

John Stuart Mill intervenes

Mill entered the debate in the House of Commons[11] on another amendment to the Bill, this time by C. Gilpin, that 'It is expedient, instead of carrying out the punishment of death within prisons, that capital punishment should be abolished.' The crime of murder, he said, was increasing under the present law but would decrease with abolition as had other crimes in the past. Mill regretted that he was opposed to what he called 'the philanthropists' since on this very subject

> we all know what signal service they have rendered. It is through their efforts that our criminal laws—which within my memory hanged people for stealing in a dwellinghouse to the value of forty shillings—laws by virtue of which rows of human beings might be seen suspended in front of Newgate—have so greatly relaxed their most revolting and most impolitic ferocity, that aggravated murder is now practically the only crime which is punished with death. And we are even now deliberating whether the extreme penalty should be retained in that solitary case.

71

He thought not. If a man were proved guilty of 'the greatest crime known to the law', to deprive the criminal of the life of which he had shown himself unworthy was the most appropriate and impressive mode of society marking the penal consequences of murder. He claimed to defend the penalty, when confined to atrocious cases, on the very ground on which it was commonly attacked, namely as being incomparably less cruel than imprisonment with hard labour for life which would impair something more precious than the life of the physical body. 'What comparison', he asked,

> can there really be, in point of severity, between consigning a man to the short pang of a rapid death, and immuring him in a living tomb, there to linger out what may be a long life in the hardest and most monotonous toil, without any of its alleviations or rewards, debarred from all pleasant sights and sounds, and cut off from all earthly hope, which was a torture of the most terrible intensity. And how were we to know the death penalty had failed as a deterrent when we could not know how many its threat had saved from becoming murderers?

He went on to say that abolition would be a fatal victory by producing 'an enervation, and effeminacy, in the general mind of the country . . . [And] is it, indeed, so dreadful a thing to die?' Was it not 'the object of all manly education to teach us to despise death which was by no means high in the list of evils and was, at all events, an inevitable one?' On the other side of the same coin it is interesting to note that on 17 May 1856 *The Economist* had said that 'With death all earthly pain, all punishment ceases. The sinner must be allowed to live that he may suffer and be a warning'.[12]

Mill also gratuitously advocated flogging as a punishment in cases of brutality.[13] As for the problem arising from the finality and irremissibility of capital punishment he said that if a condemned person were not guilty he did not consider he was likely to suffer death. The rules of evidence were if anything too favourable to the prisoner and judges and juries would let the guilty go free before the innocent would suffer. Clearly he was either not in touch with the reality or he chose to ignore it, along with the evidence given to the Royal Commission about innocent men who were convicted. Curiously, he said that he was opposed to what he regarded as the position of advanced liberal opinion.

Editorially, *The Times*[14] concluded that what it correctly described as Mill's 'remarkable speech' had considerably helped secure the defeat of the amendment for abolition which was lost by 127 votes to 23.[15] The Capital Punishment Within Prisons Bill then received its third reading, was approved by the House of Lords and given the Royal Assent on 29 May 1868. Four days prior to that saw the last of the public spectacles.

Clerkenwell gaol dynamited

The Fenian Brotherhood was founded by Irishmen in the United States in 1859. Its inspiration was the ancient Gaelic elite legion of warriors known as the Fianna, and its purpose was to secure a republic in Ireland by means of guerrilla warfare.

72

In December 1867 two members of the brotherhood, Burke and Casey, were being held in Clerkenwell gaol in London. A group of sympathisers sought to rescue them on the thirteenth of the month by exploding a barrel of gunpowder against the wall surrounding the prison yard. The force of the explosion drove 40 tons of masonry out of the wall and across the yard. Opposite the prison it completely wrecked a row of tenement houses which were separated from the prison only by a narrow lane. Nine local residents were killed instantly, three died of their wounds and 30 were seriously injured. Public outrage was summed up by a leading article in *The Times* which said 'We are confronted by a gang of reckless criminals who respect no laws, human or Divine . . . We must crush them at any cost'. The question arises in this inflammatory situation, was the necessary caution likely to be used in searching for the perpetrators?

By April 1868 five men and a woman were charged at the Old Bailey with murder, and three others with conspiracy to depose the Queen. Prosecuting counsel were attended by armed police officers throughout the trials with police also stationed on the roof of the court. In the conspiracy case two of the accused were sentenced to long terms of penal servitude. In the murder trial four of the men and the woman were acquitted.

Despite the highly charged atmosphere the fifth man, Michael Barrett, who denied being near Clerkenwell at the time, was alone found guilty and was subsequently executed outside Newgate prison on 25 May 1868. He was the last man to be hanged publicly in England. At the hanging the crowds were more sympathetic than usual owing to some doubt about his guilt, despite the optimism of Mill that no innocent person would suffer execution. The hangman at Newgate was the now more experienced Calcraft but still Barrett died in convulsions. When after some time his body had not been cut down the crowds began to shout, 'Come on body-snatcher! Take away the man you killed!' When Calcraft did so jeers and curses followed his hasty departure into the prison. Significantly, as a clue as to why public executions had to go, the *Daily News*, in writing of the crowds, stated, 'The bastard pride in [his] animal courage and the brutal delight that he died game made the law and its ministers seem to them the real murderers, and Barrett to be a martyred man'. [16]

Relief

Even *The Times* now joined in the general feeling of relief that public executions and the fearsome displays accompanying them were at an end. This relic of medieval barbarism had finally come to a stop. As Sir Leon Radzinowicz has put it, 'The spectacle once thought so essential and potent a deterrent had dwindled to little more than a notice and a certificate on the gate of a prison'. [17]

The first person hanged inside prison was Thomas Wells, at Maidstone, Kent on 13 August 1868. He was an 18-year-old Dover railway porter who had murdered his station-master after a reprimand. His execution, whilst he proudly wore his railway uniform, was generally disapproved of because of his age. Furthermore, after the drop he still took two minutes to die. The first hanging inside Newgate took place 26 days later, on 8 September when another 18-year-old, Alexander Mackay, was executed for murdering his master's wife. They

73

were part of the distressing statistic that 90 per cent of people executed at the time were under 21.

It was after executions were confined to within prison walls that the Convict Prison Department of the Home Office issued a statement on 23 April 1877 admitting that death by hanging could result:

- from strangulation
- from suffocation
- from rupture of the spinal cord (i.e. breaking the neck)
- from shock to the nerves.

It conceded that the first two, although resulting in death, were accompanied by pain and were not rapid. This was generally the case with executions by Calcraft with his two feet drop. Marwood, the statement said, claimed to pinion criminals by drawing their arms back to deprive them of the ability of hardening the muscles of the neck. The Home Office made the further admission that the death penalty, although in the nature of a surgical operation, was left almost entirely to the judgment of any 'rough uneducated man who might undertake the office of hangman'.[18] So much for the invariable public announcement after each execution that it had been carried out satisfactorily.

Home Office records also reveal dissatisfaction with the requirement after the 1868 Act that the prison bell should be tolled to ensure that it was known outside the prison that an execution was taking place. The bell had to be tolled for 15 minutes before a hanging and for 15 minutes following. An advantage, one person wrote, was that those who heard it could offer up a prayer on behalf of the 'poor wretch who is to be hurried into eternity'. The general view, however, was that whilst it did nothing for the man dazed with 'the awful certainties of his next few minutes', its effect on other prisoners was to produce a 'brutal levity'.[19] It also undoubtedly produced among them reactions of fear and depression. As a consequence the tolling of the bell before an execution was abandoned in March 1901.

In spite of the privacy then obtaining, disasters, such as Wells' agonizing last minutes, and occasional decapitations, still occurred, particularly when the hangman was worse for wear due to drink, or the rope used was too long. For instance, in Exeter prison in 1885, defective apparatus meant that three attempts to hang John Lee, who was said to have murdered his landlady in her home, proved unsuccessful. He became known as 'The Man They Could Not Hang' and as a consequence of his terrible ordeal on the scaffold he was reprieved and his sentence commuted to life imprisonment. He was released in 1907. It is debatable whether Lee received a fair trial and he may have been innocent.[20]

ENDNOTES

1 P.P., xxi
2 *The Times*, 24 February 1865

3   *Hansard* [Lords], [182] 837
4   ibid, 243
5   ibid, [184] 453
6   ibid, 1163
7   *The Times,* 8 August 1866
8   HO., 144/18/46327
9   *Hansard,* [190] 1128 (1867)
10 ibid, 1131/2
11 ibid, [91] 1047 (21 April 1868)
12 p. 532. The journal's Victorian-style full title was *The Economist, Weekly Commercial Times, Bankers' Gazette and Railway Monitor. A Political, Literary and General Newspaper*
13 *Hansard,* [191] 1054 (1868)
14 22 April 1968
15 *Hansard, op. cit.*
16 *Daily News,* 27 May 1868
17 *A History of English Criminal Law and its Administration from 1750,* iv 353, 1968
18 HO., 144/18/46327
19 HO., PCOM, 8/210
20 cf. 'John Lee: An Aborted Execution', Barry Phillips, *Justice of the Peace,* 6 July 1996.

CHAPTER 7

The Campaign at Bay

The crusade against capital punishment itself was not at an end, of course, although support diminished once public hangings had gone, and when William Ewart died in 1869 it was left without a charismatic leader. Neither Disraeli nor Gladstone felt any sympathy with this cause. Indeed, no Conservative MP supported abolition and two leading Liberals who became home secretaries in the 1880s, William Harcourt and Hugh Childers, reversed their earlier support when they took office. Whatever their individual opinion might be, they said, they had to take into account the demand of the community for retribution.

Attempts and failures

The debate resumed in June 1877, when Sir Eardley Wilmot moved in the House of Commons that the death penalty should be restricted to premeditated murder and cases where the killer knew that his act would probably cause death. But he did not support abolition, and malice aforethought and intent had long been essential ingredients of the crime of murder.

Wilmot also felt that infanticide should not be a capital offence even when it was deliberate.[1] In law, infanticide was a form of murder and treated as such despite a tendency to circumvent the death penalty by substituting the offence of concealing a birth. The Royal Commission of 1866 tried to find a compromise as did Sir James Fitzjames Stephen in his Criminal Law Code as well as a number of MPs. It was not until 1922, however, that a separate non-capital offence of a mother causing the death of her child was created by the Infanticide Act of that year.

In the debate on Wilmot's motion of 1877, J. W. Pease, a Quaker, moved an amendment for total abolition saying that experience in countries which had taken that step proved that the death penalty did not deter people from murder. 'The punishment', he said, 'must pass away from our land . . . It belongs to a much earlier day than ours, and it is no longer needed for the civilization of the age in which we live'.[2] John Bright agreed and argued that even with private executions the public mind was still poisoned by reading the newspapers which contained accounts of every little detail. 'You cannot', he cried, 'teach people to revere human life by strangling a person before the sheriff, prison governor, police, priest and hangman, with maybe a dozen newsmen looking on'. The plea fell largely on deaf ears, with Sir John Holker, the attorney-general, conceding for the government only that the notorious murder-felony rule, by which people were hanged for unintentional killing whilst committing a felony, needed revision. The motion and the amendment were both heavily defeated.[3]

Further attempts by Pease in 1878 and again in 1881, when Gladstone had become prime minister, also failed although in the latter year he secured 79 votes against 175. Between 1878 and 1881 the majority for retention had dropped from 199 to only 96. When the barrister Josiah Oldfield sent a cir to the judges and bishops enquiring whether the time had come to suspen barbarous penalty' at least experimentally, only two judges responded and an the bishops favoured retention. Thereafter the question of abolition was not the subject of a full-scale Commons debate during the remainder of the nineteenth century. In a leading article, *The Times* had stated, that 'the storm which once seemed to be gathering has subsided and has been followed by a great calm. Abolition no longer had a place among the real questions of the day'.[4] On the other hand, in another, later, leader, it was to continue its opposition, saying '99 out of 100 moral men would say that the proper punishment for homicide with true malice is death'.[5] Nevertheless, the foundations laid by men like Ewart and Bright existed for a renewal of the crusade after World War I when the earlier arguments for and against were to resurface.

A call for change

At the beginning of the last year of the nineteenth century a letter appeared in *The Times* from William Tallack, who was secretary of the Howard Association.[6] He called for a reform of the law of murder so that it would reflect the different classes of murder in terms of intent, since 'some are convicted of murder where there is no intention to kill or do harm, the offender is convicted and sentenced to death and the sentence then commuted to three or seven years imprisonment'. He called this 'an irregularity which is mischievous both to the dignity and efficacy of the law' and said '. . . this state of affairs has too long continued to be a scandal to our intelligence and to our juridical system'. He did not join in the call for a Court of Appeal which arose following .the commutation of some death sentences as he regarded the home secretary to be fully competent in regard to special appeals in capital and other offences. He believed that an appeal court would involve delay and would afford temptations to obstruct and interfere 'to which the home secretary is not liable'. He ended his letter calling for the law of homicide to be brought into harmony with both facts and justice.

In a long leading article on page eleven of the same edition *The Times* agreed with Tallack. The article, which quoted the opinions of a number of authorities, ends, 'There is no doubt that the law is not in accordance with the public conscience and that there is a genuine desire that it should be altered'.

The executions

The new century began as the old century ended: there was no shortage of executions. *The Times* reported them diligently, albeit briefly, and it is interesting to note the range of murders for which people were sentenced to death. The first individual of the century to be executed, on 9 January 1900,[7] was Louise Massett, aged 36, for the murder of her three-year-old son at Dalston railway station. She was reported as saying on the night before she was hanged 'What I suffer is just'. The execution 'was satisfactory in all respects' and the coroner stated that death was instantaneous.

February was free of hangings but on March 6 Ada Chard Williams, aged 24 was executed for the murder of a child in her care. Billington was the executioner and Lieutenant Colonel Milman, the governor of Newgate and Holloway said that the execution was carried out satisfactorily and that death was instantaneous.[8]

On May 22 Henry Grove, 26, was executed by Billington at Newgate,[9] and although there were no executions in June, three were sentenced to death in July. Alfred Highfield, 22, was executed on July 17 by Billington at Newgate for the murder of Edith Margaret Poole,[10] death, as usual, being instantaneous and the execution satisfactory. But on July 25 in response to a petition, the home secretary respited the sentence on Henry John Milstead with a view to commute it to penal servitude for life. Milstead said that he took to drink after his wife became a drunkard and was on the verge of *delirium tremens* at the time of committing the crime and thus was not mentally responsible.[11] At the trial of John Birtles a plea of insanity had been raised but he was still sentenced to death. On July 29 however, this sentence was commuted and on the basis of two Home Office reports he was transferred to Broadmoor Criminal Lunatic Asylum.[12]

August was a wicked month, at least the second half of it, with no fewer than four executions being carried out in two weeks. On August 14 William James Irwin, who was 61, was hanged by Billington for the murder of his second wife[13] and two days later there was a double execution at Leeds. A labourer named Mellor was hanged for drowning his two children whom he had vainly attempted to get into a workhouse, and Charles Benjamin Backhouse was hanged for being implicated with his brother in the murder of a policeman. The brother was reprieved two days earlier and although there had been a recommendation for mercy by the jury, this was not entertained by the home secretary. Unusually, no reporters were admitted to witness these executions but *The Times* reported that although the weather was gloomy a crowd assembled to see the black flag hoisted.[14]

On August 22 *The Times* reported the execution a day earlier of 'a coloured man', William Lacey, at Cardiff for the murder of his wife, despite efforts to secure a reprieve.[15] The executioner was Billington, assisted by his son and as reporters were admitted, together with the High Sheriff and other officials, they were able to report that Lacey walked firmly to the scaffold, was given a drop of about six feet, and that 'death appeared to be instantaneous'. Several thousand people assembled outside the prison to see the black flag hoisted.

The last of the August executions was that of Charles Oliver Blewitt, a tanner, for 'cutting his wife's throat as she sat in a rocking chair'. At the first trial the jury disagreed but he was found guilty at a second trial and hanged at Leeds by Billington assisted by his son. *The Times*[16] reported that 'the condemned man was callous and indifferent to the last and made no confession'.

There were executions on two consecutive days in October. On October 2 John Parr, who was only 19, was hanged at Newgate for shooting Sarah Willett, a girl 'with whom he had been keeping company'. Death, it was said,[17] was instant and the convict left no statement and expressed no contrition. The execution of William Barrett, a hawker from Chelmsford, on October 3 for murdering his young wife, was unusual as he was 'given a drop of over nine feet'[18] which indicates that he was extremely light in weight and that the pit beneath the scaffold was exceptionally deep.

On November 23 Henry Thomas Bland was reprieved with a view of commutation to penal servitude for life, following a recommendation for mercy from the jury.[19] Surprisingly for such a notorious murderer, there was only a small notice concerning the execution at Pentonville of Hawley Hervey Crippen ('Dr Crippen') for the murder of his wife. The executioner was Ellis and a large crowd gathered outside the prison. The Home Office had no knowledge of any confession. On December 4 the sentence of Oscar Mattson was 'respited until further notice of His Majesty's pleasure[20] but on the same day Joseph Holden, 57, was hanged at Strangeways, Manchester, for the unusual crime of murdering his grandson. He had pleaded guilty and also admitted having assaulted another grandson by hitting him with a stone. At the trial he had been full of remorse and penitence, and his sanity had been in some doubt but was 'affirmed by medical opinion'.[21]

But the year, and December, were not yet finished with capital punishment. On December 12 John Bowes, 50, was executed by Billington at Durham for the murder of his wife[22] and on the December 28 Billington was busy again, this time hanging James Bergin for the murder of his sweetheart Margaret Morrison, even though over 30,000 people signed a petition for his reprieve. No witnesses were allowed but it was said that Bergin was very penitent and paid great attention to the administrations of the Roman Catholic prison chaplain.[23]

But between these executions there was one reprieve. More than 5,000 signatures were attached to a petition for William Wood who had murdered his wife at Wigan. The home secretary said that in all the circumstances he was advising the King to respite the capital sentence with a view to commuting it to penal servitude for life.[24]

The discussion
A further ten years were to pass and many more executions were to take place before there was any serious discussion in the correspondence columns of *The Times*; in Parliament there was none. The subject was launched by a letter from Arthur G. Benson of Magdalen College, Cambridge.[25] He referred back to the execution of Dr Crippen as providing excitement and enjoyment to many and deprecated the 'hideous drama' enacted since 'this unhappy man's condemnation'. He drew attention to 'hideous delays', often due to appeals, and the prolongation of uncertainty for the prisoner and the publicity of sickening mechanical details. He attacked the so-called deterrent nature of capital punishment and said that if it were a deterrent it should be ignominious and painful and that prisoners should be racked and tortured as well. He then made an unusual suggestion: that instead of the execution taking place at a pre-arranged time, the condemned man should be able to choose, within limits, the time and manner of his death, which the resources of medical science should make as swift and painless as possible. He concluded that 'the solemn barbarity [of hanging] has an entirely debasing and degrading effect on the public mind'.

The very next day saw a riposte in the form of a letter from Sir Herbert Steven,[26] who argued that Benson's scheme would result in no less prolongation as the criminal would choose the latest time available. Furthermore, the criminal would make no choice as to his manner of death in nine out of ten cases and the tenth would make a choice that was as embarrassing as possible. Sir Herbert, unfortunately, did not elaborate on what would be an embarrassing way to die, nor on who was likely to be embarrassed. He went on to say that anyone who knows about ropes and drops knew that consciousness was lost as soon as the rope tightens and that he saw 'nothing morally wrong in forcing a man into such a situation that he will die'.

The next day saw three letters and an article. The first, from Sir Mackenzie Chalmers,[27] gave no comfort to Benson whose sympathy was 'misplaced'. Only about one third of murderers were actually hanged and then only for calculated and brutal murder. He went on, 'It's a mistake to attribute to murderers of this kind the sensitive feelings of kind and humane people . . . The gentle euthanasia that Mr Benson half-heartedly advocates would be but a poor deterrent to the type of criminal from which these murderers come'.

On the same page a letter from J.C. Chance[28] had a modern ring to it. 'In Mr Benson's sympathy for the guilty has he forgotten the victim?' Overflowing sympathy for the fate of the criminal is just as debasing to the public mind as the gloating over his fate. But also on the same page was to be found some support for Benson[29] from Carl Heath who was keen to get rid of medieval methods of capital punishment and supported George Greenwood's Law of Murder Amendment Bill which would put Britain in line with most European countries by grading murder as recommended by the Royal Commission of 1866, and that the death penalty would be reserved for murder of the first degree. He concluded, somewhat naively in retrospect, '. . . with the gradual rise in social conditions such cases will become rarer and the death penalty will then fall into disuse'.

An article, entitled 'The Modern Execution',[30] dubbed Mr Benson's letter 'impressive' but disagreed with much of it, calling his proposals for permissive suicide 'startling'. But the article did not accuse Benson of sentimentality.

> It comes in the end to this . . . how is the sentence of the law to be carried out with least pain? . . . Of course . . . death should be as swift, quiet and painless as possible. What evidence is there that executions as now practised are otherwise? . . . If there were failings in this respect we should soon hear of them. It is intelligible to oppose capital punishment altogether or to retain it for specially brutal murders. It is also intelligible to propose that the prison supply or friends smuggle in prussic acid or some other potent poison . . .

But '. . . it is not possible to strip the process of grim and repulsive elements and awful ceremony. Would it be justifiable if it were altogether devoid of them?' The article went on to question Steven's certainty and said there is much to be said in favour of electrocution. Although commending Benson for his humanity, the article concluded by pointing out that 'it is of doubtful value if it is intended to insinuate that we have the reality of justice with its power to deter bold offenders and yet be devoid of sternness; that it may do its rough work in a pleasant and gentle way . . . There is no making the scaffold decorative or unforbidding.'

The next day saw some original thoughts on the matter in a letter from Filson Young[31] who, having studied conditions of prisons and punishment in Britain found that they were incredibly more brutal and barbarous than anything that could be imagined. He believed that there are worse things than death and could see that it is reasonable for the state to decide when a person's life cannot be allowed to continue. But we have no right to punish people by killing them. Although it was difficult to get statistics, he believed that the death penalty was a deterrent and therefore if the criminal dies for the benefit of the state by frightening off other potential murderers then his death should be accomplished with a degree of dignity and honour. Half the people who become entangled in the machinery of death have been punished all their lives, by squalor, lack of education and lack of beauty and brightness in their lives. It is the 'gentle, kind, sentimental people who hang men and women and who then find the subject so unpleasant they would rather not talk about it.' Referring to Mr Benson's views, Young ends by pointing out that some correspondents felt that any attempt to show human feeling for a man awaiting death is to condone his crime, as though any mitigation of his sufferings in some way robs the victim of a benefit. On the same page *Fiat Justitia* accused Benson of being sentimental. The current method of execution is quick and the criminal is in the execution chamber for only a few seconds. As the murderer's victim did not have a choice of how to die, why should the murderer?

The next day saw four more letters on the subject.[32] Emily Lutyens deplored the fact that Christian sentiments were dismissed as 'sickly' and 'decadent humanitarianism'. An E. Arbuthnot thought it unnecessary that it is known when an execution is to take place; all that was needed was an announcement that it had. *Journalist* had witnessed two executions in Warwick. The whole business took less than a minute 'and death was instantaneous as I could see from where I was standing.' No more speedy and merciful method could be devised than the one in operation, he claimed. And, at last, some tongue-in-cheek humour, from J. D. P. who wrote:

I do not think Mr Benson goes far enough. Instantaneous and absolutely painless death, guaranteed by the government at a time of one's own choosing would suit most reasonable people. Why must I qualify for this advantage by committing murder? If Mr Benson will place me on the same footing with murderers I am with him.

The next day saw a return to solemnity.[33] Homewood Crawford, as under sheriff for London and Middlesex, had seen 12 executions and on no occasion did they fit the description of Filson Young. The prisoners were always grateful for a delay of a fortnight before being executed and news of a reprieve was not always welcome. One man had said 'Thank you for nothing. I'd rather be hanged'. Carl Heath, writing on the subject a second time, supported the Greenwood proposal. There must be a discussion of the whole concept of having a death penalty, not just the method. Agnes Grove, in a letter as confused as it was fey, was more kindly disposed to murderers than to cabinet ministers who opposed women's suffrage.

With the month barely half over Benson replied to his many critics.[34] He pointed out their misconception that any humanity extended to the criminal is inconsistent with pity for the victim. The fear of dying is more terrible than death itself yet several corespondents 'speak as though one could only express one's pity for the victim by torturing the criminal'. He did not agree that murders would increase if the present penalty was abrogated and cited the fact that thefts had not increased sine the death penalty was abolished for such crimes. Many practices 'that were once accepted on social or ethical grounds are now regarded with repugnance' and it was time to take a step forward.

Henry Smith was in no doubt where he stood and made three points.[35] The press should not be excluded from executions as the public had a right to know what goes on. He could not understand sympathy shown to cold-blooded and calculating miscreants like Dr Crippen whose 'behaviour in the dock was an outrage to decency, yet people signed petitions for a reprieve!' Finally, 'the rope is the greatest deterrent. The rope it is that is anticipated with terror.'

A short letter from K. E. B.[36] who wanted the death penalty retained but did not want the execution dates announced in advance, was followed by a very long one from A. Chichele Plowden.[37] He announced himself as a disbeliever in the efficiency of capital punishment as there was no evidence from countries where it had been abolished that the rope was a deterrent. 'We all know that crimes for which capital punishment used to be the penalty have diminished and that murders continue to afflict society. It was a fallacy to label murderers as the worst of criminals. Some people who had been blameless can be driven in a moment of frenzy into acts of violence from which they would recoil in saner moments. He then wrote a passage of great farsightedness that has relevance today. 'No-one who has not been through fire' he wrote, 'can tell what may be the effect on his self-control of a long course of studied insults and provocation on the part of a worthless wife against her husband persevered day by day, for months and even years at a stretch'. What would nowadays be seen as a sexist slant was no doubt the result of a plethora of wife murders but no or few instances at that time of wives killing their husbands. He pointed out that Dr Crippen's crime was common: he killed the wife he hated for the woman he loved. Had he met his second wife before his first he probably would have been a law-abiding citizen. It was quite clear, as with other murderers, that the deterrent effect was nil. Men fear pain not death and the 'cat' should be made part of the punishment whether capital punishment is abolished or not. Had Crippen 'been asked what he feared most, the physical pain of the lash or the death to follow—can anyone be in doubt what his answer would be?' (One would have thought a great deal of doubt; would any man really fear temporary pain more than the permanance of death?)

An interesting letter followed from W. D. Morrison.[38] Although he himself did not believe in the value of capital punishment he felt that the public were not ready for abolition. The current laws required revision to allow judges more discretion, and death should be reserved for the worst sort of murder. (This passage anticipates the Homicide Act 1957, which was unsuccessful, and the argument in the 1990s regarding the mandatory life sentence for murder). Crippen he believed to be the worst sort of murderer, a poisoner, as poisoning involves 'deliberate, cold blooded, carefully planned premeditation' (poisoning was excluded as a capital crime by the 1957 Act) and 'as long as the death penalty is in existence it will be used for murders of this character' (wrong!).

The next day, adjacent to an advertisement for a cruise to Gibraltar, Morocco and the Canaries: 23 days from £21, was a letter from J. Riccalton[39] who described how he had witnessed four executions at Salford prison, two of which were unsatisfactory, one man taking half a minute to die. On the same page Charles Mercier asked, if there is no evidence that the rope is a deterrent how can there be any that the rope is not a deterrent?—and A.W. claimed that the absence of press at executions was due to the action of under sheriffs who were acting *ultra vires* and the home secretary should stop them.

The last letter of this batch and of the decade had to wait until after Christmas and came from Sir Henry Smith. He did not like Plowden's comment that murderers were hardly criminals and he was not bothered by Crippen's coolness but by his 'flippant impudence which was an outrage on decency'. In his opinion, if Crippen was not hanged for murdering his first wife he would have gone on to numbers 2, 3 and 4! He ended his riposte: 'Mr Plowden's letter, emanating from a police magistrate still in office, is calculated to do an immensity of harm. It is pestilential—there is no other word for it—and should be stamped out like the cattle plague.' How he would go about stamping out a published letter we shall never know, and what Sir Henry was not to know was that stamping out cattle plague has not been an unmitigated success either.

ENDNOTES

1   *Hansard*, [234] 1663-70

2   ibid, 1673

3   ibid, 1715

4   *The Times*, 14 March 1878

5   ibid, 14 January 1899

6   ibid, p.13, 14 January 1899

7   ibid, p. 7, 10 January 1900

8   ibid, p. 12, 7 March 1900

9   ibid, p. 12, 23 May 1900

10   ibid, p. 13, 17 July 1900

11   ibid, p. 6, 26 July 1900

12   ibid, p. 10, 30 July 1900

13   ibid, p. 7, 15 August 1900

14   ibid, p. 8, 17 August 1900

15   ibid, p. 8, 22 August 1900

16 *The Times*, p. 10, 29 August 1900
17 ibid, p. 5, 3 October 1900
18 ibid, p. 10, 4 October 1900
19 ibid, p. 8, 23 November 1900
20 ibid. p 4, 5 December 1900
21 ibid, p. 5
22 ibid, p. 10, 13 December 1900
23 ibid, p. 4, 28 December 1900
24 ibid, p. 4, 21 December 1900
25 ibid, p. 14, 5 December 1910
26 ibid, p. 4, 6 December 1910
27 ibid, p. 11, 7 December 1910
28 ibid
29 ibid
30 ibid
31 ibid, p. 4, 8 December 1910
32 ibid, p. 4, 9 December 1910
33 ibid, p. 12, 10 December 1910
34 ibid, p. 4, 13 December 1910
35 ibid, p. 4, 16 December 1910
36 ibid, p. 3, 19 December 1910
37 ibid, p. 4, 20 December 1910
38 ibid, p. 4, 22 December 1910
39 ibid, p. 2, 23 December 1910.

CHAPTER 8

Towards a Select Committee

It is not surprising given the carnage of the first world war that following its conclusion capital punishment was not a subject of great importance. However, during the following few years questions were asked in the House of Commons, mainly by Major Christopher Lowther, which showed that the topic was by no means forgotten.

Questions and answers

In May 1919 Lowther asked the secretary of state for the Home Department (Edward Shortt, a Liberal MP who was home secretary from 1919-1922) how many people were sentenced to death in 1918 and how many reprieved, and was told that there were seven executions and that 18 death sentences were commuted.[1] Two days later Lowther asked how many females were sentenced to death in 1918 and how many sentences were commuted.[2] Shortt replied that there were nine, commuted in each case. Lowther then asked how many were sentenced to death between 1914 and 1918 for treason, espionage, etc. and how many were British, enemy or neutral; and how many sentences were carried out. The answer was a total of 19 of whom eight were enemy, eight were neutral, two were allied and one was British; 13 were executed. Mr Shortt was careful to point out that these figures excluded cases in connection with the Irish rebellion of 1916.

Lowther was quietly persistent and a couple of weeks later asked the home secretary what circumstances might make it desirable to commute the death sentence and what persons were consulted other than the trial judge.[3] But he was told by Sir Henry Greenwood that the circumstances varied so much it was impossible to detail what steps were taken.

Lowther's two Bills

Almost two years passed before Lowther intervened again and early in 1921 he introduced the Capital Punishment (Limitations) Bill.[4] Supported by Messrs Bottomly, Spoor and Kennedy Jones the Bill sought 'to prohibit the passing of sentence of capital punishment on persons who, at the time of committing the offence, have not attained the age of 21, and on persons who have been recommended to mercy by a jury'. Nothing came of it.

A year later he tried again, moving 'that leave be given to bring in a Bill to abolish in Great Britain the award of capital punishment for any crime or offence whatever'.[5] Considering that his much more modest Bill of a year before got nowhere, Lowther must have known what the fate of this all-embracing Bill would be. He first argued that it was wrong to take life in any circumstances and that it is equally wrong for the state to do so. He asked not to be thought of by the House as a 'sickly sentimentalist' but he challenged such a rigid sentence for murder that only the home secretary could modify. He recognised the need for a deterrent but felt it not beyond the wit of man to find one that did not involve taking life. Finally, he drew the attention of the House to the 'intolerable anguish' of the condemned man's family. Predictably the motion was lost, by 234 to 86. Among those supporting the Bill were Nancy (Lady) Astor, John Clynes a future home secretary, and Arthur Henderson; among those against were an ex-prime minister, Arthur Balfour, two future prime ministers, Stanley Baldwin and Neville Chamberlain, Austen Chamberlain, the only leader of the Conservative party not to have been prime minister, and Sir Samuel Hoare, a future home secretary.

The Times expresses support for hanging

A few months passed and a Mr Rapier asked the home secretary[6] how many had been sentenced to death in the past two years and how many were reprieved. There were, replied Mr Shortt, 28 sentenced, of whom three were women. Eight men and all three women were reprieved.

On 7 June 1922 a young man called Henry Jacoby, not yet 19-years-old, was hanged at Pentonville for murdering an elderly woman and this was the subject of a leader in *The Times* the next day.[7] The jury had recommended him to mercy on account of his youth and it was expected up to the last that the home secretary would commute the death sentence. But, said *The Times*,

> We are glad that Mr Shortt has been proof against the appeal of sentimentality. If the criminal law in this country in regard to murder has not . . . the support of public opinion, the sooner it is altered the better. So long, however, as the law provides that one who is old enough to play a man's part in the affairs of life is also old enough to pay a man's penalty for crime, the law must be punctiliously upheld by those who are its guardians. Henry Jacoby had, upon his own admission, committed murder . . . Upon what reasonable grounds was he entitled to special consideration?

After dismissing penal servitude as too harsh for one so young—presumably because of the length of time he would have to serve—and physical punishments, which are inflicted only after the greatest hesitation in the case of adults, this harsh article concluded, 'If capital punishment is justifiable on grounds of experience and reason, is there any but a purely sentimental argument that deprecates it at an age of discretion?' (The fact that it may not have any deterrent value was not addressed). 'The law that demands a life for a life does not survive at the whim of the legislature. It is a substantial and well-tried barrier against deeds of violence . . . [institutions of this nature] exist because public opinion finds better reason to sympathise with the victims of offences than with those who perpetrate them' (this fallacious argument has still not gone away). 'It is a rule founded both on common sense and the essential elements of human justice.'

Bywaters and Thompson

The case of Henry Jacoby was completely overshadowed by another that occurred later in 1922. Edith Jessie Thompson and her husband had as an occasional lodger Frederick Bywaters, who was a young merchant seaman. When he was on home leave he stayed at the Thompsons' and after a while he and Mrs Thompson became lovers. She became infatuated with Bywaters and in order to free herself from her marriage, probably persuaded Bywaters to kill her husband, which he did by ambushing him and stabbing him to death although without her prior knowledge. Thompson and Bywaters were quickly arrested and tried for murder.

The trial lasted from December 6 to 11 and was fully reported daily in *The Times* and elsewhere. The judge summed up on December 11 and the jury retired for two hours. When they returned Mrs Thompson had to be half carried to her place and when guilty verdicts were announced on both defendants she 'shut her eyes and seemed as if she would have fallen but for the support of the wardresses. Bywaters retained his composure'. After the death sentence was passed and the clerk asked if she had anything to say she 'threw up her arms and exclaimed, "Oh God, I am not guilty. Oh, God, I am not guilty". She then collapsed and was carried from the dock'.[8]

A few days later *The Times* was on its high horse again;[9] if it had little to say on behalf of Jacoby it had less for Bywaters and Thompson. 'There were no circumstances in the case to provoke the slightest sympathy. The crime was premeditated and long contemplated . . . Mr Thompson was stabbed to death by Bywaters on a quiet road in Ilford. The whole case was simple and sordid'. Given that *The Times* gave the trial massive coverage day by day in great detail—there was a short report daily and almost a full page devoted to the previous day's proceedings—the rest of this leader shows the most blatant hypocrisy. It continued,

. . . it is hard to understand why the entrance to the court was besieged day by day by men and women. It is extraordinary that persons should squat outside a criminal court at midnight in the hope of gaining admission next morning to hear a trial which presented really no features of romance, and which provided none of the horrors that appeal to the morbid mind . . . Such prurient curiosity in such wholly uninterested masses is happily rare.

The Times was right in one respect: the case was about a sordid and selfish murder. But although the case itself had no bearing on the future of capital punishment, the execution of Edith Thompson probably did. On December 29 the execution was fixed for January 9 at 9 a.m. and the executions were subsequently reported by *The Times* at its most terse.[10] Hidden away on an inside page under the headline, 'Ilford Murderers Executed', *The Times* announced that Bywaters was executed at Pentonville and Thompson at Holloway at 9 a.m. There were 'large crowds outside both prisons but in accordance with present custom no bell was tolled and no black flag hoisted. Instead, official notices were posted on the gates.' The *Daily Mail* carried a fuller account.[11] According to that paper, 'Bywaters had dressed and had a light breakfast by 8 a.m. He rose at two minutes to nine to meet his executioner and walked firmly the six yards to the gallows. Mrs. Thompson was awakened at a few minutes to eight. In a dazed way she nibbled at a slice of toast and an apple, breakfast of her own choice. She was dazed but appeared calm [but] when executioner Ellis entered her cell she began to moan in a distressful manner. She could have walked unaided but was supported on either side as she walked to the gallows. At the inquest relating to Edith Thompson, the governor said 'there was no hitch of any kind.' This last comment was quite untrue as other papers hinted and future events would verify.

The *Daily Mirror* unravelled slightly more of what had happened. Photos of each prisoner were printed and it was reported that after a night of semi-consciousness with a doctor in attendance Mrs Thompson was dazed but able, with assistance, to walk to the scaffold. But later in the article: 'It was afterwards learned that [she] was prostrate nearly all night and when the hour of execution arrived . . . had to be practically carried to the scaffold.'[12]

But a more accurate account, as it later transpired, was carried by the *Daily Express*.[13] On the front page there was a brief announcement of the executions but on an inside page there was a headline: 'Mrs Thompson Hanged. Nearly unconscious and unable to walk. Carried. Distressing last scenes'. Just how distressing was not to emerge for a long time. The paper reported, citing the Central News Agency, that 'Mrs Thompson was prostrate nearly all night and was continually under the doctor's care. At five o'clock she was unconscious and when the hour for the execution arrived she was in a dazed state, only partly conscious and unable to walk, so that she had to be carried. The doctor was in attendance almost up to the time of the execution'. The Exchange Telegraph Company confirmed that Mrs Thompson 'was in a state of collapse'.

The *Daily Express* claimed to have had corroboration of these circumstances from reliable sources. The article went on, 'All the women officials who have been engaged in watching Mrs Thompson have felt the strain acutely and some of them are prostrated in consequence. Many of them have declared that they would never again carry out the duty imposed on them yesterday'. The article concluded with a brief account of Bywaters' bravery. In fact, the circumstances were even more harrowing than what was reported; the governor of Holloway and the chaplain were devastated by what they had witnessed and two weeks later the executioner attempted suicide.

Whether this disturbing news had anything to do with their decision or not, one week later Shoreditch Borough Council passed a resolution to reform the penal system and abolish capital punishment. It was suggested that murder, legal or illegal, was wrong.[14]

More questions—fewer answers
The early months of 1923 saw several interventions in Parliament but with little return from the government. Whether the circumstances of the execution of Edith Thompson was the motive for Sir J. Hewitt's question in February is not known. He asked if the home secretary, W. C. Bridgeman, would consider altering the law to give judges discretion to pass sentence of penal servitude for life instead of death on a conviction of murder.[15] He was told (by Bridgeman) 'There are many reasons against it' but we do not learn what those reasons were.

88

A month later R. Morrison asked if there was any proposal to introduce legislation to enable a judge to pass a sentence of imprisonment for murder where the jury had recommended mercy.[16] The answer was short: 'No'.

A couple of months later Noel Buxton asked the home secretary for statistics on violent crimes in countries where the death penalty had been abolished for ten years or more, before and after abolition. He was told that he would see what statistics could be collected.[17] And Mr T. Thompson asked for legislation to be introduced so that it would no longer be necessary to exhibit for 24 hours notices of executions on the gates of prisons (as required under the Capital Punishment Amendment Act 1868) as children and young people had to pass. But he was told by Mr Lockyer-Sampson that there was no occasion to alter the law.[18]

Questions in the House trickled on slowly. Early in 1924 Mr J. O'Neil asked if any decision had been taken by the cabinet in regard to capital punishment, and if not would the government grant facilities for the introduction of a Bill for abolition. He was told that no decision had been made and facilities for private members' Bills were granted on the general feeling of the House.[19] One month later Edmund Harvey presented a petition from the Society of Friends with 18,639 signatures who 'view with abhorrence the continuance in Great Britain of punishment of death, and praying that a measure be introduced into Parliament for its speedy abolition'.[20] It was ignored. When Rennie Smith asked for details of death sentences and executions for men and women for every year since 1800 the home secretary, not surprisingly, was unable to furnish them. He did, however, give details from 1901 to 1924 as per the *Table 1* overleaf:[21]

The data are interesting for two reasons. Although the number of death sentences diminished during the second half of the period, with the exception of 1922, the proportion of those convicted and sentenced to death that were actually executed remained roughly the same throughout the period. The other striking feature is the tiny number of executions of women, more than half of which were carried out in one year, 1903.

One year later Mr Scurr discovered that of 40 under 21-year-olds sentenced to death 14 had been executed[22] and a month later Mr Beckitt learned that the home secretary was not prepared to appoint a Royal Commission despite 'the growth of public opinion in favour of abolition of capital punishment'.[23] When Mr Rennie Smith asked the home secretary for a list of the occupations of those condemned to death since 1901, he was told, not surprisingly, that there was not enough value for the labour of compiling it.[24]

The year 1926, in which there were massive economic problems, saw only a single question in the House concerning capital punishment when Colonel Day asked Sir William Joyson-Hicks, (Conservative home secretary 1924-1929) if he would consider a Bill to abolish capital punishment for unmarried mothers charged with infanticide, and was told that the provisions of the Infanticide Act 1922 (which had abolished hanging for mothers who killed their new-born babies) were adequate.[25] Later, the Sentence of Death (Pregnant Mothers) Act 1931 would abolish hanging for pregnant women.

Year	Sentenced men	Sentenced women	Executed men	Executed women	Percentage of men executed
1901	26	2	15	0	57.7
1902	28	5	22	0	78.6
1903	37	4	24	3	64.9
1904	26	2	16	0	61.5
1905	31	1	17	0	54.8
1906	24	3	9	0	37.5
1907	20	1	9	1	45.0
1908	23	2	13	0	56.5
1909	27	4	18	0	66.7
1910	24	4	16	0	66.7
1911	26	5	16	0	61.5
1912	24	1	13	0	54.2
1913	24	4	16	0	66.7
1914	21	3	14	0	66.7
1915	18	3	12	0	66.7
1916	12	5	8	0	66.7
1917	14	2	9	0	64.3
1918	17	7	10	0	58.8
1919	19	5	12	0	63.2
1920	32	3	21	0	65.6
1921	10	3	5	0	50.0
1922	30	4	20	1	66.7
1923	19	2	11	0	57.9
1924	13	1	9	0	69.2

Table 1

A year later Mr Pethick-Lawrence asked if recommendations were given to prison governors in regard to what information they should give at inquests following executions, and if so what they were. The home secretary replied that there was a memorandum given to governors but he would not be drawn as to the nature or extent of the instructions.[26] In the course of a speech on a variety of matters Mr Compton drew the attention of the House and the home secretary to the publication by a Sunday newspaper of harrowing details of executions, and in particular accounts embellished by an ex-hangman. He hoped that the home secretary would consider banning such accounts and guessed that 99 per cent of people would welcome the ban and that it would benefit 'working people who read this kind of Sunday newspaper'.[27]

Another new Bill

In February 1928 the Abolition of Capital Punishment Bill was introduced[28] and a few days later Sir Robert Thomas learned from the home secretary that he was not considering the substitution of the death penalty with penal servitude. [29] The Bill was introduced by Lieutenant Commander Kenworthy who began by citing the countries, and states within countries, which had already abolished the death penalty and showing that where this had happened there had been no rise in the murder rate. The first argument he advanced was that there was always a chance of a mistake and that an innocent man would be hanged, and suggested that it was better that 100 guilty men escape the gallows and undergo penal servitude for life than one innocent man be judicially murdered. Most people found it repugnant to execute women, and it must be equally repugnant to execute a man. He reminded the House that whenever it had been proposed to do away with the death penalty for some lesser crime there had been arguments against that had not been borne out in practice. Finally, he hazarded that everyone present, and 999 people out of a 1,000 would shrink from the idea of acting as hangman, and 'we ought not ask a fellow-citizen to perform a duty from which we ourselves recoil with horror'.

Permission to bring in the Bill was opposed by Mr Radford who claimed that capital punishment 'was a deterrent to any man who may contemplate committing murder'. If this were not so, he explained, there would not be such strenuous efforts to secure reprieves for those condemned. He advised against any weakening of the code of criminal law and that every deterrent should be retained that would prevent men contemplating murder from carrying it out. The Bill was carried to its second reading by the narrowest of majorities: 119 to 118.[30]

For the past few years the public had been more or less silent on the subject but later in 1928 a letter appeared in *The Times* that again sent the feathers flying. The letter was from Lord Buckmaster who was President of the National Council for the Abolition of the Death Penalty and he pointed out that a last minute reprieve of three other men because of an element of doubt raised the issue of capital punishment acutely. He agreed that Parliament could not abolish it without popular consent, but the groundswell of opinion against capital punishment that he believed to exist had no means of expression. Furthermore, although in favour of a referendum on the subject he thought it unlikely that Parliament would agree. Therefore, his council were launching a petition and urged readers to obtain forms from his office.[31]

Four days later the first response appeared, from P.G. Eckford[32] who had received a petition form and found 'it would be very easy to make mincemeat of most of the points made in the memorandum' if space permitted and that it would attract 'the usual crowd of unthinking people or those swayed by diseased sentiment'. He had signed a counter-petition and sent it to his MP. However, Rudolph B. Burney supported Buckmaster[33] and pointed out that even if capital punishment were a deterrent its exaction on that count was unsound legally and ethically. 'A man may only be punished for his own crime, and he should not be called upon to suffer for a potential tendency in others towards murder'. Thus the punishment for murder should be less than hanging which was irrevocable and retaliatory. Of course, Burney's argument that one should be punished for what one does not for what others might do has cut little ice and, even today, deterrence is cited as a justification for harsh punishments long after capital punishment has disappeared in Britain.

Barnard Laily wondered, tongue in cheek or seriously, whether there was any legitimate ground on which the community might punish at all if deterrence was unfair and retribution un-Christian[34] but Percy E.F. Hobbs (a retired major-general) was in no doubt.[35] He referred to a murder two days earlier where the victims were buried alive and asked, 'Could anything short of death adequately punish such brutality? Are the abolitionists for keeping murderers in the "comparative comfort of a prison" for the rest of their lives at public expense?'

The final letter in this batch came from Reginald Ward Pole[36] who asked why a burglar ('having entered a woman's bedroom', he added unnecessarily) would not kill to avoid detection if the penalty for the killing and the burglary were the same; this argument has been used in the 1990s *vis à vis* mandatory life sentences and discretionary sentences.

Brown has a try

In October 1929 W. J. Brown moved 'that in the opinion of this House, capital punishment for civil crimes should be abolished'.[37] Brown began his speech by covering the usual ground, showing that when abolition of the death penalty was mooted for minor theft the Lord Chief Justice in 1810 was 'convinced . . . that public expediency requires that there should be no remission of the terror denounced against this description of offence'. He then turned to experiences abroad, and showed once again that abolition was not followed by more murders. The figures showed, quoting a Home Office document, that there was a greater likelihood of being acquitted of murder than any other offence. Certainty of detection not severity of sentence was the deterrence, he said, a sentiment that is still being uttered, and still being ignored. He then pointed out that not only was death not a remedial punishment, which he believed all punishment should be, but was irrevocable and there was no moral right to administer punishment that could not be undone if the judgment were subsequently found to be wrong. The present system of capital punishment was bad for society and newspaper reports fed unconscious sadism in the public mind. Finally, he said that capital punishment debased everyone who had a practical part in its application. He quoted a prison governor who said that executions that he had had to superintend always gave him an acute sense of personal shame. He pointed out that making more widows and orphans did not help the family of the murdered man and that it would be of more practical purpose if the murderer were made to work to help support the relatives of the man he had murdered.

This was not an original speech—everything that could be said on the subject had been said many times before—nor was it emotional. It set out the case for abolition clearly and succinctly. Half-way through the debate Sir Herbert Samuel, an earlier home secretary, spoke, and moved that a Select Committee be appointed by the government. He would support capital punishment if it were a unique deterrent, but if it were not it was a terrible thing to kill a man in cold blood. He agreed that juries, believing death to be an inappropriate sentence, not infrequently acquitted, resulting in murderers going free of any punishment, and he was also convinced that now and again an innocent man had been hanged. He held that a country that could dispense with capital punishment would have reached a higher plane of civilisation and went on to dismiss some of the more superficial arguments against abolition, particularly the 'eye for an eye' argument. Pointing out that this was a principle that had never been acted on by any people nor was ever part of any code, he added dismissively, 'It is not on the principle of tit for tat that we should deal with these matters . . . This doctrine that the punishment should correspond with the crime was a wrong one.'

Just before the debate ended Vicountess Astor made an impassioned speech in favour of abolition and dismissed the need for a Select Committee on the grounds that 'there is ample evidence in existence upon which the home secretary could act'. Finally, Brown accepted the amendment, not because he was convinced of the need for a Select Committee but because Sir Herbert Samuel made it 'doubtful whether my motion will be carried' and the home secretary (Clynes) made it clear that even if it were carried 'I should have made no further advance in [my] cause'. It was then resolved 'That, in the opinion of this House, it is desirable that a Select Committee should be appointed to consider the question of Capital Punishment'. Immediately before the year ended the government ordered that a Select Committee be set up 'to consider the question of capital punishment in cases tried by civil (i.e. non-military) courts in time of peace and to report whether another penalty, and if so, of what nature, should be substituted for the sentence of death in such cases where that sentence [was] prescribed by law'. Fifteen members of the committee were named.[38] Had they known the fate of this Committee's report, the retentionists could have rested easy.

In March 1930 a petition was presented to the House signed by 88,594 'British subjects' plus corporate seals[39] and it was revealed later[40] that the cost of the Select Committee thus far was £1,200 and that further costs were likely to be small.

Controversial report

The Report of the Select Committee, published in December and avaiblable from His Majesty's Stationery Office, price 1s.6d. (7.5 pence), raised considerable controversy as six Conservative members had withdrawn on the grounds that the chairman was one-sided, and the recommendations were subsequently carried on the chairman's casting vote.[41] The conditional recommendations, if Parliament decided to maintain the death penalty, were:

- the M'Naghten Rules [on insanity] should be revised to give fuller scope to medical opinion and extend criminal responsibility to the mentally defective
- the death penalty should apply to women as it does to men and that when considering mercy the home secretary and secretary of state for Scotland should consider each case on its merits
- no-one should be sentenced to death below the age of 21, the age of full responsibility
- there might be a larger exercise of the royal prerogative.

There was not much there to satisfy abolitionists, but the definite recommendations were more far-reaching, i.e. that:

- a Bill be introduced and passed into law during the present session providing for the abolition of the death penalty for an experimental period of five years in cases tried by civil courts in time of peace
- a resolution be passed that in the meantime the home secretary and the secretary of state for Scotland would recommend reprieves in each case
- the penalty to be substituted for death should be that currently administered to reprieved murderers (usually penal servitude for life).

The predictable flurry of letters, which went on well into the New Year, began with a modest proposal from Roger Burges that the exhibition in the press of pictures of criminals and sensational presentation of their exploits should be prohibited.[42] If Mr Burges were still with us over 60 years later he would still be waiting.

H. G. Griffin, writing as 'a humble man in the street' set out the cases for and against abolition. For: justice is fallible and the innocent may be executed; there are many groundless pleas of insanity that enable real criminals to escape from justice; human life is sacred. Against: the death penalty is never inflicted where there is doubt; it is inflicted only for the most aggravated cases of murder; it is the greatest deterrent to premeditated murder; without fear of the death penalty many minor offences would lead to murder. He favoured retention as for real criminals the prospect of penal servitude for life would not be as great a deterrent as hanging and he could murder his gaoler with no further punishment.[43]

The following day saw a long letter from Dr Joseph Hunter MP who, as the result of being a police and prison medical officer for many years, could not recommend abolition. The murderer is 'a criminal of a lone class' and he could not think that 'the envisagement of penal servitude is as clear and definite to the murderer as the swift and awesome retribution of the scaffold. He 'had not a shadow of doubt that this fear deters potential murderers', and that human life was so precious that it should be protected from destruction at all costs (sic).[44]

The next day the Reverend James Barr MP, chairman of the Select Committee, defended the decision of the committee and pointed out that the report was passed by eight out of 15 members, an absolute majority (even if his was the casting vote).[45] But a few days later, Gervais Rentoul MP, one of the six who withdrew because the chairman would not allow a dissenting alternative, found it regrettable that there was no mention of this dissension in the report. He found it 'rather absurd' to talk about an absolute majority and that the report had been almost unanimously condemned by the press for both its form and substance. The chairman not only gave his casting vote but 'was the sole author of every recommendation'.[46]

On Christmas eve Douglas Hacking MP wrote to defend Dr Hunter's letter and pointed out that the recommendations were carried only by the chairman's casting vote and this should be made clear to Parliament.[47]

On the same page was a letter from a Dutchman who had lived in England for a long time. He pointed out that in Holland there had been no execution since 1860 and capital punishment had been abolished in 1870. He believed that a large majority in England who favoured capital punishment did so not out of principle but for expedience. They said that due to the imperfections of society and civilisation, for the time being the death penalty could not be dispensed with. Was it, then, he asked, the implication that the level of society in Holland had reached a higher plane than in England? For Holland was not endangering the lives of its citizens as the number of murders had dwindled. This seemed to be the experience of other European countries that had abolished capital punishment. Mr Geyl was unable to understand how a reform that had taken place in so many countries no further advanced than England in humanity, education and respect for the law was possible but could not be adopted in this country without inviting social disaster.[48] The letter writing season drew to a close on the last day of the year when Nancy Astor asked that the question of capital punishment should not be made a party political issue and urged people to read the report and make up their own minds.[49]

For abolitionists the decade ended more hopefully than it began. The tide of public opinion was edging gradually to a position less favourable to capital punishment and there had been a good deal of activity in Parliament. Nothing had been achieved, and several Bills had been thrown out, but at least a Select Committee had been set up and had made favourable recommendations. It was hoped that this would be a springboard from which abolition could be launched; it turned out to be more like quicksand.

ENDNOTES

1   *Hansard*, [115] 734, 6 May 1919
2   ibid, [115] 1084, 8 May 1919
3   ibid, [116] 201, 20 May 1919
4   ibid, [139] 1255, 15 May 1921
5   ibid, [151] 393, 1 March 1922
6   ibid, [153] 1014, 1 May 1922
7   *The Times*, p. 15, 8 June 1922
8   ibid, p. 7, 7 December 1922
9   ibid, p. 13, 12 December 1922
10 ibid, p. 10, 10 January 1923
11 *Daily Mail*, p. 5, 10 January 1923
12 *Daily Mirror*, 10 January 1923
13 *Daily Express*, p. 7, 10 January 1923
14 *Daily Mirror*, p. 2, 17 January 1923
15 *Hansard*, [160] 1284, 23 February 1923
16 ibid, [161] 2373, 30 March 1923

17 *Hansard,* [162] 323, 27 May 1923

18 ibid, [167] 288, 24 July 1923

19 ibid, [170] 84, 25 February 1924

20 ibid, [171] 1791, 31 March 1924

21 ibid, [182] 2057, 7 April 1925

22 ibid,[181] 677, 5 March 1925

23 ibid, [183] 597, 4 May 1925

24 ibid, [183] 1174, 7 May 1925

25 ibid, [193] 1654, 29 March 1926

26 ibid,[207] 2022, 23 June 1927

27 ibid, [208] 2372, 14 July 1927

28 ibid, [213] 1053, 16 February 1928

29 ibid, [213] 1778, 23 February 1928

30 ibid, [223] 1220, 5 December 1928

31 *The Times,* p. 15, 18 September 1928

32 ibid, p. 6, 22 September 1928

33 ibid, p. 10, September 25 1928

34 ibid, p. 8, 27 September 1928

35 ibid, p. 8

36 ibid, p. 6, 29 September 1928

37 *Hansard,* [232] 241-293, 30 October 1929

38 ibid, [232] 2372, 6 December 1929

39 ibid, [237] 573, 27 March 1930

40 ibid, [241] 2413, 24 July 1930

41 *The Times,* p. 16, 16 December 1930

42 ibid, p. 17, 17 December 1930

43 ibid, p. 10, 18 December 1930

44 ibid, p. 13, 19 December 1930

45 ibid, p. 13, 20 December 1930

46 ibid, p. 6, 23 December 1930

47 ibid, p. 4, 24 December 1930

48 ibid

49 ibid, p. 8, 31 December 1930.

CHAPTER 9

Peace and War

After a short lull for New Year, in 1931 E. Roy Calvert, secretary of the National Council for the Abolition of the Death Penalty, wrote to deplore the fact that the home secretary did not reprieve a man executed the previous week. He pointed out that the last century was full of precedents for reducing the number of executions in response to public opinion[1] and followed this up[2] by pointing out that between 1756 and 1772 about half of the death sentences had not been carried out; in the three years ending April 1830 the figure was 88 per cent, and in 1891 the figure was 96 per cent, and that the main reason for this reduction was the more frequent exercise of the home secretary's discretion in deference to public opinion that had not yet expressed itself as legislation. The following month yet another letter appeared from Calvert who pointed out that the six dissenting MPs on the Select Committee could not expect the remainder to scrap the report but did have a right to prepare an alternative statement. They had had plenty of time to do this and it was to be regretted that they did not.[3]

For the rest of the year the correspondence pages and Parliament were quiet but the topic rumbled on slowly. In a reply to a question the home secretary said that it was impossible to review all sentences until Parliament decided on the matter.[4] Following an execution in March further letters from H. C. L. Heywood,[5] F. H. Lyon[6] and T. S. Lascelles[7] all deprecated the sensational 'Execution Scenes' and suggested it be made a penal offence to publish anything bar the bare announcement. They were disgusted to see the cheaper press 'trading on morbid curiosity'. They would be disgusted still.

More questions and answers
In the previous five years only one person under 21 years—he was 20—had been executed[8] and since the Select Committee had reported there had been five executions.[9] There were seven executioners on the list and they were paid by the local sheriffs who fixed the amount, but assistant executioners received three guineas (£3.15). Since 1900, 19 people had been executed in Scotland, for murder. Other gems that questions winkled out were that 1,492 copies of the Select Committee report had been sold plus 205 copies of the complete transactions;[10] the cost of the committee had been approximately £1,500, including £351 to cover the cost of overseas witnesses, and receipts from sales of the report had reached £230.[11] From a question in February of the following year it was learned that since 1922 18 people between 18 years and 20 years had been sentenced to death and four had been executed.[12]

In April, Mr Mander, the Liberal MP for Wolverhampton East, asked the home secretary whether his attention had been drawn to the fact that someone who had been an approved hangman was now travelling the country fairgrounds demonstrating an actual hanging; and whether he would take steps to prevent such practices. Sir Samuel Hoare, who was then home secretary and later, as Lord Templewood, would become an ardent abolitionist, replied that he had no power to stop it.[13] At the end of the year, in answer to another question, Oliver Stanley announced to cheers that section 19(2) Children and Young Persons Act 1933, which would prevent the death sentence being passed on anyone under 18, would be brought into effect early although the rest of the Act would not come into effect until the following April.[14]

Capital punishment was being nibbled at slightly around the edges but no cracks were yet appearing, for when six months later Mr Hales asked that the use of the black cap by judges when passing a death sentence be abolished and the phrasing of the death sentence be changed it was pointed out by Sir John Gilmour, who had become home secretary, that the black cap and form of words were settled by the judges in 1903.[15] A few months later Vyvyan Adams presented a Bill 'to provide for the abolition of the death penalty for an experimental period of five years in cases covered by civil courts in time of peace'.[16]

In February 1934 the following data were provided[17] concerning the number of death sentences and executions in the previous ten years:

| Year | Sentenced to death | | Executed | | |
	male	female	male	% of men[18]	female
1923	19	2	11	58	0
1924	13	1	9	69	0
1925	28	2	19	68	0
1926	21	3	15	71	1
1927	22	3	16	73	0
1928	23	0	13	57	0
1929	15	0	7	47	0
1930	13	1	5	38	0
1931	17	1	9	53	0
1932	14	1	9	64	0
1933	16	3	10	63	0
TOTAL	201	17	123	61	1

It can be seen that the number of death sentences on males remained within a narrow band and those on females dwindled slightly (apart from 1933). However, when it comes to executions the picture is different. With the exception of 1930 when the percentage of sentenced men executed was low (as was the total number of sentences), the proportion of men condemned to death who were actually executed remained at well over half. The greatest contrast, however, is between the men and women: of 17 women sentenced to death in this eleven year span only one was hanged. Yet at the end of the year the home

98

secretary said that there was no legislation being considered to abolish capital punishment for women[19] even though *de facto* this had almost already occurred. Two days before the home secretary's announcement, however, another woman, Ethel Lily Major, had been executed at Hull for murdering her husband with strychnine. The jury had made a strong recommendation for mercy and a petition had been sent to the home secretary for a reprieve. When the home secretary declined to interfere with the sentence the Lord Mayor of Hull had sent a telegram to the King and Queen but this was merely forwarded to the home secretary. The prison governor stated that the execution was carried out (by Pierrepoint) in a humane and expeditious manner, and Dr. Barlee said that death was instantaneous.[20] Nothing had changed.

On Budget day 1935 Mr Bateman apologised to the House for choosing such a busy time to present a petition containing 52,961 signatures against the death sentence on Percy Charles Anderson but as the execution was scheduled for the next day he had had no choice.[21] The hanging took place as scheduled but Mr Bateman managed to squeeze in a question before the Budget speech when he asked what the view of the Home Office was since there was a growing feeling in the country for the abolition of capital punishment. The home secretary replied that there was no significant change on the part of the public on this subject. When Lady Astor asked whether, then, he would accept the views of prison governors throughout the world that capital punishment does no good, no reply was recorded.[22] A reply of a sort came some eight months later when he said that no alteration to the law was contemplated in the government's legislative programme.[23]

Early in the next year Mr Thurtle asked the home secretary if his attention had been drawn to a recent case at the Old Bailey in which a widow had been sentenced to death for the murder of her eight-year-old daughter, and to remarks made by the judge regarding the nature of the case, and further asked if he would consider modifying the existing law to absolve the judge from pronouncing the death sentence where such a sentence is repugnant to the public? The under-secretary replied that a modification of the law was being considered but that it was difficult, and that he would again draw it to the attention of the home secretary.[24]

As the situation in Europe became more serious the issue of capital punishment receded. When asked if any action was to be taken on the Select Committee's recommendations Sir John Simon repeated his previous answer, and when it was suggested that as the report was issued in 1930 it was time that action was taken, there was no reply.[25]

Sir John still had nothing to say almost a year later when asked by Vyvyan Adams what the government's policy was with regard to the death penalty,[26] but Adams did learn a year later that from 1929 to 1938 inclusive there had been 83 executions, including three women, showing a very marked decrease (in the case of men) over the previous decade.

The beginning of the end

The last major debate on capital punishment before the second world war came, and Parliament had more pressing uses for its time, took place in November 1938[27] when a motion moved by Vyvyan Adams and seconded by Benson 'that this House would welcome legislation whereby the death penalty should be abolished in time of peace for an experimental period of five years' was laid before the Commons. The time of peace was rapidly drawing to a close, but after debating the matter for four hours the motion was passed by 114 votes to 89. With the onset of war less than a year away and the change of government to a national coalition, the Bill progressed no further.

Not surprisingly, during the war years when millions were being slaughtered in Europe and elsewhere, whether to hang of a few people a year or not was not at the forefront of people's minds. However, one person at least, wanted to add a little to the carnage. In a Parliamentary question which for the first time for decades indicated an interest in making the death penalty a punishment for crimes other than murder and treason, Mr Bower, Unionist member for Harrow, asked if the home secretary would consider taking powers to make those people who ran gambling dens and sold bootleg liquor or otherwise endeavoured to make illegitimate profit out of the national emergency, liable to the death penalty or life imprisonment. Herbert Morrison (Labour, Hackney South), the wartime home secretary, must have realised that if the death penalty were imposed on all who profited from the flourishing black market there would be carnage indeed. One can only imagine him turning his one good eye on Mr Bower as he responded with impeccable grammar to his silly suggestion: 'While I share Mr Bower's wish that it were possible to put an end to these anti-social offences at a stroke by some dramatic and comprehensive measure, experience shows that it is only possible to attain the ends which both he and I desire by making specific amendments to the laws relating to specific offences as will enable convictions to be obtained and stern penalties to be imposed on all types of offenders who basely exploit war conditions for personal gain.'[28]

The remaining war years saw only innocuous requests for information. Rhys Davies was told by the home secretary that in 1942 there had been 25 death sentences for murder of which 15 had been carried out.[29] Ellen Wilkinson, then Parliamentary secretary to the Ministry of Home Security, told Sir A. Southby that United States forces in the UK had passed seven death penalties of which two had been carried out and one execution date had been fixed. The others were reprieved or under review.[30] One year later Rhys Davies learned that in 1943 there had been 26 sentences of death of which 15 had been carried out. The home secretary was unable, or unwilling, to give details of those sentenced to death for crimes other than murder.[31]

A few months later Mr Davies, who seemed to be carrying the baton alone, asked the home secretary for an explanation in regard to a mother and daughter sentenced to death for the murder of the daughter's 13-day-old illegitimate baby. They were in the condemned cell for nine weeks, and eleven days had elapsed after their appeal had been dismissed before they were reprieved only four days before the date set for execution. Morrison, denying that there was public disquiet over this case, pointed out that some reprieves could not be announced quickly as decisions take time and could not be hurried.[32] In less than a year the war in Europe would be over and with the arrival of peace the war against capital punishment would again be underway.

ENDNOTES

1   *The Times,* p. 8, 8 January 1931

2   ibid, p. 6, 10 January 1931

3   ibid, p. 8, 14 February 1931

4   *Hansard,* [248] 2262 (26 February 1931)

5   *The Times,* p. 13, 12 March 1931

6   ibid, p. 13, 14 March 1931

7   ibid, p. 8, 16 March 1931

8   *Hansard,* [255] 1503 (22 July 1931)

9   ibid, [255] 1688 (23 July 1931)

10 ibid, [255] 1965 (27 July 1931)

11 ibid, [205] 2101 (28 July 1931)

12 ibid, [261] 1839 (18 February 1932)

13 ibid, [264] 1398 (20 April 1932)

14 ibid, [272] 971 (2 December 1932)

15 ibid, [280] 324 (5 July 1933)

16 ibid, [283] 405 (24 November 1933)

17 ibid, [286] 934 (27 February 1934)

18 Percentages are not given in the original table

19 *Hansard,* [296] 1535 (21 December 1934)

20 *The Times,* p. 9, 20 December 1934

21 *Hansard,* [300] 1577 (14 April 1935)

22 ibid, [300] 1603

23 ibid, [307] 1940 (19 December 1935)

24 *The Times,* p. 9, 31 March 1936

25 *Hansard,* [311] 19 (21 April 1936)

26 ibid, [319] 1049 (28 January 1937)

27 ibid, [341] 954-1012 (16 November 1938)

28 *The Times,* p. 8, 20 February 1942

29 *Hansard,* [386] 1077 (4 February 1943)

30 ibid, [395] 1401 (14 December 1943)

31 ibid, [396] 1425 (3 February 1944)

32 ibid, [402] 336 (20 July 1944).

CHAPTER 10

The Silverman Amendment

The proportion of people sentenced to death who were subsequently hanged had not changed. In 1944, 20 people were sentenced to death; ten were hanged, nine reprieved and one conviction was quashed on appeal. Since 1900, 28 men under 21 had been hanged but no women under that age.[1]

Shavian suggestions

Before the war in Europe was quite over but when it was virtually won, the anti-capital punishment debate opened with a vengeance in *The Times*, launched by no less a person than George Bernard Shaw.[2] His remarkable letter, quoted here in full, contained some unusual and provocative suggestions. He wrote:

From a well-known passage in Genesis we learn that our method of executing criminals is the same as that in use at least 2,000 years ago. Is it not time to reconsider it?

We have before us the case of a girl whose mental condition unfits her to live in a civilised community. She has been guilty of theft and murder; and apparently her highest ambition is to be what she calls a gun moll, meaning a woman that thinks that robbery and murder are romantically delightful professions. She has earned her living as a strip-tease girl, which I, never having seen a strip-tease act, take to be a performance so near to indecent exposure as the police will allow, though after 20 years' observation of sunbathing I find it difficult to imagine anyone being entertained by the undress that would have shocked Queen Victoria. Clearly we have to put such a character to death or re-educate her. Having no technique of re-education immediately available, we have decided to put her to death. The decision is a very sensible one, as the alternative is to waste useful lives in caging and watching her as a tigress in the zoo has to be caged and watched.

Unfortunately our method of putting such people to death is so primitive that when it has to be practised on a girl in her teens, everyone, including the Sovereign who has to sign the death warrant and the home secretary who has to decide whether it shall be carried out or not, is revolted by it. They agree that the thing should be done, but not in this unnecessarily unpleasant way. The jury, moved by the girl's age and sex, recommend her to mercy, leaving her adult male accomplice pitilessly to his fate. As this 'mercy' takes the form of a dozen years of daily torture, demoralisation, disablement and cutting-off from all the news of the world which we call penal servitude, and is far crueller and wickeder than burning at the stake, the only people who are satisfied with it are our anti-Christians who lust after vindictive punishment, and would welcome the spectacle of a burning or flogging, and the capital punishment abolitionists, who, shrinking from killing as such, have no conception of state responsibilities, sign every petition for reprieve, and drop the case the moment the condemned person is left alive, no matter under what conditions.

Surely it is possible nowadays to devise some form of euthanasia more civilised than the rope, the drop, and the prison chaplain assuring the condemned that she has only to believe something she obviously does not believe, and she will go straight to eternal bliss in heaven. The fact that the horror of such a business will oblige the prison authorities to drug her to endure it only adds to the disgust it creates.

The matter has long been pressing. The savage superstitions of vengeance and expiation, the exhibition of executions as public entertainments, and the theory of deterrence, which depends upon an impossibility of detection in which no criminal believes, and also makes it a matter of complete indifference whether the person we hang is guilty or not provided we hang somebody, are discredited; and as the necessary work of 'weeding the garden' becomes better understood, the present restriction of liquidation to murder cases, and the exemption of dangerous lunatics (who should be liquidated as such, crime or no crime), will cease, and must be replaced by state-contrived euthanasia for all idiots and intolerable nuisances, not punitively, but as a necessary stroke of social economy.

If the strip-tease girl had been told simply that her case was under consideration, and she were presently to be found dead in her bed some morning in a quite comfortable lethal chamber not known by her to be such, the relief to the public conscience would be enormous. And the survivors would acquire a wholesome sense of public obligation to make the preservation of their lives by civilisation worthwhile.

This mish-mash of odd ideas, tongue-in-cheek suggestions and trivialisation of a serious subject would probably not have been published if it had been written by a lesser-known writer; considering that what had been done by Germany was currently being made public, at the very time that the camps were being liberated, some of Shaw's comments vary from the tasteless to the obscene. But two days later the inevitable responses came. First among unequals was Quentin Hogg, already a formidable lawyer, later Lord Chancellor and almost prime minister, pipped at the post by Lord Home. In a few swift lines he laid bare Shaw's nonsense:

As one intolerable nuisance to another may I ask Mr Bernard Shaw on what principle of 'social economy' we should both be executed by euthanasia? And as for 'idiots', why does he think they do not enjoy life as much as he? If a particular criminal is told his case is 'to be considered' and then murdered painlessly in his sleep, many of us will spend restless nights and take up wondering whether or not our bedchamber is not 'a quite comfortable lethal chamber not known by us as such'.

To make the taking of human life apparently an act of kindness is to tempt society to become a conspiracy of murderers; if we are to pass judgement on one another as to whether each serves a useful purpose here, who among us will rest with a guilty conscience? Far better than this it would be to abolish the whole beastly business; but if it has to be retained, let us not pretend it is anything but what it is—an act of violence by one person on his brother. Cain was wiser than this. He was under no illusions as to what he had done.[3]

On the same page was a curious letter from Miss F. Tennyson Jesse who had some quaint and misguided ideas of her own. Although disapproving of capital punishment she admitted that it was a deterrent and pointed out that in the USA criminals were very careful to kill only in those states that did not have capital punishment, and were careful not to kill in Canada where British law held (one can only wonder where she got these ideas from). If the criminal were put to death, she continued, more or less unconscious, the whole principle of deterrence 'goes by the board and it would only be a few days before the criminal world would know that the murderer had been mercifully put to death'.[4]

It would seem from this letter that to be put to death nicely is no deterrent at all; it is the nastiness of the passage not the eternal oblivion that deters! A letter[5] from C. F. Wood announced that he had been present at hangings of people he had tried as a magistrate in India. Re-education was not possible and his decisions had been sensible, but he agreed with Shaw that the method was 'unbearably primitive'. Eden Phillpotts also agreed about the method and hoped that the mercy extended to domestic animals might be extended to the 'hopelessly insane' for whom 'life possesses no meaning'.[6]

A curious letter from O. P. Clark cited a paper called 'Cases of Judicial Hanging' read before the Medicolegal Society in 1924 in which doctors gave their opinions that death from hanging is instantaneous and painless. A Professor Littlejohn was 'quite certain that loss of consciousness was instantaneous and also that death was instantaneous'.[7] Quite apart from the tautology of the last remark, how did these people *know* how instantaneous death is; are they in the pit when the body falls and stops? A final thought for that day came from H. P. Plumstead who believed that crime is a disease and that criminals should be used for research to prevent this disease in future generations.[8]

Two days later John Paton, Secretary of the National Campaign for the Abolition of Capital Punishment, produced data that refuted the claims of Miss Tennyson Jesse and showed that in the past few years there were fewer murders per head of population in those states without the death penalty than in those that had retained it.[9] This was supported by S. V. Sturtz who pointed out that those countries that had abolished capital punishment, including Belgium, Holland, Norway, Finland and Sweden, have seen no increase in the murder rate so the death penalty cannot be an exclusive deterrent.[10]

A table produced as a written answer to a request by Mr Taylor reveals some aspects of murders, convictions and the death penalty.[11] *Table 1* opposite is an abridged version which omits some of the detail.

It can be seen that with the exception of 1937 and 1938, when there were rather fewer murders, and 1942 and 1943, when there were rather more, the number of murders known to the police kept within fairly narrow limits year on year. The total number brought to trial in each year did not vary nearly as much as the number of murders, neither did the numbers convicted and sentenced to death—so that over a 20 year period there was little change in the number of murders committed, the numbers charged and the numbers convicted and sentenced to death. What did change was the number executed. Between 1929 and the outbreak of the second world war ten years later the annual number of executions was usually in single figures, and this reduction in executions had not led to an overall increase in murders.

Year	Murders known to police	Charged	Convicted[12]	Sentenced to death	Executed
1922	145	60	35	34	21
1923	150	58	21	21	11
1924	150	42	14	14	9
1925	160	81	31	30	19
1926	154	57	24	24	16
1927	143	50	25	25	16
1928	136	60	23	23	13
1929	131	59	15	15	7
1930	122	40	14	14	5
1931	138	57	18	18	9
1932	125	64	15	15	9
1933	141	53	19	19	10
1934	141	61	24	24	9
1935	120	52	20	20	10
1936	145	67	27	27	9
1937	114	44	14	13	7
1938	116	54	23	22	8
1939	157	64	28	25	9
1940	123	59	22	21	11
1941	146	64	24	23	15
1942	290	72	31	25	18
1943	174	75	29	27	15
1944[13]	166	48	21	21	13

Table 1

A new government
In July 1945, only a few months after the war in Europe was over but with the war in the Far East looking as if it would continue for some time (it ended a month later after two atomic bombs were dropped on Japan), a Labour government was not only surprisingly elected, but with a huge majority. Penal reformers hoped and expected that the new government would be more receptive than previous ones to calls for the abolition of the death penalty. The new home secretary was James Chuter Ede and after he had been in office for nearly a year Mr Nally asked him, if in his review of the criminal justice administration, he would consider the abolition of capital punishment. Ede replied noncommittally that he was considering all subjects. John Paton asked him if he was aware of the proposals of the Select Committee which reported in 1931 and proposed abolition for an experimental period of five years, and if he

105

would keep this under consideration, to which Ede encouragingly replied that was one of the things being considered.[14]

A new spate of letters to *The Times* was initiated a little later by Vyvyan Adams MP, whose 1938 Bill for abolition for five years had died with the onset of war. Suggesting that the present government might put it into effect, he listed his objections to capital punishment. It was of dubious deterrent effect and caused some juries to be reluctant to convict if they thought that the death penalty would follow. Society had no need of this protection since countries with no death penalty had no increase in their murder rate. Furthermore, the executioner's role was hideous and disgusting and society ought not retain him; and finally the death penalty defied Christian principles.[15] A few days later there were letters of support from Leonard F. Fountain and Margery Fry, the well-known penal reformer, who drew attention to the suffering of murderers' families and friends, and to the effect of hanging on prison officials.[16]

A letter from the mayor of Chelsea, Gerald A. Thesiger, disagreed. He hoped that if the death penalty were abolished all householders would be armed. He cited in support of this the by now unoriginal argument that if burglars were sure they would not be hanged they would not stop at killing a key witness; it would pay to kill rather than to injure.[17]

A letter from Kailas Nath Katju, minister of justice and development, United Provinces, India, was firmly in support of abolition. 'Capital punishment', he said, 'was not only barbarous but served no useful purpose. Lifelong imprisonment was far worse and was a constant reminder, whereas once a man was hanged he was forgotten. If capital punishment were the deterrent that was claimed', he pointed out, 'murders would have stopped long ago', a view supported on the same page by Frank Dawtry, Secretary for the National Council for the Abolition of Capital Punishment, who disagreed with the Mayor of Chelsea, citing European countries and states in the USA which had abolished executions.[18]

The end of the month saw a letter from C. Cyril Batten who supported Adams on the grounds that everyone had the right to have an opportunity to reform, and final judgment rested with God; and a final salvo from the mayor of Chelsea who claimed that Norway, the USA and India were different from Great Britain as they have different penal systems so could not be used as examples. 'Norway', he concluded lamely, 'is not like London'.[19] Who could argue with that?

No let-up
Possibly intrigued by unsupported claims in the press that death by hanging was instantaneous, Tom Driberg asked if any records were kept of the time that passed from the moment of hanging to the time when life was extinct, and (indicating his scepticism of instantaneity) would the home secretary state the number of minutes. Ede replied that no such records were kept and that he had been advised that unconsciousness was instantaneous. Driberg then cited reports from Nuremberg, where war criminals had been recently hanged, that sometimes

death took 12 or 14 minutes, but Ede replied that he had seen nothing to doubt the accuracy of the answer he gave.[20]

Letters in *The Times* continued to flourish. Theodora Calvert pointed out, disagreeing with Chelsea's mayor, that if Norway were not like the UK on grounds of population density, then the population density of Belgium was similar. She called for 'normal' life imprisonment as a substitute for capital punishment, that is, with a release date after a number of years. On the same page Derek Curtis-Bennett considered that to abolish capital punishment would be 'an act of the greatest folly'. He could not understand how 'anyone with experience in criminal law' could say it was not a deterrent. Life imprisonment would not stop criminals going armed to avoid capture—and as for other countries, he concluded, laying claim to being perhaps the first Eurosceptic, we did not 'need any lessons on criminal justice from outside'. For A. G. Morris it was the irreversibility of hanging that was the conclusive case against capital punishment.[21]

Ronald E. Harker[22] likened Curtis-Bennett's comment 'act of the greatest folly' with that of Lord Ellenborough, Lord Chief Justice in 1831 when Romilly was trying to get hanging abolished: 'My Lords, if we suffer this Bill to pass we shall not know where to stand; we shall not know whether we are on our heads or on our feet'—a remark no less opaque in 1946 than it was in 1831.

Two letters from members of Parliament followed. Hector Hughes acknowledged the usefulness of *The Times* correspondence but considered a commission or committee was needed to discuss the problems of capital punishment and the M'Naghten Rules,[23] and John Paton wrote that Curtis-Bennett's claim that more people would carry arms as the result of abolition of capital punishment should be put to the test. He pointed out that most murderers were not criminals and burglars but people who had committed no previous offence and were unlikely to go around armed. The experience of over 30 countries that had abolished capital punishment with no increase of their murder rate could not be ignored.[24] J. D. Caswell, on the same page as Paton's letter, suggested three degrees of murder with only the first attracting the death penalty, in order to avoid juries bringing in manslaughter verdicts where they believed the defendant guilty, but not guilty enough for the death penalty.

A few days later there was a riposte from Vyvyan Adams. 'Let [Curtis-Bennett] prove that the abolition of capital punishment will result in more murders and his case is won', he wrote. He agreed that the death penalty was a deterrent but questioned whether it was the only, or the best, one. It was certainty of detection and conviction that deterred. He pointed out that between the wars there were about 150 murders a year; on average 55 people were charged, 20 sentenced to death and ten reprieved: thus, about ten of 150 murderers were hanged. He recalled Robert Peel when he labelled the abolition of the death penalty for stealing more than £5 'a dangerous experiment'. 'We are all degraded', he concluded, 'when we do to the convicted man the very thing for which we condemned him'.[25]

This batch of correspondence concluded with a further letter from Frank Dawtry who pointed out that the Select Committee in 1930 supported a five year experimental period of abolition; this was deferred by the then home secretary (John R. Clynes) and then the government changed at the outbreak of the war. As Labour had supported the report, he wrote, some action was now needed by the present home secretary.[26] But the present home secretary showed no sign of acting.

In mid-November the House debated the Royal Address during which Mr Donovan said that there was considerable opinion in the House for the abolition of capital punishment and that it should be debated. He had been in condemned cells and had not liked what he had seen.[27] But two weeks later Chuter Ede put paid to any prospect of an early debate when, in answer to Leslie Hale, who had asked whether the government intended to implement the recommendations of the Select Committee and abolish the death penalty for five years, he replied that this would need legislation and that there was no prospect of legislation in the current session.[28] Some months later he confirmed that he was not even in a position to make a statement regarding the government's intention regarding capital punishment.[29] James Hemming, writing in *The Times* later in the month, suggested that the incidence of murder went down in some countries after capital punishment was abolished because the death penalty had been seen as a challenge by some criminals. His solution, based on this shaky premise, was to deglamourise crime which included abolishing the hangmen and gallows.[30] This must have been the first suggestion ever that hangmen and gallows were glamorous.

New hope for abolitionists
The new Parliamentary session brought with it the promise of a new Criminal Justice Bill. This was enthusiastically welcomed by the vice-presidents of the National Council for the Abolition of the Death Penalty, among whom were listed such well-known people as Sybil Thorndyke, Vyvyan Adams, Nancy Astor, Osbert Sitwell and Ernest Raymond. They hoped that the new Bill would include provision for abolition or suspension of the death penalty.[31]

Not everyone, however, shared the council's enthusiasm. Mr Curtis-Bennett, who had not had a letter published for some time, was moved to hope that the Council would have been 'halted in their tracks' by the murder of Mr De Antiquis, who was 'killed by ruffians whilst committing a felony'. One assumes it was the ruffians who were committing the felony not the unfortunate Mr De Antiquis whom Curtis-Bennett's syntax would suggest, but with curious logic he went on: '. . . it is true that the death penalty did not deter these young men . . . [but] how many more of these cases would there be were it not for the deterrent effect of the death penalty? Since two of these murderers have been executed there has been no occurrence of this type of murder so even if the National Council have not learned their lesson evil-living young persons seem to have done so'.[32]

Two days later a long letter from Hector Hughes analysed murders between 1939 and 1945 showing that there were two degrees of murder, and suggested that judges should have discretion in sentencing depending on the degree of murder.[33] There was also a letter from Gerald Gardiner KC, later to become

108

Lord Chancellor. He listed 21 countries that had abolished capital punishment with no increase in the murder rate, in refutation of Curtis-Bennett's claim that it would increase. He went on to ask, 'is there something so peculiarly brutal about Englishmen that they need a special form of deterrent which nearly every civilised country in the world has found . . . to be . . . unnecessary?' [34]

Mr R. L. Kitching claimed that at least capital punishment meant that the murderer could not kill again and that therefore, if it were abolished, murderers should never be set free; [35] and another from Theodora Calvert [36] pointed out that introducing degrees of murder was thrown out by the Select Committee in 1930 because it was difficult to define first degree murder, and for untrained jurors to assess culpability. Since the burden of the home secretary could not be abrogated to the judge as he had no time to see reports, the only thing to do was to abolish capital punishment totally. On the same page was a letter from Ethel S. Quinn who wrote movingly about one of the murderers in the De Antiquis case, [37] Christopher Geraghty, whom she once knew and who was hanged although only 20 years old. She wrote about the grief of his family and that his death did nothing to assuage the grief of the De Antiquis family. The continuation of capital punishment, she said, could only brutalise the community. Nicholas Rutherford responded that Geraghty committed a brutal murder and did not have to do so [38] and Dawtry, on the other side, replying to Kitching's letter, said that there was no justification for keeping murderers in prison for life as almost half were reprieved and eventually released, and that there had been only one instance of one of them murdering again. [39] Robert W. Orme was sympathetic to neither Miss Quinn nor Miss Calvert. Miss Quinn's account made no compelling case against capital punishment, he wrote, and murder could be divided into first and second degrees, depending on intent. Furthermore, the death penalty shows the supreme disgust of the community which any lesser penalty did not. [40]

The correspondence continued throughout the month of November, displaying a variety of views and arguments on both sides that must have been of considerable interest to members of Parliament. It was pointed out by H. A. Sams that in India there was an alternative sentence for murder and the judge could adjust the penalty; [41] and G. A. Sutherland attacked the main argument for the retention of capital punishment, deterrence. His two arguments were that hanging is the least of all penalties to follow the crime: only one man was executed for every 11 murders; and that since 90 per cent of murders were crimes of passion, the state of mind of the murderer at the time of murder is seldom such as to make him consider the consequences. [42]

Silverman's first attempt

In 1947 the home secretary, Chuter Ede, introduced a Criminal Justice Bill to amend the Criminal Justice Act 1911 in order to remove some of the harshness from criminal law and prisons. For example, it would abolish penal servitude, hard labour and whipping, and amend the law regarding probation by reforming existing methods and providing new methods of dealing with offenders liable to imprisonment. The first reading was at the end of October. [43] Sidney Silverman recognised it as a reforming Bill but felt it did not go far enough and got himself on to the committee for that stage of the Bill.

On November 21 a motion was announced, tabled by seven Labour members and one Conservative, in the name of Sydney Silverman and others, to insert a clause into the Criminal Justice Bill that would suspend capital punishment for five years.[44] At the second reading there was an impassioned plea from Reginald Paget for the abolition of capital punishment to be included with the other reforms. He said that 'judicial execution is the ultimate subjection of the individual to the state. Let the dictators have their gallows and their axes, their firing squads and their lethal chambers. The citizens of a free democracy did not have to shelter under the shadow of the gallows tree'.[45] Hector Hughes regretted that there was no mention of degrees of murder in the Bill, and Robert Villiers Grimston was attracted to the idea of two degrees of murder. Sidney Silverman announced that he had consulted the leader of the House who had agreed to allocate half a day to discussion of the abolition of capital punishment, with a possible extension.

A few days later Lord Templewood, now president of the Howard League, addressing the League's annual meeting, said he had not supported the abolition of capital punishment in 1938 when he was home secretary (as Sir Samuel Hoare) but since then he had been in a number of countries where it had been abolished and had seen no bad effects. He believed from his experience as home secretary that effective treatment for murderers would be found; many were first offenders. In Switzerland there were many reformed murderers.[46]

Again, in *The Times,* a long letter from Cicely M. Craven, honorary secretary of the Howard League, claimed that the main justification for abolition was that without it murderers could not reform.[47] Lieutenant Colonel C. Radcliffe supported Miss Quinn. He wrote[48] that actions which appeared sordid to cultured people were seen in a different light by boys of Garaghty's background. He admitted that penal servitude for life was almost as bad as hanging but believed that both were too severe for the sort of crime committed by a 20-year-old. One of the last letters of the month was from R. Chevenix Trench who claimed that abolition did not result in a decrease in the number of murders, and cited as an example Hyderabad, where the death penalty had not been abolished but where the sentence was commuted in every case. There the murder rate had increased, from 92 in 1911 to about 360 a year in the past few years.[49] Guy Kendall thought that crime was romantic, pointing to the highwayman and his gentlemanly conduct and final bravado on the scaffold, and that this romanticism must be removed,[50] an echo of James Hemmings' earlier suggestion to deglamourise the gallows

J. D. Casswell suggested that those best able to comment on the deterrent effect of the death penalty would be four groups: first, killers who had been caught, second, killers who had not been caught, third, killers who had been acquitted, fourth, killers who had been convicted. He thought useful information could be obtained from people in the last two categories and from their solicitors and prison staff. He preferred three degrees of murder, without saying what they were, and that the decision as to which degree should be left to the jury.[51] The next day Alexander Wallace wrote to say that he had witnessed many executions in India and had always been ashamed. Arguments about the expediency of capital punishment were irrelevant: it was a violation of God's natural law.[52]

This long and diverse correspondence culminated in a *Times* editorial.[53] The paper welcomed the Criminal Justice Bill and highlighted the proposal to abolish capital punishment for five years. 'In the light of the entire Bill being of a reformative nature and capital punishment abandoning hope of reform, it is logical that capital punishment should be abolished'. On the other hand, the leader went on, many believed that capital punishment was a necessary deterrent, notwithstanding that evidence from 30 countries showed this not to be the case. The article ended by agreeing that the proposal to suspend capital punishment for five years would provide both sides with the evidence they needed to make a permanent decision. How different this was from that newspaper's leader of June 8 1922 (see *Chapter 9*).

The Times may have believed that it had wrapped up the subject but public comment continued unabated. In Geoffrey Pyke's opinion, whether the death penalty was a deterrent or not should not be the criterion on whether it should be abolished. It might be that the hanging of children was a deterrent but we stopped that because it was abhorrent. The issue was whether we had the decency and self-respect to live our lives without this real or imaginary protection. A vote for retention was a vote for the barbarity of the eighteenth and nineteenth centuries.[54]

L. D. Blackford's point was that in the first world war, when desertion was punishable by death, there were few desertions whereas in the second world war when desertion was not punished by death there were thousands of deserters. How is that explained, he asked, by those who believe capital punishment is not a deterrent?[55] But this letter was somewhat overshadowed by one just above, from Bernard Shaw, 91, but no less controversial. He suggested that the terms 'capital punishment' and 'death penalty' should be dropped in favour of 'judicial homicide' or 'judicial liquidation'. There were many objections to deterrence and the punishment must be cruel for it to deter. When a crime was committed it did not matter who was punished so long as someone was. Criminals should be liquidated, he continued, using his own preferred terminology, not because they were wicked but because they were mischievous or dangerous. He quoted a Dickens character with approval: 'Much better hang the wrong fellow than no fellow'. He said that dangerous insanity should be the strongest ground for liquidation. Long terms of imprisonment were not humane and a waste of manpower; if criminals were reformable they should be reformed but the rest should be liquidated.

The response to these horrifying and outrageous ideas was less than one might have expected; perhaps by then Shaw was viewed as something of a crank. Notwithstanding, Sydney W. Carroll said that Shaw's words shocked even those used to his propensity to shock, and that perhaps Shaw himself was incorrigibly mischievous and ought to be destroyed,[56] and R. Kennard Davis wrote that respect for human personality and human life was the basis of civilization. He was surprised that Shaw could advocate a doctrine which if

111

carried into practice might endanger his own continued existence.[57] But R. Traill Thompson pointed to a recent article in the *Medico-Legal Journal* and suggested that his article might have been written by a Nazi leader in justification of some of their worst crimes. He found Shaw's arguments shocking and the extension of a 'Marxist' way of thinking.[58]

Leo Page asked whether it was worth risking the low murder rate that the United Kingdom enjoyed to keep alive about eleven murderers a year who are actually hanged. Furthermore, he wrote, we could not relate to conditions abroad. Norway and Finland had no large cities and in other countries capital punishment had fallen into disuse long before it was abolished so that 'before and after' comparisons were meaningless. He also asked whether abolitionists approved of the Nuremburg executions.[59] John R. Poole wondered what jurors thought of the death penalty as they seemed reluctant to convict. At present, he deduced, jurors seem to be saying that the death penalty was not applicable in every case. Reginald Paget MP helpfully categorised three types of murderers. The first type were those who acted in a moment of violent emotion, more than half of whom commit suicide; they gave no thought to the consequences. Second were those who planned their crimes so that they did not expect to be caught. The third group were lunatics for whom the death penalty was sometimes the main attraction.[60] Miles Irving added a fourth category: the man who had no wish to kill but goes to rob prepared to kill rather than be caught. He was the one who really presented a problem.[61] Several other replies appeared on the same page. Arthur B. Morely pointed out to Leo Page that other countries had both large cities and a reduced murder rate, citing as examples Denmark and Holland, where murderers served 16 years or less in prison. The Nuremburg executions were not a good parallel as countries that had abolished capital punishment in time of peace had also executed their own quislings—and Leonard F. Behrens suggested that if people defended the death penalty they should also defend torture which was a greater deterrent. Torture was no longer tolerated because it was beastly and abhorrent; so was the death penalty.

Theodora Calvert (chair) and Frank Dawtry (secretary) of the National Council for the Abolition of the Death Penalty answered Page in that it was not a matter of keeping alive eleven murderers a year, but was a matter of principle that would apply even if one a year were saved. They agreed that it was relevant to look at other countries and were collating information. Although the National Council were only interested in changing the law on capital punishment in this country in time of peace and could not speak for other abolitionists, the two signatories believed that the principles that underlay their disapproval of the death penalty held good for Nuremburg and for all over the world.[62]

One final, uplifting, letter of the year was from Edward Hyams who pointed to the moral benefits to a community of abolition. 'When one is told "We have no capital punishment here" it is said with pride and it is good for citizens of those countries' and showed a respect for life.[63]

The Bill

In the Standing Committee on the Criminal Justice Bill, George Benson moved an amendment to the effect that no-one under the age of 21 when committing a murder should be subject to the death penalty, effectively raising the minimum age from 18 to 21. Chuter Ede said that there was a prevalence of violence among young people and he would find it difficult to advise the House that people under 21 who appeared normal in all respects could be regarded as irresponsible. The amendment was withdrawn.[64]

On March 15 Lord Templewood again addressed the Howard League and said that the more he considered the present position the more he was convinced there was no place for capital punishment. Corporal punishment in prisons should be abolished, too. He added, with great foresight as it turned out, that the proposed detention centres would end up being short-term prisons by another name for young offenders.[65]

On March 26 a new clause in the Criminal Justice Bill, to suspend capital punishment for an initial period of five years, but with a provision that before the end of that period an address could be presented to the King praying that this be extended without limitation of time or for any new period, was urged on the House by 147 members led by Silverman. It was supported by 135 Labour members, six Liberals, four Conservatives, one Independent Labour and one Communist. Ede thought that the time was inopportune for such an amendment but would allow the House a free vote.[66]

In the course of the debate Mrs Ayrton Gould MP (Hendon North), said that after the execution of Edith Thompson (see p. 86 *et al*) the hangman committed suicide, one of the wardresses who was present went mad and the prison chaplain had a very bad nervous breakdown; and every single person who was present at the execution had left the prison service within a very short time.[67]

On the day that the Bill returned to the Commons for the report stage *The Times* ran a leader.[68] Commenting on the five year experimental period, it said that nobody would wish to retain the death penalty if an alternative sentence without risk could be found. The column gave a long, detailed and balanced argument for both sides. On the one hand, it pointed out, other countries had abolished capital punishment without any increase in the murder rate; on the other, there were fears that if abolition took effect burglars and other serious criminals would kill to escape arrest. As no-one knew which argument was correct *The Times* agreed that the five year experiment was a good idea; there was little risk and at the end of that time there would be more information on which to base a decision.

When the Bill returned to the House for the report stage on April 14, Silverman moved the amendment to suspend the operation of capital punishment for five years. He opened the debate by calling the death penalty a revolting and barbarous thing, and claimed that the proceedings were surrounded by melodrama and sensationalism. Commenting on Ede's announcement he said that although it was a free vote the government front bench would be voting against. He criticised the government for not allowing its own members a free vote as all other members were.

113

The introduction of the clause was opposed by Sir John Anderson who said that the experience of other countries was irrelevant; decisions had to be made according to the circumstances in this country. To his knowledge and belief no-one had been wrongly executed. There were some prisoners who were 'wild beasts, morons, and subjected to gusts of passion'. These should be certified as insane as there was no hope for such a person. Paton pointed out that in the previous ten years there had been a marked increase in crime including murder, yet capital punishment had not been effective in stemming this increase. Chuter Ede wound up this debate. He said that he had supported abolition in 1938 but the government would urge rejection this time, although it was a free vote. The Bill was carried by 245 to 222 and the amendment to abolish by the huge margin of 215 to 74.

The Times commented that this was a surprise result considering that members of the government had abstained, but that they would now have to abide by the decision. However, *The Times* also foresaw the Lords throwing out this clause.[69] Two days later the Bill had its third reading. The usual arguments were aired with Earl Winterton hoping that the Bill would not pass into law in its present state and the home secretary accepting both the Bill and the abolition clause as the will of Parliament.[70] *The Times* the next day called the case for abolition 'overwhelming' and discussed what the Lords were likely to do faced with a Bill carried by a divided House and a government which had abstained.[71] Two days later, Lord Simon took great exception to the word 'overwhelming' in a forceful letter.[72] He wanted to know which arguments were overwhelming since the decision to hang the war criminals at Nuremberg had had the support of *The Times*. How odd, looking back, that a man of such outstanding brilliance, who had been among other things both home secretary and Lord Chancellor, could not separate the arguments for executing a few casual villains a year from hanging some of the most wicked men ever to have walked the earth.

Lord Simon's letter was balanced by one from a past chairman of the Campaign for the Abolition of Capital Punishment, L. H. Green, who welcomed the vote and also called for more police and better pay and housing for them. Hector Hughes responded[73] by pointing out that a hundredfold increase in the police would make no difference to the crime rate but if there were different degrees of murder then major crime could be met with major penalties, etc. But Leo Page, commenting on Green's letter, said that if abolition did not result in more crime and murders, why was there a need for more police?[74] This was sharply answered by W. L. Roseveare who pointed out that no-one claimed that abolition would deter men from murdering, but the death penalty was not a deterrent. The most effective deterrent, he went on, was certainty of capture and conviction and therein lay the need for more police.[75]

Lord Simon was quickly answered, too, by Raoul Colinvaux, who first pointed out that the evidence from other countries was that the abolition of the death penalty reduced murder, and if there was any reason why that could not happen in Britain it would be discovered by the five year experiment, then asked, 'Is that argument not "overwhelming?"'[76] However, John Clarke, whose letter was printed on the same page, was of the opinion that the murder rate would go up as a result of other prevailing circumstances. He thought it would be better to defer abolition until crime had abated. He would be waiting still.

A letter from Beverley Baxter MP, who voted for the amendment, criticised the critics who had rebuked those who had voted thus. He believed that violence begat violence and that the ritual of trial and execution romanticised the whole process. Going further, he advocated an amnesty for army deserters from among whom many criminals sprang.[77] On the same page was a curious letter from Christmas Humphreys who advocated that anyone carrying a firearm while committing an offence should be given 12 months in prison for carrying a gun in addition to any other sentence. This, he continued, would have a deterrent effect against carrying firearms that the abolition of the death penalty might remove. Such naiveté from one of the most effective prosecutors of his day is astonishing: as if another 12 months more or less would make any difference to a ruthless criminal. A few days later J. L. Thomas pointed out that under section 23(2) Firearms Act 1937, in the circumstances Humphreys had mentioned, carrying a firearm, or even an imitation firearm, carried up to seven years penal servitude in addition to any other penalty.[78]

Winston Churchill (the wartime prime minister) was vehemently against abolition and had spoken in the House against it in the most scathing terms. Addressing the Conservative Women's Conference at the Albert Hall in April, he told them that 'this grave decision on capital punishment' was left to the casual vote 'of the most unrepresentative' (they had a majority of over 140) 'and irresponsible House of Commons that ever sat at Westminster'.

April 26 was the silver wedding anniversary of King George V and Queen Mary. A letter from Eric Sachs proposed retaining the death penalty for the murder of a police officer in the execution of his duty, or anyone helping him; for any prisoner with five years or more left of his sentence who murdered in prison or whilst attempting to escape; and for anyone convicted of a second murder.[79]

Ede and Eden
During the course of the debate on the third reading the home secretary, Chuter Ede, had commented on the fact that at the second reading the House had inserted a clause abolishing capital punishment for five years. He had had to decide what to do with convicted and sentenced people until this Bill became law, and had decided to advise the King to give a conditional pardon and commute to penal servitude for life in every case as a matter of course.[80] Ede had no wish to see people executed even while abolition was in process of being passed through the Parliamentary procedure so that whether a man was hanged or not depended on how his execution date matched the Bill becoming law, so this provisional decision, to be put into practice during the interim, seemed reasonable. But it was not reasonable enough for Anthony Eden, who called into question the constitutional position of this blanket advice and suggested that the home secretary should make a further statement on the subject.[81] Chuter Ede replied that he would not make a statement until the Bill came back from the

115

Lords; Eden responded that the home secretary was taking a course of action that was contrary to the law of the land and should make a statement.

Eden was probably right in regard to the constitutional issue: there was no provision in law for blanket reprieves. But it was also an occasion where Parliament could have turned a blind eye since it would have affected only a couple of murderers; hanging people during the passage of the Bill would have seemed repugnant once it had been passed; and the home secretary could have kept his own counsel and reprieved sentenced murderers anyway without announcing his intention to Parliament in advance.

A couple of days after the House of Lords debate, when Eden asked Chuter Ede whether, in view of the Bill coming back from the Lords without the capital punishment clause, he would reconsider his recommendation to reprieve people under a death sentence in all cases of murder,[82] the home secretary replied, 'Not at present', but did so a week later.[83] He said that owing to the decision by the Lords he was revoking his advice to the King and would be considering each case for reprieve on its merits. Whether what he had done was or was not constitutional was then debated but the matter was not resolved. When, months later, Sir J. Mellor asked for assurance that the home secretary was not automatically advising the King to reprieve, Chuter Ede replied that he had nothing to add to his earlier statement.[84]

Meanwhile, the Commons' decision had attracted much correspondence in *The Times*. Two letters on the same page, one from S. H. Heaton-Renshaw and the other from W. Grey believed that members of Parliament on a free vote should consult their constituents and vote according to their views; public opinion was paramount and their own consciences should come second.[85] How they were meant to canvass public opinion was not suggested. There followed a lively discussion in the correspondence columns concerning the methods by which MPs could gauge public opinion on the one hand, and how, on the other, they were elected to use their own judgment. One letter writer, A. C. Richmond, had in the past visited prisoners and claimed to have spoken to many reprieved murderers. The motive of most, he said, was mainly jealousy or uncontrolled impulse. That death by hanging would be a probable result of their crime did not affect their actions. Those whom Lord Goddard said were capable of the most revolting forms of criminal homicide were also not deterred by capital punishment. Mr Richmond urged MPs not to heed public opinion which was of no value in such matters. The right treatment for murderers, he concluded, was primarily psychological.[86]

At the end of May a White Paper (Cmnd 7419) was presented to Parliament by the home secretary. It stated that between 1 January 1920 and 31 March 1948, 267 people who had been convicted of murder in Great Britain were subsequently reprieved. Of these, 209 were released after five years or more, and 58 after less than five years.

The Lords debate

In the event this entire discussion was rendered academic by the House of Lords. The issue was raised of whether the Lords would throw out the abolition clause

116

because of the coming Parliament Bill, one of the provisions of which was to cut the suspensary veto of the Lords from two years to one.

The Lords debated the Bill and in particular the amendment to abolish capital punishment, on June 1 and 2.[87] It is impossible to summarise such a long debate but one or two contributions stand out. Viscount Samuel pointed out that although public opinion was against abolition the majority in favour in the House of Commons was actually greater than that recorded because although it was a 'free vote' ministers in favour of abolition were compelled to abstain. Next time, if the Lords threw out the amendment, the majority would be bigger still: not only would the abstainers vote in favour but those ministers who voted against on the first occasion would vote in favour. He, himself, was voting in favour of the amendment.

Early in the debate Viscount Templewood, who as Sir Samuel Hoare had been home secretary, spoke in favour of the Bill and, in particular, of the controversial abolition clause. He spoke in support of the point made in the white paper that murderers were not the worst sort of criminal; in fact, he said, until they murdered most were not criminals at all. He quoted Sir John McDonald, who some thirty years earlier was Master of the Supreme Court:

I am inclined to think that this crime is not generally the crime of the so-called criminal class, but in most cases is an incident in miserable lives in which disputes, quarrels, angry words and blows are common.

Referring to a white paper prepared by the Lord Chancellor at his request, he showed that, notwithstanding that all the material available was not included, he was still able to demonstrate that of 174 murderers since 1920 whose sentences were commuted, only five had been reconvicted for any offence and only one for murder, and the reason, he suspected, was that on release he had joined the army and had had no after-care.

He then turned to the part of the white paper that dealt with foreign experience, which he found of extreme interest and value. It confirmed his view that a large percentage of murderers could be reformed. In no case where the death penalty had been abolished had there been any dangerous result and in no case any rise in murders or even violence. He found that in Sweden, and more recently, Switzerland, after a length of time in prison the prisoner was let out on leave to visit his family and was allowed to work, and in many cases the murderer had made good. He concluded by addressing two arguments against abolition. One was that public opinion was against it. He had found, he said, that public opinion was always against changes in penal methods. Public opinion was almost inevitably ignorant of the kind of details being discussed in the debate. If during the last century they had waited for public opinion before restricting the death penalty to a few crimes they would have found public opinion almost always against the more expert views of Parliament and Whitehall.

The second argument was one that Lord Goddard, who was then Lord Chief Justice, had advanced during the debate on the second reading. Lord Goddard,

117

he reminded their Lordships, 'horrified the House . . . by the description he gave of certain terribly depraved criminals, and reached the conclusion that men of that kind should be eliminated.' He thought Goddard's argument had gone too far. 'If we reach the conclusion that these human monsters must be eliminated', he continued, 'then we must extend the death penalty—as indeed was suggested by the right reverend Prelate, the Bishop of Truro—to other crimes committed by men who are as depraved as the type of murderer to whom Lord Goddard alluded.' He thought it very dangerous to assume that their lives were hopeless and that they must be eliminated, and believed this to be too close to the totalitarian argument that eliminated people and races for that reason. He ended by claiming that capital punishment had no part in an improved penal system and that the experiment suggested could be made safely and successfully.

The views of Lord Goddard were well known. He was a 'hanging judge' not so much because of his sentencing, which was obligatory once a person had been convicted of murder, but because of his views as a whole concerning criminals, which had been alluded to in Lord Templewood's speech. Lord Goddard made three main points, the first of which was that if capital punishment were abolished, even for an experimental period, it would be impossible to re-impose it. He brought no evidence to support this assertion; a number of countries had done just this and one or two had re-abolished, but no-one interrupted to point this out. Having 'established' that abolition would be permanent he went on to say that this was not the time to do it. There was breakdown in discipline—there was certainly a post-war crime wave but that was not wholly unexpected—and he referred to that day's newspaper which had reported the battering to death of a lady of 89 years and the binding and gagging of two ladies in a flat in Kensington. 'These are the sort of things that are going on at the present time'. They were, of course, nothing new, certainly not to Lord Goddard, but he posed the question, 'Is it a safe or a proper time to carry out an experiment . . .?'

He agreed with a point that Lord Merthyr had made, namely that abolition would make juries more ready to convict for the crime of murder. But the reason was not what Lord Merthyr had in mind. 'Once they know there is little distinction, if any, between murder and manslaughter, they will not give their anxious and careful attention to cases as they do at the present time.' He cited a recent case at Worcester Assizes where the jury had retired to consider whether to bring in a verdict of murder or manslaughter and came back after only ten minutes with a verdict of murder. To a lesser man this would seem to invalidate Goddard's claim of 'anxious and careful attention', but the Lord Chief Justice put this cavalier retirement of the jury down to 'this announcement about a reprieve'.

The last point he discussed was one made by the Bishop of Truro to whom he apologised for saying at the opening of his speech at the second reading 'that I was not going to follow him in all his bloodthirsty suggestions. I did not mean it in any derogatory sense and I desire to apologise to him . . .' We were not to know in which sense he did mean it because he went on to agree with the Bishop that there are many other cases worse than murder. He agreed that it did not seem logical that if two people each shot someone and one victim died and the other was saved by some miracle of surgical skill, only one offender could be sentenced to death. But principles of law, he pointed out, were not always just and logical and although he could see merit in having the death penalty for cases other than murder, that was not what was being discussed. The amendment to abolish was massively lost by 181 to 28 and the Bill sent back to the Commons.

A compromise Bill

Correspondence continued unabated. A couple of days after the Lords' debate a letter appeared from Chief Inspector C. R. Hewitt. He wrote that in 25 years in the police force neither he nor most police officers had ever arrested a murderer, a burglar or any other desperado. The police generally did not like capital punishment and believed that if 34 other countries could cope with homicide by the use of prison and reformation, why was it still necessary for English criminals to be killed. Many believed that killing by the state devalued human life. It was often claimed that attention should be paid to public opinion before coming to a conclusion. But why, he asked, is public opinion useful when it is rejected in the case of lotteries, income tax, licensing hours and Sunday theatres? Were the public so much better informed about the death penalty than on those other matters? Many police officers would dispute that there would be resignations if the death penalty were abolished, as had been suggested, or that recruits would not come forward for fear of being shot.[88]

Mr A. Goodwin Cooke pointed to the recent decision of the USA Supreme Court, presided over by Justice Frankfurter in *Ondres v United States* which decided that in all cases where first degree murder had been proved the jury could qualify the verdict by adding 'without capital punishment' which would automatically result in a sentence of imprisonment for life.[89]

During the debate in the House of Lords on June 2 Lord Goddard had said that the home secretary's intention to advise the Crown to reprieve all people convicted of murder was 'exercising a dispensing power which has been repudiated by Parliament since the days of James II . . . action of this sort is declared illegal'. A letter from Geoffrey Bing KC, MP however, supported the home secretary.[90] He pointed out that the home secretary would not be making an overall judgment but would advise the King on each case as it came up. But this view was not supported by Dermot Morrah who noted that Ede's action would not enable the dispensation of mercy to be made on each case after full consideration of the circumstances.[91]

Lord Simon claimed that the essence of the matter was that no-one could qualify a penalty imposed by statute for murder before the murder takes place. The reprieve was a conditional pardon: the murderer being reprieved on condition that he enters penal servitude for life. No foundation existed for the argument that mercy could be exercised before the commission of the crime.[92] He cunningly ended his long letter by turning the situation on its head, for those without access to law books, by asking what the reaction would be if a home secretary announced that he would *never* reprieve a murderer no matter how extenuating the circumstances. 'Would anyone contend that this was the proper exercise of a home secretary's duty?'

Although this point was by now academic the correspondence continued. Lord Cecil joined in next day, saying that where there was little prospect of an execution being carried out the death penalty should not be pronounced. This was a most woolly comment: what was a 'little prospect', and if the death penalty was not pronounced it became no prospect. A jury's recommendation for mercy, he continued, should result automatically in lifelong imprisonment or another suitable penalty, and execution should be saved only for 'heinous and grievous crimes' (whatever they were).[93] Maurice Hayward, on the same page, was 'surprised' that no-one had mentioned section 302 of the Indian Criminal Code which gave discretion of sentence to the judge. Bing came back next day with the logic-chopping comment that the home secretary was merely announcing in advance that he would advise the King to reprieve on each case as it came up, and asked Lord Goddard to produce reasoned argument and authorities if he believed the home secretary's action wrong.[94]

A week later Sydney Silverman approached the problem from a pragmatic rather than a legalistic standpoint. He claimed that it was conceded that hanging anyone after a House of Commons decision to suspend capital punishment was unthinkable but that if the home secretary had reprieved every case without first making a statement he would not have been exposed to Goddard's charge. Thus it was only the form of words used by the home secretary that was at issue and it was not worth having a battle over the words when the substance was agreed. He further charged Goddard with making a debating speech in the form of a pronouncement of the Lord Chief Justice.[95] Lionel Heald criticised Silverman for imputing Goddard with political motives and pointed out that no-one might query the right of Lords or members of the House of Commons to say what they liked in Parliament.[96]

In advance of the Commons debate it was again pointed out, in a long letter from Hector Hughes, that the whole capital punishment argument concerned only about eleven murderers a year[97] and Russell Wakefield argued with Lord Cecil on the grounds that the jury could not make an informed pronouncement on sentencing as they did not have the offender's previous record.[98]

On June 15 the Commons debated the Bill again in the light of its having been sent back from the Lords.[99] The debate was opened by Sir Hartley Shawcross who disagreed with the Lords' amendment to delete the abolition clause. He reviewed the various arguments in favour and against capital punishment and conceded that there were instances where only the fear of a more severe punishment than prison might prevent a murder. The government would thus advise the House to retain capital punishment in cases of that kind. The new clause divided murder into capital and non-capital but at that stage did not define what was meant by either term. Any alteration to the law was opposed by Winston Churchill who relied on the 'better sense' of the second chamber to ensure that common sense and public opinion prevailed.

The motion to disagree with the Lords' amendment was carried by 332 votes to 196, a majority of 136. An amendment moved by Anthony Greenwood to substitute life imprisonment for the death penalty for a period to be at the discretion of the home secretary was defeated by 319 to 186, and the government's amendment to introduce categories of murder was carried by 307 to 209, a majority of 98, most of the government who abstained at the first debate voting in favour.[100] Finally, a Lords' amendment to retain flogging was rejected by 232 to 62, a Government majority of 170.

The Times leader the next day[101] generally welcomed the government's position although pointing out the basic illogicality of such a compromise, and praised the attorney-general for raising the standard of the debate. It pointed out that the lines of demarcation did not run between the more and the less deliberate murders but was pleased that at least poisoners, the most calculating kind of murderers, would still be subject to capital punishment.

The Lords had yet to debate the new clause and support for it came from Hector Hughes and A. M. Sullivan who believed that the matter of whether murder was capital or not should be left to the jury after direction from the judge.[102] This view was not shared by Lord Simon who pointed to anomalies in the new clause: if poison were administered as a single dose it would not be capital murder but if given in a succession of doses it would, and that a man who drowned his wife or a parent who starved his child to death could not be hanged.[103]

On July 20 the Lords threw out the government's compromise clause by a dismissive 99 to 19. Lord Llewellen called it a 'murderer's code' which could be read and learned to enable a murderer to commit a crime in such a way that his life would not be forfeit.[104] After this vote, the Lords were not inclined to argue for the retention of flogging and left in the government's clause deleting it.

Lord Cecil never gave up. He wanted the jury's recommendation to mercy to be the final arbiter and suggested that the frequency with which they gave it would be an indication of whether public opinion was swinging in favour of abolition.[105]

Another Royal Commission

In November Chuter Ede, home secretary, announced the setting up of a Royal Commission to examine whether capital punishment could be modified, limited or substituted.[106] Speaking in South Shields, he said it was impossible that certain types of murderer could be released on society, but it was also difficult to keep them captive for life under the existing prison system. This was the problem that was standing in the way of abolishing capital punishment and would be considered by the Royal Commission. The public, he believed, would not tolerate the total abolition of capital punishment until an answer could be found.

The Criminal Justice Act of 1948 (without the compromise clause dismissed as described under the last heading) had become law at the end of July. There had been no executions since February when the abolition clause first appeared, and the next executions were in November, when Stanley Joseph Clark was hanged at Norwich on the eighteenth, the same day as the home secretary announced the setting up of the Royal Commission, and Peter Griffiths at Liverpool a day later.[107] One month later the Commission members had still not been chosen, the home secretary had yet to find a chairman, and it was announced that membership and the terms of reference would not be announced before 18 January 1949.[108]

In the New Year of 1949 the terms of the Royal Commission were announced,[109] terms that were not without controversy as the following exchange during prime minister's questions demonstrated.[110] Wilson Harris asked the prime minister whether he would name the members of the Royal Commission on the Death Penalty.

The prime minister (Clement Attlee): The King has been pleased to approve the setting up of a Royal Commission on Capital Punishment with the following terms of reference:

To consider and report whether liability under the criminal law in Great Britain to suffer capital punishment for murder should be limited or modified, and if so, to what extent and by what means, for how long and under what conditions persons who would otherwise have been liable to suffer capital punishment should be detained, and what changes in the existing law and the prison system would be required; and to enquire into and take account of the position in those countries whose experience and practice may throw light on these questions.

I am glad to be able to announce that Sir Ernest Gowers will act as chairman of the Royal Commission and I hope to be able to give the names of members of the Commission before very long.

There was a serious omission in the terms of reference but it was not picked up immediately. After Harris asked that the proceedings be expedited and Attlee replied that it was up to the members, not for him to order them when to report, John Paton put his finger on it:

May I ask if the words 'limited' or 'modified' in these terms of reference would preclude the Commission from recommending the total abolition of the penalty?

Attlee: Yes, Sir. It was thought that it would be much more useful if the Royal Commission inquired into modifications or alternatives, because the straight issue of capital punishment is one on which Parliament in due course will have to take its decision. It is not very suitable to put it before a Royal Commission.

Mr Hale: Does the prime minister realise that that begs the whole case for abolition which has already been carried by this House on a free vote, and that if a Commission is appointed to express an opinion whether it should be limited or modified, the report of that Commission will be read as a report against abolition; and may I implore the prime minister to reconsider these terms of reference and to make it abundantly apparent that the Commission is to have a free vote.

Attlee: I am quite sure that is not so. I have made it abundantly clear, as I stated, that it is for Parliament to decide on that issue. I am quite sure that if we put up a Royal Commission with terms of reference to consider abolition, we should merely get majority and minority reports, and I think it is much more useful to set up a Commission with these terms of reference.

The prime minister could not, at that stage, tell Mrs Mann how many women would be included in the Commission, but in the event it was two women and ten men.

Abolitionists were not pleased. They had seen a Select Committee report in their favour and the recommendations ignored; they had had a Bill in favour of abolition for five years passed in the Commons only to see it thrown out by the Lords. Now hopes that they pinned on a Royal Commission were dashed by the Commission's terms of reference. *The Times* said that the disconcertion of abolitionist MPs was not really justified as the home secretary had indicated the terms of reference in November when the announcement of the Royal Commission was made.[111]

The prime minister agreed with Mr Blackburn that the Royal Commission should also consider the method of execution[112] but that was no consolation, and in a written answer Chuter Ede informed the House that since 1 January 1938 17 executions had been carried out where the jury had recommended mercy, and since July 1945, five.

Once again, the cause for total abolition had lost its momentum. While the Royal Commission sat little could be done and abolitionists had to await its recommendations. The chairman of the Howard League, Lord Templewood, together with the vice-chairman and secretary, wrote to *The Times* criticising the government for the terms of reference and claiming that they had 'shillyshallied' enough. A Royal Commission, he said, was not needed merely to inquire into modifications of capital punishment.[113] But that was precisely what it was to do.

ENDNOTES

1   *Hansard*, [407] 1937 (6 February 1945)

2   *The Times*, p.5, 5 March 1945

3   ibid

4   ibid

5   ibid

6   ibid

7   ibid

8   ibid

9   *The Times*, p.5, 9 March 1945

10   ibid

11   *Hansard*, [416] 1752 (29 November 1945)

12   The difference between those charged and those convicted is made up of non-prosecutions, insane on arraignment, acquitted, and guilty but insane. The numbers found insane exceeded the number of acquittals in every year.

13 Provisional figure
14 *Hansard,* [423] 2139 (6 June 1946)
15 *The Times,* p. 5, 22 October 1946
16 ibid, p. 5, 25 October 1946
17 ibid, p. 5, 26 October 1946
18 ibid, p. 5, 28 October 1946
19 ibid, p.5, 30 October 1946
20 *Hansard,* [428] 771 (31 October 1946)
21 *The Times,* p.5, 1 November 1946
22 ibid, p. 5, 5 November 1946
23 ibid, p. 5, 8 November 1946
24 ibid, p. 5, 9 November 1946
25 ibid, p. 5, 11 November 1946
26 ibid, p. 7, 13 November 1946
27 *Hansard,* [430] 279 (14 November 1946)
28 ibid, [430] 1751 (28 November 1946)
29 ibid, [434] 97 (6 March 1947)
30 *The Times,* p. 5, 21 March 1947
31 ibid, p. 5, 29 October 1947
32 ibid, p. 5, 5 November 1947
33 ibid
34 ibid
35 ibid, p. 5, 8 November 1947
36 ibid, p. 5, 11 November 1947
37 ibid
38 ibid, p. 5, 14 November 1947
39 ibid
40 ibid, p. 5, 15 November 1947
41 ibid, p. 5, 18 November 1947
42 ibid, p. 5, 19 November 1947
43 ibid, p. 2, 1 November 1947
44 ibid, p. 4, 22 November 1947
45 ibid, p. 2, 29 November 1947
46 ibid, p. 2, 4 December 1947
47 ibid, p. 5, 22 November 1947
48 ibid
49 ibid, p. 5, 15 November 1947
50 ibid, p. 5, 26 November 1947
51 ibid, p. 5, 28 November 1947
52 ibid, p. 5, 29 November 1947
53 ibid, p. 5, 27 November 1947

54 *The Times*, p. 5, 3 December 1947
55 ibid, p. 5, 5 December 1947
56 ibid, p. 5, 8 December 1947
57 ibid
58 ibid, p. 5, 12 December 1947
59 ibid, p. 5, 11 December 1947
60 ibid, p. 5, 12 December 1947
61 ibid, p. 5, 16 December 1947
62 ibid, p. 6, 23 December 1947
63 ibid
64 ibid, p. 2, 4 February 1948
65 ibid, p. 2, 15 March 1948
66 ibid, p. 2, 27 March 1948
67 *Hansard*, [449] 1060 (14 April 1948)
68 *The Times*, p. 5, 14 April 1948
69 ibid, p. 4, 15 April 1948
70 ibid, p. 2, 17 April 1948
71 ibid, p. 2, 17 April 1948
72 ibid, p. 5, 19 April 1948
73 ibid, p. 4, 26 April 1948
74 ibid, p. 5, 26 April 1948
75 ibid, p. 5, 29 April 1948
76 ibid, p. 5, 21 April 1948
77 ibid, p. 5, 20 April 1948
78 ibid, p. 5, 26 April 1948
79 ibid
80 *Hansard*, [449] 1307 (16 April 1948)
81 ibid, [451] 1236 (3 May 1948)
82 ibid, [451] 1497 (4 May 1948)
83 ibid, [451] 2370 (10 May 1948)
84 ibid, [457] 32 (1 November 1948)
85 *The Times*, p. 5, 1 May 1948
86 ibid, p. 5, 11 May 1948
87 *Hansard*, [156] 19-75 and 102-192 (1 June 1948)
88 *The Times*, p. 4, 4 June 1948
89 ibid
90 ibid, p. 5, 5 June
91 ibid
92 ibid, p. 5, 7 June 1948
93 ibid, p. 5, 8 June 1948
94 ibid, p. 5, 9 June 1948

125

95   *The Times,* p. 5, 16 June 1948
96   ibid, p. 5, 25 June 1948
97   ibid, p. 5, 12 June 1948
98   ibid
99   ibid, p. 4, 16 June 1948
100 ibid, p. 2, 17 June 1948
101 ibid, p. 5, 16 June 1948
102 ibid, p. 5, 15 July 1948
103 ibid, p. 5, 16 July 1948
104 ibid, p. 4, 21 July 1948
105 ibid, p. 5, 27 July 1948
106 *Hansard,* [458] 565 (18 November 1948)
107 *The Times,* p. 5, 19 November 1948
108 ibid, p. 4, 22 December 1948
109 *Hansard,* [460] 329 (20 January 1949)
110 ibid
111 *The Times,* p. 4, January 21 1949
112 31 January 1949, HOC [464] 355
113 *The Times*, p. 5, 28 January 1949.

CHAPTER 11

The Royal Commission

Very little could be done in Parliament, or elsewhere, whilst the Royal Commission was sitting but that did not mean that nobody was thinking about abolition; and the correspondence pages of The Times were by no means devoid of the subject. In April, that newspaper reported on Templewood's address in which he had pointed out that executions had again begun and that the wave of human feeling that had swept through Parliament had not been reflected in any change of policy,[1] and an editorial, commenting on this, stated that after the debates in the Commons it was believed that the home secretary would in effect distinguish between degrees of murder in the manner in which he recommended reprieves, yet he had reprieved fewer since the debates than before.[2] It was six months since the Commission had been set up and members had still not been appointed. So long a delay, said The Times, was 'wholly unjustified'.

The members of the Royal Commission were announced on 28 April 1949. They were: Sir Ernest Gowers (chairman); Elizabeth Dorothea Cole Cameron (Elizabeth Bowen, the writer); Norman Roy Fox-Andrews KC; Florence Hancock; William Jones; Horace MacDonald; John Mann; Sir Alexander Maxwell; Professor George Allison Montgomery KC; Earl Peel; Professor Leon Radzinowicz and Dr. Eliot Slater.[3] Gowers had had a distinguished career in public service. He had been permanent under-secretary for mines; chairman of the board of the Inland Revenue; chairman of coal mines reorganization and of the Coal Commission; senior regional commissioner for civil defence for London; chairman of the committee on the Shops Act and of the committee on the admission of women into the foreign service; and he was currently chairman of Harlow New Town.

The Commission begins work

On the same day that the commission's membership was made public, a letter from Derek Hudson, agreeing with Lord Templewood's stance (see Chapter 10), analysed murders and executions since the beginning of the debate and showed that during the interval when all were reprieved, between February and November, there was no difference in the murder rate. He also deprecated that a woman had been executed, and so had a man who had given himself up, pleaded guilty and whom the jury had recommended for mercy.[4] A month later a rather ambivalent suggestion was made by Dr Greer, Bishop of Manchester, in an address to the Diocesan Conference of Manchester. The bishop conceded that total abolition of capital punishment was not then possible as public opinion was divided, but called for abolition with regard to women in order to prepare the public for total abolition.[5]

In August the first public meeting of the Royal Commission took place. It was revealed that a detailed memorandum submitted by the Home Office contained criticisms of proposals for changes to existing law and practice. It was revealed that between 1900 and 1948, 1,178 people had been sentenced to death of whom 617 (including eleven women) had actually been executed. The remainder were commuted to penal servitude or respited to Broadmoor. There were two objections to dividing murder into two degrees: one, it was impossible to frame a definition which did not include cases that ought not be included; two, there were not two classes of murder but an infinite gradation from the heinous to the excusable. Premeditation was not enough to determine that a murder was of the first degree. The jury would have to decide the degree of murder and they were not well fitted to do such a task. The memorandum went on to assume that murderers not executed would fall into three categories:

- those convicted of less heinous crimes would be required to serve sentences comparable in length to sentences in recent years
- those who committed heinous crimes would be required to serve up to 20 years; public opinion would be revolted by longer sentences
- those who were a danger to society might never be released.

Again, there had been only one recorded case of a released murderer murdering again. The Home Office believed that hanging was as good a method as any, but they had had no experience of any other methods of execution.

The first person to give evidence to the commission was Sir Frank Newsome, permanent under-secretary at the Home Office. He did not think that the average murderer needed reforming as he was generally not of bad character. Not all murderers were insane and it would be necessary to decide what to do with those who were not executed (this was an odd remark considering that two out of three murderers were not hanged). Dr. Methven, Commissioner of Prisons and former governor of Maidstone gaol, thought it 'near impossible' for an insane person to be executed.[6]

Ian Gregg deprecated the method of capital punishment which he believed catered for peoples' sensationalism. He advocated in a letter that places of execution be far from cities so that executions did not upset other prisoners and would not attract crowds at the gates.[7] Lieutenant Colonel F. A. Barker agreed: in India executions were at early dawn before the prisoners were awake and were at a location far from the sight or hearing of prisoners. He further stated that publicity and pictures of trials and executions should be ended.[8]

The Chief Constables' Association of England and Wales and the Police Federation both opposed the proposal to abolish capital punishment when they gave evidence to the Royal Commission. They were satisfied that capital punishment was a deterrent, especially to those who were violent. If criminals did not fear capital punishment they would have gone on to kill their victims. Neither body wanted degrees of murder as the police could not always give the Director of Public Prosecutions enough details about the crime to decide what degree it was, and the criminal might adopt a method designed to show that the murder was not of the first degree. The Police Federation also said that the *existing* law should be amended so that the death penalty could be carried out even when physical deformity made it impracticable or undesirable; in such cases other methods than hanging should be employed.[9]

The following day the Director of Public Prosecutions, Sir Theobald Matthew gave evidence. He said that the prosecution should not be concerned with the punishment that was eventually to be awarded. He had full confidence in juries and had never believed that a jury had returned a wrong verdict in all the trials he had seen. He thought it dangerous to raise the age before which someone could be hanged to 21 as a considerable number of young hooligans between the ages of 18 and 21 took part in violent crime.[10] That was the end of the first public session.

When the Royal Commission resumed sitting on October 6 it first heard evidence and opinions from a panel of prison governors and a panel of chaplains.[11] The prison officers said that hanging was expeditious and humane. The governors felt that it would be better if the condemned cells and gallows were in a separate part of the prison grounds and that possibly condemned cells could be better furnished. The governor of Wandsworth prison was convinced that death was instantaneous and mentioned that there was an enormous number of applications for the job of executioner. He did not agree with the suggestion that prisoners should be given the means to kill themselves. He did not condone suicide: 'It would be a bad thing'. He disputed what had been said in the commons debate, that after Edith Thompson had been executed the hangman committed suicide, the chaplain had had a nervous breakdown, a warder went mad and that everyone connected with the execution left the prison service. If capital punishment were abolished he believed the prison staff would be in great danger. Prison officers felt that if murderers were serving life without the possibility of the death penalty, they would kill a prison officer or other prisoner with impunity. The consensus in prisons was that the present method of execution was as humane as circumstances permitted. If capital punishment *were* abolished, they were against a separate prison for murderers.

The chaplains also thought that capital punishment should be retained as it was a necessary deterrent to crime. The chaplain at Liverpool had been 'amazed' at the skill and humanity of the operation of an execution. The following day the Commissioner of the Metropolitan Police, Sir Harold Scott, said that all the police were against abolition as they believed that capital punishment offered them protection against violent criminals.

Next to give evidence was Lord Justice Denning. He did not believe that either deterrence or reform or retribution were the only justification for capital punishment: it was society's way of denouncing the crime. Too much emphasis had been placed on deterrence. He thought that the current law of murder was wrong, but neither did he like the idea of first and second degree murder. He advocated dividing culpable homicide into three categories: murder, manslaughter and unlawful killing. 'Murder' should have express, rather than implied, malice. It should be an act that is meant to kill, is premeditated and is unprovoked. All other cases then considered murder he would classify as manslaughter, which would comprise cases where there was an unpremeditated intent to kill, in the course of causing grievous bodily harm, rape or another felony. All other unlawful deaths would be reclassified as 'unlawful killing' where the death was unlawful but was not the result of another felony or intent. On balance, he was against the abolition of capital punishment as he thought that for the worst crimes the public should have a method of expressing their denunciation.[12] This was so far the most lucid and logical of the attempts to classify murders as it separated premeditation and intent, which were often confused (they still are) and introduced the concept of (unlawful) killing that was detached from both intent and any associated felony.

Hector Hughes MP still held out for two categories of murder depending on the degree of turpitude, mainly premeditaion. Basil Neald KC, MP (later to become a High Court judge, and the only judge to have sat in every Assize Court town in England and Wales) agreed with the death penalty exacted only for the first category, and added generously that the survivor of a suicide pact should not suffer death, but whether this was merciful or vindictive was not made clear.

With the New Year, 1950 came the big guns. The first to give evidence, on January 5, was the Lord Chief Justice, Lord Goddard. He saw no useful purpose in dividing murder into two categories. It was possible to introduce statutory factors that would make homicide murder with the result that all other unlawful killing would be manslaughter, but he thought that modern judges would direct juries to manslaughter verdicts if the right factors were present anyway. It would, he believed, be wholly undesirable to leave to judges the discretion as to whether or not a death sentence were passed; judges had different temperaments. Asked by the chairman whether the home secretary should always reprieve when a recommendation to mercy had been made by a jury, Lord Goddard replied, 'That would be most disastrous'. He believed that reprieves had been made much too freely of late. He also thought there was no point in doing away with the 'black cap' but agreed that posting a notice of execution outside the prison gates was unnecessary. He could not understand why women murderers should not be hanged and did not think that raising the age for execution from 18 to 21 was always right: some young gangsters should not be reprieved at any age.[13]

Mr Justice Byrne also did not want judges to have discretion to sentence to death or to life imprisonment. He thought that capital punishment was a deterrent but not for everyone. Murderers who thought themselves so clever that they would never be caught, and those who saw red and killed would not be deterred. He, too, disagreed that there should be degrees of murder and believed that women as well as men should hang—and, he added, many of the worst crimes were committed by people between the ages of 18 and 21.[14]

This stream of retentionists giving evidence to the Royal Commission prompted an editorial from the *New Statesman* that asked whether this was the country where the House of Commons in 1948 voted for abolition. No word from the abolitionist side had been heard by the Royal Commission and the newspapers had been able to report nothing but grim demands for executions from the Home Office, the prison commission, prison officers, the clergy, the police and the judges. Emphasising the timidity of some of those who gave

130

evidence they cited Sir Frank Newsome, under-secretary at the Home Office, who said that before he answered any questions he wished to make clear that questions as to his personal views might be embarassing to him and to the home secretary. The editorial looked forward to the time when the commission heard evidence from the Howard League and the British Medical Association, and reports from countries that were able to retain a low homicide rate without the death penalty.[15] This brought a swift rebuff from Harry Harley Cronin, general secretary of the Prison Officers' Association, who considered the *New Statesman's* remarks offensive and inaccurate. Prison oficers, he said, made no demands for executions. They opposed abolition but were in favour of the death penalty being waived in certain cases.[16] But the editorial was supported by the Howard League. Its general secretary pointed out that while judges did not have to watch a condemned murderer in the death cell or witness an execution, prison officers and chaplains were face to face with the condemned. Unless the home secretary set his staff free to speak their minds the Royal Commission would be a waste of money.[17]

The Howard League itself gave evidence the following month and not surprisingly could not advocate any policy other than complete abolition. In the League's opinion, the death penalty was harmful to the whole community because it periodically stirred up unhealthy emotions, concentrated the public interest in brutality, violence and vengeance, and in some cases was apt to shift public sympathy away from the victim to the murderer. A memorandum from Margery Fry, who saw Edith Thompson in 1923, said it was wrong to put onto prison officers the strain of the effect of Thompson's execution.[18]

If anybody present at the hearings entertained the possibility that the evidence given to the Commission by the Archbishop of Canterbury, Geoffrey Fisher, would be tempered by the balm of humanity and mercy they were in for a shock. Of the death sentence, he said in words that have since passed into history, 'it was intolerable that this solemn and significant procedure should be enacted when in almost half the cases the consequences would not follow'. He added, 'speaking as a churchman, so long as this awful punishment . . . is retained it should be delivered from every circumstance which may make it anything less than it is . . .' It was only his flowery turn of phrase that delayed for a moment or two the stark meaning of his words: hang the lot! He considered that unpremeditated and provoked killings were both murder and the meaning should be the same. 'Occasionally' there might be extenuating circumstances, but he would not remove mercy killing from the category of murder. He said that he did not appear before the commission as an advocate of capital punishment (which must have surprised the members) and did not commit himself to any view on the ethical side (which must have surprised even more those who believed that that was what an archbishop was for), and believed the 'black cap' should be retained.[19] During his oral evidence a female member of the public rose and asked, 'Do you think that Christ would have said what you have said today?' No reply is recorded but perhaps he did not recognise to whom she referred.

131

Lord Simon was happy with the way things were. He did not favour categories of murder; on a guilty verdict by a jury the judge had no choice but to sentence to death; since 1907 appeal to the Court of Appeal and the House of Lords was possible, which exhausted the judicial process, and reprieve by the executive was feasible. He thought the system should be left alone.[20]

In the meantime Sydney Silverman asked the home secretary what considerations he had regard to in deciding whether or not to advise the King to exercise the Royal prerogative of mercy in capital cases. Ede replied that it was neither desirable nor possible to lay down hard and fast rules. But a memorandum showing general principles followed by successive home secretaries had been sent to the Royal Commission by the Home Office and he promised to send a copy to Silverman.

Following a further question by Silverman concerning the hanging of criminal lunatics, Mr Wilkes referred to the five men who had been executed since 1945 even though the juries had recommended mercy. 'Would not the minister agree that as a jury, who listen most patiently to a case from beginning to end, probably know more about the case than anybody else, it would be advisable to treat strong recommendations to mercy as an expression of the jury's view that the man should not hang?' Ede replied that this was one of the considerations to be taken into account but he did not accept that it should be the final and determining factor. After further questions from Silverman and Hector Hughes, Ede said that the duty of considering whether to reprieve or not was difficult and delicate and that misgivings in the minds of the public would be removed if he could disclose his reasons, which he was unable to do. R. A. Butler concluded this exchange by informing Ede that the opposition had every confidence in his judgement.[21]

On the day following, 10 March 1950, an event took place that attracted very little attention. A man named Timothy John Evans was hanged for the murder of his baby daughter Geraldine.[22] His execution passed almost unnoticed but a time-bomb had been placed under the death penalty—and would explode a few years later.

In April, the commission members briefly visited Scotland for a view from North of the border. Scottish chaplains thought that executions should be carried out in a building separated from the prison as the sound of the trap falling could be heard by all. Representatives of the Scottish Superintendents' Council said that not enough thought was given to victims and too much to the murderers. The Scottish Police Federation said that murder trials should be heard by a panel of three judges as jurors were not detached enough and might be swayed by the personality of the accused. But they were all in agreement that capital punishment was an essential deterrent to crime.[23] The Lord Justice-General, Lord Cooper, informed the commission that he would deplore the abolition of the death penalty. He attached the utmost importance to the maintenance of capital punishment as a deterrent and as an indispensible safeguard for the protection of society and the maintenance of law and order.[24]

Further evidence continued to be collected. Sir Norwood East, a lecturer in forensic science, said he saw no reason to lead him to believe that infrequent

duty in the condemned cell affected prison staff adversely, but the reveren_
Joseph Walker, a former chaplain to Manchester's Strangeways prison, had
attended the execution of five men and one woman and did not agree. He knew
two prison officers who several years after their experiences in the condemned
cell were sick men, and he himself had had a heart attack which began a few
months after the execution of Margaret Allen, and he was shortly leaving the
prison service.[25]

The opinion of the Society of Labour Lawyers was that the death penalty
should be limited to cases in which prison officers were murderered by prisoners
sentenced to life. They saw no reason why in England provisions were needed
which many civilized countries found unnecessary.[26]

In September the Howard League gave evidence for a second time. They
submitted a memorandum on the effect of abolition in other countries which
showed that there was no evidence whatever that abolition had resulted in an
increase in murder, or that restoration of the death penalty when it occurred, had
resulted in a decrease. This was the experience in 30 states in which abolition
had been enacted. There was no significant trend in the murder rate or in the
murder figures. The evidence from abolitionist countries was that abolition
made no difference to the safety of its citizens, and 'it becomes unreasonable to
contend that there is something about the British people at home, either a great
brutality or a great fear of death, or both, which makes abolition an undue risk in
the United Kingdom'.[27] At the end of that hearing, the chairman, Sir Ernest
Gowers announced that the Royal Commission would meet again in November
and in the meantime the members would visit Norway, Sweden, Denmark,
Belgium and Holland.

In November the commission heard Lord Templewood (the former home
secretary, Sir Samuel Hoare). He was opposed to capital punishment in any form
in peacetime. However carefully the death penalty was inflicted, he said, a state
execution was a repulsive procedure. Capital punishment was objectionable
because it abandoned the possibility of reforming the murderer, it gave no
possibility of reversing a wrong sentence, it placed a hateful duty on all who
took part in the execution and it lowered the moral standard of the community.
Its only justification was the safety of the state. If it could be proved that
punishment of death was an indispensible deterrent against murder he would
reconsider his position. Lord Templewood concluded by hoping that the
Commission would recommend suspending the death penalty for a sufficient
period to test the effect of the substitute of life imprisonment. If capital
punishment were to be retained he would favour the reclassification of the crime
of murder and would raise to 21 the age under which no execution could take
place as the younger the offender the more chance there was of rehabilitation.[28]

The hangman's tale
One of the most useful interviews—but one that the Royal Commission was
unable to hold—would have been with a man who had been hanged, and given
the time that it took them to present their report one might have been forgiven
for believing that they had made a journey beyond the grave to do just that. At

the very least such an interview would have determined once and for all whether death, or at least unconsciousness, was instantaneous, and to what extent there was any pain, albeit brief. After all, no-one else really knows. What would have been physically possible and also useful, although undesirable for a variety of reasons, would be to interview prisoners awaiting execution, from whom one might have learned what the waiting period was like, how they felt about being killed at a precise time, if they were afraid, how they felt about the effect on their families, and so on. Both of these possibilities were out of the commission's reach, but they did the next best thing: they interviewed the one hangman who was probably responsible for more executions in this country than any other man in modern times, Albert Pierrepoint.

Pierrepoint has recorded and commented on this interview in his autobiography *Executioner Pierrepoint*[29] and from it smugness shines like a sun, which is surprising considering that in the same book he admitted that after performing 'many hundreds' of executions he believed that capital punishment was of no value and that he was not in favour of it. A hangman who disapproved of capital punishment may sound paradoxical but at least it gave him a certain detachment and professionalism which he undoubtedly had. Had he despised the prisoners whom he dispatched to eternity, or hated them and felt that their fate was well-deserved, he might have treated them with less consideration and dignity than he unquestionably did.

He was jealous of his calling and had no wish to give evidence to the Royal Commission, but had no choice. He aimed to give as little information as he could and his answers were usually succinct. When asked how many executions he had been responsible for he declined to answer. In the end he gave a figure but an agreement was reached with the chairman that the figure in the official report would be 'some hundreds'. In his evidence he said that hanging as carried out in England—the equipment was old in Scotland—was as quick and humane as possible, and was the best method of execution in the world; he could think of nothing that would improve it. Very rarely did anything go wrong, but from the running commentary that his book gives on the interview it is apparant that he is not always presenting the whole picture. He gave the commission members, who had already witnessed a dummy execution, a blow by blow account of his actions from the time he arrived at the prison until the trapdoors opened 'while the clock is still chiming the hour', and explained why it was necessary to see the prisoner in order to calculate the drop. He revealed—not to the commission members but to his readers—that he had once had to execute a dwarf at the time he was courting his wife, and boasted that he did not discuss with her the height of the noose and the drop to be calculated for someone of abnormal muscle formation; it would have been an unusual courtship if he had, but the point he was making was that he was ill-at-ease discussing these things in front of women, and two commission members and the stenographer were women.

He did not find it more difficult or more unpleasant to hang a woman. Women, he said, were braver than men—and then, in the commentary in his book, he revealed information that would have been invaluable to the commission for its revelation of the banality and sheer squalor of executions.

134

The following vivid description appeared in no official record but is more telling than any that did. Commenting to his readers on the bravery of women, for whom he seemed to have a genuine and deep respect, he wrote:

> But not the sort of glamourous bravery you used to see at the end of a spy film, with a disdainful Mata Hari slinking sexily to the execution post. Murderers are so often ordinary people, caught on the wrong foot. Ordinary men, without elequence. Ordinary women, rarely beautiful. Square-faced, thin-mouthed, eyes blinking behind National Health spectacles which I have to take off at the last moment, hair scraped thin by curlers, lumpy ankles above homely shoes, in which they have to slop to the gallows because prison regulations demand that there are no shoe-laces. It is not easy to go to die like that, but the fortitude of a woman comes through.

This simple, eloquent passage would have moved the most hardened retentionist and would certainly have nullified any beliefs that the gallows were glamourous or romantic. Unfortunately these words did not reach the Royal Commission; they were written years later.

On 6 May 1951 Sir Ernest Gowers departed for the USA. The report, he said, would be ready by Christmas.[30] The following couple of years were a quiet time as far as capital punishment went: everyone was waiting for that report. In 1951 there was a general election and Labour's slim majority which they had clung to in the election of 1950 was swept away; once again a Conservative government was in office and the chances for abolition appeared to have receded. But of far greater significance to the cause of the abolitionists, several murder trials took place that were to shock the country, rock the criminal justice process, and put the abolition of capital punishment firmly back on the Parliamentary agenda.

ENDNOTES

1 *The Times*, p. 4, 25 April 1949

2 ibid, p. 5

3 *Hansard*, [464] 355 (28 April 1949)

4 *The Times*, p. 5, 28 April 1949

5 ibid, p. 2, 28 May 1949

6 ibid, p. 2, 5 August 1949

7 ibid, p. 5, 16 August 1949

8 ibid, p. 5, 22 August 1949

9 ibid, p. 2, 9 September 1949

10 ibid, p. 2, 10 September 1949

11 ibid, p. 2, 7 October 1949

12 ibid, p. 2, 2 December 1949

13 ibid, p. 4, 6 January 1950

14 ibid, p. 3, 7 January 1950

15 *New Statesman and Nation*, p. 87, 28 January 1950
16 ibid, p. 132, 4 February 1950
17 ibid, p. 161, 11 February 1950
18 *The Times*, p. 2, 3 February 1950
19 ibid, p. 2, 4 February 1950
20 ibid, p. 2, 3 March 1950
21 *Hansard*, [472] 452 (9 March 1950)
22 *The Times*, p. 3, 10 March 1950
23 ibid, p. 2, 4 April 1950
24 ibid, p. 3, 5 April 1950
25 ibid, p. 3, 6 May 1950
26 ibid, p. 2, 8 July 1950
27 ibid, p. 3, 9 September 1950
28 ibid, p. 4, 4 November 1950
29 *Executioner Pierrepoint*, Albert Pierrepoint, London: Harrap, 1974
30 *The Times*, p. 2, 7 May 1951.

CHAPTER 12

Trials and Tribulations

In early December 1951 a man called David Ware was found guilty but insane of attempted murder by his own confession by attacking his victim with a hammer. He had previously confessed to a murder in 1947 for which Walter Graham Rowland had been hanged.

In answer to a question from Charles Hale, MP (Oldham West) the new home secretary, Sir David Maxwell Fyfe, agreed he *was* the same David Ware. When Sydney Silverman asked if it was possible that Rowlands was innocent as evidence favourable to him was not disclosed to the defence, the home secretary replied that a full inquiry into the confession had been made and concluded that Ware, who retracted his confession, was innocent. Sir Hartley Shawcross said that evidence favourable to Rowlands had been withheld by the police. Fyfe said that was the first he had heard of this and that he would look into it.[1]

Haitus

Christmas 1951 came and went but no report was forthcoming and some people were growing impatient. It was already three years after the Royal Commission was set up and Sir David Maxwell Fyfe, in answer to a question from Hector Hughes, said he still did not know when the report would be ready, as how long the commission sat was a matter for them and did he not know how many times they had met since being appointed three years earlier.[2]

A week later Maxwell Fyfe gave two written answers on the same day.[3] The first was to Silverman who had asked what steps he proposed to take in 'view of grave doubts that have arisen in recent cases', to ensure that innocent men were not hanged. The home secretary replied that he could not accept the suggestion that innocent men were hanged and knew of no foundation for any doubts. He also informed Hector Hughes that he had nothing to add to his reply of November 22 as to when the commission's report would be ready.

Two weeks later Hughes, who was obviously waiting anxiously and with decreasing patience for the report, suggested that the home secretary alter the commission's frame of reference so that it could publish an interim report, to which Maxwell Fyfe replied that they already could if four members of the commission wished to do so.[4] By early summer the home secretary told Hughes that he expected the report by late summer.[5] However, in mid-autumn, in answer to Wing Commander Hulbert, under-secretary at the Home Office, Sir Hugh Lucas-Tooth said that the report of the Royal Commission was 'likely to be presented' in the next few months.[6] Hughes could apparently not wait that long for only one month later the home secretary was obliged to tell him the same thing.[7]

Straffen's trial

On 22 July 1952 the trial of John Thomas Straffen, aged 22, opened at Winchester Assizes, before Mr Justice Cassells. He was charged with the murder of Linda Bowyer, aged five, on April 29 of that year. Straffen was a gardener and inmate of Broadmoor Institution.[8] The solicitor-general, Sir Reginald Manningham Buller, leading for the prosecution, said that no-one saw Linda being killed but she had been strangled and medical evidence would show that it was Straffen's hands that did the strangling. Straffen had escaped from Broadmoor at 2.40 p.m. on April 29 and was seen at 4.30 p.m. Linda's body was found at 5.40 a.m. next day. Although Straffen had been caught and locked up at 6.40 p.m. the same day he had escaped, the prosecution submitted that there was ample time for him to have committed the murder, for until the next morning no-one knew the girl was dead. The next day saw a minor sensation as the judge discharged the jury on account of one of their number having discussed the case outside court, and a new jury was sworn in. The trial was re-started and the prosecution repeated the evidence so far.[9]

When the defence case opened it was established that Straffen had twice been certified as mentally defective. His mental age was nine and he was said to have little or no moral sense. He had escaped on two previous occasions. Whilst he was out on licence, when he had lived with his parents, two girls, aged six and nine, were murdered five days apart. Both girls had been strangled. He was seen by police and after being charged with the second murder the judge had ruled that he was unfit to plead and ordered that he be detained in safe custody at His Majesty's pleasure.[10]

The next day a consultant psychiatrist confirmed that Straffen's mental age had not changed and that he was quite properly certified as mentally defective. He would have known what he was doing when he killed the girls but had no idea of the consequences. He said that his desire to kill was to pay back the police because he hated them. The doctor at Bristol prison said that Straffen was now fit to plead although he was not before. The judge began his summing up.[11] He warned the jury to look at the difference between 'a bit funny' and 'mentally defective' and 'insane'. He told them that to return a verdict of guilty but insane they had to believe that when the accused committed the crime he was suffering from a disease of the mind so that he did not appreciate the nature and quality of his act, or that he did not know that what he was doing was wrong.[12] These instructions would have stretched a jury composed entirely of psychiatrists; for a lay jury it was an enormous burden, and one for which no jury is fitted. They were out for just 53 minutes and found Straffen guilty of murder. He was duly sentenced to death.

An appeal was lodged on July 30 and dismissed[13] and an appeal to the House of Lords refused.[14] The execution date was fixed for September 4[15] and he was reprieved on August 29.[16] *The Times*[17] quoted *Medical World* which said that it was the law that was insane in finding that a mental defective with a mental age of nine could first be found unfit to plead and six months later guilty of murder and sentenced to death. The article concluded dryly that Straffen must have had exceptional treatment in Broadmoor.

138

The first letter in response to the trial and the reprieve was published two days later. It was from Russell Brain, President of the Royal College of Physicians.[18] He pointed out that the M'Naghten Rules had not kept up with modern knowledge of the mind. Straffen had been found guilty but although of unsound mind the jury believed he knew the nature and quality of his act and that it was wrong. He called for a new definition of criminal insanity and said that it was for society, not doctors or lawyers, to decide. Possibly a Royal Commission was required. He could have been forgiven for forgetting that one had been sitting for nearly four years.

A few days later four letters were published in connection with the trial.[19] Two were reasoned discussions of the M'Naghten Rules which needed examining if not revising, and two did not address the matter at all. Lord Harris believed that murder was murder and that insanity should not merit any special plea and should no longer be an excuse for avoiding the death penalty. George Bernard Shaw would have agreed with him but had died two years earlier aged 94. Shaw would also have found a friend in the vice-president of the Royal College of Surgeons, Reginald Watson-Jones who thought that the prevailing attitude to murder was the exact opposite of what it should have been. He reminded his readers that those who murder on momentary impulse are 'brutally hanged' while those who would go on murdering without knowing it are protected and supported. The advisability should be considered of abolishing capital punishment for those whose minds are normal, but those who murder without knowing it should be put peacefully to sleep.

It was becoming apparent to many people who were interested in the subject that the more the problem was analysed the sillier the solutions became. Any compromise was likely to prove defective in one way or another; only an absolute solution would work. However, more letters were published that discussed insanity without shedding any real light on the problem, if, indeed, a problem existed. The surgeon's letter was refuted by the secretary of the Howard League, Hugh J. Klare, who said that respect for justice, reason and humanity must come first.[20]

At the end of a month of letters discussing the mind, the will, the brain, the M'Naghten Rules and *mens rea*, no further light had been shed on the criminally insane and nobody agreed with anyone else. Perhaps this was sufficient in itself for the rules of legal insanity to be re-examined, but attention had been drawn to problems which arose when sanity was in doubt and the death penalty was an option. Later the same year another murder was committed that was to have an even greater impact on attitudes towards the death penalty by the public and in Parliament.

Bentley and Craig

On the evening of 2 November 1952, two men were spotted on the roof of a warehouse in Croydon, south London. A 999 call alerted the police who surrounded the warehouse. Several police went up on to the roof and a number of shots were heard. Police constable Sydney Miles was shot dead and detective officer J. Fairfax was wounded. Miles was a married man of 42 with two children and had been in the force for 22 years. Within a short time both suspects had been arrested. The entire incident lasted only 15 minutes but it was to rumble on for over 40 years and to have a profound effect on thinking about capital punishment.[21]

The next day Derek William Bentley was charged with the murder of constable Miles. When Bentley was questioned he said 'Craig shot him'. He was remanded in custody by Croydon magistrates. Craig was in hospital after a fall when he was captured.[22] On November 11 he, too, was charged with murder and remanded in custody. When charged and cautioned at Croydon hospital he said, 'He's dead, is he? What about the others?'[23] On November 17, after evidence was heard both were committed for trial on charges of murdering police constable Miles and attempting to murder detective officer Fairfax. [24]

The trial began on December 9 and was reported fully.[25] Lord Chief Justice Goddard presided and Christmas Humphreys prosecuted. The evidence was that Fairfax had got hold of Bentley and dragged him away. He told Craig to come out and Craig called, 'If you want us, come and get us'. Bentley got away from Fairfax and shouted, 'Let him have it, Chris'; this was followed by a loud report and Fairfax was shot in the shoulder. That shot began a gun fight in the course of which Miles was killed. Fairfax, although injured, knocked Bentley down and found in Bentley's pocket a knife and a knuckle-duster.

It was alleged that Bentley knew that Craig had a gun because when Fairfax was asked by another police officer what kind of gun Craig had, Bentley replied, 'He has a Colt 45 and plenty of ammunition, too'. Police constable Miles came straight onto the roof from the head of the stairs; Craig fired again and Miles fell dead with a bullet between the eyes. Craig shouted, 'I am Craig. You have just given my brother 12 years'. When Bentley shouted, 'Look out Chris, they are taking me down' there was another burst of firing from Craig. When he ran out of ammunition he said, 'There, it's empty' and jumped 25 feet off the roof into the arms of police constable Lowe. Craig broke his wrist in the fall, and hurt his back and chest.

The case for the Crown was that Craig deliberately shot Miles. Nine shots were fired, thus Craig had to reload, showing that his actions were deliberate. It was alleged that Bentley, who was technically under arrest, incited Craig to start shooting.

Craig's father, from the witness box, said that Christopher was the youngest of eight children. He had an interest in firearms but could not read. In 1951 he had been convicted in the juvenile court of possessing a firearm.

The next day, Craig gave evidence. He agreed that he had long been interested in guns. He also agreed that he had reloaded but said that he had fired the shots randomly and had not meant to harm anyone. He had dived off the roof because he was upset that he had hurt a policeman and wanted to kill himself. He admitted that he had shot Miles, but had not intended to do so.

Bentley said that he did not know that Craig had a gun and denied he had said anything before a shot was fired. When Fairfax had been hit he, Bentley, had stood by him and made no attempt to escape. He said he shouted 'They're taking me down' as a warning to Craig as he was afraid he might be hit.

In summing up for the prosecution, Christmas Humphreys said that each of the accused had had a common purpose to break into the warehouse. They were both armed and intended to resist arrest with as much violence as was necessary. At no time did Bentley make any sign to Craig to stop him. According to the police officers Bentley incited Craig to begin shooting.

For Craig, counsel said that he intended no harm. It was possible that the bullet ricocheted off the parapet and a million to one chance killed police constable Miles. The whole thing was a tragic accident. At this point Lord Goddard intervened, saying 'I shall tell the jury that what you are saying is not the law. I shall explain that the defence of accident is not open. A man doesn't accidentally cause injury if he shoots'. Counsel for Bentley said that before he could be found guilty there had to be an agreement between them to use violence. Bentley had shown no violence towards any police officer. He remained in the target area and made no attempt to rejoin Craig. He denied he had said 'Let him have it, Chris' and Craig said he never heard it.[26]

Summing up next day, the Lord Chief Justice said, 'If a person is arrested . . . and the arrest if effective be lawful, and that person for the purpose of escape or preventing or hindering the arrest does a wilful . . . act which causes the death of an officer, he is guilty of murder whether or not he intended to kill him or do grevious bodily harm'. The only way this could be manslaughter was if the act was not intentional. The arrest was lawful as the two men were carrying out a felony. Goddard pointed out that the jury might wonder why Craig said, 'Come on you coppers—I am only 16'. Did he mean 'Come on. I have a gun. I can't be hanged?' If the jury believed that Bentley knew that Craig had a gun there was a common purpose and both were guilty. Also, if he really did say, 'Let him have it', as sworn by three police officers, it was the most damning piece of evidence.

The jury were out for an hour and 17 minutes and returned guilty verdicts on both defendants. They added a recommendation for mercy for Bentley. Goddard told Craig he was the more guilty of the two and that when he passed to the home secretary the jury's recommendation for mercy he would tell him that Craig was one of the most dangerous young criminals that had ever stood in that dock. He then sentenced Bentley to death, and Craig to be detained during His Majesty's pleasure.[27]

A few days later it was announced that Bentley was to appeal.[28] On 13 January 1953 Bentley's appeal was heard and dismissed. The presiding judge said that he and Craig were on a joint venture and therefore both were guilty. There was nothing wrong with the summing up of the Lord Chief Justice; it was carefully, adequately and properly put. The point was made in the appeal that Bentley was under arrest at the time of the shooting but Bentley had been specifically asked if he was under arrest when the shot was fired and he specifically denied it. His answer destroyed this point.[29] The fact that Bentley was simple-minded had either not been raised or not been considered relevant.

One week later the home secretary announced that he was unable to advise a reprieve as he had failed to find any sufficient grounds to advise the Queen to interfere with the due course of the law.[30] Of course, had he been inclined to find grounds there were plenty to be found: Bentley's age, his mental age, the

141

fact that he did not fire the shot and had no gun, the fact that he was under arrest when the shot was fired, and, not least, the jury's recommendation for mercy. Singly, any one of these could be considered as a ground, but collectively they could have been considered irresistible.

Bentley's father sent a cable to the prime minister (Winston Churchill) who was returning from Jamaica, asking for him to intervene. Churchill sent a telegram back saying he had forwarded Mr Bentley's message to the home secretary, which could not have given Bentley senior much comfort. Several hundred telegrams had arrived at the House of Commons, all protesting at the refusal of a reprieve. There was also a petition with 14,000 signatures. Sydney Silverman and 45 other MPs sought a motion urging the home secretary to reconsider his decision in Bentley's case, but doubted whether such a motion would be admissible. Bentley's forthcoming execution was becoming a *cause célèbre*.

On January 27, Silverman sought leave to put the motion that 'This House dissents from the decision of the home secretary and urges him to reconsider'. He was supported, among others, by ten privy councillors, a former solicitor-general and a former under-secretary to the Home Office. The speaker, giving reasons and precedents, would not allow the motion to be put. He was urged to allow the motion by Aneurin Bevan, Desmond Donnelley, Charles Hale and Reg Paget, but to no avail; the speaker would not budge.[31] At ten o'clock that night the home secretary announced again that he could see no reason to alter his decision. The execution was due next morning and a deputation of six MPs with a petition went to see the home secretary. The deputation was introduced by Bevan and the home secretary listened to them for three-quarters of an hour, but was not to be moved. A demonstration of about 300 people gathered outside Parliament chanting 'Bentley must not die'; they then marched to the Home Office and finally to Sir David's home in Great Peter Street.[32]

The next morning at 9 a.m. Bentley was hanged at Wandsworth gaol. A large crowd outside the prison sang 'Abide With Me' and recited the Twenty-third Psalm. One man was arrested when he broke the glass-covered official announcement of the execution that had been placed on the prison gate.[33] It was all over. The speaker would not even allow Silverman to discuss the matter or to question the home secretary for an account of what took place in regard to the Bentley case.[34]

Goddard had had no choice, fettered by the law, he had to sentence Bentley to death. But in pointing out publicly that he would tell the home secretary how dangerous Craig was, and that he was the more guilty of the two, he was implicitly stating that Bentley had taken a lesser role. Sir David Maxwell Fyfe had total, unfettered choice: he chose death. Bentley was hanged and Sir David, later transformed into Viscount Kilmuir, became Lord Chancellor. But from the moment that poor, half-witted, 19 year-old Derek Bentley fell through the floor, the days of capital punishment in Britain were numbered.

There was hardly any public comment following the execution; perhaps the public were too shocked. The little known *British Weekly*, a Christian journal of news and comment, ran a short editorial in its next issue. It said that there was a

142

sore spot in the conscience of the British people after the decision not to reprieve Bentley. When justice was the letter of the law 'as a warning to evil-doers' it becomes something much less than the law. It continued, 'This three-quarter wit was seemingly hanged as an example for a murder somebody committed while he was under arrest . . . a Tory minister . . . can be trusted to show a proper concept for the conscience and convictions of the people.'[35] The only two responses to this piece were critical. T. J. Lovgreen took exception to the jibe against the home secretary whom he said *Hansard* showed he did not treat Bentley with contempt, and urged readers 'to think of the widow and orphans of the officer who was shot doing his duty.' And Rhoda Puck Took disagreed that justice is at its best when tempered with mercy and at its worst when it is merely the law. 'It is the law, no worst or best', she said.[36]

A leading article in the medical journal *The Lancet* on 'Law and Public Feeling' was reported in *The Times*.[37] The journal was of the opinion that the 'public sense of guilt seems to have been far stronger than the desire for vengeance'. If according to law and practice Bentley was justly hanged, in their view 'the perpetual public preoccupation with the condemned cell and the gallows is harmful to the mental health of society.'

Early in the New Year (1953) the Royal Commission report still showed no sign of turning up but the home secretary had some information for Hughes. The commission had been formally appointed on 6 May 1949, had held public sittings on 27 days, the last sitting was on 6 December 1951 and the report would be available in the next few months.[38] One month later Maxwell Fyfe still did not know when the report would be ready but in answer to Hughes said that as the commission was already considering the possibility of degrees of murder he was not prepared to discuss the subject. He was not aware that the delay in the report was the result of a deadlock on the commission.[39] Replying to Brigadier Medlicott two months later, the under-secretary explained that the commission's investigation concluded some time ago but writing the report had taken a long time and it was now at the printers.[40] Why the writing of the report took such a long time when the chairman of the commission was, of all people, Sir Ernest Gowers, an unchallenged authority on clear writing, was not explored, but the same response was given to the same question a month later.[41]

Christie and Evans

However, even before the home secretary was trying to explain the delay in the Royal Commission report, events began to unfold that would vie for the public attention with the forthcoming coronation of Queen Elizabeth II on 2 June 1953. In late March the bodies of three women were found in a house in Rillington Place, Notting Hill, west London. The causes of death were not apparent but the police were anxious to trace John Reginald Halliday Christie, a road haulage clerk. What made the discovery of the bodies so sinister was that in December 1949 Beryl Evans, 19, and her daughter Geraldine, aged 14 months, had been found strangled in an outhouse at the same address, and in March 1950 Beryl's husband Timothy, aged 25, was hanged for the murder of the child.[42] The next

143

day a fourth dead woman was found and one of the women had been identified.[43]

One day later saw all four bodies identified and it had been ascertained that all had been strangled. One of the women was Mrs Ethel Christie, wife of the man the police were trying to trace. Officers in charge of the case were satisfied that there were no more bodies concealed at the premises, and revealed that Mr and Mrs Christie had for some years been occupying the ground floor flat of the house.[44] The police were most anxious to interview Christie in connection with the dead women[45] and were of the opinion, as they continued to hunt for him, that there might be six, or even seven, bodies altogether.

The impact of these grisly discoveries had been somewhat diminished by the death of Queen Mary, the mother of King George VI who had died barely a year earlier, and on the same day as her burial Christie was found and charged with murder.[46] A day later he was remanded in custody for one week, charged with the murder of his wife.[47] He appeared in court again on April 8[48] and again on April 15 when he was charged with murdering three other women.[49]

On April 29 a doctor gave evidence that Christie suffered from various conditions and had been seriously injured in the first world war. Doctor Francis Camps, a pathologist, had seen the bodies and said that the four women had been dead for four weeks, eight weeks, eight weeks and 15 weeks respectively. All had been gassed with carbon monoxide and then strangled with a ligature. The case was further adjourned with Christie remanded in custody.[50] In May, the bodies of Beryl and Geraldine Evans were exhumed at the request of lawyers representing Christie.[51]

On June 22 the trial of Christie opened at the Central Criminal Court before Mr Justice Finnemore. The attorney-general, Sir Lionel Heald QC, MP prosecuted and Derek Curtis-Bennett QC led the defence. When charged with the murder of his wife on 31 March 1953, Christie had made a statement: 'I sat up [in bed] and saw she appeared to be convulsive. Her face was blue and she was choking. I did what I could to try to restore breathing but it was hopeless . . . I got a stocking and tied it round her neck to put her to sleep'. Heald pointed out that there was no such thing as mercy killing known to the law.

The defence was insanity. Christie had a long criminal record including a conviction for malicious wounding as well as a number of theft offences, although his last conviction was 20 years ago in 1933. One witness for the defence, Inspector Griffin, agreed that Mrs Evans and Geraldine had been exhumed and found to have been strangled. It was further agreed that Evans had been convicted of murdering the baby and had been hanged. More ominously, it was agreed that at Evans' trial, Christie had given evidence for the Crown.[52] He had been, in fact, the main prosecution witness.

In the witness box Christie admitted to having strangled two women and also said that he may have carried out more killings. He agreed that in 1949 he was living at 10 Rillington Place when the top floor was occupied by the Evans' and their young baby. He said that he had found Beryl Evans unconscious from gas and had opened the windows and brought her round. The following day she told him she was fed up with living and was intent on taking her own life. She

144

appealed to him to help her do it, so he did. He gassed her, and when she w. unconscious, strangled her with a stocking. He had attempted intercourse with her, but whether when she was unconscious or dead was not known. He did not agree that he had killed the baby.[53]

A psychiatrist giving evidence said that he presumed that sex was the motive for the killings, not necessarily insanity.[54] There was some evidence that he had had intercourse with his victims. In summing up, the judge said that it was admitted that Christie had killed his wife but he claimed he was insane. He told the jury that every person was presumed to be sane unless and until the contrary were proved. Christie was found guilty of murder and sentenced to death.[55]

There was little or no public sympathy for Christie but the Howard League wrote to the home secretary urging a public inquiry into the case of Timothy Evans. Recent events had thrown doubts on some of the evidence in Evans' case and the League urged that the inquiry be in public 'so that public confidence in justice be maintained.'[56] A day later it was announced that George Roberts MP would ask home secretary Sir David Maxwell Fyfe if he would order an inquiry into the execution in 1950 of Evans. During his trial Christie had said that he had killed his wife and six other women including Mrs Evans. Mrs Agnes Probert, Evans' mother, was said to have new evidence which George Rogers was sending to the home secretary. Sydney Silverman gave notice of moving a Bill to suspend the death penalty for five years. However, during the trial of Christie, *The Times* pointed out,[57] the judge had stated that 'it has been made quite plain by Inspector Griffin and by Mr Curtis-Bennett that there is no suggestion that anybody other than Evans killed the child'.

On June 29, Christie's lawyers announced that he had decided not to appeal but would apply to the home secretary for mercy.[58]

Silverman tries again

On July 1, Silverman, and eleven other members from all parties, sought leave under the ten minute rule to introduce a Bill to suspend the death penalty for five years, although he was told that this was premature in view of the production of the Royal Commission report. Silverman replied that the death penalty did not come under the terms of reference of the commission, and that there was concern among many members about evidence given in Christie's trial the week before and that his execution was fixed for July 15.[59]

That afternoon he begged to move 'that leave be given to bring in a Bill to suspend the death penalty for the period of five years.'[60] He recalled that in 1948 the House passed, by a majority of 23, a similar motion but it was defeated in the House of Lords. He saw no reason, as had been suggested, to await the Royal Commission's report since it could say nothing on the question before the House. Parliament should decide. He then turned to the finality of the death penalty and recalled that in the previous debate when he asked if it was possible that an innocent man could be wrongly hanged, he was told by the (current) home secretary that he was 'moving in a realm of fantasy when he makes that suggestion'. He wanted to know whether Maxwell Fyfe (who was not present) still believed that, since there was strong evidence, from Christie's confession in the *News Chronicle*, that he had murdered Evans' baby. It was not certain that Christie was telling the truth and a public inquiry was needed to investigate the matter, but such an inquiry was irrelevant to his present purpose.

The motion was opposed by Harry Hylton-Foster who could find no reason for suspending a penalty that some found to be a useful deterrent. All the evidence was not available on the Evans case; 'if there [was] the slightest shadow of a scintilla of doubt on that case' he hoped the home secretary would hold an inquiry to satisfy the public. The motion was lost by 256 votes to 195 and *The Times* report mentioned that the home secretary was not present to answer Silverman's claim that a man had been convicted and hanged on a false case.

The next day a number of members asked when the report of the Royal Commission would be published and Sir Hugh Lucas-Tooth informed them that he expected to receive it by the end of the month. Viscount Hinchingbrooke asked that the report be presented to Parliament and published during the recess.[61] Silverman then asked if the home secretary would order a public inquiry into the case of Evans to see if any miscarriage of justice had occurred. This question was echoed by Horace King, Anthony Greenwood, S. O. Davies, John Paton and Fred Willey. Lucas-Tooth said they would have to wait to see if Christie would appeal. Silverman emphasised that nobody was asking the home secretary to make a statement, merely to hold an inquiry as public confidence in the administration of justice had been gravely shaken—to which there were cries of 'No'. Lucas-Tooth, being clearly painted into a corner, promised that as soon as Christie had decided not to appeal, or his appeal had been determined, the home secretary would make a statement. Paton said that as the time for an appeal would expire on Sunday, could they have the statement on Monday; and that the inquiry should be public with interested parties present and available for cross-examination. Pressed, the under-secretary could not give an answer, and when Greenwood suggested that the inquiry be held 'before still another mouth is closed' he agreed that if it were considered desirable for Christie to give evidence to an inquiry 'if necessary, the date of the execution can be postponed'. Before anyone could ask what sort of co-operation they might expect from a condemned man told he would have to wait to be hanged until he answered a few questions, the Speaker halted further discussion.[62]

Scott Henderson's report

A few days later Sir David Maxwell Fyfe announced that he had appointed the Recorder of Portsmouth, John Scott Henderson, QC, to examine evidence in the cases of Evans and Christie, assisted by George Blackburn, Assistant Chief Constable of the West Riding of Yorkshire. The inquiry would not be in public and the procedure would be in accordance with the rules of natural justice not of evidence[63] which was regretted by the Howard League who asked that Evans' mother be present at the inquiry.[64]

Not only would the inquiry be private but its location was to be kept secret. The Penal Reform Group passed a resolution that it was profoundly disturbed at the nature of the inquiry into the conviction of Evans and that a secret inquiry of this kind could allay neither public nor private anxieties.[65] It was revealed next day that the hearings were being held at the Law Courts in the Strand and that Mr G. A. Peacock, secretary to the inquiry, had had a 45 minute interview with Christie at Pentonville the night before.[66] Subsequently, Scott Henderson and Blackburn, in the presence of Christie's counsel, Curtis-Bennett, interviewed Christie for an hour and a quarter.[67] There was concern in the House of Commons that the *Sunday Pictorial* had published an article purporting to be a personal confession by Christie.[68] The following day the inquiry was declared to be over. Scott Henderson had been instructed to hold the inquiry on July 6 and he submitted his report on the thirteenth of that month although he later said that he had begun reading evidence a few days earlier when the home secretary had signalled his intention. It was revealed that the two medical consultants who gave evidence at Christie's trial had been interviewed and that Evans' mother and two sisters were present.[69]

Events then moved quickly. On July 13 the home secretary announced that there would be no reprieve for Christie and that he had received Scott Henderson's report which would be presented to Parliament and published as a command paper the next day.[70] On July 14 the report was published by the Stationery Office (Cmnd. 8896, price 2s (10p).[71] Rogers and Silverman requested a debate on the Scott Henderson report before Christie was executed next morning. Rogers sought to reject the findings of the tribunal and to hold another inquiry. The speaker ruled this out on the ground that a capital sentence could be discussed only after the execution had taken place. Despite urgent pleas from a number of members of Parliament who pointed out that they were not seeking to discuss the prerogative of mercy but merely wanted to discuss the report whilst Christie was still alive as he was a material witness, the speaker again ruled the matter out of order.[72]

Christie was hanged at Pentonville at 9 a.m. on 15 July 1953 where 200 people waited outside the prison to see the notice of the execution,[73] which possibly prompted Mr Grey's request that hangings take place before 6 a.m.[74] On the day that Christie was hanged, Fred Willey asked for a transcript of the evidence of the Scott Henderson report to be placed in the House of Commons library. Maxwell Fyfe refused on the grounds that the inquiry was held in private and some of the evidence had been given in confidence.[75]

The report of the Evans inquiry stated Scott Henderson's opinion that there were no grounds for thinking that there may have been any miscarriage of justice in the conviction. An immediate debate on the report was refused. The findings were:

1. The case for the prosecution against Evans as presented to the jury at his trial was an overwhelming one.
2. Having seen all the material now available relating to the deaths of Mrs Evans and Geraldine Evans, Scott Henderson was satisfied that there could be no doubt that Evans was responsible for both.
3. Christie's statements that he was responsible for the death of Mrs Evans were not only unreliable but were untrue.

147

The report concluded: 'I have therefore to report that in my opinion there is no ground for thinking that there may have been any miscarriage of justice in the conviction of Evans for the murder of Geraldine Evans.'[76]

Later, Sidney Silverman and other Labour MPs called for a Select Committee to examine matters based on the report and asked the home secretary not to accept it.[77] Here was an inquiry set up hurriedly by a reluctant home secretary, which was held in private, whose witnesses could not be cross-examined and whose report, which was completed and presented a mere five days after the inquiry had begun, stated that everything about the Evans case had been perfectly in order, that it was Evans who had lied and Christie, a convicted multi-murderer, who had told the truth. It is possible that if Scott Henderson had had more time the report would have been more thorough but the main criticism was that even on the evidence that Scott Henderson had accumulated in the time available he had come to some bizarre conclusions. Also, he did not seem to have addressed the possibility that if Christie had been lying at Evans' trial—he had, after all, strangled at least six women and had a considerable criminal record—then Evans may have been telling the truth. In deciding 'there can be no doubt' that Evans was responsible for both murders, even though Christie had confessed to killing Mrs Evans, Scott Henderson implied that more time would not result in a different conclusion. In addition, Maxwell Fyfe declined to make public the evidence of the witnesses or of the log book kept at Pentonville which contained statements by Christie up to the moment of his execution.[78] Little wonder there was great dissatisfaction. But when Silverman asked for the appointment of a Select Committee to inquire again into the case of Evans and for a debate on that motion, the leader of the House, Harry Crookshank, said he could offer no time for this.[79]

Geoffrey Bing QC opened the debate on the inquiry by saying that the report on the Evans case was in every way unsatisfactory and that it was unfortunate that the home secretary presented it to Parliament without any explanation or provision for a debate. It turned out that the principal witness for the Crown in the Evans trial was found to have murdered six women in exactly the same way that Evans supposedly had, and in the witness box accused him of murdering two female people. It would be an extraordinary coincidence that there should be two killers killing their victims in exactly the same way, at the same address, hiding them in the same place, and acting completely independently of each other. Bing might have added, suggested Ludovic Kennedy,[80] that both of them murdered only women, both murdered only by strangling with a ligature, both murdered women who were pregnant,[81] both murdered women with no knickers on, both had intercourse with their victims at the time of their death, both wrapped the bodies in dark blankets and hid them in the wash-house, both sold their furniture to the same dealer before running away and both sold their dead wives' wedding rings. Yet that is what Scott Henderson had found had taken place (Christie's evidence had been suppressed and passed over by Scott Henderson). Bing continued at length to take various aspects of the report to pieces and added for good measure that it was cut through with prejudice. He called for the home secretary to publish the whole of the evidence

148

of the inquiry so that MPs and the public could judge whether it was a fair report or not.

Michael Foot, who spoke next, considered that Bing's 'was one of the most formidable speeches that has been delivered in the House for many years', as indeed it was: a devastating dissection of the report. He said that when the announcement of the inquiry was first made, many people, led by Sidney Silverman, criticised its form and were supported by almost all the newspapers in the country. It was rather remarkable that when the inquiry was rushed through in two or three days, that most of the same publications had prepared the same whitewash as the home secretary had been applying to the case. Foot said the report was not worth the paper it was printed on (Scott Henderson had not been paid a fee for preparing it)[82] and drew cries of 'Shame!' when he said that Scott Henderson reached the conclusion which he had before he had started. Foot concluded by saying that if the home secretary had not the courage to print all the evidence of the inquiry he should resign. Chuter Ede, who as home secretary had written across Evans' file the conventional phrase: 'The law must take its course', said that the report did not convince him and supposed that he was the person in the country who most wanted to be convinced.

In answering some of his critics, Maxwell Fyfe read out a series of questions to Detective Inspector Black, that were asked at the trial of Evans, and which indicated, as Bevan pointed out immediately afterwards, that every material fact about the murder of Mrs Evans and Geraldine, had been disclosed to the police before Evans made his confession: where the bodies were found, that they were found in the wash-house behind stacked wood, and that they had been strangled. The report, however, said that the piece of evidence against Evans that remained irrefutable was the fact that in the course of his confession he narrated incidents about the murder which could only have been known to him if he had committed the murder. Now it appeared that all the material facts had been disclosed to Evans before his confession which was thus a complete refutation of Scott Henderson's deduction.

The home secretary rejected the attack on the motives and methods of Scott Henderson and refused the further inquiry that had been asked for. Reg Paget, QC, said that the opposition were attacking the report because it deliberately concealed the truth and it was dishonest, and Bevan accused the home secretary of being more concerned with defending the reputation of Scott Henderson than with defending the integrity of British justice.[83] It was said in conclusion that at least a *prima facie* case had been made out and there should be a public inquiry into Evans' alleged guilt.[84] A motion was tabled asking for a Select Committee to be set up to inquire into the methods of procedure of the Evans inquiry.[85]

Scott Henderson himself was charged with preparing a secondary report on the inquiry and in the meantime an inquest established the identity of two women found as human remains at 10 Rillington Place as Marguerite Christine Fuerst and Muriel Amelia Eady, both of whom Christie had admitted gassing, strangling and burying in the garden some years earlier, almost five years before the Evans' moved in.[86]

Two weeks later the supplementary report on the Evans inquiry was published.[87] Scott Henderson defended his preparation of the original report and said there were no justifications for Bing's criticisms. Reg Paget said that the supplementary report 'strengthens the case for a public inquiry in which disputed evidence [could] be heard and tested in public'. He called it an even more unsatisfactory addendum to an unsatisfactory report.[88]

At Evans' trial it was easy to understand that Christie would be believed; he had been wounded in the 1914-18 war, was a special constable in the second world war with two commendations, his criminal record was trivialised (by the judge among others) as having ended nearly 20 years earlier. Evans, on the other hand, five feet five tall, slightly built, with a low I.Q. (of 68) and a mental age between ten and eleven, unable to read or write, who had confessed to two murders and then retracted his confession, who had run away to Wales at the time that the bodies of his wife and baby were discovered, came across as a foolish liar. In cross-examination, he and Christmas Humphreys were barely speaking the same language, such was the intellectual gulf between them. Softly-spoken, articulate Christie, who accused Evans of the murders was believed; inarticulate, confused Evans, who accused Christie of the murders, was not. One could at least understand how Evans came to be convicted. But when Scott Henderson, three years later, with a mass of written evidence available to him in addition to any witnesses he cared to interview, with little of the evidence seen at leisure supporting the evidence that Christie had given at his trial, concluded that *there can be no doubt* that Evans murdered his wife and child, this flew in the face of all the known facts.

A few weeks later Fred Willey opened an adjournment debate on Scott Henderson's supplementary report. After analysing the inadequacy of the original report and the final report Willey concluded that unless the home secretary held a full and public inquiry the Evans case might well become a second Dreyfus case (a French soldier cashiered for a crime he did not commit). Chuter Ede, who was home secretary at the time of Evans' trial, entered the debate. He quoted a book by Paget which said the most worrying aspect of the Evans case 'was that Evans' guilt appeared so clearly proved. There was no criticism of judge or jury or counsel or police, and yet the apparently cast-iron case was unquestionably a false one'. He continued that 'at that stage no allegation against the probity of the police was made'. He concluded, with what was to prove great foresight: 'This is not the only case in which it has been alleged that officers of the Metropolitan police manufactured or deflected evidence. If that were ever believed by the majority of the people of this country, all faith in our police and judicial systems would vanish'.

Adjournment debates may last only 30 minutes and Lucas-Tooth wound it up by defending the fact that the inquiry was held in private, before being stopped by the speaker in mid-sentence because time was up.[89]

Nothing came of this and the Scott Henderson reports were subsumed by the publication of the Royal Commission report after so long an interval. Some two years later in 1955, in a written reply to Mr Harman, the home secretary, then Gwilym Lloyd George, said that having considered the Evans case carefully in the light of all the information and views expressed in the press and elsewhere, he did not think a further inquiry would serve any useful purpose.[90] Some six months later Mr Lewis asked that, given the disquiet felt by many members of the legal profession and the general public over the Evans case, would the home secretary appoint a Select Committee to examine the whole matter. Lloyd George said that from all the relevant facts on record there was no reason to believe that any new information would be forthcoming.[91] That would seem to be that, but the time-bomb was still ticking.

Back to the Royal Commission
The events surrounding the Evans inquiry report were quickly to be overtaken by the publication of the Royal Commission report. Early in September it was stated that the report would be ready in a week or two and would be directed to criminal responsibility in cases in which insanity was pleaded by the defence.[92] Two weeks later the definitive date of September 23 was named,[93] and when that date finally arrived anyone with 12s. 6d. (62.5p) to spare was able to buy Cmnd. paper 8932 from the Stationary Office.

There were three main recommendations which, considering the report had taken four years to produce and was more than 500 pages long, did not seem much. The one main recommendation that would cause most dissent was that discretionary power should be given to the jury to decide in individual cases whether there were extenuating circumstances which would justify the substitution of a lesser sentence than death for convicted murderers. There was also a recommendation that the M'Naghten Rules be amended so that the jury would decide whether the accused was sufficiently of unsound mind as to not be held responsible; and that the statutory age limit below which a person could not be hanged be raised from 18 to 21. The report also recommended that the method of lethal injection should be examined, but electrocution and lethal gassing were rejected as alternative methods of execution. The report commented that given the few executions actually carried out, it was unsatisfactory that so many reprieves were at the discretion of the executive. Dividing murder into two degrees, and redefining murder were rejected in favour of giving the jury discretion; discretion for the judge was also rejected. The concept of constructive malice, they said, should be abolished. The report concluded that the death penalty was likely to be a deterrent although there was no convincing statistical evidence that this was so.

The Howard League said that after four years study the commission found that there was no effective way of limiting the liability of suffering the death penalty other than a jury's discretion. They should therefore conclude that the real issue was whether capital punishment should be retained or abolished. The Prison Officers' Association and the Police Federation broadly agreed with the report's findings but were not in favour of jury discretion.[94]

In *The Times,* an editorial broadly welcomed the report which, it said, should reassure the country that, assuming its conscience was at peace about retaining the gallows at all, 'we have little to reproach ourselves with about the way in which the community uses it'. The main caveat of the editorial was letting the jury have discretion. Only a judge or the home secretary had standards on which to base a decision, and a random collection of 12 people brought together for one occasion to decide matters of fact could not acquire these standards.[95]

Not everybody was so sanguine and Sydney Silverman demanded a debate on the report at the earliest opportunity, claiming that it strongly supported the case for the complete abolition of capital punishment. The proposed changes made little difference; the real question that had emerged was whether to abolish or not. *The Times* thought that the government would be in no hurry to grant a Bill but would wish to see how Parliament debated the report and how public opinion developed.[96] A book was published at about this time by Silverman and Paget called *Hanged and Innocent?* It described and discussed the cases of Rowland and Ware, Christie and Evans and Bentley and Craig; Rowland, Evans and Bentley were all wrongly hanged, the book contended. The book, said *The Times* reviewer, aired doubts but proved nothing.[97]

Evans again

The overshadowing of the Evans inquiry by the publication of the Royal Commission report was temporary. A series of questions were put down in the House of Commons relating to the taking down of the 2,000 word confession of Evans by Inspector Black, and it was suggested that such a confession could not have been taken down in so short a time, namely between 9.55 p.m. and 11.15 p.m. The home secretary replied that he had watched the re-enaction of part of it and had no reason to believe that the suggestion was well-founded.[98] But Geoffrey Bing asked for a further inquiry into the Evans case and stated that the Scott Henderson inquiry had not allayed public disquiet that a miscarriage of justice may have occurred. The case for Evans could not have been properly put in the time available from July 6 to July 13; it was too short to allow a proper case to be presented.[99] Bing, later addressing a meeting organized by Tribune, said that if the name of British justice was to be upheld there should be a further inquiry into the case. If the home secretary did not take responsibility for ordering an inquiry he should resign. This call was supported by Silverman, Rogers and Phipps.[100] Two days later a motion was set down concerning the inability of the House to accept the Scott Henderson report and resolved that a Select Committee be set up.[101] The next day, no fewer than 18 questions were addressed to the home secretary.[102]

Bing asked whether the home secretary would review the conduct of the inquiry as counsel had not been permitted to cross-examine and Scott Henderson refused to put questions to Christie and other witnesses. Some counsel were excluded from hearing the evidence of witnesses they themselves had suggested and they were not supplied with transcripts of the case of Christie. Maxwell Fyfe replied that the procedure was entirely within the discretion of Scott Henderson himself and he believed it was properly conducted. The inquiry was not an appeal, the tribunal was not a court, there were no parties to the proceedings and the examination of witnesses was a matter for Scott Henderson not for counsel. Rogers asked why the home secretary had refused Mrs Evans' request that the evidence she gave to the inquiry should be published, and Silverman asked that copies of the complete proceedings against Evans be made available to members of Parliament in the library. Sir Lionel Heald, the attorney-general, said there were no grounds for any further inquiry.

The under-secretary, Sir Hugh Lucas-Tooth, replying to Fred Willey, said that the only grounds for reopening the Evans case would be if it were shown that there had been some impropriety, and the home secretary was completely satisfied that the inquiry had been held with skill, care and impartiality.[103]

Jo Grimond (later leader of the Liberal party) asked the home secretary what action he intended to take on the recommendations of the Gowers commission. When Maxwell Fyfe replied that he was not yet ready to make a statement, Grimond asked if he would take steps to suspend the death penalty until the report had been discussed. Maxwell Fyfe declined, saying he could not anticipate a decision that could only be taken by Parliament.[104] A few days later Silverman asked if a day could be set aside to discuss the report of the commission which had made 'interesting suggestions', and was told 'not at the moment or next week'; and Hector Hughes asked if it was the intention of the government to implement the recommendations.[105] When one week later Silverman, nothing if not persistent, asked the same question and wondered if the government was going to shelve the matter altogether, he received an equivocal answer to the effect that the report had only been received in September[106] and Grimond was told by Maxwell Fyfe that he did not know when a statement would be made.[107]

As 1953 drew to a close the Evans affair ground to a halt, and there seemed little prospect of a debate on the Royal Commission report which had taken over four years in preparation and which had been published for over three months. However, the report had not gone away, merely to 'another place'.

The Lords debate the report
An editorial in *The Times* commented on the coming speech by Lord Simon that would invite the Lords to dissent from the recommendation that would place on the jury the decision whether a convicted murderer should hang or go to prison for life. The report was quoted as saying that the 'signal advantage of the jury's discretion is that . . . it would make the law of murder flexible', and *The Times* questioned if flexibility was a desirable quality in the law. For many centuries juries had been pronouncing on facts, the editorial continued, but this proposal meant that they would be pronouncing on values and their qualification to do so was questionable. It concluded, 'At bottom, the decision to hang or spare is not the less an act of policy because it is applied only to an individual case, and it ought to be taken by a minister who is responsible for policy to Parliament, and not by a chance-met company of men and women who cannot be responsible to anyone, because as a body they have ceased to exist'.[108]

Lord Simon's motion was that juries should not make any decision as to punishment in murder cases. They were not fitted to the task and were judges of fact only. It was a great mistake to try to interfere with the system. If juries had to decide a sentence by what standard were they to measure the case? Lord Jowitt agreed, but Viscount Templewood, whilst admitting the objections to the changes, pointed out that the problem of whether the law of murder was too

153

rigid remained unresolved. Other countries gave discretion to the jury and perhaps it could be tried for a period of five years.

Nobody spoke in favour of the recommendation. It had been suggested in the report that where extenuating circumstances were being considered, the judge should address the jury a second time, but Lord Goddard said that rather than take part in such a performance he would rather resign from the office he held (of Lord Chief Justice). The Lord Chancellor said he was not in a position to make any pronouncement on behalf of the government as the government had had only three months to consider the report. The motion was withdrawn.[109]

F. Scott Lindsay, who had served as a juror at the Old Bailey, wrote that the decision to hang or spare should not be added to the jury's already painful responsibility. On arriving at a proper verdict the general feeling of the jury is reluctance to find the prisoner guilty. If in such an atmosphere jurors were called upon also to determine sentence, the inevitable breakdown might well frustrate the whole purpose of justice.[110] One final letter, from the secretary of the Howard League, succinctly summed up the state of play. Hugh J. Klare pointed out that the only situation where there was no flexibility of sentencing was in the case of capital crimes. If jury discretion is too difficult to work, then in the commission's own words, 'the issue is now whether capital punishment should be retained or abolished'.[111]

It had not been a good two years for the justice system. One man, already at Broadmoor, had been sentenced to death and reprieved when barely six months earlier he had been found unfit to plead for reasons of insanity. Another man, simple-minded and only 19 years-old, was hanged even though the 16 year-old he was with had done the killing, and despite the jury's recommendation for mercy. A third man was hanged for a number of murders, and had probably committed others for which someone else had already been wrongly hanged. An inquiry into this matter was hurriedly held despite the wishes of the home secretary; the inquiry was held in private, was manifestly unsatisfactory and found that no injustice had been done. A second inquiry, into the probity of the first and carried out by the same person, found that the findings of the inquiry were sound. Finally the Royal Commission published its long-awaited report and appeared to please no-one.

The end of the Evans affair
The Evans affair died down, but the seeds of suspicion that it had sown—that a miscarriage of justice had resulted in an innocent man being hanged—began to take root. The first argument of abolitionists was that capital punishment was not a unique deterrent to murder and evidence was accumulating that this was so. The second argument, swept aside so cavalierly by Maxwell Fyfe when he said (and never retracted) that anyone who thought that an innocent man could be hanged was moving in the realms of fantasy, was that capital punishment was final and that if a mistake were made it could not be undone. Many, not least Chuter Ede, thought that a mistake had been made and that only complete abolition of the death penalty could prevent the possiblility of another.

In 1961, the home secretary, Mr R. A. Butler, refused an earnest appeal by Sir Frank Soskice for a new inquiry into the Evans conviction. In 1964 there was

154

a change of government in which Sir Frank himself became the new home secretary but he, in turn, told Sir Ian Gilmour in February 1965 that a new inquiry would serve no useful purpose. However, a groundswell of Parliamentary and public opinion caused him to change his mind and in August he appointed Sir Daniel Brabin, a High Court judge, to hold a new inquiry. The inquiry opened in November 1965 and the report, running to over one million words, was delivered in October the following year. The conclusion was scarcely credible. In the words of Ludovic Kennedy, 'Sir Daniel produced the novel idea that while Evans had probably *not* murdered his baby (for which he had been hanged), he probably *had* murdered his wife (for which he hadn't even been tried).' [112] But by then Sir Frank Soskice had been ennobled to become Lord Stow Hill and the new home secretary was Roy Jenkins. He recommended, and the Queen granted, a posthumous free pardon and the saga of Timothy John Evans was over.

Evans died unjustly but the execution of this innocent simpleton probably did more than anything to accelerate the cause of the abolitionists.

ENDNOTES

1   *The Times*, p. 4, 7 December 1951
2   *Hansard*, [494] 557 (22 November 1951)
3   ibid, [497] 146 (13 March 1952)
4   ibid, [498] 807 (27 March 1952)
5   ibid, [502] 49 (12 June 1952)
6   ibid, [505] 146 (23 October 1952)
7   ibid, [508] 77 (27 November 1952)
8   *The Times*, p. 3, 22 July 1952
9   ibid, p. 4, 23 July 1952
10   ibid, p. 3, 24 July 1952
11   ibid, p. 3, 27 July 1952
12   ibid, p. 3, 26 July 1952
13   ibid, p. 9, 21 August 1952
14   ibid, p. 4, 27 August 1952
15   ibid, p. 2, 28 August 1952
16   ibid, p. 4, 30 August 1952
17   ibid, p. 2
18   ibid, p. 5. 1 September 1952
19   ibid, p. 5, 4 September 1952
20   ibid, p. 5, 12 September 1952
21   ibid, p. 6, 3 November 1952
22   ibid, p. 3, 4 November 1952
23   ibid, p. 2, 12 November 1952
24   ibid, p. 2, 18 November 1952

25 *The Times*, p. 3, 10 December 1952
26 ibid, p. 2, 11 December 1952
27 ibid, p. 2, 12 December 1952
28 ibid, p. 2, 15 December 1952
29 ibid, p. 4, 14 January 1953
30 ibid, p. 8, 22 January 1953
31 ibid, p. 4, 28 January 1953
32 ibid, p. 6
33 ibid, p. 2, 29 January 1953
34 ibid, p.11, 3 February 1953
35 *British Weekly*, p. 6, 5 February 1953
36 ibid, p. 9, 19 February 1953
37 *The Times*, p. 3, 6 February 1953
38 *Hansard*, [510] 40 (21 January 1953)
39 ibid, [511] 2289 (26 February 1953)
40 ibid, [514] 365 (16 April 1953)
41 ibid, [515] 33 (7 May 1953)
42 *The Times*, p. 8, 25 March 1953
43 ibid, p. 8, 26 March 1953
44 ibid, p. 5, 27 March 1953
45 ibid, p. 8, 28 March 1953
46 ibid, p. 8, 1 April 1953
47 ibid, p. 4, 2 April 1953
48 ibid, p. 2, 9 April 1953
49 ibid, p. 4, 16 April 1953
50 ibid, p. 2, 30 April 1953
51 ibid, p. 4, 19 May 1953
52 ibid, p. 3, 23 June 1953
53 ibid, p. 5, 24 June 1953
54 ibid, p. 3, 25 June 1953
55 ibid, p. 3, 26 June 1953
56 ibid, p. 6, 26 June 1953
57 ibid, p. 6, 27 June 1953
58 ibid, p. 2, 30 June 1953
59 ibid, p. 6, 1 July 1953
60 *Hansard*, [517] 407 (1 July 1953)
61 ibid, [510] 577 (2 July 1953)
62 ibid, [517] 579/80, 2 July 1953
63 *The Times*, p. 4, 7 July 1953
64 ibid, p. 6
65 ibid, p. 6, 8 July 1953

66   *The Times*, p. 4, 9 July 1953
67   ibid, p. 3, 10 July 1953
68   ibid, p. 10
69   ibid, p. 3, 11 July 1953
70   ibid, p. 6, 14 July 1953
71   ibid, p. 4, 15 July 1953
72   *Hansard*, [517] 1897 (14 July 1953)
73   *The Times*, p. 2, 16 July 1953
74   *Hansard*, [518] 64 (23 July 1953)
75   ibid, [517] 2226 (15 July 1953)
76   Report by Mr J. Scott Henderson, QC, Cmd. 8896, 1953; Summary of Findings, paras. 49 and 50
77   *Report of the Inquiry into the Conviction and Execution of Timothy John Evans*, HMSO Cmd. 8896; *The Times*, pp. 3 and 8, 15 July 1953
78   *The Times*, p. 5, 24 July 1953
79   *Hansard*, [517] 2250 (16 July 1953)
80   *10, Rillington Place*, Ludovic Kennedy, Victor Gollancz Ltd, 1961. Reprinted, Grafton, 1971. This book is a detailed and painstaking account of the movements and trials of Evans and Christie, with a detailed critique of the Scott Henderson report.
81   Beryl Evans and Rita Nelson (murdered by Christie in January 1953)
82   *Hansard*, [545] 51 (18 December 1953)
83   *The Times*, p. 3, 30 July 1953
84   *Hansard*, [518] 1435 (29 July 1953)
85   *The Times*, p. 5, 31 July 1953
86   ibid, p. 3, 28 August
87   White Paper, Cmd. 8946, 4d (28 August 1953)
88   *The Times*, p. 3, 13 September 1953
89   *Hansard*, [520] 447 (5 November 1953)
90   ibid, [545] 51 (27 October 1955)
91   ibid, [551] 65 (17 April 1956)
92   *The Times*, p. 6, 5 September 1953
93   ibid, p. 8, 18 September 1953
94   ibid, p. 6
95   ibid, p. 2
96   ibid, p. 3, 25 September 1953
97   ibid, p. 8, 30 September 1953
98   ibid, p. 2, 1 October 1953
99   ibid, p. 4, 16 October 1953
100 ibid, p. 4, 20 October 1953
101 ibid, p. 4, 22 October 1953

102 *The Times*, p. 12, 23 October 1953
103 ibid, p. 3, 3 November 1953
104 *Hansard*, [520] 71 (12 November 1953); *The Times*. p. 3, 13 November 1953
105 *Hansard*, [520] 1909/1911 (19 November 1953)
106 ibid, [521] 528 (26 November 1953)
107 ibid. [521] 151 (3 December 1953)
108 *The Times*, p. 7, 16 December 1953
109 ibid, p. 9, 17 December 1953
110 ibid, p. 9, 18 December 1953
111 ibid, p. 7, 19 December 1953
112 *10, Rillington Place, supra*.

CHAPTER 13

A Quiet Report

The year changed (to 1954) but Maxwell Fyfe's high-handed manner did not. He told Hector Hughes—who asked when the Royal Commission report and the evidence on which it was based would be made available in book form—that he was not convinced it was necessary.

Sitting on the Report

A request for a debate must be made through the proper channels. Silverman reminded him that the report should not be treated with disrespect and its findings should not be ignored.[1] Later, Fyfe told Jo Grimond that he was still in no position to make a statement on what action the government would take on the report[2] and when Silverman asked if the government would set aside time to discuss it, the Lord Privy Seal, Harry Crookshank, would hold out no hope.[3] It was becoming apparent that the current Conservative government were not interested in a report of a commission set up by a previous Labour one.

In the meantime a letter was published[4] by judge Patrick Devlin concerning a lecture he had delivered the previous week at the University of London. Referring to the M'Naghten Rules on insanity, he believed that the subject was obscured by the fact that after conviction for murder the death sentence was passed automatically leading the public to think that the attitude of the law was that anyone whose case lay outside the rules deserved to be hanged. In truth, he pointed out, the rules are concerned only with the verdict, not with sentence. They were designed to be a definition of total irresponsibility which was determined by the verdict. Questions of partial or diminished responsibility were for the judge, except that in the case of murder the function that normally belonged to him was discharged by the home secretary. The distinction between judicial determination of the appropriate sentence and the exceptional act of clemency was that the former is primarily an act of justice, the latter of mercy. Although home secretaries had discharged their duties satisfactorily, lawyers could not be satisfied with the system. It was not due process of law; it meant that part of the administration of justice had been handed over to the executive. He cited several alternative procedures, each of which had objections. The first was that the judge should be given discretion; a second, that capital punishment should be abolished; a third was that the crime of murder should be limited to cases in which the public would regard death as a just sentence.

This elegant outline of the insanity rules produced not a ripple on the unruffled surface of the government pond. At the end of March the home secretary was still unable to make a statement on the government's action on the Gowers report[5] and at the end of April he declined to review the practice of burying executed prisoners in the precinct of the prison despite the fact that the bodies of executed criminals in the Nuremberg trials (in which Maxwell Fyfe

159

had played an undisputed brilliant role) were returned to their families. The Law Commission had recommended such a change but he was not yet able to make a statement about it.

The report was still receiving the government's attention, Grimond and Willey were told, but no statement was forthcoming,[6] and Charles Hale received the same (written) answer.[7] When Hale, some months later, asked if time would be given before the end of the session to discuss the report, the Lord Privy Seal said that the matter was 'engaging the immediate attention' of the home secretary, but when Silverman asked when they could consider the state of the law that the commission found unsatisfactory, Crookshank replied that if they were to debate 'all these things' they would never prorogue at all.[8] Later in the year, when Reg Paget asked if there was any likelihood of time to discuss the report, he got a very cavalier response: 'Perhaps the honourable and learned gentleman might like to make a speech about it today.'[9]

By this time there was a new home secretary, Major Gwillym Lloyd George, the member for Newcastle upon Tyne North, and although still unable to make a statement on the report he hoped the House would have an opportunity of discussing it in the not too distant future,[10] and one week later Crookshank promised a debate on the report in January.[11] This was not merely due to a thawing at the Home Office but a response to a motion on the Order Paper signed by over 50 members of Parliament criticising the home secretary. When Silverman asked if he would now give serious attention to finding time to discuss the report, Crookshank said he hoped to fix a day soon after the Christmas recess. Silverman expressed his gratitude but pointed out that it was almost 12 months since the report was produced and no time to discuss it had been found.[12]

The Report debated

The 'long-awaited debate on the Royal Commission report that had been submitted in 1953 after an inquiry that lasted four years'[13] was announced by Harry Crookshank for 10 February 1955. The motion would be to take note of the report and *The Times* anticipated an amendment to suspend capital punishment for five years. Silverman reminded Crookshank that some of the recommendations of the commission were unanimous and did not require legislation.[14] The home secretary told Fred Willey in a written answer that he would make a statement during the debate.[15]

The debate[16] was opened by Lloyd George, and after expressing the gratitude of the House for the work the commission had done he went on to say that the government had given very careful consideration to the commission's recommendations and he would indicate its provisional views, which would be examined again in the light of the debate; they would be very ready to give full weight to the views expressed and the arguments advanced.

The recommendations covered a wide field but there were three of outstanding importance. The first was that the statutory age limit below which the sentence of death might not be imposed be raised from 18 to 21. The second was that in all other cases the jury should be given discretion to decide whether there were such extenuating circumstances as to justify substituting the sentence of life imprisonment for that of death. The third was that the test of criminal responsibility laid down by the M'Naghten Rules should be wholly abrogated and that the jury should be left to determine, unfettered by any formula, whether at the time of the act the accused was suffering from a disease of the mind or was mentally deficient.

The majority of the commission, by six to five, believed that people under 21 could not be regarded as fully mature and, however heinous their crimes, were often capable of reformation. The minority took the view that the right course was to consider each case individually on its merits and not to exclude the operation of the death penalty by a rigid and arbitrary rule restricted to a particular age. The government were disposed to agree with the minority. It would be dangerous and inopportune to raise the age limit at a time when crimes of violence on the part of people between 17 and 21 were so prevalent. In 1938, people between 17 and 21 found guilty of such offences numbered 163; in 1948, 405; in 1951, 492; and in 1953 it was 603. The government could not think this was a time to remove a sanction which might deter such young men from committing murder.

Reg Paget interrupted to say that he did not understand why the government should wish to retain the death penalty for a class of youth upon a basis of statistics which seemed to show that the death penalty had been completely unsuccessful in restraining them. The home secretary replied that it was not a good idea to remove something which might be a deterrent. Turning to the second recommendation he quoted the view expressed by the commission that 'the outstanding defect of the law of murder is that it provides a single punishment for a crime widely varying in culpability'.

The commission rejected proposals for the division of murder into two degrees which were closely argued and convincing. They went on to propose that the only other way to limit the scope of the death penalty was to 'give either to the judge or the jury a discretion to decide in each particular case, in the light of all the information before the court, whether the sentence of death is appropriate, and if it appears to them that it is not, to impose or recommend a lesser punishment'. It rejected a discretion vested in the trial judge and concluded that entrusting such a power to juries worked well in other countries. He emphasised to the House that that did not amount to a positive recommendation, but only to saying that, if it were thought essential to find a halfway house between existing law and abolition of the death penalty, all the other proposals considered by the commission must clearly be rejected. The government felt little doubt that the recommendation was unworkable and should be rejected.

The third main recommendation was that the criterion in the M'Naghten Rules was so defective that it ought to be changed and that the best course was to leave the jury to decide whether the accused was suffering from a disease of the mind or mental deficiency. The government recognised that the M'Naghten Rules were open to criticism but were impressed by the difficulty of framing

161

satisfactory alternative rules when there were wide differences of opinion on the issue among doctors, lawyers and the general public.

Having disposed of the three main recommendations of the commission, Lloyd George turned to the question of capital punishment. He said that he was personally in favour of abolition provided that a suitable substitute could be found, but the government were opposed for three reasons. One, they were not disposed to reject evidence that it was a unique deterrent for professional criminals. Two, they were not convinced that the detention of some criminals for very long periods would not give rise to much more serious difficulty than the Royal Commission expected. Some of the most heinous criminals were fundamentally abnormal but many were normal and would have to be detained for a very long time. Three, the government had no doubt that it would be entirely wrong to abolish capital punishment unless there was clearly overwhelming public opinion in favour of the change and the government felt that the contrary was true.

Chuter Ede (the former home secretary) doubted whether in the last hundred years public opinion was in favour of any of the major penal reforms. Then, commenting on the Evans case he said that a mistake had been made and that he hoped that no future home secretary would ever have to feel as he did: that he had done his best but had sent an innocent man to the gallows.

At that point Sydney Silverman introduced his amendment that for a period of five years would substitute life imprisonment for the death penalty. Answering the home secretary's question, if you seek to abolish the death penalty, why suspend it for five years, Silverman responded by pointing out that none of the three objections he had cited on behalf of the government were provable one way or the other. But after a trial period it would become apparent whether any of the objections were valid or not. He then cited three examples of where the present law, which relied, he said, on mercy rather than justice, was wrong. Bentley was a mental defective who performed no act of violence himself but was hanged. A woman whom the prison doctor certified as insane was hanged. A week or two later a farmer in Wales who was convicted on clear evidence of murdering his business partner so effectively that the body was never found, was reprieved. He acknowledged that the recommendations of the commission were difficult. He asked, do we do what everyone knows ought to be done, that is, to differentiate between crimes of different moral culpability? If they could think of no other way they were driven back on abolishing the death penalty altogether, or at least for a trial period. Not one of the recommendations mattered in comparison to that, he said, and ended his argument by pointing out that 'all the other problems, the age of execution, insanity, degrees of moral culpability, and all the rest of them, cease to be problems if the death penalty goes'. He called for an end to 'this barbaric and obscene futility'.

Sir Frank Soskice, supporting the motion, took issue with the fact that the home secretary felt it would be unsafe to abolish unless he was certain that some equally effective deterrent could be put in its place. But starting from an assumption that this was a practice that was inherently barbaric, and which

162

everybody, deeply and profoundly, felt ought to be dispensed with if it possibly could be, the only justification for its retention would be convincing and irrefutable proof that without it society would be seriously harmed. He drew attention to the macabre details surrounding an execution which were published in detail in the newspapers and suggested that the whole business had a brutalising effect on society. Finally, he said that the evidence given to the Royal Commission was subjective and only an experimental period of abolition could answer those questions that needed answering.

John Paton quoted the report which said that excessive rigour in the law should not be tolerated merely because it was corrected by executive action, and recommended jury discretion as a practical corrective. He took the home secretary to task for rejecting the recommendation without putting anything in its place. The debate was wound up for the government by the attorney-general, Sir Reginald Manningham-Buller. He detected four points of view expressed in the debate. There were those who were in favour of the abolition of capital punishment and those against; there were those who were not convinced one way or another but believed that the experiment should be tried, and those unconvinced who believed that it was no time to experiment. He himself believed that the only possible ground for retention of a capital sentence was for the protection of society and that raised the question, was it a deterrent or not, and to what extent was it a deterrent. Soskice had said that those who sought to retain capital punishment must justify its retention, but the attorney-general thought otherwise: 'We have had this law for many a long year, and those who wish to change it have to prove their case for a change'.

The amendment was rejected by 245 votes to 214 and the government motion agreed. It was noted that a number of Labour MPs had changed their minds. Ede had voted against the proposal in 1948 but in favour in 1955, whilst Lloyd George had voted in favour in 1948 but against on this occasion. Attlee and Morrison had both voted against in 1948 but abstained in this debate.[17]

This setback prompted a letter from the secretary of the Howard League arguing that the government's main plank—that the death penalty must be retained because it was a uniquely effective deterrent for professional criminals—went against the whole weight of evidence of the Royal Commission report. Furthermore, the government's assertion that detention for very long periods could not be seriously maintained was also unsustainable: if other countries could solve this problem then we could too.[18] Lord Quickswood solved the problem. It was more humane, he wrote, to put a criminal to a painless death than to keep him in prison for a long time.[19]

Ruth Ellis

On 10 April 1955 a murder was committed in Hampstead, London, that would also affect the climate of opinion with regard to capital punishment. A young woman named Ruth Ellis shot dead her former lover outside a public house and the trial was scheduled for June.[20] Meanwhile, in May a general election had returned the Conservative government, and in the debate on the Royal Address that followed John Hynd (Sheffield, Attercliffe) blamed the previous

163

government for not legislating on the Royal Commission report and said that the time to tackle it was now, immediately after the election.[21] Needless to say, he was ignored.

In mid-June the trial of Ruth Ellis opened at the Central Criminal Court. Christmas Humphreys QC, who had prosecuted Timothy Evans, prosecuted Ruth Ellis and evidence was given that she made a confession to the police saying that she drove to the pub where she suspected her ex-lover David Blakely might be and shot him three times. She was a divorced single mother with two young children. She had been living with Blakely and had had occasion to complain of his conduct with other women. In answer to Christmas Humphrey's question, 'When you fired the revolver at close range into the body of David Blakely, what did you intend to do?' she replied, 'It's obvious when I shot him I intended to kill him'. Meldred Stevenson QC, opening the case for the defence, said that malice was absent from the case and that the jury could return a verdict of manslaughter rather than wilful murder.[22] The next day the trial continued before Mr Justice Havers in the absence of the jury whilst the judge delivered his response to the defence submission. He decided that Stevenson's submission had fallen short of disclosing sufficient evidence to support a verdict of manslaughter on the grounds of provocation. Stevenson said that in view of the ruling he did not consider it to be appropriate to say anything more to the jury, and Humphreys said that in those circumstances neither would he make a final speech. The judge summed up and said that the verdict of manslaughter was not open to the jury. The killing was admitted, manslaughter was excluded, the jury retired for a mere 23 minutes before returning a verdict of guilty of murder and Ruth Ellis was sentenced to death.[23]

It was decided not to appeal[24] but her solicitors advised people how to draw up a petition for her reprieve.[25] Her execution was fixed for July 13 and she asked the home secretary for clemency. Meanwhile a petition with 200 signatures was taken to the Home Office.[26] However, despite further petitions containing several thousand signatures urging a reprieve, the home secretary did not recommend it.[27] Because of her age—she was 28—her children and the fact that the killing was impulsive rather than planned and, of course because she was a woman, there was a great deal of public sympathy for Ruth Ellis and many people believed that the home secretary would relent at the last moment. It was reported that the French were shocked by the death sentence as under French law the killing would come under the umbrella of *crime passionnel* and a sentence of at most two or three years imprisonment would be imposed.[28] The night before the scheduled execution police reinforcements were called to control the crowds outside Holloway gaol who were 'demanding to see' Ruth Ellis, and a further petition had been presented to the home secretary signed by 35 members of the London County Council. One section of the crowd began chanting 'Evans—Bentley—Ellis' and the chorus was taken up by all those watching, which indicated that the public were realising that some executions were unjust and possibly that they should be done away with altogether.[29] The crowd did not disperse until 11.30 p.m. and Ruth Ellis was duly hanged at 9 a.m next morning.

164

On the day of the execution a statement was issued by a group of teachers from a school near Holloway gaol which said, 'the school was in a ferment. There were some children who waited outside the prison gates; some claimed to have seen the execution from the windows; others spoke with a fascinated horror about the technique of hanging a female. Not only was Ruth Ellis hanged today but hundreds of children were a little corrupted'. On the same day, in a written reply to Arthur Lewis (West Ham), the home secretary refused to introduce legislation to abolish the death penalty.[30]

There was little doubt that the general public found the hanging of a woman, for the first time for some years, distasteful and that opinion was shifting closer to abolition. This was picked up in a short exchange between Manny Shinwell and the home secretary.[31] Having been told that Lloyd George had no thought to abolish capital punishment Shinwell asked him if he did not agree that there was a change of public opinion and a change of opinion among MPs. He cited a case in Germany where there had been no execution for a similar case and suggested that the government might consider legislation which 'would be more consistent with the morals of a civilised country'. Lloyd George said that that was a matter of opinion and that the government's stance had not changed. The opinion of those readers of the medical journal *The Lancet* who wrote to that publication was that the execution was a disgrace. Sir Francis Walshe was severely critical of those who opposed capital punishment[32] but Dr I. H. Milner pointed out that only weeks before the murder Ruth Ellis had had a miscarriage and that she was in an unstable state. Dr J. F. Tuthill believed that everyone was responsible for the hangings whilst Dr I. Atkin believed it demonstrative of the low level of ethical development that the question of capital punishment was still being debated.[33]

In a further discussion concerning serious scenes outside the prison when Ruth Ellis was hanged the home secretary said that the metropolitan commissioner had informed him that the crowds had behaved in a quiet and orderly manner. Asked whether he could find any truth in the statement of the Holloway teachers he said that he could find no foundation for it. He told one member that between 1925 and 1954, 677 men and 60 women had been sentenced to death in England and Wales of whom 375 men and 7 women had been executed.[34] However, nobody had been hanged in Scotland since 1951.[35]

A couple of weeks after the execution of Ruth Ellis the Howard League sent a petition to the home secretary asking him to reconsider his opinion expressed in the House of Commons in February, in the absence of any factual evidence of a unique deterrent effect of capital punishment, and also that no adverse effects have been noticed in countries where capital punishment has been abolished.[36]

More Evans and Christie

A book review of *A Man of Conscience*, which was a detailed investigation into the Evans murder trial by Michael Eddowes published by Cassels in August 1955 considered that the assertion that Evans was innocent could not yet be considered the final verdict of history; counsel in the case could not speak about it until they retired[37] but a few days later a 'short notice' of the same book called it 'a timely investigation into the Evans murder trial.'[38] The next day the executive committee of the National Campaign for the Abolition of Capital Punishment issued a statement expressing a belief that a much higher percentage of the population was in favour of abolition than formerly. They announced that they were going to launch a campaign to bring capital punishment to an end at the earliest possible moment. A committee would be formed and it was suggested that abolitionists abstain from attending any place of entertainment on the eve of an execution and that shopkeepers close for an hour during the day that an execution takes place and display a notice explaining their action.[39]

Michael Eddowes responded to the comments made in the review of his book. He said that the two years he spent researching and writing the book drove him to the conclusion that Evans was innocent. He advocated that when a murder suspect was taken to a police station an independent person should be present to observe. He made a number of other suggestions, one of which was that a transcript of the whole trial of a convicted murderer should be made available to the public immediately after its completion,[40] which prompted L. Sloane Richards to suggest that a copy of the judge's summing up was available to jurors when they retired.

Concern continued to be expressed and a letter from Bilton Andrews, Sir Ian Gilmour and John Grigg (who as Lord Altrincham was one of the first to renounce his hereditary peerage) claimed that there were many people still 'profoundly disturbed' by the Evans and Christie murder cases and that no notes or record of the evidence to the Scott Henderson inquiry had been made public. It was, they said, becoming increasingly clear that his conclusions may have been based on false reasoning, and cast doubts on the efficiency of the police when it was disclosed that Christie with a bad criminal record was taken on as a special constable during the war. It traspired that the police apparently knew at the time that a skull had been dug up in Christie's garden and it was also apparent that the police knew at the time of the trial more than they saw fit to divulge. They called for a further inquiry to be held in public and with time for all witnesses to be heard to elicit the truth and restore the good name of the police.[41] The Assistant commissioner CID, Mr R. L. Jackson maintained that the skull was found a quarter of a mile away from Rillington place and that it was reported to the coroner who believed it was the skull of an air-raid victim.[42] This was true as far as it went and the coroner's opinion was a reasonable one in 1949, but the assistant commissioner should have known otherwise, and perhaps did. Christie's dog dug up the skull of Muriel Eady, one of his early victims. Christie waited until it was dark then

> went into the garden and got the skull and put it under my raincoat. I went out and put it in a bombed house next to the tennis courts in St Mark's Road. There was some corrugated iron covering some bay windows and I dropped the skull through the window where the iron had been bent back. I heard it drop with a thud as if there were no floor-boards.[43]

Some children found the skull a few days later, and via the police it found its way to the coroner. However, Andrews, Gilmour and Grigg accepted the explanation of Mr Jackson but pointed out that it was such a discrepancy between people's memories that brought Evans to the gallows. The more they studied the Evans case, they said, the more they were convinced that an innocent man was hanged and that a further inquiry was necessary.[44]

Silverman stymied

There were signs that public opinion was changing and the Liberal party passed a resolution that 'it should give a lead to enlighten public opinion by firmly declaring its opposition to the continuance of capital punishment in this country'[45] but an opportunity to introduce a private member's Bill was lost by the Labour MP John McGovern when he was not in his place in the House of Commons at the appointed time.[46] On the same day, Mr Russell asked the home secretary for the government decision on the recommendations of the Royal Commission. The home secretary said that the recommendations divided into three groups. The first group contained the major recommendations: to raise the age threshold to 21, to give the jury discretion to substitute life imprisonment for the death penalty, and to abrogate the M'Naghten Rules. The second group were less important and could not be implemented without legislation, and the government saw no prospect for legislation in the near future. The third group were administrative, accepted, and could be and were being implemented immediately.[47] Sydney Silverman sought leave under the ten minute rule to introduce a Bill, and a campaign to abolish capital punishment within a year was launched at a public meeting at Central Hall, Westminster, which overflowed. The chairman of the committee running the campaign, Victor Gollancz, announced the objective and a collection raised nearly £1,000 in 20 minutes.[48]

The House of Commons gave Silverman the leave he sought and he introduced the Death Penalty (Abolition) Bill backed by Chuter Ede and other Labour supporters, Conservatives Sir Beverly Baxter and Montgomery Hyde and the Liberal leader Clement Davies. But there was little chance of the Bill making much progress[49] although the following night a motion was tabled by 156 members of Parliament urging that time should be provided for the second reading of the Bill, and more MPs were expected to add their names.[50] However, the government were in no mood to entertain another Bill from Silverman. When he announced that since being given leave to introduce his Bill an order paper had been signed by 166 MPs of all parties, and asked if the government would provide a day for the debate, Harry Crookshank said that there was no question of the government doing any such thing and they were only at the stage of Silverman being given leave to introduce it.[51]

Any objection to a Bill at its second reading is enough to stop it going any further; predictably enough Silverman failed to get a second reading due to objections from government supporters.[52] The final nail in the coffin came from a meeting of the Conservative Home Affairs Committee, all but a small group of whom would support the government in resisting the abolition or suspension of capital punishment. At the same time Lord Chorley, a Labour peer, tabled a motion in the Lords to suspend the death penalty for a period of ten years.[53]

167

ENDNOTES

1 *Hansard,* [524] 558 (25 February 1954)
2 ibid, [525] 138 (25 March 1954)
3 ibid, [526] 1793 (29 April 1954)
4 *The Times,* p. 7, 9 March 1954
5 ibid, p. 9, 26 March 1954
6 *Hansard,* [527] 553 (6 May 1954)
7 ibid, [527] 66 (11 May 1954)
8 ibid, [531] 1383 (21 October 1954)
9 ibid, [535] 318 (2 December 1954)
10 *The Times,* p. 9, 10 December 1954
11 ibid, p. 5, 17 December 1954
12 *Hansard,* [535] 1984 (16 December 1954)
13 *The Times,* p. 4, 4 February 1955
14 *Hansard,* [536] 1272 (3 February 1955)
15 ibid, [536] 145 (3 February 1955)
16 ibid, [536] 2064-2184 (10 February 1955)
17 *The Times,* p. 4, 12 February 1955
18 ibid, p. 9, 15 February 1955
19 ibid, p. 7, 19 February 1955
20 ibid, p. 16, 13 May 1955
21 *Hansard,* [542] 230 (10 June 1955)
22 *The Times,* p. 6, 21 June 1955
23 ibid, p. 6, 22 June 1955
24 ibid, p. 4, 23 June 1955
25 ibid, p. 6, 1 July 1955
26 ibid, p. 3, 9 July 1955
27 ibid, p. 8, 12 July 1955
28 ibid, p. 6, 13 July 1955
29 ibid, p. 8
30 *Hansard,* [543] 196 (14 July 1955)
31 ibid, [544] 541 (21 July 1955)
32 *The Lancet,* 30 July 1955
33 ibid, 20 August 1955
34 *The Times,* p. 12, 22 July 1955
35 *Hansard,* [544] 108 (26 July 1955)
36 *The Times,* p. 4, 4 August 1955
37 ibid, p. 11, 18 August 1955
38 ibid, p. 11, 25 August 1955
39 ibid, p. 4, 26 August 1955
40 ibid, p. 9, 7 September 1955

41 *The Times*, p. 11, 16 September 1955
42 ibid, p. 7, 17 September 1955
43 Christie's Statement to Chief Inspector Griffin on 8 June 1953, quoted in *10 Rillington Place*, Ludovic Kennedy, Victor Gollancz Ltd., 1961. Reprinted, Grafton, 1971
44 *The Times*, p. 9, 23 September 1955
45 ibid, p. 9, 26 September 1955
46 ibid, p. 7, 10 November 1955
47 *Hansard*, [545] 219 (10 November 1955)
48 *The Times*, p. 8, 11 November 1955
49 ibid, p.10, 16 November 1955
50 ibid, p. 6, 17 November 1955
51 ibid, p. 6, 18 November 1955
52 ibid, p. 4, 19 November 1955
53 ibid, p. 6, 20 November 1955.

CHAPTER 14

Another Victory: Another Defeat

The first main event of 1956 as far as capital punishment was concerned was the publication of a report by the Inns of Court Conservative and Unionist Society called *Murder: Some Suggestions for the Reform of the Law of Murder in England*. The report was proposed by eight barristers under the chairmanship of Sir Lionel Heald. They agreed with the Royal Commission that the doctrine of constructive malice should go as they believed that intent was even more important for such a serious offence as murder. They recommended, however, that an exception should be made when a firearm was used; even if the firearm went off accidentally and killed somebody the offender, and any accomplice, should be subject to the death penalty. They further felt that when mental abnormality was not serious enough to come under the M'Naghten Rules, 'diminished responsibility' was a useful addition.[1] In *The Times* an editorial commented that whereas the adoption of these proposals would probably not reduce the number of executions it would certainly restrict the number of death sentences passed, which was a good objective in itself.[2] A couple of days later the Society of Labour Lawyers passed a resolution protesting against government inactivity in regard to the recommendations of the Royal Commission two years after the report was published.[3]

Another Bill: Another amendment

In the Commons, Sydney Silverman asked for a debate on capital punishment that would not be academic but one leading to some kind of action if the House should so decide. The Lord Privy Seal and Leader of the House, R. A. Butler, replied that he realised that the matter was pressing and would bear it in mind.[4] Over a week later Hugh Gaitskell (later leader of the Labour party) asked when the capital punishment debate was coming up, and whether it would be a free vote[5] and Butler replied that it would be within three weeks, and a week later confirmed that the vote would be free.[6] To give the House of Commons Bill a chance, Lord Chorley postponed his motion in the Lords but *The Times* believed that the prospect of the Bill making further progress was slender.[7] An amendment by Chuter Ede that the death penalty be abolished or suspended for an experimental period was tabled when the government announced its Bill and proposal 'that this House is of the opinion that while the death penalty should be retained the law relating to the crime of murder should be amended'. At the National Liberal Club that evening a motion to abolish the death penalty, proposed by Gerald Gardiner QC and opposed by Tudor Reece, a barrister, was carried by 64 votes to 26. Two Conservative members of Parliament, Kirk and Langford-Holt, as well as Hughes, added their names to the Ede amendment.[8]

An article in the weekly legal journal *Justice of the Peace*, 'The Law of Murder and the Death Sentence', noted that it was over two years since the

Royal Commission report was published. It pointed out that the Society of Labour Lawyers regretted the government's refusal to state whether or not it concurred with the unanimous recommendations of the report that the law of murder relating to malice, provocation, suicide pacts, mental deficiency and other matters should be amended; and also that the Inns of Court Conservative and Unionist Society had issued a report calling for amendments to the anomalies and anachronisms in the law. The *Justice of the Peace* article concluded by saying that the time had probably come to transfer the onus of proving their case to those strongly in favour of retaining the death penalty as their case was what they feared would happen whereas the abolitionists relied on what has happened in other countries.[9]

Meanwhile a number of eminent educationists recorded their conviction that capital punishment should be abolished for three reasons. One, because execution is final and irrevocable, it presupposes the absolute certainty of guilt; two, executions and their surrounding publicity excites hysteria and morbidity which is contrary to the spirit of education; three, it replaced rehabilitation with a philosophy of retribution and despair.[10] Three more Labour members of Parliament added their names to the amendment and *The Times* predicted a close vote.[11] In an editorial the paper recalled that eight years ago they had expressed the view that 'public opinion was clearly not ready for abolition'. They now broadly agreed with the 'Heald' proposals that there was a strong case for redefining the law, and that the government and the House must make up their minds whether the adoption of the Scottish rules on murder with diminished responsibility should be applied to weak-minded killers who were not insane.[12]

With this increased activity further correspondence was not long in coming. A. L. Goodhart disputed whether the Heald recommendations were any better than those of the Royal Commission. He agreed that the plea of provocation should be extended to cover words as well as acts but viewed this as of minimum importance since no case had hinged on this in the past ten years. Commenting on the doctrine of constructive malice where firearms were used, Goodhart pointed out that that doctrine had hardly ever been applied in cases where an offensive weapon was not used, and that a change would have little practical result: it would not, for instance, have affected the case of Bentley and Craig. However, he did approve of the recommendation concerning diminished responsibility but pointed out that someone like Christie, obviously not normal, would not be hanged whereas normal people like Ruth Ellis would be, and he doubted whether any of Heald's recommendations would do anything to allay the fears of the public that innocent people may from time to time be convicted.[13]

This letter drew two responses on the next day. The reverend Dr Leslie Weatherhead, past president of the Methodist Conference, said that if he were an MP he would vote for abolition since 'clearly capital punishment fails to turn the criminal into a useful citizen'. He would not let the murderer off easily, however, but would make him serve the community for the rest of his own life in a way that would make him penitent and a good citizen. But Sir Cyril

171

Atkinson, an ex-judge, said that hanging should not be abolished as murderers would kill to avoid capture.[14]

Heald responded to Goodhart's letter, disputing that the points he made were 'minimal'. There were instances where constructive malice played a part even when a dangerous weapon was not used, such as the man who keeps watch not knowing that his accomplice is armed. Nor did he find it strange that the abnormal Christie should be reprieved while normal murderers should hang: 'that was the whole point'.[15] But on the same page the secretary of the British Council of Churches, Kenneth Slack, hoped that Parliament would abolish or suspend the death penalty.

On the day of the debate *The Times* again entered the fray with a long editorial. The debate that evening, it said, would not turn on the government's proposals for reform but on the direct clash between movers of the resolution who want to retain capital punishment for some murders and movers of the amendment who want to make an end of it. The modern penal system was predicated on the deterrence of others from committing crimes and on reforming the criminal to prevent him from returning to lawbreaking. The defenders of capital punishment have to sacrifice the second element when they maintain that the death penalty is a unique deterrent. *The Times'* own opinion was that it was necessary that the punishment of murder by death should be retained, however widely murder was interpreted, and that some executions should be continued to be carried out when the facts of the case justified it.[16] However, the National Council for Civil Liberties stated that it had record support for abolition. Errors in the administration of justice manifestly did occur, and there was general doubt in regard to the outcome of the Evans and Christie cases.[17]

The debate

On the afternoon of February 16, after debating the extermination of rabbits, the distribution of vegetables, health surveys in the potteries and Farne Island seals, at 3.47 p.m. the House of Commons finally got round to debating the death penalty.[18]

The debate was opened by the home secretary, Gwilym Lloyd George. The government, he said, were asking the House to consider the straight issue of retention or abolition, and that they had themselves reached the conclusion that capital punishment should be retained. In outlining the arguments for and against, he said that the most important argument in favour of the abolition of capital punishment was that there was no clear proof that capital punishment was an effective deterrent. Evidence from other countries had been cited but he pointed out that the Royal Commission had emphasised that differences in law, custom and statistical methods made strict comparison between one country and another impossible. We should not assume, therefore, that what holds good in one country would hold good in Britain.

The commission had not said that capital punishment was a uniquely effective deterrent but that the figures provided no reliable evidence one way or another. He suggested three reasons for the lack of reliable statistical evidence. First, few countries kept records of the number of crimes known to the police as

172

distinct from the number of convictions. Second, in a number of countries capital punishment fell into disuse some time before it was formally abolished. The third reason, he said, quoting the commission report, was that it was impossible to be sure that variation in homicide statistics before and after abolition were due to abolition or that 'if the figures remain[ed] constant, abolition did not have some effect which was cancelled out by some other cause'. It is difficult to believe that Sir Ernest Gowers, of Plain English fame, could have been party to such an obscure sentence.

Lloyd George then began to split hairs, possibly in case any members present believed that the Royal Commission leaned towards abolition. He pointed out that when the Royal Commission said 'there is no clear evidence that the abolition of capital punishment had led to an increase in the homicide rate   ' they did not mean there had been no increase, but that there was no clear evidence that there had been. He did not add that, equally, there was no clear evidence that there was an increase, or that in the whole of Europe no country had reinstated capital punishment.

He then turned to the argument that there was a risk of an innocent man being hanged. Showing how unlikely this was he said that before an innocent man could be hanged the same mistake would have to be made by the police, the judge, the Court of Criminal Appeal and the home secretary. He did not believe that an innocent man had been hanged in this country. If there was a scintilla of doubt the home secretary would recommend a reprieve.

Passing to more general considerations he said that the first function of capital punishment was to give society's emphatic expression of its abhorrence of murder: the reservation of the gravest punishment for the gravest crime. He then quoted a most odd statement from the Royal Commission report: 'The fact that men are hung for murder is one great reason why murder is considered so dreadful a crime', a comment as silly as it is (astonishingly) ungrammatical. The opinion of the police and prison service was that it was the death penalty which was the main reason why lethal violence was not more prevalent and why criminals did not carry firearms. The professional criminal was prepared to accept imprisonment as an occupational risk, but not hanging. Inevitably, the home secretary continued with the argument that if imprisonment were the penalty for both burglary and murder there would be nothing to stop a burglar from shooting the only witness to his crime. The murder rate in Great Britain was as low as any in Europe but it could not be assumed that this would continue if the one effective deterrent were removed. However, not everything was satisfactory: the number of murders had risen by about a third above the pre-war figure; crimes of violence and serious sexual offences against women had trebled.

Turning from abolition to the recommendations of the Royal Commission the home secretary was dismissive. Alteration of the statutory age limit for executions, giving discretion to the jury, the alteration of the M'Naghten Rules: 'the government remain of the opinion that all these proposals are unacceptable to them'. The government were in greater sympathy with some of the more minor recommendations. It was agreed that the law on constructive malice was

173

unsatisfactory and that the law on provocation should be amended. It was also accepted that the survivor of a suicide pact who did not actually kill the other member of the pact should be guilty only of manslaughter.

Sir Lynn Ungoed-Thomas interrupted to point out that none of those proposals would have had any effect on the cases of Evans, Bentley or Ellis, but as the home secretary believed that these three people had been rightly hanged Sir Lynn's intervention left him unmoved.

After Lloyd George sat down Chuter Ede formally introduced his amendment. Sir Lionel Heald still thought that Evans was guilty of murder. Both Christie and Evans were implicated and the only injustice was that Christie was not hanged earlier. The Labour member for Glasgow, Govan, William Reid, told how shocked he was when informed by a prison governor that the body must hang for an hour before being examined by a doctor, and the reason was that death was not always instantaneous but would always take place within an hour, if not by a broken neck, by strangling. James Stuart, secretary of state for Scotland, replied that this practice was abolished in 1954 (only two years earlier) and the examination was carried out within a few minutes.

Mr Rogers took the home secretary to task for his dogmatism that Evans was guilty. 'Mark these words, Mr Speaker: I will make the home secretary eat those words before I am much older . . . I will demonstrate that Evans was innocent and the judges were wrong'. Later in his speech Rogers revealed that he himself had taken Ruth Ellis' young son into his home 'to try to save him form the horror of the day of execution'.

Sydney Silverman wound up for the amendment. He admitted it was not possible to advance anything very new. The unsatisfactoriness of the present law was unanimously accepted and nobody liked the death penalty any more than anyone likes murder. It was an attractive proposition to come to a compromise between the retentionists and the abolitionists and retain the death penalty for some capital crimes and abolish it for the others. He recalled how Lord Simian had said during the Lords debate in 1948, that people might accept the abolition of the death penalty for some murders but went on to define five categories of murder for which he said the public would never tolerate the abolition of the death penalty. Lord Simian, a great lawyer, had told them that an attempt at compromise would not work. He quoted the Royal Commission report which had said that a compromise was 'chimerical and that it must be abandoned'.

Silverman concluded his speech by reminding the House that every jury was told not to convict if they had a reasonable doubt of guilt. Those who supported the amendment were entitled to ask the House not to retain the death penalty if they had a reasonable doubt about its effectiveness. There must be remaining in their minds the fear that from time to time an innocent man would be taken out of his cell and have his neck broken. He was assured in 1948 by Sir John Anderson (later Lord Waverley) and Sir David Maxwell Fyfe (later Lord Kilmuir) that this could not happen, yet within two years Evans was hanged. There was a free vote on the amendment, he reminded the House (though not on the substantive motion), and ended, '. . . let us as free men, free women, free

174

members of Parliament in a free society, go forward and wipe this dark stain from our statute book forever.'

In his first speech as Leader of the House R. A. Butler wound up by putting the view of the government. Worried that members may 'base their judgment on the question whether innocent people are in fact being hanged' he stated 'quite frankly and firmly . . . no innocent man has been hanged within living memory'. In particular, they 'did not accept that there was a miscarriage of justice either in the case of Evans or in the case of Rowland.' He ended by warning the House that it would be unwise without waiting for the government amendments to the law to abolish the death penalty.

When the House divided that the proposed words (i.e. the amendment) be left out there were 262 in favour and 293 against, a majority of 31. It was then resolved 'That this House believes that the death penalty for murder no longer accords with the needs or true interests of a civilised society, and calls upon Her Majesty's government to introduce forthwith legislation for its abolition or for its suspension for an experimental period'. When Chuter Ede asked the government to take steps to implement the decision of the House, Sir Anthony Eden said they would give it full weight.

The government's dilemma

The Times[19] called the result a great victory for the abolitionists and pointed out that in view of the heavy programme that confronted Parliament the passage of legislation to abolish the death penalty for murder might not be possible for some time. They also anticipated the same conflict with the Lords as had happened in 1948. In an analysis of the voting it was revealed that 36 government supporters went into the lobby with the abolitionists, 253 Labour members of Parliament voted for the amendment and seven voted with the government, whilst 257 Conservatives voted for the retention of the death penalty. There were 41 members of Parliament who abstained or were absent and a majority of these were Conservatives. However, the next day an amended figure showed that 48 Conservatives voted for the amendment among whom were 17 new members.

A rather sour letter from Sir Thomas Moore MP offered up the opinion that the will of Parliament is not always the will of the people. Sometimes Parliament was misled and misguided as to what people really felt. He thought that the capital punishment debate was a classic example of this.[20] A few days later came a response from one of the new members of Parliament, Anthony Kershaw, who said that he was well aware that voting against the death penalty was against the wish of the people and having spent the past weekend among them he was certain of this. But he also believed that he was elected to exercise his judgment and that he had done to the best of his ability.[21]

The government were now faced with having to implement a motion of Parliament into legislation that they totally disagreed with. There were suggestions that they might seek a way out of that dilemma by providing facilities in the Commons to consider Silverman's Death Penalty (Abolition) Bill which provided for suspension of capital punishment for ten years.[22] This was an astute forecast but not even *The Times* could foresee what skulduggery and trickery the government would employ in order to retain the death penalty. The Commons vote aroused keen interest as far away as New Zealand. The death penalty had been abolished there in 1941 and reinstated in 1950 due to the high murder rate in the preceding three years.[23]

The accuracy of *The Times'* forecast was not long in being proved. A week after the debate Eden announced that the government would find time for Silverman's Bill and that this would be on a free vote. Hugh Gaitskell asked why they could not just act on the vote on the amendment but Eden was not to be drawn. Silverman pointed out that in 1948 the Labour government were faced with an identical situation and had adopted the remaining stages of the Bill as a government measure. Lloyd George said it would be unconstitutional if he and the secretary of state for Scotland were to abrogate capital punishment by administrative action in anticipation of the law changing. In the meantime, each case for reprieve would be decided on its merits. In answer to a rather trivial question from Montgomery Hyde, the home secretary said there were eight executioners on the list; they could get up to 15 guineas (£15.75) per execution plus travel and lodgings, and assistants earned five guineas.[24]

Abolitionists felt that the government were guilty of something like sharp practice. They had the impression that the prime minister and Butler had committed the government to accept, and themselves to act on, the decision of the House and the government were in a dilemma: they could not produce a Bill they felt would be against the public interest; only three cabinet ministers who sat in the Commons were in favour of the Bill.[25] Meanwhile, Albert Pierrepoint, the chief hangman since 1946, asked the prison commissioners to remove his name from the list of hangmen.[26]

The prevailing uncertainty began to appear. In sentencing a convicted murderer, Jan Moczygemwa, to death, Mr Justice Greenfield pointed out to him, almost by way of an apology, that until there was a change in the law he had no choice but to pass the sentence he had.[27] Two relevant books were published at this time. Sir Ernest Gowers, who had become a convert to the abolitionist cause since chairing the Royal Commission, had published *A Life for a Life?* and Gerald Gardiner's *Capital Punishment as a Deterrent,* though lacking Gowers' literary skill according to *The Times* reviewer, skilfully attacked capital punishment as a unique and necessary deterrent.[28] In the House there was criticism of the government for finding time for a private member's Bill on abolition rather than sponsoring a Bill themselves. A motion was tabled by three Labour members of Parliament calling on the government to implement the will of the House.[29]

An article by Arthur Koestler in *The Observer*[30] caused a flutter of excitement in the House of Lords. Entitled 'The Alternative to Hanging', Koestler quoted instructions to prison governors dated 10 January 1925 which said 'Any reference to the manner in which an execution has been carried out should be confined to as few words as possible, e.g. it was carried out expeditiously and without a hitch'. The truth, said Koestler, was that some prisoners struggle, both in the condemned cell and under the noose and some

176

had to be carried tied to a chair or dragged to the trap with their arms pinioned behind them, limp and deprived of bowel control. By recalling the execution of Edith Thompson and the suicide of Ellis, her executioner, a short time afterwards, the prison chaplain, Glanville Murray, said that when they were all gathered together there it seemed impossible to believe what they were there to do. This article was raised in the Lords by Viscount Waverley and answered by Lord Mancroft, under-secretary to the Home Office, who disputed what Koestler had said. Viscount Hailsham said that the matter should be referred to the Press Council.[31] The subject was defused, however, by an apology in the following week's *Observer* by Koestler, who said that he was not in possession of the full instructions to prison governors in regard to executions nor was he aware that the allegations about Thompson's execution were without foundation. This statement was accepted by the government.[32]

This was merely a distraction to Silverman's Bill which was coming up in the next week. There was strong pressure from the constituencies on the 48 members of the government side who voted for abolition as the outcome would largely depend on them[33] and already a number of government supporters led by Sir Robert Villiers Grimston, chairman of the Conservative Home Affairs Committee, had tabled an amendment that Silverman's Bill be postponed for six months.

The second reading of the Abolition Bill was proposed by Silverman and opposed by Grimston. Lloyd George said that there was no record of any failure or mishap with an execution to date and the fact that it was a deterrent was only common sense. 'How could anybody', he asked, 'think that hanging could not be a deterrent?' Mr Logan, a Labour member, said that the Bill was the most fallacious and damnable thing affecting the liberty of the people ever to be brought to the House of Commons. It gave a licence to kill without a penalty and should not be allowed. Notwithstanding this outburst from a member of Silverman's own party, the vote was 286 to 262 in favour, a majority of 24, and the Bill was read for a second time.[34]

Government manoeuvres

Government supporters were shaken by the result of the second reading debate and their only hope of wrecking the Bill before it got to the Lords was to weaken it in committee. Various amendments were tabled. One was to retain the death penalty for the murder of serving or retired members of the police force, prison service or state security organizations; for the murder of serving or retired judges or judicial officers and for prisoners convicted of a second murder. Another amendment was that the substitute sentence should be prison for the lifetime of the prisoner. Other amendments were to retain capital punishment for a murderer who commits murder in the furtherance of a felony or whilst escaping, or who was armed or who was in concert with another person who was armed, or for a person convicted of premeditated murder.[35] Further amendments sought to delay the abolition of hanging until 1961, Sir Thomas Moore proposed that the Bill should commence in June 1960 and others proposed that hanging should be retained where the murder was by the administration of poison or something similarly destructive.[36] When Silverman asked what progress was being made with the Bill, Butler replied that it would be treated like any other outstanding piece of legislation.[37]

Edith Thompson may have been dead for some 30 years but she certainly was not forgotten and she attracted more attention than she ever would have had had she still been alive. Reg Paget asked the home secretary whether he would issue new instructions to prison governors with regard to executions, and whether he would publish the information in his possession concerning the execution of Mrs Thompson. Lloyd George, in a written answer, said that before the execution the governor of Holloway prison, who was also the medical officer, gave Mrs Thompson sedatives. At the time for the execution the governor considered it would be more humane to spare her the necessity to walk the few yards to the execution chamber so he had her carried there and she was supported on the scaffold. There was no truth in the allegation that she had 'disintegrated as a human creature' or that she had 'fought, kicked and screamed and protested her innocence to the last, and that it required about five men to hold her down whilst being carried to the gallows . . .' or in the story that 'her insides fell out'. Nothing occurred that called for any change in the instructions to governors. The instructions were confidential and like his predecessors he refused to publish them.[38]

This answer was not very convincing. It would be stretching humanity to its limit to spare someone who was going to be killed in a few seconds the necessity of walking five or six steps by having her carried. The quotes that the home secretary said were without foundation must have arisen from somewhere. A couple of days later Sir Robert Boothby (Conservative) and Fenner Brockway (Labour) both asked for the full facts surrounding Mrs Thompson's execution as well as the full instructions to governors. When Lloyd George had nothing to add to his written answer Boothby pointed out that the answer he gave was markedly different to answers that his department had previously given to both Houses of Parliament. He was told that he, Lloyd George, could not be responsible for what his predecessors had said and that most of the statements came from people outside. When Brockway said that in view of the admission that Mrs Thompson had to be carried to the scaffold a full inquiry would assure the public that all the facts have been revealed, Lloyd George assured him that there were no facts that had not been revealed.

Responding to a comment by Kenneth Younger that the home secretary's need to amplify previous statements had engendered a deal of distrust, he rejected the accusation and blamed Koestler's article in *The Observer*. He had been attacked constantly and he would not take any responsibility for what happened in 1923. Younger replied that statements comparable to Koestler's had been made for years and that Koestler was misled as to the true instructions to governors only because the Home Office had not made them public.[39] But the home secretary was not in the mood to make them public then, and there the matter stood. But only until the following day.

When Sir Robert Boothby made the same point the home secretary made the same reply: he had nothing to add, but Boothby said that his earlier reply

178

was different from that which the Home Office had hitherto given to both Houses. Fenner Brockway went further; in view of the home secretary's reply he asked for a full inquiry so that the public should be quite sure that the facts had all been revealed.[40]

The Death Penalty (Abolition) Bill was due to be discussed in committee towards the end of April and by the middle of the month over 50 amendments had been tabled, mostly designed to weaken or wreck it. A group of Conservative members of Parliament including a number of lawyers, under the chairmanship of Captain Charles Woodhouse, were busy preparing a new batch of amendments, most of which sought to exclude certain classes of murder from the Bill. One of them was to retain the death penalty for any murder involving the use of an offensive weapon, and others to retain hanging for murders committed in the course of escaping or attempting to escape from prison, or in the course of robbery, burglary, housebreaking or rape, or by poisoning or while attempting to escape from the custody of a police or prison officer.[41] Of course, if only a few of these amendments were accepted the Bill would be wrecked.

After the first day of the committee stage of the Bill no changes had been made. There had been only two divisions, both on amendments that sought to limit the application of the Bill, and both were rejected by 20 votes.[42] During the discussion on the amendments there were contributions from Sir Thomas Moore, Reg Paget and Philip Bell, but Silverman objected to any limiting amendment. He said that Britain's good name in countries that had abolished the death penalty was being harmed by what was regarded as obstinacy in clinging to it. He realised he would not sway the invincible supporters of retention and said he was addressing himself only to the waverers. He objected to concessions or compromise. He said that there were currently eleven or 12 executions a year and asked how many would be executed if the amendments were carried. Lady Tweedsmuir said that members should vote according to their own judgment and not according to what their constituents thought—public opinion, once so popular, was now being sidelined as it moved towards abolition—as it was sometimes necessary for Parliament to lead public opinion. Captain Pilkington, the Conservative member for Poole, confirmed that public opinion was changing. An opinion poll taken in February by the *News Chronicle* showed that 45 per cent were in favour of abolition compared with only 26 per cent. in 1948.[43]

Owing to the fact that there were still over 30 amendments outstanding, a second day was set aside for the committee stage and it was extended by two hours until midnight. Retentionists were pinning their hopes on an amendment tabled by Sir Hugh Lucas-Tooth that would retain hanging for murders committed in the furtherance of various other offences.[44] When the hearings were resumed one amendment was passed, by the slender margin of four votes, that would retain hanging for a murder committed by a person already serving a sentence of life imprisonment. Silverman had attacked the amendment as an attempt to retain the solemnity of the gallows, the black cap and the paraphernalia of a barbarous anachronism to protect society against an imaginary mischief. Other amendments, to protect police officers, and for

179

retention for murders committed in the furtherance of other offences, or by the use of an offensive weapon, were all defeated.[45] In an interesting intervention during the discussion of Lucas-Tooth's amendment, Viscount Hinchingbrooke pointed out that if the amendment were passed, Miles Gifford, who had battered his mother and father over the head and then thrown them over a cliff, would not hang, whereas Craig would.[46] A group of Conservative members of Parliament tabled a novel amendment that, in addition to any other penalty imposed, male murderers should be liable to be privately whipped if they had murdered in the furtherance of robbery with violence, armed robbery, housebreaking or burglary.[47]

Despite further amendments that had been tabled in advance of the report stage, the Bill was expected to pass intact. The only amendment so far carried would be removed by the promoters on the ground that it had less merit than others that the House had rejected.[48] The promoters of the Bill believed and hoped that the Bill would become law before the summer recess. They could not believe that the Lords would reject it as they had done in 1948 as it would be a rash act to throw out a Bill passed by the Commons in two Parliaments, one with a Conservative and the other with a Labour government. But as Lord Chorley's motion had never been put to a debate the Lords' opinion had not recently been tested.[49]

Silverman's 'sleight of hand'

On the evening of June 18, the Death Penalty (Abolition) Bill was debated on a free vote. At the report stage the home secretary said that the Bill, if passed, might result in more murders being committed, and would remove the most powerful deterrent against criminals being armed. Mr Simon asked for flexibility in sentencing as an alternative to hanging as the Royal Commission had pointed out that the crime varied widely in culpability. Silverman replied that once the death penalty was abolished it would be safe to leave other questions to the discretion of the home secretary who would have the sentences under constant review. William Deedes asked that the alternative penalty should be extremely harsh.

A proviso had been inserted at the committee stage (the only one passed) that the Act 'shall not apply to any case where a murder is committed by a person already serving a sentence of imprisonment for life'. Sir Hugh Lucas-Tooth had tabled an amendment in similar terms after the committee stage was concluded, the beginning of which was a clause to remove the proviso as redundant. In a skilful manoeuvre Sydney Silverman first persuaded Lucas-Tooth to move his amendment on the grounds that it was almost a replica of the proviso. He then asked the House to agree to the first part of the amendment, which was to delete the proviso. This was carried by 162 to 139. He then asked the House to vote on the insertion of the second part of the amendment and this motion was rejected by 158 votes to 133. After these two motions Lucas-Tooth's amendment consisted of just three words: 'provided that this'. The three word amendment was now quite meaningless and after a heated discussion involving the speaker, Silverman moved to delete the three pointless words; this was agreed without a division. This skilful manipulation of the system was a tactical victory for Silverman who had thereby removed from the report stage the only real limitation on the Bill which had been inserted in committee by only four votes, namely to retain hanging for murder by people already serving life. The tactic was criticised by a Labour colleague, Turner-Samuels QC, but supported by Boothby and Elliott who upheld Silverman's right to use Parliamentary tactics to support his case.[50] That concluded the report stage and they immediately went on to the debate on the third reading.

In moving the third reading, Silverman asked the government what the attitude would be in the Lords. He pointed out that every possible examination of the Bill on a free vote of the house had now been taken. Nothing had been hasty or ill-considered. He asked that the government should take over the Bill (which was still a private member's Bill) and make itself responsible for all its future stages as a government measure.

Lloyd George responded that the attitude of the government was clear. He was still of the opinion that the death penalty was a unique deterrent and that the public should not be deprived of its protection. He also felt that abolition, resulting in long terms of imprisonment, would bring its own moral and administrative problems for home secretaries. He regretted that the House had not at least accepted amendments giving protection to police and prison officers, or to discourage criminals from carrying arms. He pointed out that men of extremely bad character would have to be released from prison, as opposed to those reprieved murderers now released after an average of nine years because their reprieve meant there were extenuating circumstances. He emphasised that Britain had the lowest homicide rate in the world, and he would recommend that the House vote against the third reading. Joan Vickers said that a majority of women members of Parliament were in favour of abolition. She herself favoured life imprisonment which she believed was a far greater deterrent than hanging. Angus Made said that there was an inevitable trend towards abolition and he was wholly in favour of it.

At the third reading, the voting was 152 to 133 in favour, a majority of 19. There were handshakes and back-slapping all round for Silverman, for his skilful handling and what many believed his ultimate victory.[51] The next day, *The Spectator* celebrated the result by reprinting an article by William Temple, Archbishop of York (and an active member of the Labour party when the article was originally published on 25 January 1936, in an era when the government would not even find time to discuss abolition). The article was entitled 'The Death Penalty' and after briefly discussing the principles of punishment the Archbishop turned his attention to the death penalty itself. With tongue in cheek, he dismissed the reformative possibilities of hanging as that could occur, he wrote, only on the hypothesis of immortality and he doubted whether murderers had a sufficiently vivid faith in a future life to accept the sentence of death as a temporary discipline. He found little evidence that the death penalty was a deterrent if only because more people were reprieved than were executed which introduced an element of uncertainty into the punishment, and it was the certainty of the result that deterred, not always the severity. There was always the risk of a mistake and subsequent discovery of a hanged man's innocence could not avail him in this life. For these reasons the death penalty should be removed from the statute book. Where the state takes life, he concluded, it undermines regard for life and therefore eventually encourages murder. Few public actions would so much demonstrate and secure an advance in the ethics and civilisation as the abolition of the death penalty.[52]

The Lords strike again

The Times[53] noted that no Bill had yet passed into law under the amended Parliament Act by which the period in which the House of Lords could hold up a measure passed by the Commons was reduced from two years to one. The Lords were to debate the Abolition Bill shortly and if they were to reject it on the second reading the promoters could bring it forward again in the Commons in the next session of Parliament. If it were then rejected a second time by the Lords, provided a year had passed the Bill would still receive Royal Assent. Two days had been allocated and although more than 40 peers had expressed a wish to take part in the debate it was decided that extra time would be allowed on the second day if necessary, but that there would be no third day.[54] A day later the number wishing to speak had risen to 56 and *The Times* forecast rejection at the second reading.[55]

Whatever *The Times* thought, *The Spectator* came out strongly in favour of the Bill in an editorial in anticipation of the Lords' debate. They believed that the criminal population of the country had not been encouraged by Silverman's Bill, nor had the murder rate gone up. In fact, the number of murders between the second and third readings was 55, lower than in any year since 1953. Whereas the choice in 1948 had been between a little hanging and quite a lot of hanging, the choice then was between a little hanging and no hanging at all. The proper course for the Lords, they advised, would be to acquiesce in the decision of the Commons however much they might dislike it. Retentionists would be hard put to find good constructive grounds for throwing out the Bill.[56]

By now over 60 peers were to take part in the House of Lords debate, including both Archbishops and the bishops of Chichester and Exeter. The debate would be on a free vote.[57] It had been suggested that the Lords would be justified in rejecting the Bill on the grounds that only 289 members voted in the Commons. In a letter[58] Silverman rejected that suggestion and pointed out that on other occasions 559, 542 and 474 members voted. There had been a good deal of pairing at the third reading and compared with votes on other major issues there was a higher percentage poll than what was usually accepted as normal.

The Lords' debate[59] was opened by Lord Templewood by saying that the existing law of murder was 'evasive and sophistical'. Two methods of mitigating it were often used: the Royal prerogative and the use of the M'Naghten Rules. Both were unsatisfactory. It had not been shown that capital punishment was not an effective deterrent against murder. But an execution is a horrible and repulsive act that could be justified only if it could be shown to be essential to the security of the state. There was always the chance of an irrevocable mistake. When he was home secretary (as Sir Samuel Hoare) he had had 47 death sentences to deal with. He advised a reprieve for 24, four were insane and 19 were executed. He admitted he did not know if he had made any mistakes.

The Lord Chancellor (Lord Kilmuir, who as Sir David Maxwell Fyfe had been the home secretary before Lloyd George) said that the government was unequivocally of the view that capital punishment must be retained. At the crux of the question was whether capital punishment was a uniquely effective deterrent greater than life imprisonment. Statistics were unreliable, he said, with logic-chopping audacity, because it was the murders that had not been committed that mattered. He maintained his belief that within living memory no mistaken execution had been carried out.

The debate was the occasion for two maiden speeches. Viscount Malvern was satisfied that capital punishment was a deterrent. In a curious and astonishingly irrelevant argument he feared that if the Bill for total abolition was passed into law it could be imposed on one of those territories overseas which were not ripe for total abolition. But it was his maiden speech—and he need not have concerned himself; many of the territories he no doubt had in mind, now independent, to this day execute enthusiastically and with a vengeance.

The Archbishop of York, Michael Ramsey, used his own maiden speech to support the Bill but Viscount Hailsham was convinced by the Lord Chancellor's argument. He said that if the Bill became law they would have the government against them, the judiciary against them, the police, the prison officers and the public all against them. Lord Oaksey, a former trial judge, was not convinced that the death penalty was not a deterrent. He wanted no changes in the law as he felt its flexibility was a great virtue, which was surprising given that the punishment for murder was the one inflexible penalty.

The Bishop of Exeter announced that he had changed his mind and would vote for the Bill. If the death penalty was supposed to be a mark of detestation of murder it defeated itself. It cheapened human life and detracted from its sanctity. Lord Russell of Liverpool was also in favour of the Bill. He did not believe that hanging was a unique deterrent but did believe that mistakes could be made. When the debate was resumed on the second day The Bishop of Chichester declared himself in favour of the Bill but the Archbishop of Canterbury, Geoffrey Fisher, he who had told the Royal Commission that too many condemned men were reprieved, was in a dilemma. He was neither in favour of total abolition nor in favour of the current system. He would vote for the Bill but hoped it would be given a second reading and then amended in the Lords. He said, and presumably believed, that by bringing the House to agreement it would be an act expressing the general will of the community for the defence of society, as well as a solemn vindication of the laws of God.

Viscount Samuel found himself in an even worse situation and admitted he was in a dilemma. He could not accept the advice of the Lord Chancellor which was to throw out the Bill without replacing it with an alternative policy. He could not accept the view of Lord Templewood which was to pass it with a view to its becoming law as it stood. Nor could he accept the view that the Bill should be passed and amended. Poor Lord Samuel, he was in a double dilemma and did the only thing possible: he abstained. At the division the voting was 95 votes for the Bill and 238 against, a majority of 143. The Lords had done it again.

ENDNOTES

1   *The Times*, p. 5, 19 January 1956
2   ibid, p. 9
3   ibid, p. 10, 23 January 1956
4   *Hansard*, [548] 372 (27 January 1956)
5   ibid, [548] 1083 (2 February 1956)
6   ibid, [548] 1814 (9 February 1956)
7   *The Times*, p. 4, 2 February 1956
8   ibid, p. 4, 11 February 1956
9   *Justice of the Peace*, p. 83, 11 February 1956
10 *The Times*, p. 3, 13 February 1956
11 ibid, p. 8
12 ibid, p. 9
13 ibid, p. 9
14 ibid, p. 5, 14 February 1956
15 ibid, p. 9, 15 February 1956
16 ibid, p. 9, 16 February 1956
17 ibid, p. 13
18 *Hansard*, [548] 2536 (16 February 1956); *The Times*, p. 4, 17 February 1956
19 *The Times*, p. 8, 17 February 1956
20 ibid, p. 7
21 ibid, p. 9, 21 February 1956
22 ibid, p. 8, 23 February 1956
23 ibid, p. 7
24 ibid, p. 5, 24 February 1956
25 ibid, p. 8
26 ibid, p. 3, 27 February 1956
27 ibid, p. 8, 1 March 1956
28 ibid, p. 11
29 ibid, p. 5, 2 March 1956
30 *The Observer*, p. 2, 4 March 1956
31 *The Times*, p. 4, 9 March 1956
32 ibid, p. 4, 14 March 1956
33 ibid, p. 6, 8 March 1956
34 ibid, pp. 4/5, 13 March 1956
35 ibid, p. 10, 14 March 1956
36 ibid, p. 6, 15 March 1956

37 *The Times*, p. 5
38 *Hansard,* [550] 189 (27 March 1956)
39 ibid, [550] 2344 (29 March 1956)
40 *The Times,* p. 3, 31 March 1956
41 ibid, p. 5, 19 April 1956
42 ibid, p. 4, 26 April 1956
43 ibid, p. 14
44 ibid, p. 13, 11 May 1956
45 ibid, p. 10, 17 May 1956
46 ibid, p. 4
47 ibid, p. 5, 18 May 1956
48 ibid, p. 10, 28 May 1956
49 ibid, p. 6, 16 May 1956
50 ibid, p. 8, 29 June 1956
51 ibid, p. 3
52 *The Spectator,* 29 June 1956
53 *The Times,* p. 10, 3 July 1956
54 ibid, p. 10, 5 July 1956
55 ibid, p. 5, 6 July 1956
56 *The Spectator,* p. 4, 6 July 1956
57 *The Times,* p. 4, 7 July 1956
58 ibid, p. 7
59 ibid, p. 6, 10 July 1956.

The Homicide Act 1957

Following the defeat of the Bill in the Lords *The Times* considered that an interesting constitutional issue had been raised but in the view of Sydney Silverman there was no question of a constitutional crisis.

Silverman defends the Lords

Silverman agreed that the Lords had a perfect right to reject the Bill, but thought that a serious constitutional crisis *would* arise if the government were to be induced by the decision of the Lords to fail to give effect to the decision of the Commons.[1] Commenting on the Lords' vote in the following week *The Spectator* was impressed by the size of the abolition vote which was about double what might have been expected. Furthermore, the 'quality' of the abolitionist vote was good whereas that of the 'retentionist army' was largely composed of 'hitherto unknown rustics, who thought, perhaps, that abolition was in some way connected to blood sports'. *The Spectator* continued that it was humiliating for the government that its penal policy was being run by Silverman and it was difficult to see what could be done about it. The editorial concluded, 'nobody has been executed since last August. Hanging cannot be turned on and off like a tap, and it would be ridiculous if it were to be restored only to be stopped again when the Sydney Silverman Bill is brought up for the second time in the House of Commons. It would also be shocking. Until the House of Commons reverses itself, an execution is unthinkable'.[2]

On the day following *The Spectator's* editorial, the *New Statesman* printed a main leader headed 'Government from the Backwoods'. It predicted that although the House of Lords might have delayed the abolition of hanging it had hastened its own abolition. The heredity peers were united in their determination to use their medieval powers to maintain a medieval institution. The government were faced with two clear alternatives. The first was to permit Sydney Silverman to reintroduce his Bill and to give it all facilities and allow a free vote. In the meantime, all executions should be suspended. But the *New Statesman* doubted whether the government had the political courage to take that course. The second alternative would be to introduce government legislation to amend the law of murder but still retain hanging in certain cases, but the technical difficulties of drawing up such a Bill had already proved overwhelming. From the dilemma that faced the government it was evident that the time had come to abolish the legislative powers of the House of Lords.[3]

It was announced[4] that Sydney Silverman would ask the prime minister if he would make a statement about government policy in respect of the Death Penalty (Abolition) Bill following the vote in the House of Lords. A Labour MP, Stephen Swingler, asked if the prime minister would bring in legislation to abolish the Lords. On the morning of the day that these questions were to be asked, a letter from Silverman confirmed his view that the Lords were as entitled under the constitution to reject his Bill as the Commons were to pass it. They had voted according to their individual consciences and were probably right to prefer the merits of the Bill in principle to any nice calculation of consequences. He emphasised the difference between the law of murder and the penalty for murder. Whereas there was no constitutional crisis about the Lords' rejection, if the government were to reject the decision of the Commons in deference to the opinion of the Lords, that would create the gravest constitutional crisis for many years.[5] The prime minister told the Commons that the government were giving consideration to the whole question of capital punishment in the light of the Lords' rejection. He would make a statement before the end of the session, but there was no constitutional conflict between the two Houses.[6]

An editorial in *The Times* said that the government should attempt to bring the Houses together on the subject of hanging by producing a solution of their own. The threat of execution should continue to hang over the heads of all potential murderers capable of being deterred, but that requirement had to be reconciled with the reduction of hangings to the least frequency consistent with effective deterrence, and that death sentences not likely to be carried out should not be pronounced. There was a mass of information on the topic and there was a need to draft a Bill so that it combined constructive amendments with the collective wisdom of Parliament.[7]

Before the parliamentary session ended the Lords were defended, first by Viscount Astor, a leading abolitionist, who, despite the Lords' vote, thought that the level of discussion had been better than in the Commons[8] and once again by Sydney Silverman, who said that the Lords had a perfect right to pour through the 'No' lobby, but that the House of Commons had an equally perfect right to make its will prevail. No useful purpose would be achieved, he concluded, in attacking the House of Lords for exercising its constitutional rights.[9]

The government stonewalls

During the long recess both the abolitionists and the retentionists were silent. The Conservative party conference of 1956 was held in Llandudno and during the debate on the death penalty, retentionists were loudly cheered whereas the few in favour of abolition were jeered and drowned out. There were some 33 resolutions expressing opposition to the abolition of the death penalty or amending the law of murder. The motion actually debated stated 'that this conference emphatically opposes the terms of the Death Penalty (Abolition) Bill and urges that the law of murder be amended so as to limit the imposition of the death penalty'. The motion was carried by an overwhelming majority and was similarly carried at an overflow meeting in a nearby cinema. One supporter of the resolution expressed his disgust with those Conservative MPs who supported the Bill. 'Thank God for the House of Lords' he cried, to loud cheers. A speaker who opposed the motion was silenced by slow handclapping.[10]

Less than a week later the prime minister was presented with the names of 2,500 people, leaders of the professions, social services and trades unions who called upon the government to legislate for the abolition of capital punishment.

The names were drawn up on a petition by the National Campaign for the Abolition of Capital Punishment and people signed in their personal capacity. No attempt was made to get as many people as possible on to the list. Included among the names were Christmas Humphreys, senior counsel to the Crown at the Central Criminal Court and Lord Merthyr, chairman of the Magistrates' Association. Among 160 authors were C. Day Lewis, E. M. Forster, J. B. Priestley, Edith and Osbert Sitwell and Rebecca West. Twelve Bishops were among 351 Church signatories. From the arts were Sir Arthur Bliss, Benjamin Britten, Jacob Epstein and Peter Pears. The editors of the *Observer, Manchester Guardian, News Chronicle, Daily Herald* and *Reynolds News* all signed as did the editors of many provincial newspapers. Representatives from stage and film included Alec Guiness, Bernard Miles, Flora Robson, Moira Shearer, Alistair Sim, Sybil Thorndyke and Emlyn Williams.[11]

In reply to a question by Sydney Silverman concerning the government's policy on the progress of the Death Penalty (Abolition) Bill, Eden said that the government were preparing legislative proposals in the form of a new Bill in relation to capital punishment which would be laid before the House early in the next session. Silverman replied that the government were acting contrary to their own pledge and to constitutional propriety by basing their policy not on the judgment of the Commons but on that of the Lords. Eden said that the government were dealing with an appeal made in the Lords that the government should try to find a measure that would meet common agreement. Concluding this exchange, Sydney Silverman pointed out that the government had pledged that they would base their policy on the Commons decision taken on the second reading of his Bill, whereas the compromise proposal made in the Lords was precisely that which the Commons had decisively rejected twice.[12]

When Eden announced that he had read the memorial containing 2,500 signatures and had made clear the government's intentions, Sydney Silverman replied that it was the first occasion since the days of Charles I that a group of distinguished citizens had found it necessary to call on the government to govern its policy in accordance with the majority view of the House of Commons.[13]

Silverman had a great deal of support outside the House of Commons, and much of that support was in the form of forthright criticism of the government. In an article in *The Spectator*[14] Lord Templewood denounced government plans to bring in a Bill of their own which he believed was intended to torpedo a Bill that already held a constitutional place under the Parliament Acts. The government could end up with two contradictory Bills before the House, each of which had presumably passed a second reading. He said he would oppose any proposals that assumed that hanging was indispensable as a deterrent against murder. An editorial comment on Templewood's article said that

By adopting its present course a government has sacrificed a principle, consistency and common sense on the altar of party expediency. But it may even now become unstuck. It has presumably calculated that on a free vote there is still an abolitionist majority in the Commons, otherwise it could have afforded to behave properly and give time to the Sydney Silverman Bill. And if this abolitionist majority manages to secure a second reading for the Sydney Silverman Bill the government can hardly execute anybody, even if it passes its own Bill into law and obstructs the later stages of the Sydney Silverman Bill. Whether or not this happens, any execution from now on will not be judicial but political killing—the result of the government bowing not to the will of the House of Commons but to the Llandudno mob. [15]

Patrick Campbell wrote in to complain about the phrase 'Llandudno mob' which he thought 'unpleasant' but the editor commented that it was the scenes during the hanging debate that were unpleasant. [16]

The *New Statesman* was at first more conciliatory, pointing out that technically the prime minister was constitutionally correct in bringing forward a new Bill to amend the law of murder. When the Lords rejected Sydney Silverman's Bill the government was not automatically compelled to set the Parliament Act in motion but could put forward a compromise and see if it was acceptable to the House, which is what it proposed to do. The *New Statesman* rather ingenuously added that the new Bill, which would amend the law of murder, would not of itself conflict with a private member's Bill along the Silverman lines which would seek to abolish the death penalty. [17] But if that was not the government's intention what was the purpose of the new Bill?

It did not take long for the scales to clear from the *New Statesman's* eyes. Two weeks later they described the provisions of the new Bill as cruelly illogical as the worst of legal systems could devise. Would murder, they asked, in the furtherance of theft, taking and driving away or poaching for rabbits be a capital offence, whilst poisoning in order to benefit from the victim's death remained non-capital? The only approach for abolitionists was to 'oppose the whole stupid Bill'. [18]

In an article in the same issue [19] entitled 'Murder and Constitution' Sydney Silverman pointed out that the government refused to bring in the Death Penalty (Abolition) Bill itself and refused facilities for anyone else to do so. Meanwhile it gave its most urgent priority in its programme to its Homicide Bill in a desperate attempt to forestall the abolitionists from embarrassing the Commons. The Homicide Bill itself, he continued, was an elaborate device to circumvent the Parliament Act. Four of its five parts were not concerned with the death penalty at all. Although Part II alone dealt with the death penalty it was in effect the Death Penalty (Abolition) Bill with certain amendments already rejected by the Commons and had no organic connection with the rest of the Bill at all. For the Parliament Act to be triggered the Death Penalty (Abolition) Bill would have to pass its third reading before the following April since 12 months had to elapse between the second reading in the first Parliamentary session and the third reading in the second. If the Homicide Bill passed all its stages before that time then the Death Penalty (Abolition) Bill itself would be murdered. It had been estimated that the Homicide Bill would prevent the execution of five or six of the approximate 12 people executed a year, so, he concluded, the whole basis of representative government in a Parliamentary democracy was at risk in order to kill a few murderers a year.

189

The government shows its hand

The Queen's Speech contained the following words: 'My ministers will bring forward proposals to amend the law on homicide and to limit the scope of capital punishment.'[20] John Hervey, seconding a motion on the Royal Address, said that the proposal of the government to amend the law on homicide and to limit the scope of capital punishment would commend itself not only to the majority in Parliament but to a great majority of people they represent.[21] But it did not commend itself to Sydney Silverman. He asked the government not to introduce any measure regarding the death penalty in anticipation of any private members' Bills. Butler replied that it was the government's intention to introduce a Homicide Bill very soon, the next day, in fact. Silverman thought this an unfair procedure but Butler did not agree.[22]

It is useful to note in passing at this point that the United Kingdom was currently embroiled in what later became known as the 'Suez Crisis'. The Suez Canal had been owned by a corporation dominated by Britain and France. On 26 July 1956 the President of Egypt, Gamal Abdul Nasser, nationalised the canal and seized the Suez Canal Company, intending to use the canal tolls to finance a new dam at Aswan. Fearing the closure of the canal to international traffic France and Britain made secret military plans to regain control of the canal. Israel allied herself with these plans and on October 29—a week before Parliament reopened—invaded Egypt and defeated the Egyptian forces. The UK and France sent in a 'peacekeeping' force but public opinion within Britain and France, plus opposition from the Soviet Union and the United Nations, resulted in withdrawal of all British, French and Israeli forces. Nasser became a hero to the Arab peoples whilst Britain, France and Israel were reviled. Sir Anthony Eden's career was fatally damaged and his health, which had been poor for the past few years, was broken. It was in this tumultuous atmosphere that the same government were ducking and weaving, and pulling out every Parliamentary stop in order to prevent an Abolition Bill from being debated.

The Homicide Bill that was published on November 7 sought to reduce the scope of capital punishment. There were to be five sorts of capital murder: murder committed: in the furtherance of theft; whilst resisting or avoiding arrest; of a police officer or prison officer; and by shooting or causing an explosion. The sentence for non-capital murders would be imprisonment for life. The first part of the Bill would abolish the doctrine of constructive malice and deal with the legal effects of provocation. Killing as part of a suicide pact would become manslaughter rather than murder.[23]

Dirty tricks

Immediately after this first reading, R. A. Butler, as Lord Privy Seal, introduced a long motion limiting the way in which members could introduce motions.[24] This was a further attempt to block the introduction of an Abolition Bill that would get in the way of the government's own Bill. Sydney Silverman wished to add at the end of Butler's motion, 'unless such notice of motion or such Bill shall be concerned with legislation having as its principle objective the abolition of the death penalty.' Silverman actually apologised to the House for bringing in what might appear to be a trivial amendment in the midst of the crisis that was raging, but Butler, unruffled as ever, said it was impossible to make an exception in his case as there were other private members' Bills waiting to be introduced. Hector Hughes said it was wrong to bulk the Abolition Bill with other possible private members' Bills, as this Bill (the Death Penalty (Abolition) Bill) had actually been passed in the House and rejected by the Lords. Butler replied that the government was about to introduce the Homicide Bill next day and this did not preclude the introduction of a private member's Bill dealing with the abolition of the death penalty on the lines of the old Bill. On the government Bill the whips would be out, but on the private member's Bill there would be a free vote.

The Bill was welcomed by the general secretary of the Prison Officers' Association. Sydney Silverman said that parts of the Bill were a useful piece of legal reform, and the secretary for the National Campaign for the Abolition of Capital Punishment said that the general effect of the Bill was to institute degrees of murder which had always been opposed. Hugh Klare, general secretary of the Howard League, thought the Bill illogical. Jack Howard MP said that he supported the Bill but could not go so far as wanting complete abolition.[25]

The Times editorial was largely neutral and pointed out that uncompromising abolitionists would have no truck with the Bill which would presumably pass. Retentionists might ask whether cold-blooded schemers would organize non-capital murders. It was pointed out that Sydney Silverman had been promised a free vote on his Bill for total abolition but no more than ordinary facilities had been given to private members. Yet if that Bill passed the Commons a second time its enactment under the Parliament Act would be automatic and that would happen unless some of Sydney Silverman's supporters changed sides and extinguished the small majority he had in the last session.[26] On the eve of the debate it was not expected that the abolitionists would oppose a second reading but would try to move amendments at the committee stage which would have the effect of removing or restricting categories of capital murder.[27]

Few people doubted that what was taking place was a skilful, lawful, desperate and shameful attempt by the government to scupper Silverman's Bill and override the will of the Commons. Few doubted that they would succeed.

The debate

The second reading of the Homicide Bill took place on 15 November 1956. In the opening speech[28] the home secretary, Lloyd George, said he believed that a majority of people in the country were not in favour of abolition. There was, nevertheless, in the minds of many people uneasiness about the scope of capital punishment and a desire that it should be in some way limited. The government had been considering for some time how to maintain safeguards of law and order and also to give effect to the wish to see the scope of capital punishment restricted. Greater use could be made of the Royal prerogative but it was thought by many that the executive should not interfere with the decisions of the courts.

191

The home secretary then went through the various clauses of the Bill.[29] Clause 1 abolished the doctrine of constructive malice; unless the murderer intended to kill or do grievous bodily harm it would not be murder. Clause 2 adopted the Scottish doctrine of diminished responsibility. If the accused had shown that he was suffering from an abnormality of mind at the time that the killing took place so that his responsibility was substantially diminished he would be entitled to a verdict of manslaughter. The M'Naghten Rules would still apply but would lead to a verdict of guilty but insane. Clause 3 dealt with provocation; where there was evidence that the accused was provoked to lose his or her self-control the jury could consider whether the provocation was sufficient to justify a verdict of manslaughter, even if the provocation was by words alone. Clause 4 relegated suicide pacts from murder to manslaughter.

So far, there was little that many people would disagree with. Then came the controversial clause 5. This clause created five classes of capital murder (outlined above). Clause 5(2) provided that if two or more people were found guilty of murder within one of these classes, only the one who actually killed would be guilty of capital murder. Clause 6 retained capital punishment for people convicted of two or more murders on different occasions. There were also other clauses dealing with courts martial, simplifying the wording of the death sentence and abolishing the notice at the prison gate.

Lloyd George said that the effect of the proposals would substantially reduce both the number of people who would be convicted of murder and the number of those convicted who would be sentenced to death, and in consequence, the total number of executions.

During a lengthy two day debate Anthony Greenwood said he hoped to see the verdict of guilty but insane abolished as it was a legacy from Queen Victoria's days.[30] He said that the Labour party would support the second reading but would leave clauses 5, 6 and 7 during the committee and report stages to a free vote for members on that side of the House.[31] Bob Mellish pointed out that for 16 months there had been no capital punishment and as far as he could judge no public harm had resulted. Lloyd George replied that because there were no executions it did not mean there was no capital punishment: the punishment was not executed. On the second day Sydney Silverman attacked the Bill as an elaborate device to circumvent the Parliament Act. He pointed to the various illogicalities in the Bill and said that if Ruth Ellis had used a hatpin instead of a revolver she would not be able to be hanged under the new Bill. Sir Lionel Heald wondered why poisoning was excluded from the list of capital murders and Mr Treeth thought that murder in the course of rape should be a capital offence. The second reading was passed without a division.[32]

The day after the debate a note in *The Spectator's* 'Notebook'[33] savaged the new Homicide Bill. Whereas Lloyd George had recently said (referring to the Royal Commission recommendations) that it would not be useful to distinguish between differing degrees of murder, that is precisely what the government was doing. Lord Salisbury had said that the chief objection to the Sydney Silverman Bill was that the British people had not been consulted; consultation had still not taken place. R. A. Butler had said earlier that imprisonment was infinitely more cruel than capital punishment; the Bill ensured that many of the worst murderers would be imprisoned and the less bad hanged.

In advance of the committee stage, 12 Conservative MPs, headed by Sir Lionel Heald, tabled a proposed amendment to the Homicide Bill to incorporate poisoning as a capital offence.[34] For the other side, it was announced that a Death Penalty (Abolition) Bill would be introduced into the Commons by Alice Bacon who was one of three Labour MPs who drew places in the private members' ballot.[35] Her Bill to abolish or suspend the execution of the death sentence on the conviction of murder and to substitute an alternative penalty therefore, was supported by Bevan, Ede, Soskice, Silverman, Baxter, Paton and others[36] and was published one week later.[37]

When the Homicide Bill was considered in committee[38] all attempts at varying the Bill were lost. The committee sat again on the next day[39] and again all attempts at variation defeated. The committee next sat on December 4[40] and again on four further occasions in January. Sydney Silverman and the abolitionists lost every division to alter the Bill and it was finally reported without amendments to be read a third time.

An insight into the curious thinking of the government was to be had when an amendment by Sir Lancelot Joynson-Hicks supported by Mr Treeth, that murder in the course of committing rape should be made capital, was tabled. The home secretary said that rape was an offence of sudden impulse. There was no premeditation and any deterrent effect of capital punishment was unlikely to operate. Murdering rapists were not infrequently abnormal and on them deterrence would be likely to have even less effect. As the result of this incredible response the amendment was withdrawn.[41]

Britain, by force of international pressure, had been forced to climb down over Suez. Eden's political career was in ruins and his position as prime minister, after such a long apprenticeship—he entered Parliament in 1923 and had been foreign secretary three times—seemed to be untenable. His health, latterly poor, worsened and he took a holiday in the Caribbean to recuperate. His health improved but not his political standing and on 9 January 1957 he did the honourable thing (which senior public figures did in those days when they made serious mistakes) and resigned. Harold Macmillan became prime minister and on January 13 shuffled Eden's cabinet slightly. His main change was to sack Lloyd George as home secretary; he was dispatched to the Lords as Viscount Tenby, and Butler, already Lord Privy Seal and Leader of the House, became home secretary too.

Sir Lionel Heald, the former attorney-general, was determined to persuade the government to retain poisoning as a capital offence[42] and at the end of January he introduced in committee his amendment on clause five to that effect, with the exception that mercy killings carried out by the use of poison should be omitted. This amendment was rejected by a decisive 346 votes to 2. Sydney Silverman did better; his amendment to remove the death penalty for murder whilst resisting arrest was rejected by 187 votes to 139.[43]

Further sleight of hand

At the beginning of February 1957 it became clear that there would be no time for Alice Bacon's private member's Bill to abolish hanging for murder to be debated on second reading, which was, of course, what the government had engineered. As a consequence, Sydney Silverman and other abolitionists tabled a reasoned amendment for the rejection of the government's Homicide Bill which was due to come up for reading in the following week. This was a last attempt by the abolitionists to rally the support of the Conservative backbenchers who voted with them on Sydney Silverman's Bill in the previous session. But the amendment was expected to be defeated.[44]

A remarkably long debate which took place on the Advertisements (Hire Purchase) Bill left no time for Alice Bacon's Bill. She said with considerable justification that it was a deliberate attempt to stop her Bill from going on. When it was called objection was taken and the second reading deferred for a week.[45]

The third reading of the Homicide Bill took place on February 6[46] and the debate was opened by Butler with his first speech as home secretary. His long oration, which covered the usual ground—there really was nothing new to say on the subject—opened with a fulsome tribute to Sydney Silverman for his sincerity and tenacity. Silverman did not return the compliment; he said, '[T]his House, while welcoming the removal of certain anomalies from the law of murder and the abolition of capital punishment for certain offences, cannot assent to a Bill which is an affront to constitutional propriety, fails to satisfy the public sense of justice and is in defiance of the principle which this House has already approved, namely, that the death penalty for murder no longer accords with the needs or the true interests of a civilized society'. Silverman was extremely annoyed that the government had by-passed his Bill which had got through the Commons, and replaced it with a watered-down substitute. In a speech lasting 50 minutes he attacked and dissected the Bill and his amendment was seconded by Alice Bacon.

Miss Bacon pointed out that since 1955 no executions had taken place and that there were nevertheless fewer murders rather than more. Fenner Brockway, who had been within prisons on four occasions when men were executed, gave a moving account of the effect on the prisoners and the prison staff. He described how a chief warder broke down and cried in his presence because the next day he had to accompany to the scaffold a man whom he had got to know extremely well in the preceding three weeks.[47]

The debate on the third reading became a debate on Silverman's amendment and lasted for almost six hours, but little was said that was new. In the end the House divided on the amendment which was lost by 270 votes to 131 and the Bill was read a third time and passed. Commenting on clause 2 which related to mental abnormality, Butler said, rather fatuously, that it was all part of a new approach to problems of the mind which he hoped would exercise the Home Office in the months and years to come. He added that reprieves would continued to be made on merit, but Sydney Silverman alleged that Conservative members had been assured that the execution that took place in

August 1955 would be the last.[48] This was denied. It was made clear on behalf of the government that no such assurance had been made.[49]

The Bill was debated in the Lords two weeks later. After the Archbishop of Canterbury (Geoffrey Fisher) spoke in favour of the Bill, saying that the state had a right in the name of God and society to impose the death penalty, Lord Templewood said that a Bill that contained complications and anomalies of that kind could not possibly be permanent. It was nothing more than an expedient to extricate the government from a difficult position. Sooner or later total abolition would come and in the meantime he was not prepared to support a law that would satisfy neither the retentionists nor the abolitionists. Lord Chorley said that the Bill was a great disappointment to forward-looking people in matters of crime and punishment, and he protested against the unscrupulous evasion of the Parliament Act. The Bill was read a second time and went to committee in the Lords.[50] Consideration in committee was relatively brief. An amendment by the Earl of Hadington, supported by Lord Templewood, that the minimum age at which the death penalty could be imposed be raised to 21 was withdrawn after the Lord Chancellor (Lord Kilmuir) said that a great number of crimes were committed by people aged between 17 and 21. An amendment by Lord Amulree that lethal gas be substituted for hanging was also withdrawn, and the committee stage was concluded.[51]

After a very brief discussion the Homicide Bill was read for a third time and passed;[52] after passing through the House of Lords without further amendment it received the Royal Assent,[53] and the Homicide Act 1957 was law. [54]

Review
It is worth briefly reviewing the order of events over the previous 15 months in order to see clearly how the government exploited its majority in the House of Lords to use Parliament for its own ends by lawfully nullifying a Bill that had already been passed.

In February 1956 the Commons debated a government Bill that would modify the law of murder but retain the death penalty. An amendment that the death penalty be abolished or suspended was passed with a majority of 31. Prime minister Anthony Eden said that a motion calling for the government to introduce legislation for the abolition or suspension of the death penalty would be given 'full weight'. One week later Eden said the government 'would find time' for Sydney Silverman's Bill; but the House could have voted on the successful amendment. The government was in a dilemma and starting to engage in sharp practice, but there was more to come.

Attempts to delay the Silverman Bill by six months failed and in March it was passed with a majority of 24 and read a second time. No amendments were made in the committee stage. The Bill went to the Lords who rejected it by a majority of 143. The government could have invoked the Parliament Act whereby if the Commons voted in favour again after a year's delay the Bill would become law, thus overriding the decision of the Lords. But they did not choose to do so.

In July, Eden told Silverman that the government were preparing proposals in relation to capital punishment to be laid before the House in the next session. The Homicide Bill was introduced in the Queen's Speech in early November 1956. The government refused to bring in an abolition Bill and refused facilities—indeed, made it impossible—for anyone else to do so. After the first reading a motion was passed making it even more difficult for private members to introduce motions. From then on events moved quickly. The second reading of the Bill took place in mid-November; in December Alice Bacon introduced her Abolition Bill; the Homicide Bill went through committee without amendment; in February 1957 Bacon's Abolition Bill was talked out. The Homicide Bill passed through the Lords unaltered and became law in March.

A foundations for chaos

On the day before the Homicide Act 1957 became law a judge at Birmingham Assizes explained to a convicted murderer that the new Homicide Act did not apply to murder cases in which the indictment for the offence was signed before the Act; thus the prisoner would be sentenced under the old Act. He did, however, use the new form of words in pronouncing sentence: that the condemned person 'shall suffer death in the manner authorised by law'.[55]

Although the sections of the Homicide Act dealing with implied malice, provocation and suicide pacts to some extent rationalised the law of murder, and the new (in England) defence of diminished responsibility was introduced, section 5, with such inconsistencies as killing a rape victim to destroy your only witness was not punishable by hanging whereas killing a pursuing farmer in panic whilst poaching was a capital offence, would prove to be a minefield. The government had won again but their victory was to prove to be relatively short-lived. As cases under the new Homicide Act 1957 came and went the inconsistencies of the Act became glaringly apparent. The abolitionists had not gone away; their case grew stronger and their support even greater.

ENDNOTES

1   *The Times*, p. 6, 11 July 1956
2   *The Spectator*, p. 51, 13 July 1956
3   *New Statesman*, p. 29, 14 July 1956
4   *The Times*, p. 10, 16 July 1956
5   ibid, p. 11, 17 July 1956
6   ibid, p. 10, 18 July 1956
7   ibid, p. 7, 21 July 1956
8   *New Statesman*, p. 70, 21 July 1956
9   ibid, p. 104, 28 July 1956
10 *The Times*, p. 3, 13 October 1956
11 ibid, p. 4, 24 October 1956

12 *The Times,* p. 4, 24 October 1956
13 ibid, p. 4, 26 October 1956
14 *The Spectator,* p. 560, 26 October 1956
15 ibid, p. 556, 26 October 1956
16 ibid, p. 608, 2 November 1956
17 *New Statesman,* p. 507, 27 October 1956
18 ibid, p. 611, 17 November 1956
19 ibid, p. 618
20 *Hansard,* [560] 18 (6 November 1956)
21 ibid, [560] 24
22 ibid, [560] 43
23 *Hansard,* [560] 118 (7 November 1956); *The Times,* p. 4, 9 November 1956
24 *Hansard,* [560] 119 (7 November 1956)
25 ibid, [560] 446 (9 November 1956)
26 *The Times,* p. 11, 9 November 1956
27 ibid, p. 10, 14 November 1956
28 *Hansard,* [560] 1148 (15 November 1956)
29 ibid, [560] 1153
30 ibid, [560] 1163
31 ibid, [560] 1165
32 *The Times,* p. 4, 16 November 1956
33 *The Spectator,* p. 671, 16 November
34 *The Times*, p. 8, 19 November 1956
35 ibid, p. 6, 20 November 1956
36 *Hansard,* [560] 1755 (25 November 1956)
37 *The Times*, p. 6, 5 December 1956
38 *Hansard,* [561] 244-355 (27 November 1956)
39 ibid, [561] 404-538
40 ibid, [561] 1073-1198
41 *The Times,* p. 6, 5 December 1956
42 ibid, p. 6, 19 January 1957
43 ibid, p. 5, 24 January 1957
44 ibid, p. 6, 6 February 1957
45 ibid, p. 3
46 *Hansard,* [565] 454-568 (6 February 1957)
47 ibid, [565] 504-5
48 *The Times,* p. 8, 8 February 1957
49 ibid.
50 ibid, p. 11, 22 February 1957
51 ibid, p. 4, 8 March 1957
52 ibid, p. 11, 20 March

53 *Hansard*, [567] 584 (21 March 1957)
54 *The Times*, p. 6, 21 March 1957
55 ibid, p. 7.

CHAPTER 16

Confusion

After the frantic efforts by the government to ensure that its Bill went through there was a lull in abolitionist activity, but not for long. The long lull in executions—the last was in August 1955—was also about to end.

First Vickers ...

The first conviction for murder under the Homicide Act 1957, of Ronald Dunbar, convicted on May 16, was reduced to manslaughter on appeal. But a few days later, on May 23, John Vickers, aged 22, was sentenced to death and the confusion that the Act was to cause in the following few years was laid bare. His appeal to the Court of Criminal Appeal[1] was dismissed and the attorney-general refused him leave to appeal to the House of Lords which was somewhat surprising since a ruling by the Law Lords on confusing or difficult to interpret new legislation is generally welcomed and sometimes deliberately engineered.

A motion of censure on Sir Reginald Manningham-Buller, the attorney-general, was tabled by Sydney Silverman and about 50 other Labour MPs. The full motion was 'that this House deeply deplores the refusal of the attorney-general to grant his fiat to enable John Wilson Vickers to appeal against his conviction to the House of Lords so as to establish from the highest judicial authority whether or not section 1 Homicide Act 1957 effectively abolishes the doctrine of constructive malice and prevents a man from being liable to be convicted for murder who had no intention either to kill or do grevious bodily harm, as the government assured the House was its purpose during the debate on the Homicide Act'.[2] One might have thought that the attorney-general might have been at least indifferent and possibly even pleased at an opportunity to have a tricky new provision interpreted by the Lords, especially as a man's life depended on it, but Manningham-Buller pointed out that the five Appeal Court judges were unanimous in dismissing the appeal. Reg Paget pointed out that the evidence in the case was that the blows struck were intended to prevent the victim from interfering but not to maim.[3]

The following day Butler, replying to Silverman, said there was no government time to debate the motion and remained unmoved when Silverman said it was a matter of statute involving an immediate question of life and death.[4]

On the day before Vickers was due to be executed the attorney-general confirmed that he was unable to reconsider his decision and refused an appeal to the House of Lords. Kenneth Younger, Labour MP for Grimsby and Gerald Gardiner QC had an hour long meeting with the attorney-general who then issued a statement that his statutory powers did not enable him to entertain a fresh application.[5] Vickers was executed on 23 July 1957, almost two years since the previous execution.

One week later Silverman withdrew his motion criticising the attorney-general but tabled a new motion 'that this House regrets the execution of John Wilson Vickers, is of the opinion that his conviction of capital murder is contrary to the declared intention of Her Majesty's government when they recommended the Homicide Act to Parliament, and deplores the failure of Mr Attorney-General to grant his fiat to enable Vickers to bring a further appeal to the House of Lords.'[6] *The Times* sided with Manningham-Buller. In an editorial it opined that given there was complete confidence in the Court of Criminal Appeal, the attorney-general was the right man to decide whether a further appeal to the House of Lords should be made and that there was no sufficient reason for changing the present system.[7] Of course, if confidence in the Criminal Appeal Court really was 'complete' there would never be a reason to appeal to the House of Lords. Only years later were people to realise just how mistaken the Appeal Court could be and shudder at the judicial carnage that would have resulted had capital punishment still been extant.

In the discussion of his motion Sydney Silverman said that in the Vickers case every factor favouring reprieve was present. Vickers was young (22), his crime was unpremeditated, he had no criminal record, and had no particular animus against his victim. He suggested that if the Appeal Court had allowed the appeal, the attorney-general would have given himself a fiat to go to the House of Lords. The attorney-general suggested that the degree of violence was more severe than Silverman had acknowledged and the motion was negatived.[8]

The retentionists had not gone underground but few would have recognised comments reproduced in *The Times*[9] as coming from the pen of a vicar. Writing in his parish magazine, the Reverend Blagden-Gamian said he was prepared to produce a petition demanding the death penalty for child murders. There was a 'terrible' increase in the number of child murders since the death penalty was suspended as the result of 'agitation by sentimental fools'. He also urged the introduction of flogging, sterilization for sex crimes against children and that murderers' families should be responsible for maintaining the victims' dependants.

Sir Thomas Moore asked how long the government would retain the Homicide Act given the increase in the number of murders. He asked how many had been committed in the six months since May 31 of that year. Mr Butler replied that between April and September 1957, there were 128 with a variation between 34 and 11 a month, corresponding with a total of 82 for the same period in 1955. This was, in fact, a 50 per cent increase but Butler said it was too early to assess the effect of the Act, or to contemplate a further change in the law.[10]

On November 19, Dr Leon Radzinowicz, Director of Criminal Science at Cambridge, gave an address on Sir Samuel Romilly to mark the bicentenary of his birth. Romilly, he said, was bitterly disappointed as on his death the criminal law was unchanged from how he had found it. But his cause, in the end, proved triumphant. Romilly always maintained the right of the state to inflict death, and declared it absolutely impossible, even if it were to be wished, to omit death for atrocious crimes from the catalogue of human punishments.[11]

200

Then Spriggs ...

The year 1958 began much as the old one had ended: the death penalty was on the back burner. But the year would end with a killing that would revive the activity of the abolitionists with a vengeance.

It was not long, however, before the behaviour of the attorney-general was again called into question, not, this time, by Sydney Silverman, but by Mr Howell, by private notice. He asked the attorney-general whether he would reconsider his decision not to grant his fiat to J. S. Spriggs to appeal to the House of Lords against his conviction for capital murder. Sir Reginald Manningham-Buller replied that he would not and further, that the statutory period for making the application had expired so that he had no power to reconsider his decision even had he wished to, which he manifestly did not.

Mr Howell pointed out that the case was a precedent, it was the first time that an appeal on the ground of diminished responsibility had been entered under the new Homicide Act. He went on, 'In view of the comments of the Lord Chief Justice during the appeal, in respect of the extreme difficulties of juries in assessing the point in this case—the difference between emotional instability and mental instability—and the fact that the trial judge himself did not attempt to direct the jury at all on the difficulties of this matter but contented himself with circulating to them a copy of the relevant portion of the Act and leaving it to them to decide whether it was a case of capital murder or of manslaughter, is it not very regrettable indeed that the special circumstances of this precedent should not have been allowed to go to the House of Lords?' He again asked him to reconsider that which many members of the legal profession considered 'highly regrettable'.

But the attorney-general reiterated that he had no power to reconsider and said that the case did not involve a point of law of exceptional public importance. Patrick Gordon Walker suggested that when new and difficult ideas are introduced into the law, the opportunity should be taken to have a final and definitive decision on those matters. Manningham-Buller said that because it happened to be the first case under the Act that did not make it a point of exceptional importance. Hale tried again: even the trial judge said he had the greatest difficulty in understanding the section and that he read it to the jury telling them to make up their own minds as to what it meant. It was thus a matter needing a determination at the earliest opportunity. But the attorney-general was not to be moved. He did not accept Hale's summary of what had occurred and insisted he saw no ground for saying it was of exceptional public importance.[12] The attorney-general, for the second time in a few months, was unmoved and unrepentant but Mr Spriggs did not suffer as a result; he was later reprieved by the home secretary.

A few weeks later in the Commons, Mr Page wished to present a petition from Robert Alexander McGeoch calling attention to the increase in the number of murders and incidents of wounding which had occurred since the passing of the Homicide Act in 1957, and the anxieties of womenfolk and children who walked along roads and streets in fear of being attacked by some sexual maniac, in the absence of the deterrent effect of a potential death sentence. The petition

201

concluded with the prayer that the Act would be repealed or amended so that those persons found guilty of murdering a female or young male would be sentenced to death.[13] Such a petition would have had little chance of getting further at the best of times but couched in such vague and sentimental terms, it had none.

At the annual conference of the Scottish Unionist Association delegates overwhelmingly condemned the operation of the Homicide Act 1957 as being 'contrary to a proper feeling of public safety and security' and demanded the restoration of the death penalty for all murderers.[14] But at the other side of the world the government of Ceylon passed a Bill to suspend the death penalty for three years as an experiment with a view to abolishing capital punishment.[15] A draft Bill for the restoration of the death penalty in West Germany was tabled by a right wing German party, but since a two-thirds majority of the Bundestag was necessary to pass it there seemed no prospect of the Bill progressing further.[16]

Sir Thomas Moore asked the home secretary if he was aware of the opinion of recent womens' conferences which had demanded the restoration of corporal punishment for crimes of violence, and of the death penalty for all crimes of murder. But Mr Renton, for the Home Office, pointed out that the number of crimes of murder known to the police in the six months September 1957 to March 1958 was lower than for a comparable period before the passing of the Homicide Act. There seemed to be no ground for thinking, Renton said, that there should be an amendment of an Act so recently passed by Parliament. Moore was not convinced by the figures and said that the British people would not tolerate much further delay.[17]

Speaking at the Conservative party conference in Blackpool, the home secretary, R. A. Butler, referring to a call for an extension of capital punishment, said they had got capital punishment for a great variety of types of murder. He, personally, would have preferred to have it for poisoners, too. He continued, 'When you ask me whether it would be possible to get through Parliament a new Homicide Bill I tell you frankly I do not consider it to be possible, at any rate in the present Parliament, nor is it our intention to attempt to do so'. He emphasised that there was no chance of legislation to include the death penalty in the current Parliament, nor, as far as he could see, for some time.[18]

Then Marwood . . .

The opinion of the home secretary seemed to be accepted. Vickers was hanged. Spriggs was reprieved. Silverman was angry. Manningham-Buller was unrepentant. The home secretary was soothing. All was quiet again and 1958 seemed to be gliding towards the next year—an election year—until police constable Raymond Henry Summers was killed.

A fight among youths broke out in Seven Sisters Road in North London late on the night of December 14. Police constable Summers went to break it up, apprehended one man and shortly after this collapsed. He died soon afterwards. There appeared to be no wounds on the body but a post mortem was carried out.[19] The post mortem revealed next day that Summers, who was 23, had died from a single stab wound in the back.[20] The following day a small dagger was found in a front garden about a quarter of a mile away from where police constable Summers was stabbed.[21] A number of youths were held at Holloway police station in connection with the stabbing. The coroner announced that death had been due to a stab wound at the back of the chest that had penetrated the aorta; death would inevitably have been quick.[22] More youths were questioned and subsequently released[23] but no arrests made. Christmas and the New Year of 1959 came and went. It looked as if police constable Summers' murder would remain unsolved. Then, out of the evening gloom, Ronald Henry Marwood, aged 25, who the police wished to interview in connection with the stabbing, walked into the police station in Caledonian Road on 27 January 1959, and was interviewed.[24] Marwood was charged with murder and the next day taken to North London magistrates' court where he was remanded in custody for a week.[25]

Marwood was remanded again and during this second remand it is safe to suppose that the decision of the Cambridge Union debating society which voted by 81 to 53 to abolish capital punishment[26] went virtually unnoticed. When he came to court for a third time, to be remanded for a further week, Marwood said in a statement that on the night in question he was at Seven Sisters Road and that he saw his friend Mick a couple of yards in front of him, being pushed by a policeman. He went to catch up and as he reached them the police half turned round and said, according to Marwood, 'Clear off' or 'Go away', and hit him with his fist on the shoulder. The next part of Marwood's statement was to prove crucial. He said that his hands were in his pockets. He pulled out a hand intending to push him away 'but must have had the knife. I struck him with the intention of pushing him away. I didn't realise the knife was in my hand'.[27] Michael David Bloom, the 'Mick' of Marwood's story, confirmed that a policeman had hold of his arm. He said he heard a loud bang behind him, the policeman had let go and he, Bloom, had run away.[28]

At the end of the committal proceedings at North London magistrates' court, the stipendiary magistrate, Frank Milton, sent Marwood for trial at the Old Bailey. During those proceedings, a police officer who gave evidence of his interview with Marwood said that Marwood said 'I did stab the copper that night. I'll never know why I did it'. Marwood's solicitor, Mordechai Levine, submitted that there was no case to answer. He added that there was no shred of evidence to connect Marwood with anything at all except what Marwood had said himself.[29]

At his trial Marwood had claimed that the policeman he had caught up with, who was holding Bloom, turned round and told him to clear off and had hit him on the shoulder and he had punched him back. He denied that he had anything in his hand. Later, the police had written things down that he had not said. He had signed the statement because he was tired after ten hours questioning.[30] After being out for two hours the jury found Marwood guilty of capital murder and he was sentenced to death.[31]

In the House of Commons, Cyril Osborne took over from Sir Thomas Moore and asked the home secretary if he would introduce legislation 'at once' to restore hanging for crimes committed against women and children and old people. Butler declined, pointing out that the homicide figures had not gone up in the previous two years: between 1952 to 1956 the monthly murder rate was 14.2 whereas for 1958 to 1959 it was 14.3. Osborne was not really interested in facts. He pointed out that in the past eight weeks two small girls had been murdered and that hanging was too good for men who committed such crimes and that 'mothers expected him to do something'. But Butler did nothing.

In 1946 the astonishingly diverse career of Thomas Inskip had come to an end one year before his death. He was a Conservative MP for eleven years during which short time he became solicitor-general and attorney-general. He was knighted in 1922 and made a Viscount (Caldecote) in 1939. He was briefly Lord Chancellor from 1939 to 1940 and then became Lord Chief Justice. He was succeeded in this post by the first non-political appointment to it, Lord (Rayner) Goddard, a tough but intellectually rigorous lawyer. Now, in 1958, at the age of 81, Goddard retired on the grounds of failing hearing and eyesight—though he was to live on for another nine years, dying at the age of 94—and on 21 October 1958 a new Lord Chief Justice was introduced into the Lords, Lord Parker of Waddington.

Marwood's appeal was heard on 20 April 1959 before Lord Parker, Mr Justice Donovan and Mr Justice Salmon. The ruling was that Marwood's statements conflicted with what he had said in court and that the trial judge had summed up carefully. Thus there were no grounds for interfering with the verdict and the appeal was dismissed.[32] A week before Marwood was due to be hanged, over 150 members of Parliament, mostly, but not all, Labour, signed an appeal pointing out that there was no evidence of premeditated violence, or that Marwood was trying to escape or that he was of bad character.[33] A few days later a second petition was handed in.[34]

The day before the execution the home secretary announced that he could find no grounds to justify a reprieve[35] and late efforts by relatives of Marwood to secure last minute intervention were unsuccessful. There were protests reported of prisoners at Pentonville shouting and banging chairs in their cells. On the evening before the execution some 500 people gathered outside the prison gates and stood in silence until after ten o'clock.[36] By dawn the following day more people began to gather outside the prison and before 9 a.m. almost 1,000 people stood, many joined in prayers. As the fateful hour approached the crowd grew silent, but two men were arrested.[37] One, who had held a banner saying 'Save Marwood', was later given a 12 month conditional discharge for wilfully obstructing a police officer.[38]

The *Times* editorial[39] commented adversely on the crowd scenes which, it claimed, made the job of the home secretary more difficult. It is hard to see how this could possibly be the case as by the time crowds gather the home secretary's participation is complete and the execution is imminent, but even if it were true, did *The Times* really believe that the crowd, who disapproved of the execution, should try to lighten the job of the home secretary? The editorial admitted it was legitimate to try to save the condemned man but 'mob rule' (people standing in silence) could 'set a dangerous precedent': but there was a centuries-old precedent for people gathering at the scenes of executions. The article concluded that Marwood had had a fair trial and appeal in which case it was diffi⸍ understand how it would be legitimate to try to save him from the gallc. he had had a fair sentence, too. Rarely had *The Times* leader been so muddled.

The day before Marwood was executed, Lord Templewood died[40] aged 79. As Sir Samuel Hoare (he succeeded his father, the first baronet, in 1915) he was Conservative MP for Chelsea for 34 years. He had had a distinguished career, marred only by his forced resignation as foreign secretary in Baldwin's cabinet, when his plan with Laval to resolve Italy's claim on Abyssinia was repudiated by his cabinet colleagues. However, he soon bounced back as First Lord of the Admiralty and served as home secretary between 1937 and 1939. In 1944 he gave up his Commons seat, and was created a Viscount, to devote his time to penal reform. His time as home secretary had turned him into an ardent abolitionist. In February 1947 he accepted the presidency of the Howard League for Penal Reform and a month later became chairman of the Magistrates' Association. He voted against the death penalty consistently in the House of Lords and with his death the abolitionists lost a good friend.

Few friends for the Homicide Act

The conviction and execution of Marwood had once again highlighted the inadequacy of the Homicide Act 1957 and caused some public unease. Two days after Marwood was hanged Canon Collins delivered a scathing attack on the Act from the pulpit of St Paul's Cathedral. He called for the Act to be amended and dubbed the execution of Marwood 'a sin committed by the nation'. 'In a democracy', he said, 'we are all guilty'.[41] Nor was Sydney Silverman slow to go on the attack. Less than a week after the execution he had tabled yet another motion. Inviting the House to abolish capital punishment and supported by seven Labour members and one Conservative, Howard Johnson, the motion referred to the Marwood case and stated that, 'This House regards with the deepest anxiety and distress the anomalies of the Homicide Act 1957 which discriminates between capital and non-capital murder by arbitrary categories which bear no relationship to the comparative wickedness of the crime and are an abiding offence to the sense of justice and the good sense of the community. The House therefore considers that capital punishment should now be abolished.[42]

Cyril Osborne lost little time in trying to sink Silverman's motion when he and about 50 Conservative MPs tabled an amendment which would turn Silverman's motion into a plea for capital punishment to be retained, and to reinstate hanging for murder by poisoning and for the murder 'of old people and little children'.[43] Mr Matthew asked that the place and date of executions should be kept confidential and that people should not be allowed to congregate outside prisons. Butler replied negatively and pointed out that prison commissioners have no authority to prevent people assembling on a public highway outside prisons.[44]

The inconsistencies and injustices inherent in the Homicide Act 1957 were becoming clear to many people but in September 1959 none other than the Lord Chief Justice himself delivered a stinging attack on the Act. Speaking at a meeting of the Canadian Bar Association, Lord Parker criticised the indiscriminate commuting of death sentences and called the British system of capital punishment 'ridiculous'. He said, 'If a man kills and robs, he hangs; if he kills and doesn't rob, he doesn't hang'. That provided an unfair advantage for a man who intended to rob but found no money on his victim. Again, he went on, 'if a man shoots a woman, he hangs; but if he stabs her, he doesn't. If he kills a policeman in any manner, he hangs; if he poisons, a cold-blooded crime, he doesn't hang'. He considered the whole thing a political compromise, but a bad one. He concluded that rather than permit that sort of confusion he would rather see the death penalty abolished entirely.[45]

There were three unrelated events at the end of September. On September 24, Günter Poldola, a German national, was convicted and sentenced to death for the murder of detective sergeant Raymond Purdy. He was hanged six weeks later,[46] an execution which correspondent Michael Astor called macabre and shoddy.[47] Then a few days later Miss Sheila Peggy McKenzie, who had been the fiancée of the unfortunate police constable Summers (the victim in the Marwood case), collapsed and died at the age of 21 at a club in St John's Wood.[48] Thousands of miles away, the cabinet of the Ceylon government decided to repeal the suspension of the death penalty and reintroduce it without delay, in response to a spate of assassinations.[49]

When the home secretary was asked if he had given consideration to the introduction of further legislation to extend or limit the penalties for homicide or treason he replied in a written answer that there were no proposals in that field at that time.[50] Cyril Osborne, who no doubt a hundred years earlier would have been pressing for executions to continue to be carried out in public, asked the home secretary if hanging could be carried out in secret to avoid undesirable exhibitions and demonstrations by a 'minority of the public' (it would have needed 30 million to demonstrate for it to be a majority), but Butler replied that he was required by section 11(2) Homicide Act 1957 to publish the time and place of executions.[51]

After the clamour resulting from the cases of Vickers, Spriggs and Marwood in the preceding three years, 1960 began quietly but the lull was brief. The pro-hangers were most vociferous, but getting nowhere; the abolitionists had stepped backwards for a better leap. Lord Morris of Kenwood, speaking in Canada, said not only that capital punishment should be retained in Britain but flogging should be re-introduced for crimes of violence.[52] The ever-watchful Sir Thomas Moore tried a statistical tack. He said that in view of the fact that 78 per cent of the population favoured the restoration of corporal punishment for crimes of violence and 74 per cent favoured capital punishment for all types of murder, the home secretary should reconsider his policy regarding crime and punishment. Mr Butler replied that he was not prepared to propose further changes to the law relating to capital punishment until sufficient time had elapsed for the effect of the Homicide Act to be assessed.[53]

The Act was not without some positive effect, however. In an answer to Dr Johnson the home secretary revealed that since 21 March 1957 66 people originally charged with murder were found guilty of manslaughter by reason of

206

diminished responsibility following section 2 of the Act. Dr Johnson asked that that section of the Act be carefully watched as it seemed in some instances the more horrible the crime the lighter the penalty. Butler pointed out that the law was interpreted as passed by Parliament and the only way of altering it would be by fresh legislation and there was no chance of that at the present time.[54]

The curious appeals of gypsy Joe Smith

A murder had been committed before these gentlemenly exchanges the effects of which were to rumble on for many months. At the beginning of March police constable Leslie Meehan approached a car in Woolwich, south-east London. It accellerated away but not before the officer had clung to the offside driver's window. He was struck by oncoming cars and finally fell into the path of one of them and was killed. He was 34 years old, married with four children.[55] The next day, Joe Smith was remanded in custody at Woolwich magistrates' court, charged with the murder of Meehan. When cautioned he said 'I didn't mean to kill him. I didn't want him to find the gear'. When charged he said 'I didn't kill him like murder. Murder's ridiculous'.[56] At the preliminary proceedings at Woolwich court the evidence from the drivers of the oncoming cars was that the driver was trying to get the police constable off his car and was swerving from side to side to do so. The officer was knocked into two cars and was thrown under the last car.[57] Smith was sent for trial at the Old Bailey charged with the murder of Meehan.[58]

Smith first appeared at the Old Bailey on 4 April 1960[59] and three days later was found guilty of capital murder and sentenced to death. The prosecuting counsel, Mervyn Griffiths-Jones, said that Smith had had some stolen scaffolding clips in the back of his car. He was told by police constable Meehan to pull up at the kerb, but instead of doing so he accellerated, zig-zagging at speed along Plumstead Road brushing the officer against oncoming cars until he fell off. Smith later returned to the scene and admitted he was the driver of the car and that Meehan had been flung off. Smith was a gypsy and could neither read nor write. The foundation of his defence was that it was a pure accident and he was not really conscious that the officer was still hanging on to the car. Mr Justice Donovan, in his summing up, said there was a limit to human credulity and that the jury might believe that the defendant's explanation had gone past it. If they came to the conclusion that he did know that the constable was hanging on to the car 'I do not know how you can properly find that this was an accident'. He accepted, and assumed the jury accepted, that Smith did not intend to kill the officer.[60]

Smith appealed against conviction and the appeal was heard by Mr Justice Byrne, Mr Justice Sachs and Mr Justice Winn. The first ground was that of misdirection of the jury. The test of whether Smith intended to cause grevious bodily harm was a subjective one; the 'reasonable man test' advocated by the judge was objective and wrong. The second ground was that it was wrong to say that if a man intended to commit grevious bodily harm, did it, and death resulted, that was murder. There had to be malice aforethought. Since the Homicide Act 1957 implied malice had gone and there was no express malice in

207

this case.[61] Thus the appeal was firmly rooted in an interpretation of the 1957 Act.

The appeal was allowed and a verdict of manslaughter and a sentence of ten years imprisonment were substituted.[62] The full judgment was delivered a week later by Mr Justice Byrne.[63] He said that the jury rejected the defence of accident after which there was room only for a verdict of capital murder or manslaughter. At no time was it submitted that Smith intended to kill the police officer, but the prosecutor said that such an intention was to be inferred. The defence said that the intention was not established as an inference from the facts. In the present case the degree of likelihood of injury to the police constable was not such that serious injury was certain to result. Also, there was the question of whether Smith really appreciated the degree of likelihood of serious injury during the relevant ten seconds when he drove the car with the officer hanging on to it. The 'reasonable man test' was not appropriate; the only question was what was the actual state of mind of the accused. It did not seem safe to assume that the jury fully understood the position.

Thus the matter appeared to be resolved and some uncertainties of the Act resolved. But a curious twist was imminent. Two weeks after the Court of Appeal judgment the Director of Public Prosecutions was granted a certificate to appeal to the House of Lords against the decision of the Appeal Court quashing the conviction for murder and substituting a manslaughter verdict. The home secretary announced that if a murder conviction were restored he would recommend a commutation of the death sentence.

The appeal to the House of Lords[64] was heard before the Lord Chancellor, Lord Kilmuir, a former home secretary, Lord Goddard, former Lord Chief Justice, Lord Parker, current Lord Chief Justice, Lord Denning and Lord Tucker, as dazzling an array of 'judicial stars' as might be found. They sat for several days during June and on 1 July 1960 the appeal ended with the Lord Chancellor announcing that they would take time for consideration[65] and three weeks later their decision was delivered.

The law lords restored the conviction of capital murder. The judgment was detailed but in short they found that the trial judge's summing up could not be criticised and on the facts of the case it was impossible to say that the harm that the defendant must be taken to have contemplated could have been anything but of a very serious nature coming well within the term grievous bodily harm which was to be defined as having its everyday meaning. There had been a further contention that section 1(1) Homicide Act 1957 had abolished malice constituted by a proved intention to commit grievous bodily harm and that accordingly the appeal in R v. Vickers, which held the contrary, had been wrongly decided. It was sufficient to say that in their Lordships' opinion the Act did not in any way abolish such malice.[66] Thus the Homicide Act was definitively interpreted. On the application of the Director of Public Prosecutions the appeal of Smith was dismissed and the conviction of capital murder restored.[67] The death sentence was commuted by the home secretary.[68]

Four men plus one Act equals confusion

Even before the appeal by the Director of Public Prosecutions began, on the night of June 25 all was to be thrown into turmoil yet again. Alan Edward John Jee, 23, was walking home late at night. Four men, who had been drinking heavily and were out to commit burglary, changed their minds when they spotted Jee (who the previous day had become engaged to be married). They waylaid him, knocked him to the ground, went through his pockets and then kicked him into unconsciousness. He died from his injuries, which included a fractured skull, two days later. The four men were Norman James Harris, 23, Christopher Louis Darby, 23, Francis Robert George Forsyth, 18, and Terrence Lutt, 17. They were all charged with murder committed in the furtherance of theft and all pleaded not guilty. The prosecutor, Mervyn Griffiths-Jones, said that he did not suggest that any of the defendants intended to kill, but they certainly intended to do grievous bodily harm.[69]

After a successful submission from the defence by David Weitzman QC, Mr Justice Winn told the jury that he ruled that there was no case for Darby to answer on a charge of capital murder but the case would proceed against him on a charge of non-capital murder. The charge of capital murder remained in relation to the other three defendants, however.[70] The case for the defence was that all four had been drinking considerably and were out to commit burglary, but there was no intention to rob.[71]

In his summing up the judge said that before any one of the accused could be shown to be guilty of murder by an action done by someone else—another of the accused—it was necessary to establish that not only was he a party to a common enterprise but that he contemplated that it might involve an act of violence, such as, of course, the death of Jee. On September 26 all four were found guilty: Darby of non-capital, and the other three defendants of capital murder. The brutal and wanton killing of one man by four drunken men acting together resulted in the following sentences: Darby (non-capital murder) was sentenced to life imprisonment; Harris and Forsyth (capital murder) were sentenced to death; Lutt, 17 (capital murder) was sentenced to be detained during Her Majesty's pleasure on account of his age.[72] It was all rather clear cut; they had killed in the furtherance of theft; but they all contemplated whether to appeal.[73] With the execution date for Harris and Forsyth fixed for October 18, three gave notice of appeal[74] but Lutt left it to the last possible date.[75]

If three different sentences for four men who jointly had committed a single offence did not sufficiently highlight the confusion wrought by the Homicide Act 1957, an article by the distinguished academic lawyer Glanville Williams rekindled past confusions. He discussed the case of Joe Smith who was convicted by the jury of murder, had the conviction reduced to manslaughter on appeal followed by the Lords restoring the murder conviction (see p. 207 *et al*).

The point made by Glanville Williams was that constructive malice, which had been abolished by the Homicide Act 1957, now meant that murder without intent, even when committing another offence other than grievous bodily harm, was not capital murder. Because the law was so confused he suggested that possibly the time had come to abolish the rule that one who intends to commit grevious bodily harm is a murderer if death results; in other words a murder conviction would need an intent to kill in all cases.[76]

A letter from Professor C. F. Parker of the law faculty at Exeter University pointed out that before the appeal by the Crown to the Lords in *DPP v. Smith* the home secretary had already announced that Smith would not hang in any event. It might be argued, he said, that the Lords were thus arguing a hypothetical and academic case which English judges proclaim they cannot and must not do. He asked whether it was certain that their decision would have been the same if they had known that Smith would hang.[77]

Irrespective of academic considerations arising from a previous case, the prospect of a double execution in the current one, one of which was of an 18-year-old youth, attracted considerable public attention. A letter in *The Times* was signed by many well-known public figures which included Kingsley Amis, A. J. Ayer, J. B. Priestly, Donald Soper, Julian Huxley, Christmas Humphreys and Victor Gollancz from whose address, 14 Henrietta Street the letter was sent. The letter begged that at least Forsyth be spared execution as it was an affront to kill a youth of 18 whatever his crime.[78] But this plea for mercy drew a swift riposte from Norman Bower who thought that many correspondents would be 'gravely affronted' if Forsyth were not called upon to pay the penalty for a brutal and cold-blooded crime.[79] On the same page was a letter similar in tone from A. S. M. Wilson and three others. It said that if Forsyth did not wish to run the risk of being hanged he should not have become involved in crime. He had been found guilty of an unusually brutal murder and would have to take the consequences. His age had little bearing on the matter. The letter concluded that it was a pity that the 'star-studded panel from 14 Henrietta Street' could spare no thought for future victims of crime and no sympathy for the victim of that one.[80] Nor did John Murray have any sympathy.[81] He had declined to add his signature to the letter of November 1, because it seemed to place Forsyth above the law by claiming immunity for him whatever crime he may have committed. He was joined by N. C. Marshall who asked if nothing could be done to stop the 'nauseating tendency' to sympathise with the criminals and not the victims and those who loved them.[82]

Next day there were several letters of similar ilk[83] including one from M. N. Clark who warned that if Forsyth were reprieved nobody could be safe and 'they' might well have signed the death warrants of their own wives and children. But there were also letters in support of Forsyth. R. N. Heald asked why a plea for mercy for a murderer should be thought to imply lack of sympathy for his victim, and there was a further letter, signed by well over 100 people who wished to associate themselves with the letter of November 1. Alice Just quoted Sir Bernard Spilsbury: 'There's a perfectly simple way of avoiding capital punishment. Don't commit murder.' Was Sir Bernard, a world famous forensic pathologist, really so sanctimonious? But on the same page[84] Alwyn Smith pointed out that it was an absurd notion that the death of a murderer in some way mitigated the suffering of his victim.

[Elizabeth Howard, the deputy secretary of the Howard League for Penal Reform drew attention to the situation of Norman Harris, the other young man due to be hanged. She pointed out that no evidence was offered at the trial that Harris had struck a single blow at the unfortunate victim. A petition containing about 2,000 signatures was handed in to the Home Office urging a reprieve for the two men sentenced to death[85] but on the next day the home secretary announced that he was unable to find grounds to recommend a reprieve. Forsyth's mother sent a telegram to the Queen, and another petition, signed by 41 members of the London County Council and their chairman, was organised by Mr W. Bentley, father of Derek Bentley.[86]

The letters, the petitions and the telegram were of no avail. At 9 a.m. on November 10 both youths were hanged, Forsyth at Wandsworth and Harris at Pentonville, Harris aged 21 and Forsyth aged 18. Groups of people stood outside both prisons until after nine o'clock; before its weekly debate, the Oxford Union adjourned for a token period as a protest against the executions.[87]

Sydney Silverman, no doubt sickened and angered by this double execution of two young men, wasted no time. On the day of the executions he asked the home secretary if he would explain his reasons for not recommending a reprieve for the men hanged that morning. Butler declined, as Silverman knew he must, in accordance with the tradition of his predecessors. But Silverman said it was not really a proper discharge of his functions to refuse to render any account whatever of the mercy he administers or withholds 'not on his behalf but on behalf of ourselves and the nation'.[88]

Christopher Mayhew asked the home secretary if he would amend the Homicide Act in such a way as to confine murder to acts committed with intent to kill. In a written reply, Butler replied that he had no proposal to amend the Act.[89] When two months later Elwyn Jones asked the same question, Butler gave the same reply.[90]

Whether or not it was the execution of the two young men that was the trigger, the National Campaign for the Abolition of Capital Punishment, which had suspended its activities since the passing of the Homicide Act almost three years earlier, launched a new campaign to be 'continued unremittingly until total abolition has been assured'. They believed that the cases of Harris and Forsyth had increased support for abolition enormously. Lord Harewood was named chairman of the Committee of Honour; Gerald Gardiner, QC, and Victor Gollancz were named as joint chairmen of the campaign and Lord Altrichnam as treasurer. Other members of the committee included Bertrand Russell, Augustus John, Graham Sutherland, Henry Moore, Edith Sitwell and Rebecca West.[91] On the same day Alice Bacon tabled a new amendment to the Criminal Justice Bill to prohibit sentence of death being passed on any person under the age of 21.

The next day Sydney Silverman followed this up by drawing attention to a motion on the paper challenging the correctness of the home secretary's decision in the two recent capital cases. Asked if there would be time for the House to discuss it, bearing in mind it was a challenge to his personal decision, Butler replied that he was aware of the position and the gravity of the decisions and the seriousness of the issue. But he found difficulties in finding time. Silverman, not one to mince words, pointed out that this was a personal vote of censure and the

211

home secretary ought not to be willing to leave out such a motion on the order paper without giving an opportunity of considering it.[92]

A few days later an article was published in *The Times* by its political correspondent[93] which drew attention to Silverman's motion calling the home secretary to account, to Alice Bacon's tabled amendment and to the National Campaign for the Abolition of Capital Punishment. Silverman, said the article, was one of the most resourceful and pertinacious of Parliamentarians, and he had hit upon a line of attack which Mr Butler as the home secretary—from whom the initiation of the prerogative of mercy sprang—was bound to find embarrassing. Since the Homicide Act had been passed there had been 29 convictions for capital murder in England, Wales and Scotland and 16 people had been executed, ten reprieved and in three cases verdicts of manslaughter had been substituted on appeal. The only woman on the list had been reprieved, and four of the men were under 21. The following table was included in the article:

	Age	Date of conviction	Result
Ronald Dunbar	24	16 5 57	Manslaughter subs. on appeal
John Vickers	22	23 5 57	Executed
Franklin Macpherson	22	28 6 57	Manslaughter subs. on appeal
Dennis Howard	24	18 10 57	Executed
John Spriggs	29	19 12 57	Reprieved
Arthur Matheson	52	30 1 58	Manslaughter subs. on appeal
Vivian Teed	24	18 3 58	Executed
Mary Wilson	66	29 3 58	Reprieved
Arthur Bosworth	20	30 4 58	Reprieved
George Collier	67	22 5 58	Reprieved
Matthew Kavanagh	32	3 7 58	Executed
Frank Stokes	44	23 7 58	Executed
Brian Chandler	20	29 10 58	Executed
Ernest Jones	-	10 12 58	Executed
Joseph Chrimes	30	4 3 59	Executed
Ronald Marwood	25	19 3 59	Executed
Michael Tatum	24	23 3 59	Executed
David Di-Duca	21	14 4 59	Reprieved
Bernard Walden	33	1 7 59	Executed
Günter Podola	30	24 9 59	Executed
Jim Smith	26	-	Manslaughter subs. on appeal; capital murder restored by Lords; reprieved
Mihaly Pocze	25	1 6 60	Reprieved
John Constantine	22	22 7 60	Executed
Norman Harris	21	26 9 60	Executed
Francis Forsyth	18	26 9 60	Executed
John Rogers	20	20 10 60	Reprieved
Scotland			
Peter Manuel	31	29 5 58	Executed
Donald Forbes	23	25 9 58	Reprieved
Alexander Stirling	24	9 3 60	Reprieved

After Butler had announced the business for the following week, Silverman asked him why it had not been possible to find time to debate the motion on capital punishment standing in his name. Butler replied that there was no time to take the motion before Christmas. But when Silverman asked is the home secretary assuring the House that he would find time for the motion at the earliest opportunity, Butler said he could give no guarantee.[94]

Immediately before the Christmas recess Silverman was on his feet again. He called attention to the motion that other Labour members had put down recording their profound regret that the home secretary had failed to reprieve Forsyth and Harris. The case had aroused considerable influential anxiety as the correspondence in *The Times* had made clear and some explanation was due to the House. Two other members regretted that there was no time to debate their motions and Butler said that the government had to consider different motions on their merit. He agreed that Silverman's motion was of the 'greatest possible importance' but it had to be borne in mind that it was very unusual to have a motion of that kind. Silverman said that of course motions of that kind were rare, but did the home secretary know of an instance in which a motion had been put down and not debated. Butler replied that he did not know of any as he had not the records with him. It was impossible to give the House a satisfactory answer regarding reasons for reprieves or absence of reprieves as there might be repercussions if he answered in full.[95]

ENDNOTES

1   *R v. Vickers* [1957] 2 QB 664, [1957] 2 All ER 741, [1957] 3 WLR 326, 121 JP 510, 101 Sol Jo 593, 41 Cr App Rep 189, CCA

2   *The Times*, p.10, 18 July 1957

3   ibid, p. 7

4   ibid, p.13, 19 July 1957

5   ibid, p. 4, 23 July 1957

6   ibid, p. 5, 1 August 1957

7   ibid, p. 9

8   ibid, p. 4, 2 August 1957

9   ibid, p. 4, 16 October 1957

10 ibid, p. 4, 15 November 1957

11 ibid, p. 5, 20 November 1957

12 *Hansard*, [580] 1256 (23 January 1958)

13 ibid, [586] 495 (18 April 1958)

14 The Times, p. 4, 10 May 1958

15 ibid, p. 5

16 ibid, p. 5, 17 May 1958

17 *Hansard*, [591] 1423 (17 July 1958)

18 *The Times*, p. 7, 10 October 1958

19   *The Times*, p. 8, 15 December 1958
20   ibid, p. 6, 16 December 1958
21   ibid, p. 6, 17 December 1958
22   ibid, p. 6, 18 December 1958
23   ibid, p. 5, 19 December 1958
24   ibid, p. 8, 28 January 1959
25   ibid, p. 4, 29 January 1959
26   ibid, p. 10, 11 February 1959
27   ibid, p. 6, 12 February 1959
28   ibid, p. 4, 14 February 1959
29   ibid, p.13, 20 February 1959
30   ibid, p. 8, 19 March 1959
31   ibid, p. 6, 20 March 1959
32   ibid, p. 3, 21 April 1959
33   ibid, p. 10, 30 April 1959
34   ibid, p. 4, 2 May 1959
35   ibid, p. 6, 7 May 1959
36   ibid, p. 7, 8 May 1959
37   ibid, p. 4, 9 May 1959
38   ibid, p. 6, 25 May 1959
39   ibid, p. 7
40   ibid, p. 6
41   ibid, p. 4, 11 May 1959
42   ibid, p.14, 13 May 1959
43   ibid, p. 7, 14 May 1959
44   ibid, p. 4, 15 May 1959
45   ibid, p. 10, 3 September 1959; p. 8, 4 September 1959
46   ibid, p.13, 6 November 1959
47   ibid, p. 13
48   ibid, p. 8, 28 September 1959
49   ibid, p. 5, 3 October 1959
50   *Hansard*, [612] 66 (5 November 1959)
51   *The Times*, p. 4, 13 November 1959
52   ibid, p. 10, 3 March 1960
53   ibid, p. 4, 16 April 1960
54   *Hansard*, [623] 1460 (19 May 1960)
55   *The Times*, p. 12, 3 March 1960
56   ibid, p. 8, 4 March 1960
57   ibid, p. 12, 18 March 1960
58   ibid, p.18, 22 March 1960
59   ibid, p. 8, 5 April 1960

214

60 *The Times*, p. 8, 8 April 1960
61 ibid, p. 16, 10 May 1960
62 ibid, p. 10, 11 May 1960
63 ibid, p. 6, 19 May 1960
64 ibid, p. 9, 28 June 1960; *DPP v. Smith* [1961] AC 290, [1960] 3 All ER 161, [1960] 3 WLR 546, 124 JP 473, 104 Sol Jo 683 44 Cr App Rep 261, HL
65 ibid, p. 12, 2 July 1960
66 ibid, p. 5, 19 July 1960
67 ibid, p. 10, 30 July 1960
68 ibid, p. 10, 1 August 1960
69 ibid, p. 3, 21 September 1960
70 ibid, p. 7, 23 September 1960
71 ibid, p. 3, 24 September 1960
72 ibid, p. 3, 27 September 1960
73 ibid, p. 7, 28 September 1960
74 ibid, p. 7, 30 September 1960
75 ibid, p. 7, 7 October 1960
76 ibid, p. 13, 12 October 1960
77 ibid, p. 15, 15 October 1960
78 ibid, p. 13, 1 November 1960
79 ibid
80 ibid
81 ibid, p. 4, 4 November 1960
82 ibid
83 ibid, p. 7, 5 November 1960
84 ibid, p. 7, 7 November 1960
85 ibid, p. 7
86 ibid, p. 7, 11 November 1960
87 ibid
88 ibid, p. 5
89 *Hansard,* [630] 1256 (24 November 1960)
90 ibid, [633] 47 (26 January 1961)
91 *The Times*, p. 6, 8 December 1960
92 ibid, p. 5, 9 December 1960
93 ibid, p. 8, 12 December 1960
94 ibid, p. 4, 16 December 1960
95 ibid, p. 3, 21 December 1960.

CHAPTER 17

The Trend Towards Abolition

Ludovic Kennedy's book *10 Rillington Place* was published by Gollancz towards the end of 1961. After the Christmas recess George Rogers asked the home secretary what new evidence he had received concerning the Evans case and whether he intended to order a new inquiry. Sydney Silverman suggested that the home secretary ask the Queen to grant a posthumous free pardon as Evans' conviction and execution had been shown to be a miscarriage of justice. But R. A. Butler, the home secretary was not convinced of the value of a fresh inquiry and said he was examining Kennedy's book carefully.[1]

The Homicide Act under attack

Silverman was not finished. He then asked the leader of the House (also Butler!) if there was any hope of ever discussing a motion which had been on the order paper a long time (concerning the home secretary's refusal to reprieve Evans). He said that if the answer was 'Never' it would be better to say so frankly. Butler said that he 'never used the word never' but it would be difficult to find time to debate the issues in that particular motion. Cyril Osborne interjected to point out that since 1 December 1960 there had been more than 50 murders. There was mounting feeling that the death penalty should apply to all people of sound mind who committed murder, and he asked whether time could not be found to discuss that.[2] Butler replied that he could not at present indicate when there would be time, but that the had asked for an analysis of murders so that he could see whether the Homicide Act needed reviewing.[3]

A leading article in *The Times* commended Butler's cautious approach. It agreed that the Homicide Act 1957 was in some respects unsatisfactory but said that reform had to proceed from cool deliberation and from rational premises. The distinction which the Act had made between different types of murder left out of account degrees of moral culpability—and for that reason the law was unsatisfactory. Responsibility and culpability were not addressed by classifying types of murder.[4]

Emrys Hughes asked the secretary of state for Scotland if he would introduce a Bill to abolish the death penalty in Scotland or to amend the Criminal Justice Acts so that no one could be hanged in Scotland under the age of 21. The Scottish secretary, John Maclay, replied that he was not convinced that a case had been made for amending legislation. Sir Thomas Moore wanted an amendment to the Homicide Act to give Scottish courts power to impose the death penalty for murder when accompanied by rape.[5] This found immediate favour with Anthony Courtney MP who in a letter to *The Times* advocated immediate modification of the Homicide Act to make murder accompanied by 'sexual attack' a capital offence.[6] Unsurprisingly, Sir Thomas Moore agreed with Courtney and publicised his view that murder with rape should be a capital offence. He disagreed with *The Times* editorial and said that the differentiation between different types of murder should be left to the courts.[7] This latter point found a resonance with Edward Gardner QC, the member of Parliament for Billericay, and 16 other backbench Conservatives, who tabled a motion 'to consider the value of the death penalty in preventing murder and protecting society, with a view to repeal or amendment of section 5 of the Homicide Act 1957.'[8]

While all this was going on, Silverman was collecting signatures for a motion criticising a ruling by the speaker: 'This House respectfully regrets and unhesitatingly dissents from the ruling by Mr Speaker that a question sought to be put down by the honorary member for Nelson and Colne [Silverman], asking the home secretary to order an inquiry whether a miscarriage of justice had occurred in the case of George Riley (see p.218), was not in order, and expresses a view that the ruling was not in accord with the precedent and practice of the House and imposes new unnecessary and undesirable limitations on the ability of honorary members to discharge their public duties'. The speaker, Sir Harry Hylton-Foster, said that he was driven reluctantly to the conclusion that he was governed by precedent and should rule the question out of order. It might be that one day the House might want to alter its practice but 'that I would not do myself'.[9]

On February 16 in the House of Commons there were two petitions and questions to the home secretary. One of the petitions, from Godman Irving on behalf of a constituent, asked 'that the law known as the Homicide Act 1957, may be utterly revoked or so amended in Parliament as to restore fully the aforementioned deterrent protection of the penalty of capital punishment for each and every male and female person against any crime of murder that might be committed against any one of these persons, which protection they had and cherished before the law known as the Homicide Act 1957, deprived and took away from them this ancient and well-established protection in law'. Gerald Nabarro thought it 'a very good petition' and it was to lie upon the table.[10]

Four questions were initially asked of the home secretary. Commander Kerans asked whether, 'in view of the increased number of murders in recent weeks' he would consider revision of the Homicide Act. Gresham Cooke asked for murder whilst committing criminal sexual acts to be made a capital offence. Sir Thomas Moore asked for the same thing for rape (which was and is a criminal sexual offence), and Jo Grimond asked if the home secretary would institute an inquiry into the operation of the Homicide Act. To all this Butler replied that he was not convinced of the appropriateness of any amendment to the Act 'at present'.

Kerans said that there were people who could not leave their children unescorted after dark and that people were restrained from coming to Britain because of the crime in London. Butler replied that there was not a great difference in the murder rate between 1957 to 1960 and 1953 to 1955. Gresham Cooke said that between mid-December and the end of January, 17 women and girls had been murdered, most of whom were subject to sexual attacks. The deterrence of capital punishment should be restored for sexual attacks (presumably those accompanied by murder). Butler said that he shared this anxiety and was having the matters analysed by his research unit. Eric Fletcher said that there was dissatisfaction with the Homicide Act among both retentionists and abolitionists and the Act needed revision, but Butler reiterated that not enough time had passed since the Act became law for an accurate picture to have emerged.[11]

At the debate on Sydney Silverman's motion criticising the speaker, Silverman said that George Riley was convicted of a capital crime and hanged without there being a scrap of evidence against him. The evidence was not that he had committed the crime but that he had said he did. Silverman said that the police had told Riley lies: that his footprints, fingerprints and blood group matched those at the scene of the crime. Although that entire area had been copiously splattered with blood there was none on Riley. There was plenty to enquire into, but if the ruling of the speaker was correct, that an inquiry could not be made, they were prevented from doing their duty. Butler moved as an amendment 'that this House upholds the well-tested rule under which in any case involving a capital sentence the circumstances on which the exercise of the prerogative of mercy depends should not be made the subject of a question or discussion in this House while the sentence is pending'. Butler said he was satisfied that Riley had been rightly convicted of murder committed in the furtherance of theft. He had had no other possibility but to take the course he did. After the Labour whips had made it a free vote the motion was rejected by 253 votes to 60, a majority of 193.[12] An article by *The Times* Parliamentary correspondent said that:

> the House could not but admire the thoroughness and compassion with which Sydney Silverman argued the case for his motion 'unhesitatingly dissenting' from the speaker's ruling against the admissibility of a question asking the home secretary to order an inquiry into whether an injustice had occurred in the case of George Riley.[13]

Addressing the Howard League for Penal Reform at Caxton Hall, Glanville Williams said that retaining the death penalty for murder committed in the course of theft but not in the course of rape was one of the Act's great weaknesses. He said,

> It seems indefensible that the robber who uses violence he doesn't intend to be fatal should be guilty of capital murder when the rapist who deliberately kills his victim in order to prevent her from giving evidence should not.

Williams said he believed that there was no evidence showing the efficacy of capital punishment and that all the murders would have been committed since the Act was passed whether it had existed or not.[14] However, section 2 of the 1957 Act had saved some lives. In 1958 there were 25 people convicted of manslaughter by reason of diminished responsibility, in 1959, 21 and in 1960, 23,[15] many of whom would otherwise have been hanged.

An attempt by the Standing Committee on the Criminal Justice Bill to introduce a clause to prohibit the death penalty for murder on anyone under the age of 21 failed by one vote, 16 to 15. All the Labour members voted for the clause as did Joan Vickers; Julian Critchley (Conservative) abstained. William Deedes said that if there had been any real hope that sentences of 20 to 25 years would be the alternative to the death penalty he would have been willing to vote to support the clause. As there was no such hope he opposed it. Other committee members expressed horror at the suggestion that such long terms of imprisonment could even be considered.[16]

On March 14, five Labour MPs voted against the army estimates and air estimates; two days later the Labour whip was withdrawn from Sydney Silverman and four other Labour MPs (including Michael Foot, a future leader of the Labour Party).[17] This had absolutely no effect on Silverman's activities.

Another attempt was made to raise the age to 21 before the death sentence could be passed when a motion to include a new clause in the Criminal Justice Bill was tabled by Alice Bacon supported by two other Labour MPs MacColl and Weitzman.[18] The motion was debated a month later when the opposition but not the government were allowed a free vote. Sir Henry d'Avigdor-Goldsmid argued that the public interest could best be defended by treating these urchins as the irresponsible creatures they were and not giving them the treatment of adults which they had done nothing to deserve. It was unlikely that Sir Henry meant that the urchins would prefer to be treated as adults by being hanged, but his heart was in the right place and he was the only Conservative who voted with Labour. The home secretary said that the government found it absolutely repugnant to condemn young men to death but it was not wise to make the change 'at present' and perhaps give young people the idea that capital murder was not a heinous and terrible crime.[19]

It was announced in May that Brian Allen, who had assisted his father at five executions in British prisons, was resigning his post as assistant hangman.[20] He had recently qualified as a mental nurse and felt that the outlook of the two occupations were not compatible. A motion tabled by Edward Gardner QC, noted that sentences for murder in recent years had averaged only nine years and urged the government to take immediate steps to ensure that a sentence of life imprisonment should mean at least 25 years, unless a court ordered otherwise.[21] The motion was supported by a group of Conservative backbenchers.[22]

Mr Osmington Mills wrote to The Times[23] to say that he was surprised to receive a letter from the National Campaign for the Abolition of Capital Punishment asking for his signature on a memorial. It had said 'we are inviting leading men and women from all walks of public life to sign this memorial', and it was signed by Gerald Gardiner and Victor Gollancz. Mr Mills wondered how many of the signatures would be of people perturbed about the death penalty or of those flattered into joining Mr Gardiner, Mr Gollancz and other leading men and women from all walks of public life. Some weeks later a letter from T. Burnaby agreed that the memorial in question could have little value unless it carried the names of those who refused to sign as well as those who supported it.

e himself had sent the card back saying 'Please include my name on the memorial as one who feels unable to support the proposed abolition of the death penalty.'

Evans resurrected

Timothy Evans had not been mentioned in the House of Commons for some six months but in mid-June Patrick Gordon Walker initiated a debate on his case. He said there were two points: whether Evans was rightly convicted and whether his remains should be returned to his mother to be buried in consecrated ground. The weight of opinion that Evans was wrongly convicted was increasing and would continue to increase. His mother, whose only son had been hanged, would receive great comfort if she were allowed to bury his remains, which was her wish.

Sir Hugh Lucas-Tooth, who had been under-secretary at the Home Office at the time of Christie's trial, said that there was no evidence not available to the Scott Henderson inquiry that was currently available. He thought that Ludovic Kennedy's book was 'tendentious' and had misled a great many people. He also said that it was an extraordinary coincidence that two stranglers had lived in the same house at the same time, but there was no reason why this should not have occurred. But Chuter Ede, who never really recovered from his failure to reprieve Evans, was damning. The Scott Henderson inquiry, he said, had been a travesty of judicial procedure recognised by the law of the land. He then told a hushed House how R. A. Butler had come to him one night and asked him, as a friend and former home secretary, what he (Chuter Ede) would have done, and had said, 'I am advised that I must not say that this man Evans was innocent.' The matter would remain before the home secretary until it was cleared up. Could he still regard the man as guilty beyond all reasonable doubt? The evidence of doubt in the case was overwhelming, and if the House was going to carry out an act of grace, they should do it gracefully and graciously and say there are grave doubts about the position in the case. The home secretary should recommend to the Queen that she grant a free pardon to Evans. If there was no precedent for this, the time had come where the situation demanded the creation of one.

Chuter Ede's was a powerful and low-key speech whereas Sydney Silverman was more forthright. He conceded that Scott Henderson was elderly and unwell, but they had a duty to justice, to the dead and to themselves. He said that no honest man with that evidence before him could have made the report that Scott Henderson made. He must have known it was not true. George Rogers believed that Butler was big enough and generous enough to agree to another inquiry to set the country's mind at rest on the issue. Sir Frank Soskice also appealed to the home secretary that there should be a further investigation into the facts of the case (but a few years later, when home secretary himself, declined precisely that).

Butler, closing the debate, said he had studied *10 Rillington Place* with great care but could not find that Kennedy had produced any significant new facts. Since the facts as they were known by no means pointed exclusively to the innocence of Evans, he did not think an inquiry would help. There was no reason to think that any further evidence would be brought to light. A free pardon could not be granted unless there was certainty that Evans was innocent which was not possible in that case. A reprieve might have been granted if all the facts had been known at the time, but for him, while there was doubt he could not grant a free pardon.[24]

(The Anti-Violence League opened a campaign to secure the repeal of the Homicide Act and the imposition of sterner penalties including corporal punishment for crimes of violence) Prominent among the league's leaders was Sir Thomas Moore.[25] An editorial in *The Times* said that the Anti-Violence League sounded good—everyone was against violence—but there was a danger that the sensational and exaggerated talk of its organizers would breed hysteria and make more unlikely the serious consideration that those grave problems deserved. Recalling the words of Leon Radzinowicz, it agreed that there was an almost universal inclination to exaggerate the potential influence of criminal legislation and of penal systems on the state of crime.[26]

Charles Pannell took a small step forward when he was given leave to introduce his Burial of Offenders Bill. The Bill would amend section 6 Capital Punishment Amendment Act 1868 which stated that the body of every offender executed should be buried within the walls of the prison where he was executed. He wanted the home secretary to be able to give back the body to the next of kin; this could be done with the body of Evans. Pannell regarded the burial of bodies within the precincts of prisons as ghoulish and out of keeping with the times.[27]

Pros . . .
The Lower House of the Convocation of Canterbury which met in October 1961 debated capital punishment. The motion to welcome the abolition of capital punishment or at least its suspension for five years was moved by the Reverend F. D. Coleman. He believed that even though hanging had been removed from public view the act was still horrible and degrading. There was no evidence from other countries that the removal of the death penalty resulted in an increased murder rate. The Reverend Hawthorne said that the increase in armed robbery made it clear that the death penalty was not a deterrent. However, the Archdeacon of Dudley, the venerable A. V. Hurley, felt sure that the death penalty was a deterrent. He said there should be different classes of murder and that execution should remain on the statute book but be used as sparingly as possible. They should not, he concluded, be misled into voting for what looked like a nice pious resolution. Canon F. F. G. Warman moved an amendment adding to the motion the provision for the treatment of convicted people and suitable compensation for the relatives of victims of homicide. His amendment was accepted and agreed.[28]

In a sermon at Canterbury Cathedral the Bishop of Woolwich, the Right Reverend J. A. T. Robinson, said that '. . . hanging will go at the next really big push'. He said that the death penalty might well deter normal people but most murderers were not normal and the glamour of the death penalty acted as an actual incitement. 'Earlier this year', he told the congregation, 'we had a most dramatic example of this. On May 25, Victor John Terry was hanged at Wandsworth prison for the murder of a bank guard. He did that murder one hour after the hanging of Forsyth and Harris, and Terry knew them both. Far from having been deterred by the fate of his friends, the execution and the publicity that went with it seemed to have incited him to share it'.[29]

... and Cons

At the Conservative party conference at Brighton a motion was moved by one H. P. Lucas calling on the government to extend capital punishment to cover all murders where insanity was not proven. Geoffrey Howe responded that the number of murders on average since the Homicide Act was passed was about the same as that during the two years before the Act, and below the average over the past half century. He said 'There is certainly insufficient evidence to justify this conference trying to reverse the compromise that Parliament evolved only four years ago.' Butler said that any comparison of murder statistics was difficult because since the Act many killings were classified as manslaughter. He promised to keep the question under perpetual review.[30]

The point made by Geoffrey Howe was taken up by *The Times*. In an editorial[31] about a publication by the Home Office Research Unit called 'Murder', the paper agreed that the murder rate had been remarkably stable over the previous 30 years indicating that the Homicide Act was operating as intended, and concluded that capital murderers were mainly thieves who killed in the pursuit of criminal activities while non-capital murders were more likely to be committed in the heat of emotion.

Given that most capital murders were committed by family members on each other, and that slow poisoning was a non-capital offence, there was little to be said for this analysis. Indeed, D. J. Bentley found the reasoning hard to follow.[32] He thought that the point of retaining the death penalty for capital murders was to check such murders but neither rate had gone down since 1957.

A far sounder analysis was to be found in a letter from the joint chairmen for the National Campaign for the Abolition of Capital Punishment, Gerald Gardiner and Victor Gollancz. They said it was generally agreed that the Homicide Act had neither a moral nor rational basis and had resulted in practice in indefensible anomalies and ought not be left as it was. The publication of the pamphlet 'Murder' showed that the murder rate over the past 30 years had been unaffected by the general increase in crime. Since the Homicide Act there had been only a small increase in capital murders and a small decrease in non-capital murders. This indicated that capital punishment was no more a deterrent than any alternative punishment. Commenting on the vote at the Conservative party conference, the motion of the lower House of Convocation and the recent decision of New Zealand to abandon capital punishment, they expressed the hope that the government would do so too.[33]

A debate in the House of Lords on the pamphlet 'Murder' turned into a general debate on the abolition of capital punishment, but it was largely shunned by those on the Conservative benches. The Lord Chancellor (Lord Dilhorne) refused to be drawn except to make a diffident defence of the Homicide Act. In a throwback to Jeremy Bentham (see *Chapters 3* and *4*), the Conservative Lord Teviot suggested that the possibility of reciprocal punishment for murderers should be investigated. For example, one who stabs his victim to death should himself be stabbed to death. Perhaps Lord Teviot was about 500 years too late with his suggestion for it received no approval, not even from his own benches. Lord Stonham felt that the publication showed conclusively that the case for abolition was unanswerable, a view not shared by Lord Conesford. Lightening the mood, Lord Stonham recalled how he had obtained a reprieve for a murderer in 1958. The murderer had written to him: 'as one of your constituents I am writing to you on a matter of some importance . . . I am to be hanged on Tuesday week . . .' and ended, 'hoping this finds you as it leaves me'.[34]

Murder on the A6

On the evening of 22 August 1961 Michael Gregsten, a married man, had an assignation with his lady-friend Valerie Storie which began with a drive in his car and ended with probably another innocent man being hanged. During the course of the evening, night and early hours of the following morning a man with a gun demanded to be driven around and to be given food. Gregsten drove at gunpoint and they all three ended up on the A6, a little north of the village of Clophill, on a stretch of road prophetically known as Deadman's Hill. They stopped in a lay-by and as Gregston was taking something from the boot of the car their hijacker panicked and shot him dead. Shortly afterwards, the killer forced the distraught Valerie Storie to show him how to drive a car, sexually assaulted her and then shot her. He believed she was dead and drove off; she was, however, still alive, but her legs were paralysed. She lay semi-conscious on the ground then, after it became light, managed to attract the attention of a passing motorist by waving her petticoat. The police and an ambulance were called and she survived.

On October 11 James Hanratty was arrested in Blackpool and three days later was identified by Valerie Storie as the man who killed her lover and shot her. Hanratty was charged with murder. At the trial that began on 22 January 1962, Hanratty ran an alibi defence but on February 17 he was convicted and sentenced to death. His appeal was turned down on March 13, but it was widely believed that he was innocent and that another man, who had been arrested later and released, may have been the murderer. Despite a petition containing some 90,000 signatures calling for a reprieve, the home secretary, R. A. Butler, allowed the law to take its course and Hanratty was hanged on April 4.[35]

There was considerable unease about Hanratty's conviction and execution and a year later Fenner Brockway, MP for Eton and Slough (in whose constituency Gregston and Storie's fatal assignation began), after investigating the matter for more than a year, called for an inquiry into the hanging of Hanratty. But at the end of a debate lasting two hours the home secretary, Henry Brooke, could not agree to re-open the case or appoint an inquiry.[36]

Whether Hanratty was unjustly hanged has never been finally resolved as it was in the case of Evans. But the public unease that the execution generated undoubtedly helped the abolitionists, although by the time the first book on the subject was published on 21 October 1965, by Earl Russell of Liverpool, capital punishment in Britain was on the threshold of abolition.

Extra-Parliamentary activity

At the same time that James Hanratty was being tried, convicted sentenced and executed (but without alluding to that case at the time) there came, in 1962, a renewed plea for the ending of the death penalty from the Committee of Honour of the National Campaign for the Abolition of Capital Punishment. The situation had been changed by the pamphlet 'Murder' which, they said, powerfully reinforced the case against capital punishment being a greater deterrent than any other form of punishment. The committee also drew attention to the vote of the Lower House of Convocation, the proceedings of the Conservative party conference and the New Zealand decision. Among many signatures were the Bishops of Birmingham, Chichester, Manchester, Ripon, Sheffield, Woolwich and Southwark, as well as Julian Huxley, Compton McKenzie, Henry Moore and Leonard Woolf.[37]

It was announced that in anticipation of the meeting of the bishops as the Upper House of Convocation in Canterbury, the Bishop of Southwark, Mervyn Stockwood, would lead a discussion on a motion in his name inviting the bishops to support the introduction of a Bill in Parliament providing for the abolition of capital punishment or at least its complete suspension for a period of five years.[38] When the meeting took place this resolution received unanimous support. Dr Stockwood recalled that in 1810 the Archbishop of Canterbury (who was Charles Manners Sutton) and six bishops voted against the abolition of the death penalty for stealing five shillings. But in 1956 both archbishops and eight of the nine bishops present voted for abolition or suspension. He indicated the absurdity of the Homicide Act, which he said was more appropriate to Alice in Wonderland, with a number of interesting scenarios. He said that if a man killed his wife with the nearest weapon to hand and that was a gun he committed capital murder; if it was a hatchet it was not capital murder. Even more pointed: if a man raped a girl then strangled her and took her handbag this was capital murder; if he didn't take the bag it was not. The Archbishop of Canterbury, Michael Ramsey, associated himself with the resolution.[39]

In a leading article, *The Times* noted that with the notable exception of William Temple, bishops of the Church of England had taken no part in the movement for the abolition of capital punishment up to the middle of the present century. In 1956 Dr Fisher, the Archbishop of Canterbury, and the Archbishop of York, though voting for the second reading of the Death Penalty (Abolition) Bill, both disagreed with the notion that the death penalty was always un-Christian and wrong. Dr Ramsey had supported that Bill outright; Fisher supported the Homicide Act whilst Ramsey found it morally shocking.[40]

A statement was issued by the executive committee (meeting for sufferings) of the Society of Friends in Great Britain which described judicial hanging as a barbaric and degrading act. They pledged their active support of the National Campaign for the Abolition of Capital Punishment. 'As members of a democracy,' they said, 'we are involved in the wickedness of capital punishment and therefore feel bound to raise our voices against it'.[41] But an article by *The Times* political correspondent said that there was no intention to amend the Homicide Act in the lifetime of the present Parliament. Opponents and supporters of capital punishment agreed that the Act created anomalies that would be better removed. There was no doubt, said the article, that the Commons as then composed was not radical enough to carry such an amendment. It was reckoned that all but five or six Labour members would support abolition, but perhaps no more than 60 to 70 Conservatives. Many members of the public would accept abolition of the death penalty if it were replaced by imprisonment for the rest of the murderer's life or a length of sentence that reflected the degree of the crime. There were signs that this was the forward direction in which the home secretary wished to move.[42]

The National Campaign for the Abolition of Capital Punishment in a statement on imitative crimes said that the death penalty might be an incentive to murderers who had suicidal or exhibitionist disorders.[43]

Butler's cautious support

The home secretary, R. A. Butler, had exchanges with backbenchers who were leaders in the National Campaign for the Abolition of Capital Punishment. He reiterated that there was no hope of an amendment to the Homicide Act in the lifetime of that Parliament. It was widely believed that Butler had much sympathy with the abolitionists' case but saw no chance of removing anomalies or of abolishing hanging in the House as it was then composed, nor would he allow a free vote on it as it was a free vote that produced those very anomalies that were known to be disturbing the judiciary and the lawyers.

The representative backbenchers were Sydney Silverman, Chuter Ede, Jeremy Thorpe, and two Conservatives, Peter Kirk and Julian Critchley. Silverman said 'the home secretary quite clearly realised that the trend of events is towards abolition. I think it is fair to say he did not dispute any of the actual propositions put in front of him. He indicated that . . . he has an open mind and is keeping the situation constantly under review. He invited us to keep in touch with him if we wished and promised to consider very carefully everything we had said.' The deputation claimed that although the number of executions had gone down from about 12 a year to about three, there had been no appreciable effect on the murder rate.[44]

However, Gerald Gardiner was not happy with the phrase 'produced those very anomalies that were disturbing to the judiciary . . .' and disputed it. He said that while the Labour and Liberal parties had had a free vote the then government put the whips on and refused to allow one word to be altered from the original Bill in spite of numerous attempts to improve it made by abolitionist members. One of the reasons why the Homicide Act was as hopeless as it was, was because it was not passed on a free vote but was forced through by the then government with the whips on.[45]

When Mr Carol Johnson asked the home secretary whether he would review the provisions of the Homicide Act, Butler, in a written reply, said he would certainly look into any evidence but that it was only fair to say that he saw no prospects of early legislation on the subject.[46] A similar verbal answer to a similar question from Tom Driberg two weeks later resulted in one of the few discussions on the subject in the Commons at that time.[47] Driberg wanted to know if he was considering longer prison sentences for murderers sentenced to life imprisonment. Butler replied that the length of time to be served depended on the circumstances of the case. Each case was decided on its merits. In what could be regarded as the average case the period was about nine years but he thought that many prisoners detained for non-capital murders would have to serve longer than hitherto. Sir Thomas Moore said that the Act could not be reviewed, 'illogical and pernicious though it may be', as there would not be enough space to hold all the prisoners. Alice Bacon welcomed the Home secretary's explanation of life sentences as there was a great deal of misunderstanding. Sydney Silverman asked whether revisions or alterations in the law could be submitted to a vote in the country (as Moore had suggested). Moore replied, 'A general election'. Silverman replied that there was division along party lines and that a referendum might be more appropriate, but Butler would not undertake that the House would be given a free vote on the matter. One of the difficulties about the present law was that there had been very great doubt about it and he doubted whether a free vote would settle the matter.

Meanwhile, the British Council of Churches, at their half-yearly meeting at Hoddesden, Hertfordshire passed a resolution urging the government to abolish capital punishment. The arguments put forward were based on moral grounds and the anomalous results of the Homicide Act. The Bishop of Blackburn put forward two suggestions, passed by the meeting, that the sentence substituting the death penalty should be a substantial term of imprisonment, and that the dependants of the victim should be compensated.[48]

Some weeks later, Dr Harland, the Bishop of Durham, said that he was unable to vote for the motion to abolish capital punishment. He had, in the past, ministered to six different men in their condemned cells and described to the meeting his ministrations to one of them, who had committed a particularly brutal murder. He said that by the third week in the condemned cell, life, death, God and the next world became a reality to the men. In those circumstances he found it difficult to vote against capital punishment. The hardest task he had ever had, he concluded, was having to break the news to two men that they had been reprieved, for then they had the task of making good again. Notwithstanding the bishop's past difficulties, the motion was carried by an overwhelming majority.[49]

Not surprisingly, the bishop's odd comments drew some correspondence. Edmund Carpenter, the Treasurer of Westminster Abbey, said that if a man's immortal destiny depended on the reflection which the expectancy of death brings with it, then logic would demand the extension of capital punishment rather than its abolition. G. W. H. Lampe and Hugh Montefiore went further. They asked that if the prospect of hanging fitted men for eternity, ought one not press for the extension of hanging for all crimes? Why, indeed, should a crime be a requisite at all?[50]

A deputation led by Lord Harewood on behalf of the National Campaign for the Abolition of Capital Punishment went to Admiralty House to present a memorial to the prime minister and home secretary calling for the abolition of the death penalty. Others in the deputation were the Bishop of Exeter, Chuter Ede, Gerald Gardiner and Victor Gollancz. The memorial, which Lord Harewood said greatly impressed the prime minister and Mr Butler, was signed by 6,825 people including 39 bishops.[51]

Changes at the top
On what later became known as the 'Night of the Long Knives', on 13 July 1962 Harold Macmillan reshuffled his cabinet. Seven ministers were ousted. Among the changes, one of the few to be promoted rather than sacked, R. A. Butler moved from the Home Office to become first secretary of state and deputy prime minister. Sir Reginald Manningham-Buller, who was attorney general, replaced Lord Kilmuir (who 'resigned' and was later made an Earl) as Lord Chancellor and was made a Baron (he later became Viscount Dilhorne); and Henry Brooke became home secretary. Hugh Gaitskell called the reshuffle a 'political massacre which could only be interpreted as a gigantic admission of failure'. He called for a general election.[52]

When he addressed the City of London Young Conservatives, Sir Peter Rawlinson, the solicitor-general, said that the distinction in the Homicide Act between capital and non-capital murder was operating as was intended. He said, 'Many people believe that the death penalty should be abolished but there are more, I believe, equally intelligent and sincere people who believe that the penalty must be retained. The Act should be reviewed only after a substantial period of time'.[53]

Another change at the top
Throughout January 1963 Hugh Gaitskell, the leader of the Labour party, was in poor health which suddenly worsened, and on the evening of January 18 he died at Middlesex Hospital at the age of 56.[54] He had been party leader since 14 December 1955 and after the funeral the ballot for a new leader was organized as soon as was seemly.

There were three candidates: George Brown, James Callaghan and Harold Wilson. At the first ballot early in February Callaghan polled only 41 votes and was eliminated; as neither of the others received the requisite number of votes there was a second ballot one week later.[55] The second poll took place on the same day that Alf Ramsey took over as manager of the England football team and when the result was announced by Charles Kee, one of the principle scrutineers, Harold Wilson, as had been expected, won by 154 votes to 103, most of Callaghan's votes going to Wilson.[56] Three and a half years later, in 1966, both Wilson and Ramsey were to be extremely successful, Wilson winning a majority of almost 100 and Ramsey the World Cup.

The last quiet act by the Conservatives before hell broke loose for them with serious repercussions for the party, the government, and indirectly for capital punishment, was a meeting of the Young Conservatives in London. They

227

voted against a resolution urging the abolition of capital punishment by about two to one on a show of hands. They were addressed by Henry Brooke, the home secretary, who said he accepted that the Homicide Act 1957 was not perfect but had seen no suggestion for a better demarcation line or fewer anomalies if the country was to accept the idea of a death penalty for certain murders but not others.[57]

Profumo and the fall of Macmillan

The turmoil that was ultimately to bring down the government began quietly and almost insignificantly. A rumour that John Profumo, better known to the public as the husband of the popular and elegant film actress Valerie Hobson than as secretary of state for war, had offered his resignation to the prime minister was denied. When asked if there was any reason why he should resign he replied 'None whatsoever'.[58]

One week later, he denied in the House of Commons that he was having an affair with Christine Keeler, who as a bound witness at the an Old Bailey trial had disappeared, or that he knew her whereabouts. He added that there had been no impropriety in their relationship and followed this up by successfully suing a French and Italian magazine for libel.[59]

Profumo's 'House of Cards' was brought down by a Dr Stephen Ward, who moved in the same social set as the war minister. Ward revealed that he had sent a letter to the home secretary claiming that Profumo's personal statement to the House on March 22 was untrue. When this allegation was put to him on behalf of the prime minister, Profumo stuck to his guns, but his position was unsustainable. On June 4 he saw Martin Redmayne the government chief whip, and admitted that he had lied. He said he wished to resign as minister and as an MP by applying for the Chiltern Hundreds and the next day formally resigned his office and Commons seat, admitting that he was guilty of a grave misdemeanour in deceiving the House of Commons.

Profumo was politically ruined. He and Keeler disappeared from public view but the government were not out of the woods. It came to light in the course of an enquiry that Miss Keeler made herself available not only to Profumo but also to a Soviet diplomatist in the same social set, a Captain Ivanov. Even before Profumo had resigned, Lord Dilhorne, the Lord Chancellor, had begun enquiries into the security implications of the case and it was quite clear that unless Dilhorne could dispose of every lingering doubt concerning Ivanov, Macmillan's personal position could be threatened.[60]

On June 20 a motion in the Commons was debated 'that John Profumo, in making a personal statement to this House on March 22, which contained words which he later admitted to be untrue, was guilty of a grave contempt of this House.' The motion was agreed and the debate was short, but there were two interventions that were interesting. Mr Warby said that the home secretary already knew that Mr Profumo had been engaged in an improper association, but denied, when challenged by the speaker, that he was accusing the home secretary of personal dishonesty; and Sydney Silverman showed that his humanity did not stop at opposing capital punishment. He agreed that what

Profumo had done was a contempt of the House but he hoped that that was the end of the matter. He said that Profumo, who was in a difficult personal situation, had made a bad mistake but had paid for it. He had left the government and his distinguished political career was ruined. He was surrounded by public obloquy of a serious kind which it would take him a long time to live down. He ended, 'I do express the hope that he may not be persecuted or prosecuted further, and that we can all now agree to leave him alone.' Selwyn Lloyd personally thanked Silverman for what he had said.[61]

In an article on the debate[62] in *The Times* Silverman's words headed the column:

Not for the first time Mr Silverman showed that he needs no antennae to divine the mood of the Commons at any given moment and he put with great felicity what most members today obviously felt. Mr Selwyn Lloyd, in a couple of sentences seemed touched by the gravity and dignity of Mr Silverman's utterance, and Mr Silverman and his speeches seldom command agreement of any kind on the Tory benches. But then Mr Silverman is large on charity though small in stature. Not everyone in the House, however, would take his advice.

On the day of the debate there was a by-election for the seat held by Hugh Gaitskell (Leeds, South). Merlyn Rees retained the seat for Labour with a majority of over 13,000.

The government was fatally damaged by the Profumo affair. Harold Macmillan had been prime minister for seven years and had been ill for some months. His long-standing illness gave him an excuse to resign and the announcement came from Middlesex Hospital at 10.30 a.m. on October 17. At 11.15 a.m. the Queen visited him in hospital and shortly after noon the Earl of Home arrived at the palace where he was invited to form an administration. Home's appointment was a surprise—the smart money was on Butler—and when he arrived at Downing Street just after 2.30 p.m. it was by no means certain how many ministers in Macmillan's government would be willing to serve under Home, particularly Lord Hailsham, R. A. Butler and Reginald Maudling, who had all been in the running.[63] However, Home created a cabinet without too much difficulty[64] and all the rivals for the leadership accepted posts: Butler became foreign secretary (replacing Home), Hailsham became Lord President of the Council and minister for science and Maudling remained chancellor. Henry Brooke remained home secretary and Lord Dilhorne remained Lord Chancellor.[65]

The year ended with the creation of six Labour Life Peers, two of whom were Hugh Gaitskell's widow, Dora, and Gerald Gardiner QC.[66] Gardiner's elevation was an enormous boost for the abolitionists—he was still joint chairman of the National Campaign for the Abolition of Capital Punishment and worked hard for the cause—for in becoming a peer he was seen as a Lord Chancellor in waiting. It was widely rumoured at the Bar that he had declined the appointment to a High Court judgeship in the late 1950s because he was not prepared to pass the death sentence.[67]

Wilson's strong hints

As many people had predicted, Sir Alec Douglas Home, as he became after renouncing his hereditary earldom, was a weak, some would say inadequate, prime minister, and by the turn of the year a general election could not be long delayed. During an appearance on the ITV programme *This Week,* Harold Wilson was asked what a Labour government would do about the abolition of capital punishment which had been in the party programme since 1924. Wilson answered that it would be left to a free vote in Parliament and with a Labour majority he knew what the outcome would be.[68]

When a number of cuts were made by the Lord Chamberlain in a play about capital punishment called *Hang Down Your Head and Die* to be presented by the Oxford University Experimental Theatre Club the producer, Mr Braham Murray telephoned Lord Gardiner as chairman of the National Campaign for the Abolition of Capital Punishment. After a visit by Gardiner, Lord (Ted) Willis and Kenneth Robinson MP, the cuts were restored, the point having been made that by cutting the strongest arguments against capital punishment political censorship was being exercised.[69]

A view of what the attitude of a Labour government might be towards capital punishment was emerging. Addressing the Society of Labour Lawyers, Harold Wilson indicated some of the early legal reforms that an incoming Labour administration would make. Referring to the Homicide Act 1957 he said that it was generally agreed that the Act had neither a rational nor a moral basis and few people could be found to defend the law as it stood. He felt that as this was an issue on which people had strong views and which was to some a matter of conscience, It should be left to a free vote in the House, and they would be prepared to find government time for that.[70]

The Labour party published its manifesto on 11 September 1964[71] but it made no mention of capital punishment or its abolition. The general election was held on October 15, the same day that Cole Porter died, and Lynn Davies won the long jump and Britain's third gold medal at the Tokyo Olympics. So close was the result that it was not known until quite late on October 16 that Labour had definitely won. They finished with 317 seats (gained 61, lost five). The Conservatives had 302 (gained five, lost 63), and the Liberals nine (gained four, lost two) and the other parties two: a majority over the Conservatives of 15[72] and an overall majority of just four seats.

One of the first announcements the new prime minister made was his appointment of Lord Gardiner as Lord Chancellor; this was followed shortly by the appointment of Sir Frank Soskice as home secretary.[73] Other appointments included F. Elwyn Jones as attorney-general and Dingle Foot as solicitor-general.

The new government had inherited a muddle from its weak predecessor, and it had a heavy legislative programme of its own to push through with a tiny majority. The issue of capital punishment was not an important one, and abolition was by no means universally popular; but for abolitionists in and out of Parliament the finishing tape was in sight, and Sydney Silverman, the man who

230

would carry the baton across the line, who had been waiting to do so for more than two decades, was ready and waiting still.

ENDNOTES

1 *The Times*, p. 4, 27 January 1961
2 ibid,
3 ibid, p. 12
4 ibid, p. 7, 28 January 1961
5 *Hansard*, [633] 101 (31 January 1961)
6 *The Times*, p. 13, 1 February 1961
7 ibid, p. 11, 2 February 1961
8 ibid, p. 5, 4 February 1961
9 ibid, p. 12, 8 February 1961
10 *Hansard*, [634] 1729 (16 February 1961)
11 ibid, [634] 1730-32; *The Times*, p.18, 17 February 1960
12 *The Times*, p. 13, 16 February 1961
13 ibid, p.14
14 ibid, p. 18, 17 February 1961
15 *Hansard*, [634] 73 (16 February 1961)
16 The Times, p. 4, 24 February 1961
17 ibid, p. 4, 17 March 1961
18 ibid, p. 6, 18 March 1961
19 ibid, p. 12, 13 April 1961
20 ibid, p. 6, 6 May 1961
21 ibid, p. 16, 2 June 1961
22 ibid, p. 6
23 ibid, p. 15, 5 June 1961
24 ibid, p. 21, 16 June 1961
25 ibid, p. 6, 17 July 1961
26 ibid, p. 11
27 *The Times*, p.14, 19 July 1961
28 ibid, p. 6, 6 October 1961
29 ibid, p. 6, 9 October 1961
30 ibid, p. 13, 27 October 1961
31 ibid, p. 12, 26 October 1961
32 ibid, p. 11, 1 November 1961
33 ibid, p. 13, 26 October 1961
34 ibid, p.14, 10 November 1961
35 *Who Killed Hanratty?*, Foot, P, Jonathan Cape Ltd., 1971
36 *Hansard*, [682] 795 (2 August 1963)

37 *The Times*, p. 9, 2 January 1962
38 *The Times*, p. 6, 5 January 1962
39 ibid, p. 7, 18 January 1962
40 ibid, p.11
41 ibid, p. 15, 13 February 1962
42 ibid, p.12, 15 February 1962
43 ibid, p. 15, 20 February 1962
44 ibid, p. 5, 9 March 1962
45 ibid, p. 13, 13 March 1962
46 ibid, p. 17, 16 March 1962
47 *Hansard*, [656] 1535 (29 March 1962)
48 *The Times*, p. 5, 5 April 1962
49 ibid, p. 8, 16 May 1962
50 ibid, p.13, 18 May 1962
51 ibid, p. 9, 6 July 1962
52 ibid, p. 8, 14 July 1962
53 ibid, p. 6, 13 September 1962
54 ibid, p. 8, 19 January 1963
55 ibid, p. 12, 14 February 1963
56 ibid, p. 10, 15 February 1963
57 ibid, p. 6, 18 February 1963
58 ibid, p. 12, 15 March 1963
59 ibid, p. 8, 23 March 1963

60 ibid, p.12, 12 June 1963
61 ibid, p. 7, 21 June 1963
62 ibid, p. 12
63 ibid, p. 12, 18 October 1963
64 ibid, p. 6, 21 October 1963
65 ibid, p. 10, 21 October 1963
66 ibid, p. 6, 24 December 1963
67 Her Honour Jean Graham Hall: personal communication
68 *The Times*, p. 5, 17 January 1964
69 ibid, p. 6, 8 February 1964
70 *The Times*, p. 10, 21 April 1964
71 ibid, p. 6, 12 September 1964
72 ibid, p. 6, 16 October 1964 (several editions published, updating the result)
73 ibid, p. 12, 19 October 1964.

CHAPTER 18

Abolition

Harold Wilson had promised a great deal of action in the first 100 days of his administration. Law reform would be pursued under the leadership of the new Lord Chancellor, Lord Gardiner, and this would include setting up an Ombudsman system to examine private grievances of public administration. But barely a week after the election Herbert Bowden, Lord President of the Council, raised the possibility of the Capital Punishment Bill being introduced by a private member[1] and a promise was made that a Bill would be mentioned in the Queen's Speech. Sure enough, between items regarding the strengthening of the police and preventing and treating delinquency, and the remuneration of ministers and MPs, the Queen said, 'Facilities will be provided for a free decision by Parliament on the issue of capital punishment.'

Prominent abolitionist MPs were confident that the session would see the complete abolition of the death penalty. Time would be found by the government but the initiative would have to be taken by a backbencher. Many MPs believed that it would be an acknowledgement of his devotion to the cause if Sydney Silverman were to be in charge of the legislation in the House of Commons. He could introduce the Bill under the ten minute rule and a substantial majority could be forecast.[2] *The Times* had no doubt that such a Bill would carry in the Commons as it was then composed,[3] and in an article commenting on the contents of the Queen's Speech[4] the abolition of hanging was counted as one of eight major pieces of forthcoming legislation.

However, the retentionists were already girding their loins for battle. During the debate on the Queen's Speech, Edward Gardner suggested that the question of capital punishment should be referred to a committee in preparation for a debate which would ultimately have to be the business of the whole house.[5] Thomas Iremonger went further. He thought that government members should not accept the 'popular dogma' that the Homicide Act was a foolish measure. It was not. He found it 'distressing' that the House was getting a free decision on capital punishment without some kind of improvement in the current life sentence arrangements.[6]

The Conservative leadership quickly decided that their own rank and file should also have a free vote on the legislation to abolish capital punishment and it was announced that Sydney Silverman was ready to introduce a Bill as soon as the first opportunity presented itself.[7]

The Parliamentary correspondent of *The Times* sensed that the time was near when an MP would seek leave under the ten minute rule to introduce a Bill to end capital punishment and explained what would happen. When the Bill was introduced, Sir Frank Soskice, the home secretary, would formally offer government facilities for the second reading and for a division on a free vote for all parties. With a prime minister personally pledged to their cause, and a Lord Chancellor who was treasurer of the Howard League for Penal Reform and on the committee of the National Campaign for the Abolition of Capital Punishment, the first to step across the boundary between law and politics to put the hangman out of business, the abolitionists seemed set to succeed at last. Prominent Conservatives who were also abolitionists included Sir Edward Boyle, the shadow home secretary, Selwyn Lloyd, Angus Maude and Iain McLeod.

It was possible that if the new Bill were piloted in the Lords by Lord Gardiner it might bring about the first clash between the Labour government and the Conservative majority in the Lords. There was no reason to suppose that the Lords had changed since Silverman's Bill was rejected so decisively in 1956. Notwithstanding, the correspondent concluded that the hangman could begin to coil up his rope for the last time as he was hardly likely to be allowed to use it again in Britain.[8]

Even before the Bill was presented, the retentionists were trying to weaken it. Sir Richard Glyn (Conservative, Dorset North) wanted to retain the death penalty for murder by shooting. He said that without that amendment the Bill was a licence for gangsters to shoot their way out and the Bill as it stood would greatly increase the number of innocent people who would be shot dead. He was supported by the former attorney-general, Sir John Hobson, who said that if that amendment were not passed the criminal classes would not only go armed but would use their arms. There would be armed gangs of thugs ready to use their arms against each other in gang warfare as well as for thieving. Another ardent retentionist was Sir Peter Rawlinson. When he addressed a meeting of the Baron's Court Constituency Conservative Association he said he hoped ministers would survey the views on abolition of all the police forces in the country. They were the guardians of society, and Parliament and the public should at least be told of their judgement.[9] Henry Brooke was more moderate; he asked Sir Frank Soskice what period of imprisonment he was considering as a substitute for the death penalty. The home secretary replied that he was reluctant to make it higher than nine or ten years because that was the maximum period a prisoner could undergo before his personality deteriorated, but if it was in the interests of society he could be kept inside longer.[10]

The new Bill

When Sydney Silverman presented his Bill for the abolition of capital punishment it was not expected to run into organized opposition from the diminishing number of Conservative backbenchers who held a different view. Even the most convinced opponents of abolition recognised that the new House of Commons could not fail to carry an abolitionist Bill which would have government support. It was possible that an attempt would be made to retain hanging for the protection of the police when arresting armed criminals.[11]

An article in *The Times* entitled 'The End of the Road for Hanging' published the day after Silverman introduced his Bill into the Commons opined that the two men who had been hanged on 13 August 1964 (see the *Preface* to this work) would be the last to be hanged in Britain. The situation in Parliament was both clearer and more confused than it was eight years earlier when the

234

Homicide Act was passed. Clearer because the government were offering Parliament the opportunity to abolish the death penalty, and they had a Lord Chancellor long known to be an advocate of abolition and who regarded the Homicide Act as 'hopeless'. More confused because some argued that the correct course was not general abolition but an extension and redefinition of categories of capital murder. There was also the problem of the alternative penalty. A life sentence of an average eight or nine years was not generally believed to be a deterrent; those who suggested a minimum sentence of 20 to 25 years were at odds with those who argued that such a long term would institutionalise the offender totally. The attitude of two former home secretaries, Butler and Brooke, with their personal experience of having to decide whether to recommend reprieves, would carry great weight.[12]

The abolition of the death penalty was regarded as a virtual certainty. Silverman introduced the Murder (Abolition of Death Penalty) Bill; there were no prisoners awaiting execution and no death sentence would be carried out while the subject was debated.[13] The long title of the Bill was 'A Bill to abolish capital punishment in the case of persons convicted in Great Britain of murder or a corresponding offence by court martial, in connection therewith, to make further provision for the punishment of persons who are convicted'. Further provision will be a proposal to allow judges to prescribe long sentences'. This meant, in effect, that the Bill would substitute a sentence of life imprisonment but the length of sentence was not defined. Supporting Silverman as sponsors were Humphrey Berkley, Bessie Braddock, Chris Chattaway, Michael Foot, Sir Geoffrey de Freitas, Leslie Heal, Emanuel Shinwell, Jeremy Thorpe, Shirley Williams, Reginald Paget and Arthur Newens.

Hugh Klare, secretary of the Howard League for Penal Reform, welcomed the Bill. He said that life imprisonment should be an indeterminate sentence the length of which should be decided by the home secretary on the basis of an assessment programme.[14] Sir John Hobson, attorney-general in the previous government, wrote a letter analysing murder and capital murder before and after the Homicide Act. He claimed that capital punishment since 1957 had deterred robbers, thieves and gangsters from committing murder, and that it would be foolish to remove the deterrent,[15] but it was unlikely that the figures he quoted were statistically significant. A few days later Hugh Klare wrote again, quoting figures from the Home Office Research Unit which showed that the proportion of capital to non-capital murders had remained broadly similar.[16] However, Norman Kendall considered the point made in Hobson's letter 'unanswerable' and thought that the proposition that the fear of death is no deterrent was manifestly ridiculous.[17] He was joined by George A. Floris who wrote 'after succeeding in abolishing the death penalty let us hope that our penal reformers will turn their attention to abolishing murder'.[18]

The retentionists rally their forces
Meanwhile in the House of Commons, Sir Peter Rawlinson asked the home secretary if he would conduct a survey of all the chief constables as to whether capital punishment for murder by gunshot and in the course of theft should be

retained. Soskice replied that he would not, but that he would always consider any views that chief constables might express.[19] In answer to a further question by Rawlinson the home secretary published the following table:[20]

YEAR	No. executed for capital murder	No. convicted of capital murder (executed)		
		theft	*shooting*	*theft & shooting*
1958	4	8(5)	-	-
1959	6	3(2)	2(2)	-
1960	3	7(5)	-	1(-)
1961	7	5(2)	3(2)	1(1)
1962	3	2(1)	2(2)	-
1963	2	2(2)	2(-)	-
1964 (to December)	2	3(2)	2(-)	-

Edward Gardner wrote that there was disquiet by the majority about the abolition of capital punishment and they were more concerned with the victim than with the murderer. Before the death penalty could be removed with safety an alternative and fully discouraging penalty had to be substituted. Life imprisonment was a vague and indeterminate sentence and was unlikely to frighten anyone but the potential victim.[21]

The introduction of the Bill had given new life to the correspondence columns. Dr T. E. Williams wrote citing a case where a woman had received a depressed fracture of the skull during a robbery. She survived, but he asked whether, had she died, were we prepared to abolition the death penalty for such a dastardly blow and allow the criminal freedom again even after a long term of imprisonment? But F. E. T. S. Langton, an ex-parish priest, was glad about abolition although worried about the condition of those kept in prison for a very long time. He thought that a life of hopelessness should not be substituted for death. Hugh MacGregor thought that the majority view should be adopted; the death penalty should be retained but there should be a more humane and civilised means of its administration. And one of the most smug letters of all, from G. I. Howell, said that the best way to abolish capital punishment was to refrain from murder. 'No-one is compelled to commit murder and a man has only himself to blame if he is hanged'.[22]

The second reading of the Bill was barely two weeks away and one of the amendments that Conservative backbenchers were preparing would subject it to renewal every five years. Although the opposition agreed that there should be a free vote they had been disturbed by the adverse comment received from many in the legal profession concerning the terms of the Bill. The opposition was dividing into three schools. One backed Silverman and the substitution of life imprisonment; the second wanted the death penalty retained for the murder of prison officers and police officers; the third group wanted discretion on the length of sentence to pass from the home secretary to the courts. Around 30

236

Conservatives signed a motion tabled by Thomas Iremonger inviting the House to refuse the Bill a second reading because it made no provision for 'a substitute deterrent of comparable gravity' to the death penalty.[23]

Martin Sullivan, the Archdeacon of London, said that he had been a staunch advocate of capital punishment but had changed his mind. The death penalty was final and absolute and infallibility was not something that could be claimed for British justice. If murder was a gross crime then taking the life of the murderer merely repeated the crime.[24] Hugh MacGregor disagreed: capital punishment should be retained but administered in a more civilised form, but what form that should take was not stated.[25] And life went on. On the same day Ronald John Cooper, 26, was sentenced to death at the Old Bailey for shooting Joseph Hayes, 67.[26] He was due to be hanged at Pentonville on 5 January 1965.[27]

At the cabinet meeting on December 15, it was recorded that the Murder (Abolition of Death Penalty) Bill was to be committed to a committee of the whole House. The free vote was to be preserved but ministers who supported retention 'should preferably abstain from voting rather than vote against the Bill'.[28] Whilst that was going on, the indefatigable Edward Gardner was tabling another amendment to the effect that the penalty for murder should be 'life imprisonment unless the court in its discretion orders otherwise'.[29]

For the first time since the Homicide Act became law, section 6 was invoked. Three youths were convicted of killing Terrance Buckingham, 20, in Wakefield jail. Two of them, Roy Powell, 20, and Martin Morgan, 21, were sentenced to life imprisonment, but Peter Dunford, aged only 18, had on 9 December 1963 been detained at Her Majesty's pleasure for the murder of Francis Crayton, and so was sentenced to death since a second murder was a capital offence.

A letter from Lord Colyton announced that he used to be an abolitionist but had changed his mind due to the increase in the number of murders and acts of violence. He thought that the assumption that Sydney Silverman's Bill would pass through the Lords without being held up was wrong. He quoted a poll taken a few weeks earlier (November 5 to 8) on the question, 'Would you like to see the death penalty kept or abolished?' which produced the following result (percentages):

	All	Con.	Lab.	Lib.
Kept	65.5	73	62	64
Abolished	21.3	17	26	26
Don't know	13.2	10	12	10

The overwhelming opposition to abolition should be taken into account in the House of Commons, he said.[30] Although the Police Federation, not surprisingly, called for the death penalty to be retained for the murder of policemen, it was still expected that the Bill would pass comfortably on a free vote despite a sizeable group of Conservative MPs who were expected to force a division on the second reading.[31]

The Times itself had changed its mind. A leading article entitled 'The Death Penalty' claimed that that penalty was no longer a sanction against murder. There were two executions in 1962 and two in 1963, although there were 133 and 142 murders in those years, respectively. Such a system could not be an effective deterrent. Furthermore, legislative opinion had moved closer to abolition over the previous ten years and the time had come to take the last step. The suggestion that judges should determine sentences, as they do for any other conviction, should not be lightly dismissed, but more thought should be given as to the responsibility for when a convicted prisoner should be released.[32]

David Walter MP announced that he would vote for the Bill[33] but would prefer the courts to have discretionary sentencing rather than a mandatory life sentence. He was planning to propose 'imprisonment for life or such other term of years as the court may decide'. He also made one point that nobody else had made: that even after the Bill had passed, treason would still be a capital offence. On the day of the debate on the Bill, Sir Dingle Foot QC, the solicitor-general gave three reasons why he intended to vote for abolition. First, there was always the possibility of a mistake being made. He believed that Evans would never have been convicted if any jury had known what afterwards came to light. Second, he believed that juries in capital cases were influenced by the knowledge that a guilty verdict would result in a death sentence. This sometimes induced them to acquit when otherwise they would convict. Third, after seven years of the Homicide Act, it was not possible to justify the distinction between capital and non-capital murder.[34]

Sir Thomas Moore, on the other hand, believed that imprisonment for life was either 'a few relaxing years in prison or for the rest of the murderer's natural life. Watching people rot away was too horrible to contemplate so the death penalty should be the punishment for all types of murder'.[35]

The second reading debate

The debate on the second reading lasted for seven hours. It was opened by Sydney Silverman who spoke for 74 minutes without notes. He admitted that he had nothing new to say as all the arguments had been advanced many times before, and concluded by asking whether it was worth taking so much trouble over a Bill which might save two lives a year in a century that had already killed 80 million, and answered by saying 'We can at least light this small candle and see how far its tiny gleam can penetrate the gloom'. He no doubt had in mind Portia's comment:

How far that little candle throws its beam!
So shines a good deed in a naughty world.[36]

However, the climax of the debate was not Silverman but Henry Brooke, known already not only as one of the worst home secretaries but also for his stubbornness. On this occasion, in a speech widely dubbed 'courageous', this stubborn man publicly admitted he had been wrong. He confessed that he had once been in favour of hanging all murderers but despite the Homicide Act

1957, his years at the Home Office had convinced him that the death pena'
was no longer justified. It was useless to draw a demarcation between cap....
and non-capital murder. It was, for him, not a moral principle but he felt that the
taking of life by the state was only justified if it were a unique deterrent and the
statistics did not support that.

The motion was opposed by Sir Peter Rawlinson who said that although
capital punishment did not stop the ordinary murderer the Homicide Act was a
deterrent for professional criminals. He feared that the new Bill could lead to
gang warfare, more crimes of armed violence, the killing of witnesses and the
necessity of arming the police.

Brigadier Terence Clarke (Conservative, Portsmouth West) made a personal
attack on Silverman. He said not only that all murderers should hang but
Silverman and Soskice should hang, too. He believed that British juries never
made mistakes, or if they did, the odd man executed in error was well worth
while in the cause of saving innocent children. More children were going to be
killed and it was all Mr Silverman's fault. When Silverman pointed out that
child murder had not been a capital crime since 1958,[37] Clarke retorted that
lawyers could prove anything.

The second reading was carried by a resounding 355 votes to 170, a
majority of 185. The result was loudly cheered by the abolitionists who
surrounded Silverman, shaking his hand and slapping his back.[38] It was revealed
that 80 Conservatives voted in Silverman's lobby; of the nine Liberals eight
voted in favour and one against. One Labour backbencher, Frank Pudney, voted
against the Bill; there were 54 Labour votes uncast and 47 Conservatives were
absent. Among the six Conservative women members who voted against the Bill
was Margaret Thatcher, the future Conservative prime minister.[39]

The home secretary said that while the Bill to abolish the death penalty was
going through he felt it wrong to abrogate capital punishment by administrative
action in anticipation of amendments to the law (which was, of course, the trap
into which his predecessor, Chuter Ede had fallen) and that the circumstances of
each case would be considered.[40]

The debate and the result were a triumph not only for Sydney Silverman,
who must take much of the credit, but also for the government and the cabinet.
Within only a few weeks of taking office they had obtained a massive majority
for a Bill that would have little real effect (because so few convicted murderers
were actually being executed) and which was far from popular in the country at
large. It was not only a political achievement; it was also a moral
accomplishment.

Christopher Hollis wrote to say that there was no evidence that abolition of
capital punishment was likely to increase the danger for the police. In the USA it
had been shown that the killing of policemen was no more frequent in
abolitionist states than in those that had retained the death penalty. The
argument that the police were at risk under abolition lacked any factual basis.[41]
The more enlightened views of the Archbishops and bishops did not seem to
have filtered down to the foot-soldiers of the church. A former prison chaplain
attacked in his parish magazine what he called 'Silverman's Thugs' Charter' to

abolish capital punishment. Reverend Harold Lethbridge hoped that the House of Lords would throw out Silverman's Bill. He was in favour of a more humane method than hanging, however, not for the sake of the condemned prisoners but to avoid the strain on prison officers who have to prepare a man for hanging![42]

Committee stage

1965 saw the Conservatives rallying for a last ditch stand to preserve the death penalty for certain types of murder which they hoped to advance in the committee stage. Under their amendments the penalty would be retained for murder by shooting or causing an explosion or in the course of theft. Seven Conservatives tabled an amendment to ensure that any convicted murderer who murdered a second time whilst serving life imprisonment would be liable to the death penalty. One amendment being led by Edward Gardner would result in sentences of not less than 25 years unless a court ordered otherwise. At an Imperial College Union debate he said that the Bill was 'no more than an irresponsible attempt to abolish capital punishment without putting in its place the power to impose in proper cases severe and deterrent sentences of imprisonment'.[43]

Sir Peter Rawlinson deprecated the refusal of the government whips to allow the committee stage of the Bill to be taken on the floor of the House.[44] Sir Tufton Beamish agreed with Rawlinson's criticism of the government, adding that a poll in January showed that 70 per cent of the public were in favour of retaining the death penalty whilst only 23 per cent were abolitionists. As the Tories voted two to one in favour of retention they roughly reflected public opinion whereas the 'socialist party', who voted 268 to 1 for abolition, did not.[45] He was quickly answered by Mr Hickford-Smith who said that the public had no great depth of understanding of the problems surrounding the death penalty, and pointed out that public opinion was not sought when compulsory education or universal adult suffrage were introduced.[46] When Sir William Anstruther asked Herbert Bowden whether, in view of the murder a few days earlier of a policeman and the wounding of two others by gunmen, he proposed to allow government time for the remaining stages of the Bill, Bowden said that that had always been the government's intention.[47]

William Deedes (Conservative, Ashford) wanted to exclude the Bill for those who killed by explosives or guns. He said 'If the deterrent of hanging is removed it will encourage a tendency among criminals to carry and use arms'. Alice Bacon, minister of state at the Home Office, replied that a more efficient police force and better firearms legislation were a better deterrent against armed criminals than capital punishment. She said that if the amendments were carried they would create the same anomaly as in the Homicide Act. The amendment was supported by Sir Peter Rawlinson who thought the death penalty a good deterrent against armed criminals.[48]

In a reply to Richard Glyn, Soskice said that between 1940 and 1967 in England and Wales 17 people had been executed for reasons other than murder; two for treason and 15 under the Treachery Act 1940[49] and that since the end of 1957 16 people had been reprieved and they were all in custody.[50]

240

The Conservative proposal to retain the death penalty for murder by shooting was defeated in committee by 24 votes to 10. Both Sir Edward Boyle and Henry Brooke voted against the amendment.[51] Whilst Parliament was debating whether to hang one or two people a year it was announced that, in 1964, 7,820 people were killed on the roads and more than 95,000 were seriously injured.

A second committee stage

On March 5, the government hit a stumbling block. They had contrived to hold the Standing Committee 'upstairs' where the small number of committee members would comprise a majority of abolitionists (33 to 17 according to Richard Glyn who said that if the Standing Committee had been allowed to continue, the Bill would have come up for its third reading exactly as originally presented[52]) who would ensure that the committee stage would pass through quickly and not take up time on the floor of the House. They came unstuck. Forbes Hendry (Conservative, Aberdeen West) proposed that the Standing Committee be discharged and that the Bill be committed to a committee of the whole House and his motion was passed by 128 votes to 120. This resulted in all progress on the committee stage of the Bill being wiped out and the government would have to find time for a debate by the whole House.[53] Silverman wrote that it was natural for Sir Richard, a retentionist, to be disappointed that the amendments were defeated, but it was also natural that the committee voted against them[54] and Reg Paget pointed out that with only two closures in 15 hours there had been every opportunity for discussion.[55]

Herbert Bowden neatly side-stepped this. He proposed that the committee stage of the Bill should take place on the floor of the House at the same time as it had hitherto taken place upstairs. They could not continue from the point reached but would have to start afresh. With the committee stage sitting every Wednesday from 10.30 a.m. to 1 p.m. it had been calculated that eight weekly meetings would be needed to complete the committee stage. By holding sittings in the mornings the government frustrated one of the aims of the opposition, which was to eat up government time when business was congested.[56] Bowden then allowed a full day for the procedural motion on the Bill.[57] The motion to bring the committee onto the floor of the House one morning a week was debated from 3.53 p.m. to 10 p.m.[58] A number of Conservative MPs with other jobs in the mornings were unhappy but Bowden said that in all these things Parliament must come first despite the inconvenience of sitting in the mornings. The motion was passed by 299 votes to 229.[59] Silverman said it was a matter of indifference to him where the Bill was debated so long as it was passed.[60]

A new batch of amendments was tabled by Conservative backbenchers for the new committee stage.[61] They were debated at the first meeting of the full House as a committee[62] without a vote being taken[63] but when the debate was resumed the following week the amendment concerning the death penalty for a second murder was defeated by 138 votes to 237;[64] the amendment retaining the death penalty for killing a police officer in the execution of his duty was lost a week later by 115 votes to 265.[65]

Henry Brooke and five other Conservative backbenchers tabled a new amendment which proposed that the Act would continue in force until the end of July 1970 and would then expire unless Parliament decreed otherwise by an affirmative resolution of both Houses. If no action was taken to prolong the Act the law would revert to its present, that is, 1965, state.[66] An amendment from William Rees-Davies to retain the death penalty for killing a prison officer was defeated by 105 votes to 157 and the motion accepting clause 1 of the Bill was carried by 164 votes to 115.[67] At the resumed meeting[68] several amendments were lost; retaining the death penalty for murder in the course of theft by 78 votes to 180 and the amendment from Sir John Hobson excepting murder by shooting or explosion by 76 votes to 180.[69]

An unexpected problem
On May 12 the smooth progress of the Bill with the successive defeats of Conservative amendments came to a sudden and unexpected halt. Twelve Labour members, including Alice Bacon and George Thomas, arrived late for the meeting (they later claimed that the division bell had not rung where they were) and two amendments concerning the length of sentence that would be substituted for hanging were passed, one by 12 votes and the other by six.[70] The first amendment was to delete the word 'life' from the clause that read 'no person shall suffer death for murder, and a person guilty of murder shall subsequent to subsection 4, be sentenced to imprisonment for life'; this was carried by 160 votes to 148. The second part of the amendment, to add instead of 'life', the words, 'a period of not less than 25 years unless the court in its discretion rules otherwise' was defeated by 169 votes to 163. The clause as amended thus read '. . . a person guilty of murder should be sentenced to imprisonment for' which, as Soskice pointed out would mean for an indefinite period. Silverman isolated the problem by pointing out that if the word 'life' could be replaced the problem would be solved, but procedural experts believed that the deleted word could not be restored although words conveying the same meaning could be substituted. Silverman said that the only options he had were to accept a form of words of which he basically disapproved or to send through the Bill with a gap, to be filled at the next stage. An amendment by Hobson to add 'such a period as the court shall determine' was lost by 128 votes to 184 and the clause went through with the gap in it. The discussion during these proceedings was quite hilarious, so much so that Reg Paget protested at the frivolity.[71]

The following week the committee again discussed the 'life-less' clause. Hobson moved an amendment to add to the end of the clause 'such period as the court shall determine'. Silverman suggested that the word 'life' could not be put back then, but could at the report stage, and that is what he advised. He recognised that that meant sending the Bill forward with a hole in its principle clause but there was little alternative. He also recommended the rejection of the amendment as nobody, abolitionist or retentionist, thought that if the death penalty were abolished there should not be the power to keep a man in suitable

242

cases in detention for the rest of his life. The amendment was duly rejected by 184 votes to 128 and clause 1, as it stood, carried by 156 votes to 84.[72]

In the Lords, Lord Byers asked whether the government would appoint a committee of inquiry to determine the guilt or innocence of Timothy Evans. Lord Stonham, under-secretary at the Home Office, said that the home secretary considered he had no grounds to think that a further inquiry 15 years after the event could be useful. Byers pointed out that in the last Parliament Sir Frank Soskinse had pleaded most strenuously to reopen the case to clear Evans' name and asked why there had been a change of attitude. Stonham replied rather lamely that a further three years had passed and that Scott Henderson had died in November 1964. Lord Brockway pressed further, but Stonham would not be moved.[73]

The Police Federation were, not surprisingly, unhappy and at their conference at Llandudno voted unanimously against the rejection of (i.e. in effect for) the amendment to retain the death penalty for killing a policemen. A spokesman said that Parliament was flying in the teeth of public opinion and abolition had no support in the country generally. There was some bitterness as since the war 12 police officers had been murdered.[74]

The proposal by Henry Brooke that the Act should continue until 31 July 1970 was accepted after a long debate by 176 votes to 128.[75] A number of members were against the amendment on the grounds that if abolition were discontinued the law would revert to the Homicide Act 1957 which nobody liked. Norman St John Stevas thought that five years was too short but Peter Bessel (Liberal) urged the government to accept the amendment. It was then agreed to report the Bill to the House by 139 votes to 90 and the committee stage was finally completed.[76]

It was announced in the Queen's Birthday Honours that Victor Gollancz had been made a Knight Bachelor.[77] A few days later a petition against the Murder (Abolition of Death Penalty) Bill was presented to the House of Commons by Joseph Hiley (Conservative, Pudsey) from the League for Justice and Liberty. Hiley enigmatically said that the date (June 15) was significant, but whether he was referring to the date in 1215 of the signing of the Magna Carta by King John, or to the date in 1381 when Richard II met Wat Tyler and promised economic reforms, remains unknown. After a long quasi-religious preamble, the petition with 50,000 signatures concluded, 'Your petitioners pray that the death penalty be retained in cases of murder with malice aforethought and that justice with mercy be done throughout the land'.[78]

Still in the balance
Although things had gone pretty well for the abolitionists *The Times'* political correspondent said that the Bill was still in the balance and more Conservative amendments would come up for consideration, and he (rightly) doubted whether the report stage could be completed in one day. It was also expected that the Bill would be strongly opposed in the Lords.[79] Unless the government would be willing to grant more time it was doubtful whether the Bill would reach the statute book in the current session as there was still the completion of the report

stage and the third reading debate to be held. On the second day of the debate Sir John Hobson moved a new clause which provided that no-one convicted of murder should be released on licence unless the secretary of state first referred the question to a judicial review tribunal. This was rejected by 120 votes to 78 and an amendment concerning release on licence failed by 122 votes to 80. There was no further time for amendments to go to a vote.[80]

Although Sydney Silverman seemed optimistic, in a long letter he showed his frustration at the slow progress of the Bill. He pointed out that the second reading passed by 355 votes to 170 and that every subsequent amendment had been defeated by proportional majorities. Although the will of the House had been made clear, after more than six months since the second reading they had still been unable to conclude the House of Commons stages, for which he blamed the complex Parliamentary procedure.[81] Within days it was announced that the Bill would be given special facilities by the government so that it could pass through the Commons in the following few weeks.[82]

The Times supported the government's decision to provide time for the Bill. A leading article said that suspicion must be widespread that opposition to the Bill had been less concerned with its merits than with the possibility of clogging up the government's timetable. No government could allow the opposition to dictate what use could be made of Parliamentary time. It was unfortunate that the government had insisted on having the committee stage upstairs instead of on the floor of the House as when this was reversed three months work had been wiped out. It was time to realise that the Bill was not about the reform of sentencing procedures at large; all it could do was to add two or three extra prisoners to those already serving sentences.[83]

An ingenious solution

When the Bill was considered further, several amendments were rejected and the problem of the unresolved clause was not resolved[84] but the Bill was considered finally in mid-July. They began with the amendment that had been left over, which would leave out '. . . sentenced to imprisonment for . . .' and insert '. . . liable at the discretion of the court to imprisonment for life'. The sticking point for Silverman was that the amendment gave the court the power to impose a sentence of life imprisonment or no imprisonment at all: in other words the sentence became mandatory. But Silverman was famously tenacious and possessed formidable political skill. He first put the question that '. . . sentence to imprisonment for . . .' stand part of the Bill and this was passed by 193 votes to 92.[85] Now Silverman showed his ingenuity. Christopher Woodhouse had tabled an amendment to add 'Such a sentence shall be of indefinite duration subject only to the prerogative of mercy'. Silverman moved another amendment to replace the word 'life' at the end of the clause and pointed out that unless his amendment was agreed to, Woodhouse's amendment would be meaningless. Woodhouse readily agreed. After a short debate the insertion of 'life' was agreed by 207 votes to 86[86] but Woodhouse's amendment was lost by 83 votes to 196.

Third reading debate

Rawlinson's amendment which would substitute imprisonment for life was rejected by 193 votes to 92, the report stage was concluded and Silverman moved the third reading. He began his short speech by quoting from Shaw's *Caesar and Cleaopatra*:

> . . . murder shall breed murder
> Always in the name of right and peace
> Until the Gods get tired of blood and
> Create a race that can understand.

He said they had been trying to create such a race for the past 150 years. That number of years ago there were between 200 and 300 capital crimes.

> Sir Samuel Romilly fought ineffectually for year after year after year and never gave up . . . one hundred years ago those capital crimes that had disgraced the country had been reduced to four. For one hundred years no-one had been executed in this country for anything except murder. [Some had been executed for treason] . . . This was good progress but slower . . . than in other parts of Europe where the death penalty was abolished . . . years ago.

The average number of people convicted of capital murder had been two or three a year. He said: 'All the excitement, fuss and bother, all the late night sittings, the committee stages . . . all the prolonged discussions and repeated arguments . . . have been in order that we should go on executing two people a year'. He concluded: 'The thing . . . which we hope to complete is to rid at last this green and pleasant land of the shadow of the gallows.'[87]

Sir John Hobson, opposing, feared that abolition would lead to an increase in murder and armed robbery as well as break-outs from prison. They were discussing whether two or three executions a year did or did not provide a proper protection for society and law and order. He had always thought that the exceptions preserved in the Homicide Act were right and correct exceptions. Edward Gardner called the Bill bad, dangerous and likely to be carried in contempt of public opinion. Henry Brooke disputed that the idea that a life sentence was no deterrent and suggested that life imprisonment for murderers should mean 15 years in jail unless there were compassionate circumstances. The debate was short, and the closure motion from Reg Paget was carried by 187 votes to 73. When the result was announced at 12.26 a.m. —that the third reading had been carried by 200 votes to 98—there were loud cheers with Labour members once more crowding round and slapping Silverman on the back and shaking his hand[88]

Twenty-three Conservative members including nine former ministers went into Silverman's lobby and voted for the third reading. Among them were four former cabinet ministers: Henry Brooke, Sir Edward Boyle, Sir Keith Joseph and Enoch Powell. The other ministers were Sir Hugh Fraser, Chris Chattaway, Sir Hugh Lucas-Tooth, Miss Mervyn Pike and Peter Thomas. All the Liberals voted for the Bill.[89]

Debate in the Lords

Later that same day the Bill was brought from the Commons and read for the first time in the Lords[90] and in the following week the second reading debate was opened by Baroness Wootton of Abinger.[91] She spoke for half an hour saying that the main effect of the Bill would be to provide an automatic life sentence following any conviction for murder, or if committed by a person under 18, detention during Her Majesty's pleasure; the final clause of the Bill would be that it should remain in operation only for five years unless both Houses deemed otherwise. The Bill was opposed by Lord Dilhorne who, whilst commending Wootton's brevity and clarity, did not think it provided a proper alternative to the death sentence and that it was a bad Bill. He said to cheers that if it were rejected the vast majority of people in the country would welcome the decision.

Lord Parker, the Lord Chief Justice, said he was in favour of the Bill and would vote for the second reading[92] but would vote finally against the Bill unless there were suitable safeguards. It had been the absurdities of the Homicide Act that had turned him into an abolitionist. He saw only three choices. One was to amend the Homicide Act which he did not think possible. The second was to go back to the position before the Homicide Act and the third was to go forward and abolish. He said there might be cases where the death penalty was a deterrent but the potency of the deterrent weakened if only three out of 190 murderers were hanged. The Bill should be strengthened so that life imprisonment should be longer than the nine or ten years suggested but under conditions where prisoners would not rot. Lord Redsdale was sure that public opinion was in favour of abolition but Viscount Locke believed that 75 to 80 per cent of the public were against.

The resumed debate on the following day lasted a further seven hours. The Earl of Harewood, who had been in the Lords for 18 years, spoke there for the first time[93] and urged the House to vote for the Bill. Lord Chuter Ede was for the Bill and the Archbishop of Canterbury said that the abolition of the death penalty in Britain would set the nation in the way of progress and rid it of a system that punished killing with a penalty that helped devalue human life. Lord Kilmuir was angry. He said that after more than 40 years in politics he never thought he would see the day in any legislative assembly where public opinion had been swept aside and sneered at from the bench of bishops and every other part of the House. The objects of punishment were not merely deterrence or reform, but also retribution. Society and the courts had to express by punishment the revulsion that the ordinary citizen felt. Some crimes demanded the most emphatic penalty of all and the anomalies of the 1957 Act were not grounds for altering it; the anomalies should be ironed out.

The debate was wound up by a long and brilliant speech by the Lord Chancellor (Lord Gardiner).[94] He first pointed out in great detail that the level of murders had barely changed and had always been between three and four per million of population per year; even though other crimes rose, the murder rate remained constant. He then compared various abolitionist and retentionist countries in Europe and elsewhere and showed that the rate did not change according to whether the death penalty was practised or not. Lord Gardiner quoted Lord Kilmuir when on an earlier occasion he had said it was not the right time to make changes because of the increase in crime. He had read every Lords debate since 1810 and on each occasion somebody had said it was not the right time. He refuted the suggestion that abolitionists did not think of the police or the victims and cited Margery Fry who had fought for years to get compensation for victims of crimes of violence, and he quoted an American whose only daughter had been raped and strangled, who wrote in support of abolition: 'If it is an eye for an eye and a tooth for a tooth it will soon be a blind and toothless world'.

Lord Gardiner concluded by pointing out that when the punishment for treason of hanging, drawing and quartering was abolished it was not because there was sympathy for traitors but because of the view that the punishment was no longer consistent with self-respect. The police in Norway and in Rhode Island—two differing abolitionist states—did not want the return of capital punishment. He ended by quoting Romilly: 'You think crime will increase if you abolish [capital punishment] but it will not because the great deterrent to crime is not severity of punishment but certainty of conviction' and John Bright: 'A deep reverence for human life is worth more than 1,000 executions in the prevention of murder'.

The Lords then divided and voted by 204 to 104 for the second reading. It had been expected that the Lords would give the Bill a rough ride but with the Lord Chancellor, the Lord Chief Justice and the judges, plus the Archbishop of Canterbury and the bishops in favour, this unexpected majority of 100 was reached.

A few days after this historic vote in the House of Lords, Sir Frank Soskice had a discussion with an all-party deputation concerning the Evans case. Eric Lubbock said that the meeting made representations and the home secretary had undertaken to consider them and give his decision in due course.[95]

During the report stage of the Murder (Abolition of Death Penalty) Bill an amendment by Lord Parker to abolish the fixed penalty for murder and prevent life imprisonment from being the only sentence that could be passed was carried by the Lords by 80 votes to 78. Lord Parker hoped that a judge would be able to give anything from probation to life imprisonment. Meanwhile, Sir Alec Douglas Home had resigned as leader of the Conservative party and Edward Heath was elected in his place, gaining 150 votes to Reginald Maudling's 133 and Enoch Powell's 15.[96]

Another Evans inquiry
A campaign was launched to press for re-consideration of the Evans case; a committee was formed whose members included Chuter Ede and Ludovic Kennedy.[97] Lord Conesford continued to attempt to weaken the Bill during the report stage but all his efforts were defeated[98] and after agreeing to a number of amendments concerning the release of prisoners who had been convicted of murder, the report stage in the Lords on the Murder (Abolition of Death Penalty) Bill was concluded.[99]

Soskice finally conceded to an inquiry into the Evans matter and the terms of reference were announced by the Home Office. Briefly, the inquiry was to examine the evidence given in the trials of Evans and Christie, to hear any witnesses or any other information, and to report its conclusions as to whether Evans did or did not kill either his wife, his baby or both. The inquiry would be conducted, mostly in public, by Mr Justice Brabin.[100] Because of the renewed interest in the affair, copies of both of the Scott Henderson reports were reprinted by the Stationery Office.[101] A few weeks later a preliminary meeting was held before the judge to discuss how the inquiry could best be conducted.[102]

The final stages of the Murder (Abolition of Death Penalty) Bill were drawing to a close, but not to everyone's liking. Dr J. A. Imrie, Chief Medical Officer of Glasgow, addressing the annual conference of the British Burial and Cremation Authorities, said it was unfortunate that 'do-gooders' were succeeding in introducing a Bill for the abolition of hanging at a time when crime was on an upward trend.[103]

Carried in the House of Lords
For Dr Imrie, a surprising number of 'do-gooders' were to be found in the unlikely location of the House of Lords. At the same time as Dr Horace King was being elected the first Labour speaker following the death of Sir Harry Hylton-Foster, the Lords' debate on the third reading was underway. It was opened by Baroness Wootton who concluded her brief speech by saying:

> What we are here to do today is to remove the differentiation between the murderer who takes sixpence from his victim's pocket and the one who does not . . . between those who murder by shooting and those who bludgeon their victims to death . . . the differentiation which leaves the poisoner and allows the person who shoots in hot blood to be hanged. I am sure . . . we in this House shall not hesitate to align ourselves with the practice which prevails in the greater part of the civilised world.[104]

Lord Colyton remained convinced that capital punishment was a deterrent and that abolition would lead to an increase in murders; the Bill did not have the support of the overwhelming mass of the people. He intended to divide the House. The Archbishop of York was unashamedly for abolition and Lord Parker urged the House to consider the position of the judges who were almost to a man behind him in favour of abolition. Were they, he asked, to go through the farce and tragedy of sentencing people to death when everybody knew that the death penalty would never be carried out? To cheers, he asked those who threatened to divide the House to think again. The Lord Chancellor closed by saying that when the traps had been removed from the prisons 'we shall not only be a safer country but a much saner and healthier one'. The Bill was passed without a division[105] while Sydney Silverman watched in silent satisfaction from the gallery above.

The Times, commenting on the long campaign that was about to end, said that the Bill received its most compelling support from the inequitable workings of the Homicide Act. During the protracted Parliamentary procedure judges

248

were obliged to pass sentences of death on capital murderers even though they and the prisoners knew they would never be carried out. Only two amendments were added from the committee stages in the Commons and one in the Lords. One limited the Bill initially to five years duration and the other would enable the trial judge to recommend to the home secretary a minimum period of detention before a murderer was released on licence. *The Times* leader ended, 'Public sympathy may not be with this Bill or its promoters or supporters. But it is right that it should be passed at last'. [106]

The Bill was returned from the Commons with the amendments agreed to [107] and on Monday 8 November 1965 the Murder (Abolition of Death Penalty) Act 1965 received the Royal Assent and became law. The whole ghastly business was finished.

ENDNOTES

1   Bowden, H, 27 October 1964, PRO. CAB, 129/119
2   *The Times*, p. 6, 4 November 1964
3   ibid, p. 11
4   ibid, p. 12
5   *Hansard*, [701] 101 (2 November 1964)
6   ibid, [701] 136
7   *The Times*, p. 6, 13 November 1964
8   ibid, p. 6, 16 November 1964
9   ibid, p. 5, 28 November 1964
10 ibid, p. 5, 25 November 1964
11 ibid, p. 10, 3 December 1964
12 ibid, p. 9, 5 December 1964
13 ibid, p. 8
14 ibid, p. 7, 7 December 1964
15 ibid, p. 11
16 ibid, p.13, 9 December 1964
17 ibid, p. 13, 10 December 1964
18 ibid.
19 *Hansard*, [703] 145 (7 December 1964)
20 ibid, [703] 146
21 *The Times*, p. 5, 8 December 1964
22 ibid, p.13, 11 December 1964
23 ibid, p. 12, 12 December 1964
24 ibid, p. 11, 14 December 1964
25 ibid
26 ibid, p. 10, 15 December 1964
27 ibid, p. 4, 19 December 1964

28 PRO. CAB, 128/39, 15 December 1964

29 *The Times*, p. 6, 16 December 1964

30 ibid, p. 11, 18 December 1964

31 ibid, p. 4

32 ibid, p. 11

33 ibid, p. 7, 19 December 1964

34 ibid, p. 5, 21 December 1964

35 ibid, p. 7

36 *The Merchant of Venice*, William Shakespeare, Act V, Scene 1

37 Seemingly, because s. 5 Homicide Act 1957 made no special provision for the murder of children. Such a murder would only be capital if it satisfied one of the other capital criteria (as with an adult victim) e.g. by shooting. Such a child murder would be highly unusual, and other s. 5 criteria generally inapplicable

38 *The Times*, pp. 4/10, 22 December 1964

39 ibid, p. 5, 23 December 1964

40 ibid, p. 8, 24 December 1964

41 ibid, p. 11, 31 December 1964

42 ibid, p. 13, 6 January 1965

43 ibid, p. 10, 3 February 1965

44 ibid, p. 11

45 ibid, p. 11, 11 February 1965

46 ibid, p. 9, 13 February 1965

47 *Hansard*, [706] 202 (16 February 1965)

48 *The Times*, p. 7, 18 February 1965

49 *Hansard*, [705] 219 (1 February 1965)

50 ibid, [707] 189 (1 March 1965)

51 *The Times*, p. 7, 4 March 1965

52 ibid, p. 18, 10 March 1965

53 ibid, p. 6, 6 March 1965

54 ibid, p. 13, 11 March 1965

55 ibid, p.13

56 ibid, p. 16/17, 12 March 1965

57 ibid, p. 17, 17 March 1965

58 *Hansard*, [708] 1486-1616 (18 March 1965)

59 *The Times*, p. 9, 19 March 1965

60 ibid, p. 14

61 ibid, p. 10, 20 March 1965

62 ibid, p. 6, 25 March 1965

63 *Hansard* (24 March 1965)

64 *Hansard*, 1571-1620 (31 March 1965)

65 ibid, [710] 405-428 (7 April 1965)

66 *The Times*, p. 5, 27 March 1965

67 *The Times*, p. 16, 8 April 1965
68 *Hansard*, [710] 1325-1372 (14 April 1965)
69 *The Times*, p. 6, 15 April; p. 16, 29 April 1965
70 *Hansard*, [712] 460 (12 May 1965)
71 *The Times*, p. 16, 13 May 1965
72 ibid, p. 18, 20 May 1965
73 ibid, p. 18, 20 May 1965
74 ibid, p. 10, 21 May 1965
75 *Hansard*, [713] 529-566 (26 May 1965)
76 *The Times*, p. 8, 27 May 1965
77 ibid, p. 6, 12 June 1965
78 *Hansard*, [714] 213 (15 June 1965)
79 *The Times*, p. 8, 25 June 1965
80 ibid, p. 6, 26 June 1965
81 ibid, p. 13, 30 June 1965
82 ibid, p. 12, 2 July 1965
83 ibid, p. 13, 6 July 1865
84 *Hansard*, [714] 2113 (25 June 1965)
85 ibid, [716] 358 (13 July 1965)
86 ibid, [716] 402
87 ibid, [716] 412
88 *The Times*, p. 8, 14 July 1965
89 ibid, p. 7, 15 July 1965
90 *Hansard* [Lords] [268] 153 (14 July 1965)
91 ibid, [268] 456 (19 July 1965)
92 ibid, [268] 480
93 *The Times*, p. 8, 21 July 1965
94 *Hansard* [Lords], [268] 699 (15 July 1965)
95 *The Times*, p. 14, 22 July 1965
96 ibid, p. 10, 28 July 1965
97 ibid, p. 10
98 ibid, p. 13
99 ibid, p. 6, 6 August 1965
100 ibid, p. 8, 27 August 1965
101 ibid, p. 6, 1 September 1965
102 ibid, p. 5, 19 October 1965
103 ibid, p. 6, 30 September 1965
104 *Hansard* [Lords], [268] 554 (26 October 1965)
105 *The Times*, p. 12, 27 October 1965
106 ibid, p. 13
107 *Hansard*, [716] 735 (26 October 1965).

251

CHAPTER 19

The End of the Rope

Shortly before the Murder (Abolition of the Death Penalty) Act 1965 received its Royal Assent, a Home Office spokesman declined to confirm that permission had been given for the body of Timothy John Evans to be exhumed from his grave at Pentonville prison for reburial but said a licence could be applied for when the Bill became law.[1] However, the very next day the Home Office granted permission for the reburial on the grounds that the passing of the Act would repeal the provision that executed people must be buried in prison grounds.[2] Events then moved quickly.

Evans laid to rest
On the night of 9 November 1965, Evans' body was exhumed[3] and reburied the next day in St Patrick's cemetery, Leytonstone.[4] A week later it was announced that the new inquiry would start in a few days and was expected to last for three to four weeks;[5] it duly opened on November 22 and began with the complete retelling of the evidence and facts of the case.[6] Sebag Shaw QC, counsel for the Evans family, said that he intended to pursue Evans' claim that he had confessed to the Rillington Place murders through fear of the police. Mr Shaw said that he regarded it as his right to consider matters that were not reviewed at the trial.[7] The inquiry, which adjourned on December 23 until 10 January 1966, continued through the remainder of November, all of December and finally ended on January 21 after 32 days of hearings.

At the end of a closing speech lasting nine hours, Mr E. W. Everleigh QC, asked the chairman to consider the possibility that Evans killed his wife and their daughter. During the inquiry five shorthand writers wrote more than a million words and the typescript ran to more than 2,000 foolscap pages. It was not surprising that Mr Justice Brabin said it would be some time before he reported.[8]

Election
Sir Frank Soskice, who was 63, announced that he would not be seeking re-election to Parliament in the forthcoming general election so his retirement from the Home Office was expected. Immediately before Christmas, Harold Wilson took the opportunity to shuffle his cabinet[9]—he had paid his dues to those who had stuck out 13 years of opposition—and strengthen his team. Soskice became Lord Privy Seal and Roy Jenkins, who took over at the Home Office, was to become one of the most effective and reforming home secretaries ever. Although capital punishment had been abolished—or strictly speaking, suspended for five years—feelings still ran high among the retentionists. Towards the end of the general election campaign Frank Lofthouse, the Conservative candidate in Wythenshawe, Manchester, said that electors should vote for him as the only candidate there committed to bringing back hanging. He

said that he had not intended to make the death penalty a main issue but it was the subject raised most frequently by voters during canvassing.[10]

Polling day was 31 March 1966 and among the results announced on the following day[11] it could be seen that among the Conservatives who lost their seats in Labour's sweeping return to power (with a majority of 97) was Henry Brooke, and that Sydney Silverman had doubled his majority. Patrick Downey, an uncle of Lesley Anne Downey who was one of the victims of the moors murderers Ian Brady and Myra Hindley (the murders were recent and the moor not far from the Nelson and Colne constituency) stood against Silverman on the single issue of capital punishment, and polled 5,117 votes. Speaking to the Oxford University Conservative Association some weeks later, Humphrey Berkley called this the most melancholy result in the whole election. He said most of those who voted for Downey were Conservatives who voted for a man whose sole programme was to revert to a law under which on average two people a year were hanged.[12]

A boost for restorationists

After the election the subject of the death penalty faded but was suddenly given a new lease of life when three policemen were shot dead in Shepherds Bush a short distance from Wormwood Scrubbs prison, in London. The Police Federation immediately called for the restoration of capital punishment for the murder of police officers or, failing that, to arm the police. Their spokesman said that since 1910 when five policemen were shot, three of whom were killed, 24 police officers had been killed on duty.[13] Sir Richard Glyn was quick to point out[14] that in a previous letter to *The Times* in 1964 he had warned that a life sentence would not be an adequate deterrent. A duty was owed to the police to impose an effective deterrent to violent criminals, but arming the police was not the right solution.

Branches of the Police Federation in Sheffield and Derbyshire wrote to their MPs urging the return of the death penalty for the murder of a police officer. But Humphrey Berkley, former Conservative MP and now treasurer of the Howard League for Penal Reform, asked politicians to resist being stampeded into changing the law as was being called for by Duncan Sandys. The period of five years was necessary before the effect of abolition could be properly assessed despite the tragic happenings when policemen were killed. Between 1958 and 1961 (when the Homicide Act 1957 was in force) eight policemen had lost their lives.

Ted Leadbitter, Labour MP for Hartlepool, said he felt strongly about the 'uncivilized ritual' but believed that if hanging should not be re-introduced then alternative punishments had to be found to fit the crime. If not, hanging would have to return and society would have failed.[15] Sir John Hobson MP QC, wrote that the death penalty should have been retained and ought to be restored, at least for murder by shooting or murdering police officers or prison officers. How many more people must be killed, he asked, before 'the socialist government' could be persuaded to grant public servants the protection of the only deterrent which would be respected.[16]

Lord Goodman was more restrained. He joined in the correspondence by calling for careful consideration before any decision was made about hanging. He said it was a great public disserve to inflame public anxiety by suggesting that party political decisions were responsible for the deaths of three young policemen, or that it was possible to say with any certainty that had hanging been in operation this tragedy would not have taken place. Sam Silkin MP QC, wrote on similar lines. He abhorred Hobson's attempt to make party political capital out of the events at Shepherd's Bush and pointed out that the Bill to abolish hanging was supported by majorities of more than two to one and included members of all parties. But M. J. Carter, a serving police officer, urged readers to support a Bill to reintroduce the death penalty for killing police officers or prison officers.

On the same page[17] the main leader entitled 'The Rule of Law' commented on the Bill that Sandys proposed to introduce in the next Parliament for the reintroduction of the death penalty for the murder of policemen. *The Times* believed the Bill would not succeed for three reasons. First, there was no reason to suppose that the Commons were any less opposed to capital punishment than they were a year ago; second, drafting might prove difficult if there were an attempt to categorise the types of murder regarded as the most heinous; third, the abolition Act was due for review in 1970 by which time its virtues and defects would have become obvious.[18]

Sandys' Bill to restore the death penalty for the killing of police officers and prison officers was receiving all-party backing by the middle of summer, but Nigel Fisher, a Conservative MP who had voted for abolition said he was still in favour of abolition in general but believed that something needed to be done to give the police extra protection and thought that possibly hanging was a deterrent when the police had to deal with professional criminals.[19]

Pardoned

Sir Daniel Brabin was quite right when he said that his report would take some time; it had been in gestation for exactly nine months and 'The Case of Timothy John Evans' (Cmnd. 3101 Stationery Office, 12/6d (62.5p.)), which ran to 158 pages, was born on October 12.[20] The main finding was that Brabin believed it probable that Evans murdered his wife but that Christie murdered Evans' daughter. Given that Evans was not even accused of murdering his wife but was actually hanged for murdering his daughter, and that Christie was never even accused of murdering Evans' daughter, these were surprising findings indeed. *The Times* editorial[21] said that there was widespread scepticism among the public when asked to believe earlier that two murderers using similar methods could live in the same house at the same time without each other knowing, but that if the Brabin report was fiction it would be put down half-read because it was inherently incredible. There could be no certainty even after the report about what had really happened; capital punishment was dreaded by those who feared a miscarriage of justice and it looked as if this case came close to it. That risk had probably gone with the coming of the Abolition Act.

The Evans family's solicitor was considering whether to ask for a free pardon for Evans, and Eric Lubbock, who had asked for the second inquiry, said the report was highly unsatisfactory and full of largely speculative conclusions. Roy Jenkins, the home secretary, hoped to make an early statement in the House of Commons. He said that a posthumous free pardon was without precedent and foresaw serious legal difficulties.

Meanwhile, at the Conservative party conference in Blackpool a call for the restoration of the death penalty was greeted with loud applause; but Jonathan Aitkin said that they had to be certain that the reintroduction of hanging would really make the lives of police officers and prison officers more safe and that people should consider the question nearer the end of the five year period.[22]

The Timothy Evans committee noted with satisfaction one of Brabin's conclusions, namely that no jury knowing what had come to light would convict him of the murder of either his wife or daughter, and called on the home secretary to recommend a free pardon.[23] Jenkins obliged. When he announced that the Queen, on his recommendation, had granted Evans a posthumous free pardon there was a full-throated cheer from the crowded Commons benches. Recalling Brabin's conclusions, Jenkins commented that in all the circumstances he did not think it right to allow Evans' conviction to stand. 'This case has no precedent and will I believe and hope have no successor', he said. Sydney Silverman and Michael Foot pressed for an opportunity to debate the Brabin report. Silverman said the report still left uncomfortable feelings that Brabin had drawn a balance of probabilities in a wholly wrong way; Foot said that the Scott Henderson report had been shown to be absolutely unfounded.[24]

Sandys tries his luck

The number of MPs who had signed Sandys' motion for restoration had reached 170 and included seven Labour backbenchers and two Liberals. Sandys' two principal supporters were Sir Peter Rawlinson QC, a former solicitor-general, and William Deedes, a former minister of state at the Home Office.[25] But when Sandys asked Richard Crossman, Lord President of the Council, if time would be found for a debate on his motion, Crossman replied that he could see no early opportunity for reopening a question that the House had decided by a large majority on a free vote quite recently.[26] As if to underline the *status quo* the Home Office announced that all the gallows except one at Wandsworth had been dismantled; one was being kept in store to meet any emergency that might arise under the existing law that still permitted hanging as the ultimate sentence. However, all the condemned cells in prisons, even at Wandsworth, had been abandoned and used for other purposes.[27]

A Police Federation newsletter commented that Jenkins was not only wrong, but completely and tragically wrong in his blank refusal to acknowledge that the murders of policemen in the short period since abolition did not constitute fresh evidence for a review of the whole question of capital punishment. It said that the stand he was taking on the issue put him into head-on conflict with the overwhelming majority of the police,[28] a position that Jenkins seemed to tolerate with equanimity. He did, however, assure the Prison

Officers' Association that there would be a free vote on the Sandys motion to restore the death penalty for the murder of police officers and prison officers.[29] But if Sandys had the support of MPs of other parties he did not have the total support of his own. A letter from fellow Conservative MP Charles Fletcher-Cook QC, predicted that if Sandys' Bill for restoration for the murder of a police officer became law it would fail even quicker and more vaingloriously than the 1957 Act because in place of the weapon he had chosen the victim as criterion. Imagine, he wrote, the public reaction if a thug escaped hanging because his bullet missed a policeman and killed a layman, perhaps one coming to the assistance of the policeman. He called for the death penalty to be available at the discretion of the trial judge. He thought both the 1957 and 1965 Acts were false remedies and hoped that Duncan Sandys would not produce another.[30] He need not have worried. Sandys was refused leave to introduce his Bill by a majority against of 122; however about 12 MPs who voted with Silverman were believed to have changed sides.[31]

A quiet year

After Duncan Sandys' effort to bring in another Bill was frustrated, the question of capital punishment virtually disappeared and for more than a year the subject was rarely heard. After all, there were more than three years to go before the matter need be discussed again and with a Labour government with a large majority there was little chance of an early return to the death penalty.

In September 1967, when Edward Heath, leader of the Conservative party, addressed representatives of the Glasgow Conservative Association, two women interrupted with cries of 'Shame!' when Heath declined to give assurances for the reintroduction of corporal punishment and hanging. He said that in the Commons moral questions were left to individual MPs, adding 'As long as I am leader I am not going to lay down a party line on these matters. We must get the facts then act at the end of the five years. We can then form a cool rational judgment'. Another woman jumped to her feet saying, 'By the time we wait five years all decent people will be killed or have emigrated'.[32]

The next Conservative party conference gave Sandys renewed hope. He and a small army of volunteers had been collecting signatures for a petition for the restoration of the death penalty, and by the time the conference began already 25,000 had been collected. In a letter circulated to over a thousand newspapers Sandys added two new arguments. First he showed that Home Office figures indicated that there had been 67 'capital murders' since capital punishment had been abolished, compared with 32 in the two years prior to abolition. Second, he said that the number of offences in which firearms had been used had risen from 731 in 1964 to 1,511 in 1966. In response, the Home Office said the figures were correct but the interpretation dubious. Taking like with like, since 1957 there were 20.5 capital murders a year in the seven years before the death penalty was suspended and 33.5 in the two years since: too short a time for comparison. The firearms figures were also correct but their interpretation in relation to capital punishment was in doubt.[33]

256

James Callaghan, the chancellor of the exchequer, had pledged himself to maintain the $2.80 parity with the pound sterling. Once the decision to devalue (to $2.40) had been taken by the cabinet on November 16 and announced on November 18, he told Wilson he saw it as a point of honour not to stay on as Chancellor. Although he was willing to return to the back benches, Wilson was unwilling to lose him, so in a straight exchange of cabinet posts, Callaghan became home secretary and Roy Jenkins became the new chancellor of the exchequer.[34]

'His motives were always noble'

It is rare for the illness of a backbench MP to get even a couple of inches in the national newspapers let alone the front page, but Sydney Silverman was no ordinary backbencher. He had been in the House for over 30 years representing the same constituency (Nelson and Colne). He had criticised his own party and leader when he believed them to be wrong, voted against the leadership, and had the whip withdrawn. He was on the left wing of his party when it was unfashionable to be so and had fought for unpopular causes. He was an incisive speaker, a tenacious fighter and an outspoken critic. Add to all this that he was short, stocky and a Jew and one might have expected him to be widely disliked. On the contrary, he was greatly admired by both sides of the House and respected by even his extreme adversaries, for his outspokenness was tempered by great courtesy and his strongly held views did not blind him to the fact that other people held opposite views equally strongly and sincerely.

At the end of January 1968 Silverman had been taken to the Royal Free Hospital from his home in St John's Wood believed to be suffering from exhaustion[35] and the next day it was announced on the front page of *The Times* among other papers that he had suffered a 'relatively severe stroke'.[36] His condition slowly deteriorated and on February 9 he died in hospital in Hampstead.[37] He was 72. His obituary linked his name with capital punishment in the headline.[38] *The Times'* tribute was of a fulsomness usually reserved for popular statesmen. It recalled that at the end of 1964, when the Commons gave a second reading to his Bill by a majority of 185, they conceded to him the most satisfying triumph of his political career. It was the reward of nearly 30 years of dogged endeavour. After 1957 his conviction that the death penalty was a revolting and barbaric outrage by civil standards gave him no rest from the fight to remove it completely. 'He was short of stature but there was a dynamic and impressive quality about him with his snowy crop of hair and aggressively bearded chin. When he was at the University of Liverpool he was prominent at the Labour club as a debater with a tongue as sharp as his brain.' He was survived by his wife Nancy, whom he had married in 1933, and three sons.

Nearly 100 people attended his funeral at Golders Green crematorium two days later. The eulogy was given by Rabbi John D. Rayner of the Liberal synagogue at St John's Wood. Rabbi Rayner said, 'His uncompromising passion for justice and his ardent concern for the victims of injustice burned inside him like a fire, gleamed in his eyes, resounded in his voice and drove him on in dedicated endeavour to right the wrongs of society. Not everything he said and

257

did pleased everybody but everybody respected him, his integrity, his earnestness, his knowledge and skill. And above all they respected him because they knew his motives were always noble.'[39]

Last gasps for the noose

The Prison Officers' Association, like the Police Federation, did not give up. At the POA annual conference in May there was a unanimous call for reinstatement at the earliest opportunity of capital and corporal punishment for prison offences. A Mr K. Forster of Durham prison said that they believed that the vast majority of the public wished to see both corporal and capital punishment introduced, and that prison officers were being used as guinea-pigs for a dangerous social experiment.[40]

Councillor Walter Wober, of Glasgow City council distributed 100,000 forms asking people if they wanted a return of corporal punishment and hanging for some classes of murder. He planned to take the 100,000 signed forms in a lorry to London and dump them outside the Home Office and ask to see the home secretary in order to get action;[41] that the home secretary might have been more inclined to meet them without 100,000 sheets of paper left outside his front door did not seem to have occurred to him.

A Home Office report[42] showed that in 1966 there was the lowest increase in the crime rate since 1955 but that the number of murders had increased. In 1966 there had been 143 murders and, in 1967, 172. Duncan Sandys commented that in the three years since capital punishment had been suspended there had been twice the number of capital murders compared to the three years before. He said that since the deterrent of the death penalty had been removed criminals no longer hesitated to carry guns.

Alan Muir, Chief Constable of Durham told the Durham Young Liberals[43] that although capital punishment was irrelevant to the problem of murder it would be more sensible to quietly eliminate people like the 'Great Train Robbers'. He said that some people were beyond correction and society was right 'to chuck them out'—a novel euphemism for killing them. He was not too keen on hanging but thought that a dose of hemlock might be the answer. His remarks not surprisingly angered many people. Even Gerald Nabarro MP, a long-standing supporter of capital punishment, asked the home secretary whether he would call on the chief constable to retire[44] and an editorial on Muir's comments called them eccentric and extravagant whilst pointing out in great detail that the rate of murder had barely changed.[45]

In May the police officers and prison officers got their response. In a written answer to a question by Sir Cyril Osborne, James Callaghan, home secretary, said that he would not restore capital punishment for murder in agreement with their request.[46]

Duncan Sandys was once again calling for the restoration of the death penalty, which prompted Hugh Klare, secretary of the Howard League for Penal Reform, to point out that Sandys had three grounds for his argument: the capital murder rate had increased; offences involving the use of firearms had increased; many people wanted the death penalty back. Klare said that having only recently abolished the death penalty, statistics covering three years were too little on which to base new legislation. In the United States of America data from adjacent abolitionist and retentionist states covering 30 years showed that the incidence of murder was affected by factors other than the retention or abolition of capital punishment.[47]

But Sandys' proposed Bill was not a simple call for restoration as his previous one had been. Giving details of what he was attempting, he said that he proposed to delete the words 'requiring resolutions from both Houses'; this would secure that the prolongation of the suspension of capital punishment would require an Act of Parliament and could not be decided by a simple resolution. His Bill did not seek to prejudge the issue but was concerned only with the legislative process by which the decision would be taken.[48]

On midsummer day, just before members of Parliament went on holiday, Sandys sought leave to bring in his motion.[49] There was only a short debate and only Sandys spoke in favour, his main point being that crime in general and murder in particular had risen since the 1965 Act was passed. The speaker opposing was Geoffrey de Freitas who pointed out that for two and a half years not a single policeman had been killed although in November 1966 Sandys had said that unless capital punishment was reintroduced the police would be in particular peril of being killed. He said that in the age of the gas chamber and mass executions, countries had found a new safeguard and dignity by refusing the state the right to take life. The Murder (Abolition of Death Penalty) Act 1965 was intended to be permanent; the provision limiting the life of the Act for five years was accepted by the sponsors of the Bill as a compromise. At the vote, Sandys was refused permission to introduce his motion by 256 votes to 126.[50]

An end to the suspense?

Although it was not required under the Act to come to a final decision about abolition before July of the following year (1970) the government had hinted at the possibility that a decision could be made much earlier to turn suspension into permanent abolition. In a long analysis in *The Times*[51] entitled 'An Early Decision on Capital Punishment', Norman Fowler thought that the government were likely to decide what they intended to do within a couple of months. The view among Home Office ministers was that the future of capital punishment would not be decided exclusively on statistics but the moral arguments would also be important, as was the argument that the presence of the death penalty meant the risk of an irretrievable mistake. It had been trailed that a report from the Home Office Research Unit would show that capital punishment was not a unique deterrent as some people supposed. The latest figures showed that although there were 53 capital murders between 1962 and 1964, compared with 129 between 1966 and 1968, although, of course, the later figures had to be estimated and it was difficult to allocate homicide between murder and 'capital murder', or predict how juries would have behaved.

The government could wait until the following year but the earliest meaningful figures for 1969 would not be ready until May, so how much different would the decision be if it were taken on the basis of four years instead of three? It was doubtful if the figures would be statistically conclusive anyway; it would be possible to extend the period of abolition for another five years. Fowler concluded that whereas the burden of proof in re-establishing capital punishment lay with its supporters it would be a pity if the chance to provide both objective and complete evidence were ignored.

Another Conservative party conference, another Sandys petition. In Brighton he was given a petition signed by 8,000 people living in Sussex. Sandys said that all over Britain about 85 per cent of people approached had readily signed his petition. He expected to present the full petition to Parliament before the government introduced resolutions to make the abolition of the death penalty permanent. [52] The following day at the conference during the law and order debate, an amendment to restore the death penalty was carried by 1,117 to 958, a surprisingly narrow majority of 159. However, the decision had no binding effect although it could act as a powerful influence. Peter Jenkin-Jones, who moved the amendment, said he supported Edward Heath on every other issue except capital punishment, but Lynda Chalker, chairman of the Greater London Young Conservatives said that she could not support the restoration of the death penalty. [53]

Dr W. Lindesay Neustatter claimed to have examined over 100 people charged with murder. Of 62 cases he had examined, 31 had had no previous convictions and 16 of those suffered from depressive illnesses; a further 12 had committed only 'irrelevant' offences and 16 of the 62 were psychotic. Neustatter concluded that those who had killed were neither vicious nor intrinsically violent, and that although those who killed deliberately and with premeditation for gain deserved any punishment, capital punishment in America did not seem to have been a very effective deterrent. He concluded that the question needed to be decided detachedly by those with special knowledge, not by a referendum which could only reveal the attitude of the voters. [54]

The final battle begins
The results of a Marplan Survey were published in October 1969. The question asked was, 'Do you think that the law should allow hanging for all types of murder, for certain types only, or not at all?' The results are set out in *Table 1,* opposite. The poll clearly indicated that the majority of the electors wanted the hangman to be kept ready for some categories of murder, but not all. [55]

At the beginning of November it was announced that the Home Office Research Unit had completed its report setting out the facts and figures of the abolition experiment. There had been an increase in crimes of violence, and also a trend to increases in crimes of murder during the experimental period, but as the party leaders agreed that it would be wrong for that kind of issue to become a party political matter there was a general disposition to dispose of it early, in the current session rather than waiting until the middle of 1970. [56]

It was foreseen that the opponents of abolition would use the statistics as ammunition in their campaign to restore the death penalty, but the government was not going to retreat under public pressure. Lord Gardiner was believed to

260

have made it known that he wanted the abolition campaign to be resumed in order to counter the demand for capital punishment. It was also understood that Callaghan would not be prepared to continue as home secretary if he had to advise the Crown on applications for reprieve. It was recognised that a situation would arise that few people wanted to see: a disparity of punishment under which some murderers would be hanged whilst others who had committed their crimes during the experimental period would still be in gaol, or even have been released.

		WOULD VOTE			
	All	Conservative	Labour	Liberal	Other
	%	%	%	%	%
All types	38	38	37	31	31
Certain types only	47	51	45	45	52
Not at all	12	8	16	19	7
Don't know	3	3	2	2	10

Table 1

The report, called *Murder 1957-1968*, published by the Stationery Office priced 12s.(60p.)[57] showed that murder was still largely a family crime committed mainly for emotional reasons. *Table 2* below (which appeared as *Table 1* in the original report),[58] showing the murder rate over ten years was most revealing.

	No of victims			No per million population England and Wales	
	Murder	s. 2 Manslaughter	Total	Murder	Murder and s. 2
1957	135	22	157	3.0	3.5
1958	114	29	143	2.5	3.2
1959	135	21	156	3.0	3.4
1960	123	31	154	2.7	3.4
1961	118	30	148	2.6	3.2
1962	129	42	171	2.8	3.7
1963	122	56	178	2.6	3.8
1964	135	35	170	2.8	3.6
1965	135	50	185	2.8	3.9
1966	122	65	187	2.5	3.9
1967	154	57	211	3.2	4.4
1968	148	57	205	3.0	4.2

Table 2

The risk of being murdered had not changed as the rate still stood at three in a million, as it was ten years earlier. What had increased, steadily since 1957, was the incidence of section 2 manslaughter, i.e. homicides reduced to manslaughter by reason of diminished responsibility. The figure for murder in the year following the passing of the Murder (Abolition of Death Penalty) Act 1965 was the lowest although it rose in the two following years. Table 20[59] showed that murder by blunt instrument or strangulation remained constant; the use of sharp weapons increased almost 100 per cent over the 12 years (apart from a slight fall in 1968); and murder by shooting increased from 1965 but still accounted for only ten per cent of the total. Louis Blom-Cooper said, 'The report re-inforces the view that evidence about murder is really irrelevant to the issue of capital punishment, which remains purely a moral issue'.[60]

Under the main leader 'The Punishment for Murder'[61] *The Times* said that murders that previously attracted the death penalty had increased since the suspension of capital punishment but it did not follow that the suspension was wholly or mainly responsible for the increase or that restoration of the death penalty would reverse or moderate the trend. There was an increase in violent crime in general but the article contended that the conclusions were too tentative to justify restoration. The sentence was irrelevant, there could be a miscarriage of justice, the Homicide Act was unsatisfactory and the procedure of the death penalty was repugnant to many people. The leader concluded that the right course would be to extend the suspension so that the trend could be more properly studied.

When asked if he would consider legislation to restore capital punishment for the murder of law enforcement officers the home secretary, Callaghan, gave the terse answer: 'No'. When it was pointed out that for vicious men already in prison a prison sentence could not be a deterrent, Callaghan replied that no prison officer had been killed by a prisoner for many years.[62] In a written answer Elystan Morgan, under-secretary at the Home Office, confirmed that in England and Wales the death penalty still applied for offences of treason, piracy with violence under the Piracy Act 1937, arson in dockyards under the Dockyards Protection Act 1772 and for various offences under the Navy Discipline Act 1957 and the Army Act 1955 and Air Force Act 1955.[63] When, later, Elystan Morgan was asked if there was any intention to abolish capital punishment for various offences for which it could still be ordered, he replied 'not at present'.[64]

An end to suspension

Although it had been agreed that the matter should not become a party political issue, the opposition front bench tabled a motion calling on the government to wait the full five years before the Act was reviewed, rather than reviewing it when it still had eight months to run and the figures for 1969 were unobtainable. But the government thought it better to settle the question before it became an election issue.[65]

Barely two weeks before the Christmas recess the government acted. Callaghan and William Ross, the secretary of state for Scotland, tabled a motion to renew the Abolition Act of 1965 and drop the proviso of the five year experimental period. A similar motion was tabled in the Lords by Lord Gardiner; both Houses would debate the motions before Christmas. If the motions were not passed by both Houses the 1965 Act would expire on 31 July 1970 and as there was no intention of bringing in any further legislation, Parliament had a clear choice between unqualified abolition or a return to the 1957 Act. Callaghan again let it be known that he would resign as home secretary rather than preside over the administration of the 1957 legislation. Both government and opposition confirmed that there would be a free vote on the issue. Meanwhile, polls showed that around 85 per cent of the population did not want hanging abolished permanently.[66] Although the government, with their large majority, were likely to get home comfortably even on a free vote, the situation in the Lords was not so certain. It was becoming clear that many peers would vote against the motion because they believed that Parliament was being rushed into a decision before the 1969 murder figures were available. Lord Brooke, former home secretary, thought it wholly inappropriate for the government to seek to hasten a decision, considering that the law did not require one until the following summer.[67]

The opposition were even less pleased and the shadow cabinet tabled a censure motion deploring the government's action in asking Parliament to reach a conclusion on the continuance of the 1965 Act at an unnecessarily early stage in disregard of the will and intention of Parliament as declared in the Act itself. That the government would 'see off' the censure motion and win the debate was in no doubt, but in the Lords Lord Dilhorne asked for the experimental period to be extended to July 1973 and Lord Brooke wanted the Lords to postpone any decision until the figures for 1969 were available, which would be between March and May—which the government argued was too close to the general election.[68] Immediately before the Commons debate a petition was laid before the House by Duncan Sandys praying that Parliament would restore capital punishment for murder,[69] rather a hopeless prayer in the circumstances.

The petition made the front page headline in The Times[70] which predicted that the censure motion would be rejected by a comfortable majority as it was a whipped debate. Nor was it thought that the retentionists had much chance of winning in the government's debate the next day, even though they were backed by Quentin Hogg, the shadow home secretary. The Times did think that the government's motion in the Lords would be narrowly rejected leaving the way open for a final decision the following July. On the same day it was announced surprisingly that the Young Conservatives national committee voted by 23 to 14 to oppose the restoration of the death penalty; however, a survey of 4,000 members showed that only 23 per cent thought the death penalty should not be brought back in any circumstances.

On another page[71] a long article concluded there were insufficient data to come to a firm decision, a letter signed by 35 prominent criminologists headed by Leon Radzinowicz pointing out that not only was there no statistical material about murder and the death penalty, there was no conclusive evidence as to the penalty's special deterrent effect and such evidence as there was suggested that the rate of murder in society was a function of infinitely more complex social and psychological factors. A return to the 1957 Act would be the most unfortunate compromise course that Parliament could take. The issue was far simpler for Sir John Lomax who wrote that the conclusion that capital punishment was not a deterrent was rejected by the majority on grounds of common sense. The problem was that not enough convicted people were hanged. Hanging was a deterrent proportionate to its use: more executions would deter most criminals.

The day before the debate it was announced by Callaghan that crude figures for murders and alleged murders for 1969 would be produced in time for the debate.[72] Duncan Sandys presented his petition and Quentin Hogg opened the censure debate, moving 'that this House while recognising that the decision on capital punishment must be a matter for individual members deplores Her Majesty's government's action in asking Parliament to reach a conclusion on the question of the continuance of the Murder (Abolition of Death Penalty) Act 1965 at an unnecessarily early stage in regard of the will and intention of Parliament as declared in that Act and declines to come to a decision on it until after the publication of all relevant and available statistics covering the full year 1969'.[73]

A number of abolitionists spoke in favour of the motion, their point being that they would prefer to have a full five years' statistics and the government was being overhasty. A further point was made that public opinion had swung against abolition. But Shirley Williams, minister of state at the Home Office, pointed out that the 1965 Act made no mention of a five year trial period but merely expired unless the necessary Parliamentary resolutions were carried by 31 July 1970. She said it was hard to believe that a few more murder figures would tell the House much that it did not already know. There was no prospect of the final figures being analysed before the Act expired.

James Callaghan wound up the debate by reiterating that no further data could be properly collated before July 1970. The House had had the figures for all of 1968 for several months as they were published in full in July. There had been time enough to consider the issue and it was time to make a decision. After a debate lasting six hours the motion to renew the Abolition Act of 1965 and drop the proviso of the five year experimental period was put and defeated by 241 votes to 303, a majority of 62.

Between the two debates a letter from Ewen Montagu appeared.[74] He wrote that during the days of hanging although a few thugs were undeterred and carried weapons the vast majority of criminals did not take the risk for the reason that they might be tempted to use them and hang. He would be prepared for ten undeterred thugs to hang if that deterred one other crook and saved the life of one policeman. Graham G. Weekes had a simpler view. He was unmoved by statistics but believed that the basis of punishment should be retributive justice. He thought that punishment must have precedence over the reform of the criminal and a just punishment for murder was the death penalty.[75]

On the following day the home secretary (James Callaghan) opened the substantive debate when he moved 'that the Murder (Abolition of Death

Penalty) Act 1965 shall not expire as otherwise provided in section 4 of that Act'[76] and asked the House to reaffirm the decision to do away with capital punishment which was taken in December 1964 on the second reading of the Bill 'introduced by our late colleague Sydney Silverman.' He said it was necessary for Parliament to reaffirm the decision because, if the 1965 Act merely expired, the law would again operate as though it had not been passed. That would mean reverting to the Homicide Act which represented an attempt to do that which the Royal Commission concluded was not practicable, namely, to categorise murder into capital and non-capital offences, an attempt which had failed. Executions fell to two a year in 1962, 1963 and 1964. He suggested that even those who believed in the deterrent effect of capital punishment would surely regard as grotesque a situation where capital punishment was still part of the panoply of the law but came to be so little used. It simply was not credible that the structure of law and order should depend on the execution of two criminals a year.

Callaghan then discussed the murder of different groups. On the murder of policemen he noted that since the end of the war 17 police officers had been murdered on duty; five between 1958 and 1964 when the Homicide Act was in force; two in 1965, before abolition. Since abolition there had been four murders, three in a single incident at Shepherd's Bush. He concluded, 'I simply do not believe, on the basis of those figures, that it can be established that capital punishment is necessary for the protection of the forces of law and order'.[77] Nor did he think that the facts supported the case of the Prison Officers' Association: only one prison officer had been murdered, in 1965, by a borstal trainee. Incidents of violence against prison officers had not increased. Turning to the murder of children for sexual motives, three were murdered in 1957 and three in 1968; in the years between the number had varied between one and five.

In response to requests for up to date figures he was able to say that the crude figure for the number of murders in 1969 was 172, compared with 208 for 1968. Similar figures were quoted for Scotland.

Towards the end of his speech, which lasted just under an hour, the home secretary said that he was conscious of the fact that public opinion was in favour of retention, but wondered if their constituents realised to what extent murder was committed within the family, by the mentally abnormal, or whether they would welcome a return to the Homicide Act. He concluded, 'There are times when Parliament has to act in advance of public opinion and give a lead. On penal questions it is not uncommonly the case; Parliament has done it before and Parliament was not wrong. Let us give a lead again today'.[78]

Quintin Hogg, speaking against the motion, began by disposing of what he called the 'bogey of the Homicide Act'. He said that if Parliament wanted to abolish the death penalty permanently it should pass the motion; if Parliament wanted to defer the decision, it could. It could defer until 1973, it could legislate, it could do anything it pleased. But nobody wanted a perpetual see-saw between abolition and retention. That would be morally unacceptable and ridiculous in practical terms. Rather than going back and forth he would prefer complete abolition.

Dr Michael Winstanley was opposed to capital punishment on five grounds. First, it was not a deterrent. If there were any clear evidence that it was, and reduced the number of murders, he would re-examine his position; but he was not convinced. Second, he believed that the press and other reports exerted an unwholesome effect on unstable minds and might even increase violent crime. The whole obscene ritual of hanging led to reports in the press. Third, he believed that those involved in any way with the carrying out of executions were harmed: it was a wholly macabre ritual. The last time the Home Office sought an assistant hangman there were many applications, some from people known to be unstable. Fourth, the death penalty was irreversible. There had been people hanged who were innocent and it was impossible to guarantee it would not happen again. Finally, the state should set an example. While judicial hanging remained, the work being done to rid the community of violence must fail.

The debate lasted for seven hours and the motion was carried by 343 votes to 185, a massive majority of 158 which was greeted by cheers of relief from members of Parliament and prompted a rare front page banner headline in *The Times*: 'MPs vote "No More Hanging"'.[79] It was revealed that 51 Conservatives voted for abolition, as did all nine Liberals and three others. Two Labour members, Dunnett and Doig, voted against.[80]

Whereas the debate in the Commons fitted comfortably into a single day, the debate in the Upper House spread over two and began the day after the Commons debate', on December 17.

The Lords' debate, initially on an amendment by Lord Dilhorne that the current position be extended for a further three years, was opened, and some might say shut, by Gerald Gardiner, the Lord Chancellor.[81] He pointed out that the rate of murder per million of the population had not really altered in the past ten years, quoting the actual figures: 1900-1909, 4.4; 1910-1919, 4.0; 1920-1929, 3.8; 1930-1939, 3.2; 1940-1949, 3.9; 1950-1959, 3.7; 1960-1968, 3.8.[82] The data spoke for themselves. A vote for Dilhorne's amendment, he said, was the same as voting against the government's motion. There were really only two alternatives: either the House passed the motion or the Homicide Act came back in July. He did not think it was right to put men and women to death in cold blood, telling them a fortnight beforehand that you were going to do it.

Lord Brooke made it clear early on that he was not going to press his amendment calling for a postponement of a decision until all the available statistics for 1969 were known and from then on it was a straight fight between a postponement for three years and the acceptance of the government's motion and permanent abolition. The Marquess of Salisbury said that the permanent abolition of the death penalty would affront the consciences of the majority of the British people. The right action was to hold a referendum. The Bishop of Durham said that one person hanged in error seemed too high a price to pay and human error was irrevocable. Furthermore, hanging was negative, incoherent and devoid of any creative possibility. Lord Goodman said that what was required was not the retention of an abominable anachronism but the certainty of conviction. Hideous penalties produce hideous social consequences.

The fact that all three party leaders in the Commons had voted in the abolition lobby influenced many peers. The debate on the second day lasted barely three hours.[83] Summing up, Lord Gardiner recalled that in 1820 the Commons passed a Bill abolishing capital punishment for cutting down a tree. To laughter he quoted his predecessor on the woolsack who had said:

> It undoubtedly seems a hardship that so heavy a penalty as that of death should be fixed to the cutting down of a single tree or the killing or wounding of a cow. But if the Bill passes in its present state a person might root out or cut down several acres of plantations or destroy the whole stock of cattle of a farmer without being subject to capital punishment.

Gardiner concluded by saying that human beings who were not infallible ought not to choose a form of punishment that was irrevocable. To cheers he called for the Lords to take the view that the three party leaders in the Commons were right in thinking that the time to abolish capital punishment had now come.

Lord Brooke's amendment was not moved; Lord Dilhorne's amendment was defeated by 220 votes to 174 and the Lord Chancellor's motion was agreed to without a division. Once again *The Times* was moved to a banner headline: 'Capital Punishment Ended by Majority of 46 in Lords'.[84]

After the debate, the Archbishop of Canterbury, Michael Ramsey, said[85] that the abolition of capital punishment once and for all would help to create a more civilised society in which the search for the causes of crime and experiments in penal reform could be continued. Perhaps he expected too much.

ENDNOTES

1 *The Times*, p. 12, 5 November 1965
2 ibid, p. 5, 6 November 1965
3 ibid, p. 12, 10 November 1965
4 ibid, p. 17, 11 November 1965
5 ibid, p. 5, 20 November 1965
6 ibid, p. 13, 23 November 1965
7 ibid, p. 12, 24 November 1965
8 ibid, p. 12, 22 January 1966
9 ibid, p. 8, 23 December 1965
10 ibid, p. 14, 28 March 1966
11 ibid, pp. 7/10, 1 April 1966
12 ibid, p.15, 21 May 1966
13 ibid, p. 1, 13 August 1966
14 ibid, p. 9, 15 August 1966
15 ibid, p. 8, 16 August 1966
16 ibid, p. 9
17 ibid, p. 9, 17 August 1966

18 *The Times*, p. 9, 17 August 1966
19 ibid, p. 1, 18 August 1966
20 ibid, p. 1, 13 October 1966
21 ibid, p. 13
22 ibid, p. 10, 14 October 1966
23 ibid, p. 8, 15 October 1966
24 ibid, p. 1, 19 October 1966
25 ibid, p. 12, 20 October 1966
26 ibid, p. 16, 21 October 1966
27 ibid, p. 13. 3 November 1966
28 ibid, p. 10, 9 November 1966
29 ibid, p. 1, 15 November 1966
30 ibid, p. 13, 23 November 1966
31 ibid, p. 1, 24 November 1966
32 ibid, p. 2, 9 September 1967
33 ibid, p. 2, 23 October 1967
34 ibid, p. 1, 30 November 1967
35 ibid, p. 3, 30 January 1968
36 ibid, p. 1, 31 January 1968
37 ibid, p. 1, 10 February 1968
38 ibid, p. 10
39 ibid, p. 12, 12 February 1968
40 ibid, p. 5, 31 May 1968
41 ibid, p. 2, 4 June 1968
42 ibid, p. 2, 25 July 1968
43 ibid, p. 1, 26 February 1969
44 ibid, p. 4, 27 February 1969
45 ibid, p. 9
46 *Hansard*, [783] 118 (8 May 1969)
47 *The Times*, p. 11, 13 June 1969
48 ibid, p. 2, 16 June 1969
49 *Hansard*, [785] 1228 (24 June 1969)
50 *The Times*, p. 4, 25 June 1969
51 ibid, p. 6, 25 August 1969
52 ibid, p. 5, 9 October 1969
53 ibid, p. 1, 10 October 1969
54 ibid, p. 13, 17 October 1969
55 ibid, p. 10, 24 October 1969
56 ibid, p. 2, 3 November 1969
57 ibid, p. 10, 6 November 1969
58 *Murder 1957 to 1968*, Gibson, E and Klein, S, p. 2, London: HMSO (1969)

59 ibid, p. 24
60 *The Times,* p. 1, 6 November 1969
61 ibid, p. 11
62 *Hansard,* [791] 1484 (20 November 1969)
63 ibid, [791] 283
64 *Hansard,* [792] 344 (4 December 1969)
65 *The Times,* p.1, 27 November 1968
66 ibid, p.1, 9 December 1969
67 ibid, p. 2, 10 December 1969
68 ibid, p. 1, 11 December 1969
69 *Hansard,* [793] 893 (15 December 1969)
70 *The Times,* p. 1, 15 December 1969
71 ibid, p. 9
72 ibid, p. 1, 16 December 1969
73 *Hansard,* [793] 939-1062 (15 December 1969); *The Times,* p. 4, 16 December 1969
74 *The Times,* p.11, 16 December 1969
75 ibid
76 ibid, [793] 1149 (16 December 1969)
77 ibid, [793] 1153
78 ibid, [793] 1169
79 *The Times,* p. 1, 17 December 1969
80 ibid, p. 17
81 *Hansard* [Lords], [306] 1107-1258 (17 December 1969); *The Times,* p. 11, 18
    December 1969
82 ibid, [306] 1113
83 ibid, [306] 1264-1318 (18 December 1969); *The Times,* pp. 1, 4, 19 December 1969
84 ibid, p.1
85 ibid.

Afterword

Although capital punishment for murder was suspended in 1965 and finally abolished in 1969, it was retained for several other offences including treason in its various manifestations, piracy and a number of offences under military law including mutiny and assisting the enemy. However, no execution has taken place for any reason in Britain since 1964 so it is high time that these offences were removed from the statute book.

As a member of the European Union Britain should be subject to Protocol 6 of the European Convention On Human Rights which is designed to remove capital punishment for any offence from all countries of the Union. However, as much as the Labour government under prime minister Tony Blair wishes to abolish capital punishment totally, it balks at doing this by signing up to Protocol 6, as it is of the opinion that it is a matter for Parliament to decide, rather than the Council of Europe.

However it is achieved, it is almost a certainty that capital punishment for any offence will be removed from the statute book before the end of the millennium, and that unlike the present century—which began with the execution of a woman (see p. 77)—the new one will begin with the state denied all opportunity for judicial killing.

Milestones to Abolition

Hanging appears to be an Anglo-Saxon or German invention. Tacitus, in *Germania*, noted the German habit of hanging traitors and deserters. Perhaps the Saxons brought it to Britain when they invaded since it certainly was practised by the Anglo-Saxons.

As noted in *Chapter 1*, William the Conqueror abolished the death penalty, preferring visible and lasting mutilations as a deterrent. But by the reign of Henry I hanging was re-established as a punishment for felony. Beheading was reserved as a more honourable death for members of the aristocracy and burning at the stake for women. From the twelfth century only royal courts had the power to hang, although many lords and bishops continued to inflict cruel tortures.

As the value of property increased, more and more offences were made capital and more and more men, women and children were hanged. Throughout the reign of Henry VIII there was an average of 2,000 executions a year and the average under Good Queen Bess was not much less. Hanging reached its zenith in the nineteenth century when there were over 200 capital offences in the 'Bloody Code'.

1810   London described as the 'City of the Gallows'. Romilly commences crusade against the death penalty.

1832   Death for shoplifting to the value of five shillings or less abolished.

1833-37 Following the Reform Act of 1832, punishment of death is removed from two-thirds of capital crimes.

1841   Hanging for rape abolished. Death inflicted only for crimes of murder and treason.

1866   Majority of Royal Commission favours end to public executions and the introduction of degrees of murder, but no statute enacted for the latter.

1868   Executions to take place only *within* prisons.

1908   Death sentence for children under 16 years of age abolished.

1921   Howard League for Penal Reform founded.

1922   New offence of infanticide by a distracted mother effectively reduced this from murder.

1925   National Campaign for the Abolition of Capital Punishment formed.

1930   Parliamentary Select Committee recommends suspension of the death penalty for a trial period of five years. Not adopted.

1931   Execution of pregnant women prohibited.

1932   Capital punishment for people under 18 years of age abolished.

1938   Free vote of House of Commons in favour of abolition of capital punishment. Not acted upon.

1948	Sydney Silverman's motion for abolition carried in the House of Commons but heavily defeated in the Lords.
1953	All the principal recommendations of the Royal Commission under Sir Ernest Gowers rejected.
1956	A Commons motion in favour of abolition approved. Sydney Silverman's Bill given a second and third reading but rejected in the Lords.
1957	Homicide Act 1957 divides murder into capital and non-capital offences. Introduces defence of diminished responsibility and abolishes constructive malice.
1965	Murder (Abolition of Death Penalty) Act 1965 becomes law. Death penalty suspended for five years.
1969	Death penalty for murder totally abolished by both Houses of Parliament.

Prime Ministers from 1800 to 1970

1783	William Pitt
February 1801	Henry Addington
May 1804	William Pitt
December 1806	Lord Grenville
1807	Duke of Portland
1809	Spencer Percival
June 1812	Lord Liverpool
April 1027	George Canning
September 1827	Viscount Goderich
January 1828	Duke of Wellington
November 1830	Earl Grey
July 1834	Viscount Melbourne
December 1834	Sir Robert Peel
April 1835	Viscount Melbourne
September 1841	Sir Robert Peel
July 1846	Lord John Russell
February 1852	Lord Derby
December 1852	Earl of Aberdeen
February 1855	Viscount Palmerston
February 1858	Lord Derby
June 1859	Viscount Palmerston
October 1865	Lord John Russell
June 1866	Lord Derby
February 1868	Benjamin Disraeli
December 1868	W. E. Gladstone
February 1874	Benjamin Disraeli
April 1880	W. E. Gladstone
June 1885	Lord Salisbury
February 1886	W. E. Gladstone
August 1886	Lord Salisbury
August 1892	W. E. Gladstone
March 1894	Lord Rosebery
June 1895	Lord Salisbury
July 1902	Arthur Balfour
December 1905	Sir Henry Campbell-Bannerman
April 1908	H. H. Asquith
December 1916	David Lloyd George
October 1922	Andrew Bonar Law
May 1923	Stanley Baldwin
January 1924	J. Ramsay MacDonald
November 1924	Stanley Baldwin

June 1929	J. Ramsay MacDonald
June 1935	Stanley Baldwin
May 1937	Neville Chamberlain
May 1940	Winston S. Churchill
July 1945	Clement Attlee
October 1951	Winston S. Churchill
April 1955	Anthony Eden
January 1957	Harold Macmillan
October 1963	Sir Alec Douglas-Home
October 1964	Harold Wilson
(to 1970)	

Home Secretaries from 1800 to 1970

1794	Duke of Portland
July 1801	Lord Pelham
August 1803	Charles Yorke
1804	Lord Hawkesbury
1806	Earl Spencer
1807	Lord Hawkesbury (Lord Liverpool from 1808)
1809	Richard Ryder
June 1812	Viscount Sidmouth
January 1822	Robert Peel
April 1827	William Sturges Bourne
July 1827	Marquis of Lansdowne
January 1828	Robert Peel ('Sir' in May 1830)
November 1830	Viscount Melbourne
July 1834	Viscount Duncannon
December 1834	Henry Goulburn
April 1835	Lord John Russell
September 1839	Marquis of Normanby
September 1841	Sir James Graham
July 1846	Sir George Grey
February 1852	Spencer Walpole
December 1852	Viscount Palmerston
February 1855	Sir George Grey
February 1858	Spencer Walpole
February 1859	Thomas Sotheron-Estcourt
June 1859	Sir George Cornewall-Lewis
July 1861	Sir George Grey
June 1866	Spencer Walpole
May 1867	Gathorne Hardy
December 1868	Henry A. Bruce
August 1873	Robert Lowe
February 1874	Richard A. Cross
April 1880	Sir William Vernon Harcourt
June 1885	Sir Richard A. Cross
February 1886	Hugh C. E. Childers
August 1886	Henry Matthews
August 1892	Herbert H. Asquith
June 1895	Sir Matthew White Ridley
July 1902	Aretas Akers-Douglas
December 1905	Herbert Gladstone
February 1910	Winston S. Churchill
October 1911	Reginald McKenna

May 1915	Sir John Simon
January 1916	Sir Herbert Samuel
January 1919	Edward Shortt
October 1922	W. C. Bridgeman
January 1924	Arthur Henderson
November 1924	Sir William Joynson-Hicks
June 1929	John R. Clynes
August 1931	Sir Herbert Samuel
September 1932	Walter Elliot
June 1935	Sir John Simon
May 1937	Sir Samuel Hoare
September 1939	Sir John Anderson
May 1940	Herbert Morrison
May 1945	Sir Donald Somervell
July 1945	James Chuter Ede
October 1951	Sir David Maxwell Fyfe
December 1954	Gwilym Lloyd George
January 1957	Richard A. (known as R. A. or 'Rab') Butler
July 1962	Henry Brooke
October 1964	Sir Frank Soskice
December 1965	Roy Jenkins
November 1967	James Callaghan
(to February 1970)	

Select Bibliography

Reports and Collections

Hansard 1810, 1821, 1826/7, 1830/31, 1837, 1841, 1864, 1866/7, 1868, 1899-1969
Journals of the House of Commons 1830
BM. Add. MSS. 40,393. f.65 (Bentham) and 27,826. f.14 (Francis Place)
Parliamentary Papers (P.P.) xvi. 1818
P.P. xxxvi 1836
P.P. xxxi 1837
P.P. xxi 1866 (Capital Punishment Commission Report).
P.P. lxxiii 232
Public Record Office HO 45/681, HO 144/212/A486697D, PCOM. 8/210, PCOM. 8/212

Newspapers

Daily News 1846, 1868
Pall Mall Gazette 1885
St James Gazette, 1885
The Standard, 1884
The Times, 1801, 1837, 1849, 1860, 1865, 1866, 1867, 1868, 1899-1969

Books, Journals etc.

Anon, *Hanging Not Punishment Enough* (1701)
Andrews, H B, *Criminal Law: Being a Commentary on Bentham on Death Punishment* (1833)
Andrews, William, *Bygone Punishments* (1931)
Beccaria, Cesare, *Dei Delitti e delle Pene* (1769 edn.)
Blackstone, Sir William, *Commentaries* (1770)
Blake, William, 'Milton' in *Poems and Prophecies* (1927 edn.)
Boswell, James, *Life of Johnson* (1961 edn.)
Boyle, Thomas, *Black Swine in the Sewers of Hampstead: Beneath the Surface of Victorian Sensationalism* (1990)
Cadogan, Edward, *The Roots of Evil* (1937)
Cale, Michelle, *Law and Society. An Introduction to Sources for Criminal and Legal History from 1800*, PRO Readers' Guide No. 14. (1996)
Carlyle, Thomas, *Latter Day Pamphlets* (1872 edn.)
Coke, Sir Edward, *Institutes,* vol. 3 (1797 edn.)
Cooper, David D, *The Lesson of the Scaffold* (1974)
Dickens and Hogarth, *The Letters of Charles Dickens* (1882)
Dyer, C J, *Reports* (1561)
Dymond, Alfred H, *The Law on Trial, or Personal Recollections of the Death Penalty, and its Opponents* (1865)
Edinburgh Review, 1811/12
Fielding, Henry, *A Proposal for Making an Effectual Provision for the Poor etc.* (1753); *An Inquiry into the Causes of the Frequent Executions at Tyburn* (1725)
Foster, Sir Michael, *Crown Law* (1762)
Fraser's Magazine, 1840
Gatrell, V A C, *The Hanging Tree: Execution and the English People, 1770-1868* (1994)
Gentleman's Magazine, 1736, 1767, 1783
Goldsmith, Oliver, *The Vicar of Wakefield* (1852 edn.)
Griffiths, A, *The Chronicle of Newgate* (1884)
Hay, Douglas, *Albion's Fatal Tree* (1975)
Hibbert, Christopher, *The Roots of Evil* (1963)

Hodgkinson, Peter and Rutherford, Andrew, (eds.) *Capital Punishment: Global Issues and Prospects* (1996)

Holyoake, George Jacob, *Sixty Years of an Agitator's Life* (1902 edn.)

Hood, Roger, *The Death Penalty* (1996 edn.)

Hostettler, John, *Thomas Wakley: An Improbable Radical* (1993); *The Politics of Punishment* (1994); *Politics and Law in the Life of Sir James Fitzjames Stephen* (1995)

Justice of the Peace and Local Government Law (1996)

Koestler, A and Rolph, C H, *Hanged by the Neck* (1961)

Laurence, John, *A History of Capital Punishment* (1963)

Linebaugh, Peter, *The London Hanged:Crime and Civil Society in the Eighteenth Century* (1991)

Mackintosh, Sir James, *Miscellaneous Works* (1846)

Madan, Reverend Martin, *Thoughts on Executive Justice* (1785)

Mandeville, Bernard, *An Enquiry into the Causes of the Frequent Executions at Tyburn etc* (1725)

Marks, Alfred, *Tyburn Tree: Its History and Annals* (1908)

Miller, John, *An Inquiry into the Present State of the Statute and Criminal Law of England* (1822)

Ollyffe, George, *An Essay Humbly Offer'd for an Act of Parliament to Prevent Capital Crimes etc* (1731)

Paley, William, *Principles of Moral and Political Philosophy* (1786 edn.)

Parry, L A, *History of Torture* (1933)

Pettifer, Ernest, *Punishments of Former Days* (1992)

Phillips, Charles, *Vacation Thoughts on Capital Punishment* (1856)

Potter, Harry, *Hanging in Judgment. Religion and the Death Penalty in England from the Bloody Code to Abolition* (1993)

Radzinowicz, Sir Leon, *A History of English Criminal Law and its Administration from 1750*, 5 vols (1948-86)

Reade's Weekly Journal (1740)

Romilly, Sir Samuel, *Observations on a Late Publication Intituled Thoughts on Executive Justice* (1786)

Observations on the Criminal Law of England as it relates to Capital Punishment, etc (1810)

Scott, G Ryley, *History of Corporal Punishment* (1950)

Sheehan, W J, *Finding Solace in Eighteenth-Century Newgate* (1977)

Spedding, *Letters and Life of Bacon* (1869)

Stephen, Sir James Fitzjames, *A History of the Criminal Law of England* (1883)

Stowe, John, *Survey of London* (1603)

Swift, Jonathan, *Poetical Works* (1833 edn.)

Taylor, A S, *The Principles and Practice of Medical Jurisprudence* (1894)

The Chronicles of Newgate (1884)

The Newgate Calendar (1824 edn.)

The Ordinary of Newgate, *His Account of the Behaviour, Confessions and Dying Words of the Malefactors Executed at Tyburn* (1736)

The Rambler, No. 114 (20 April 1751)

Tuttle, Elizabeth, *The Crusade Against Capital Punishment* (1961)

Wakefield, Edward Gibbon, *The Hangman and the Judge* (1833)

Walpole, Horace, *Memoirs of the Last Ten Years of George II's Reign* (1847)

Westminster Review, 1832

Wrightson, Thomas, *On the Punishment of Death* (1837).

Index

280

283

Putting justice into words...

Sir William Garrow

His Life, Times and Fight for Justice
by John Hostettler and Richard Braby
Foreword by Geoffrey Robertson QC

The lost story of Sir William Garrow and its rediscovery will prove intriguing for professional and general readers alike and will be an invaluable 'missing-link' for legal and social historians.

ISBN 978-1-904380-69-6 | Paperback | Jan 2011

Famous Cases

Nine Trials that Changed the Law
by Brian P Block and John Hostettler

The authors have painstakingly assembled the background to a selection of leading cases in English law. From the Mareva case (synonymous with a type of injunction) to Lord Denning's classic ruling in the High Trees House case (the turning point for equitable estoppel) to that of the former Chilean head of state General Pinochet (in which the House of Lords heard the facts a second time) the authors offer a refreshing perspective to whet the appetite of general readers, students and seasoned practitioners alike concerning how the English Common Law evolves on a case by case basis by creating 'precedents'.

ISBN 978-1-872870-34-2 | Paperback | 2002

Browse our catalogue online at **WatersidePress.co.uk**

Evans - Old Bailey - important cases

Edith Thompson - Bailey - important cases